Real-Time Applications of Machine Learning in Cyber-Physical Systems

Balamurugan Easwaran
University of Africa, Toru-Orua, Nigeria

Kamal Kant Hiran
Sir Padampat Singhania University, India

Sangeetha Krishnan
University of Africa, Toru-Orua, Nigeria

Ruchi Doshi
Azteca University, Mexico

A volume in the Advances in
Computational Intelligence and
Robotics (ACIR) Book Series

Published in the United States of America by
    IGI Global
    Engineering Science Reference (an imprint of IGI Global)
    701 E. Chocolate Avenue
    Hershey PA, USA 17033
    Tel: 717-533-8845
    Fax: 717-533-8661
    E-mail: cust@igi-global.com
    Web site: http://www.igi-global.com

Library of Congress Cataloging-in-Publication Data

Names: Easwaran, Balamurugan, 1975- editor.
Title: Real-time applications of machine learning in cyber physical
  systems / Balamurugan Easwaran, Kamal Hiran, Sangeetha
  Krishnan, and Ruchi Doshi, editors.
Description: Hershey, PA : Engineering Science Reference, an imprint of IGI
  Global, [2022] | Includes bibliographical references and index.
Identifiers: LCCN 2021043068 (print) | LCCN 2021043069 (ebook) | ISBN
  9781799893103 (ebook) | ISBN 9781799893080 (h/c)
Subjects: LCSH: Electronic security systems. | Medical informatics. |
  Agriculture--Decision making--Data processing. | Cooperating objects
  (Computer systems) | Machine learning--Industrial applications.
Classification: LCC TH9737 (ebook) | LCC TH9737 .H36 2022 (print) | DDC
  621.389/28 23/eng/20211--dc27
LC record available at https://lccn.loc.gov/2021043068

This book is published in the IGI Global book series Advances in Computational Intelligence and Robotics (ACIR) (ISSN: 2327-0411; eISSN: 2327-042X)

British Cataloguing in Publication Data
A Cataloguing in Publication record for this book is available from the British Library.

All work contributed to this book is new, previously-unpublished material.
The views expressed in this book are those of the authors, but not necessarily of the publisher.

For electronic access to this publication, please contact: eresources@igi-global.com.

Advances in Computational Intelligence and Robotics (ACIR) Book Series

ISSN:2327-0411
EISSN:2327-042X

Editor-in-Chief: Ivan Giannoccaro, University of Salento, Italy

MISSION

While intelligence is traditionally a term applied to humans and human cognition, technology has progressed in such a way to allow for the development of intelligent systems able to simulate many human traits. With this new era of simulated and artificial intelligence, much research is needed in order to continue to advance the field and also to evaluate the ethical and societal concerns of the existence of artificial life and machine learning.

The **Advances in Computational Intelligence and Robotics (ACIR) Book Series** encourages scholarly discourse on all topics pertaining to evolutionary computing, artificial life, computational intelligence, machine learning, and robotics. ACIR presents the latest research being conducted on diverse topics in intelligence technologies with the goal of advancing knowledge and applications in this rapidly evolving field.

COVERAGE

- Synthetic Emotions
- Brain Simulation
- Intelligent Control
- Natural Language Processing
- Evolutionary Computing
- Algorithmic Learning
- Fuzzy Systems
- Artificial Life
- Cognitive Informatics
- Computer Vision

IGI Global is currently accepting manuscripts for publication within this series. To submit a proposal for a volume in this series, please contact our Acquisition Editors at Acquisitions@igi-global.com or visit: http://www.igi-global.com/publish/.

Titles in this Series

For a list of additional titles in this series, please visit:
http://www.igi-global.com/book-series/advances-computational-intelligence-robotics/73674

Biomedical and Business Applications Using Artificial Neural Networks and Machine Learning
Richard S. Segall (Arkansas State University, USA) and Gao Niu (Bryant University, USA)
Engineering Science Reference • © 2022 • 394pp • H/C (ISBN: 9781799884552) • US $245.00

Integrating AI in IoT Analytics on the Cloud for Healthcare Applications
D. Jeya Mala (School of CS&IT, Jain University, Bangalore, India)
Engineering Science Reference • © 2022 • 312pp • H/C (ISBN: 9781799891321) • US $245.00

Applications of Artificial Intelligence in Additive Manufacturing
Sachin Salunkhe (Vel Tech Rangarajan Dr.Sagunthala R&D Institute of Science and Technology, India) Hussein Mohammed Abdel Moneam Hussein (Helwan University, Egypt) and J. Paulo Davim (University of Aveiro, Portugal)
Engineering Science Reference • © 2022 • 240pp • H/C (ISBN: 9781799885160) • US $245.00

Handbook of Research on Lifestyle Sustainability and Management Solutions Using AI, Big Data Analytics, and Visualization
Sailesh Suryanarayan Iyer (Rai University, India) Arti Jain (Jaypee Institute of Information Technology, India) and John Wang (Montclair State University, USA)
Engineering Science Reference • © 2022 • 415pp • H/C (ISBN: 9781799887867) • US $395.00

Socrates Digital™ for Learning and Problem Solving
Mark Salisbury (University of St. Thomas, USA)
Engineering Science Reference • © 2022 • 383pp • H/C (ISBN: 9781799879558) • US $215.00

For an entire list of titles in this series, please visit:
http://www.igi-global.com/book-series/advances-computational-intelligence-robotics/73674

701 East Chocolate Avenue, Hershey, PA 17033, USA
Tel: 717-533-8845 x100 • Fax: 717-533-8661
E-Mail: cust@igi-global.com • www.igi-global.com

Editorial Advisory Board

Table of Contents

Detailed Table of Contents

   Sujith Jayaprakash, NIIT, Ghana
   *Shanmugapriya N., Dr. S. N. S. Rajalakshmi College of Arts and
       Science, India*
   Chitra K., Rathnavel Subramanian College of Arts and Science, India
   *Kathiresan V., Dr. S. N. S. Rajalakshmi College of Arts and Science,
       India*

The cyber-physical system encompasses physics and cyber systems, which are highly interconnected and networked. Considered to be one of the fascinating inventions of today's world, CPS applications include autonomous vehicles, industrial control systems, medical monitoring, automatic pilot avionics, etc. Autonomous or semi-autonomous vehicles, also known as self-driving or driverless vehicles, are automobiles that require less or no human intervention for operating or controlling them. CPS has brought in several advancements in the automobile industry by providing a seamless human interaction with physical and cyber systems, which includes IoT, artificial intelligence, machine learning, etc. Machine learning algorithms play a major role in enhancing autonomous vehicle models. This chapter focuses on the various machine learning algorithms that are used commonly in building robust autonomous vehicles. This chapter also focuses on the evolution of autonomous vehicles and the backed cyber advancements.

Cyber-physical systems, in short CPS, is a the term coined by Ellen Gill in the year 2006. It is a kind of embedded system. It is a kind of next generation computing systems that comprises the interacting digital, analog, physical components by integrated physics and logic. This CPS is associated and allied with other technologies and concepts such as big data analytics, cloud computing, internet of things (IoT). Furthermore, cyber-physical systems is making smart things by enabling smart grid, smart cities, and other intelligent and smart things, for example, cars, buildings, homes, manufacturing, hospitals, appliances. This chapter discusses the aspects of cyber-physical systems including its basics, features, functions, and emerging and possible roles. Moreover, this chapter also discusses the current trends on educational programs, training programs in the areas of cyber-physical systems internationally with potentiality in Indian context, and it depicts many opportunities in the contemporary scenario.

Chapter 3

The agriculture science system is facing lots of problems from environmental change. Machine learning (ML) and cyber physical systems (CPS) are the best approaches to overcome the problems by building good and effective solutions. Crop yield prediction includes prediction of yield for the crop by analysing the existing data by considering several parameters like weather, soil, water, and temperature. This project addresses and defines the predicting yield of the crop based on the previous year's data using a linear regression algorithm into which you can type your own text.

A cyber physical system (CPS) is a mechanism that monitors and controls entire devices which are connected together. Secured data transmission in CPS systems is a major problem. To provide information security for CPS applications, certain privacy preservation strategies need to be followed. Encryption and anonymization are existing traditional privacy preservation techniques which are not suitable to provide information security for advanced systems called CPS. Differential techniques is an emerging privacy technique where a required amount of noise is added using various mathematical algorithms with data while sharing information between devices in CPSs. The process of adding noise with data is called data perturbation. There are three major data perturbations mechanisms followed to provide information security. They are exponential mechanism, Laplace mechanism, and Gaussian mechanism. This chapter presents a detailed review about applications of CPSs, significance of implementing differential privacy techniques, challenges, and future research directions of CPSs.

Chapter 5

Brain tumors are prevalent and aggressive disease, with a relatively short life expectancy in their most severe form. Thus, treatment planning is an important element in improving patient quality of life. In general, image techniques such as computed tomography (CT), magnetic resonance imaging (MRI), and ultrasound imaging are used to examine tumors in the brain, lung, liver, and breast. MRI scans are used in this study to diagnose brain tumors. As a result, a reliable and automated classification technique is required to prevent death. Automatic brain tumor detection using convolutional neural networks (CNN) classification is proposed in this chapter. Small kernels are used to conduct the deeper architectural design. In machine learning, brain tumor classification is done by using a binary classifier to detect brain tumors from MRI scan images. In this chapter, transfer learning is used to build the classifier, achieving a good accuracy and visualizing the model's overall performance.

Kanakambika K., Vellalar College for Women, India
Thamizhendhi G., Sri Vasavi College, India

Technological advancement in the recent decades enhanced the calibre of human life. Contemporary research in machine learning (ML) exhibits a mock-up to make decisions on its own and is applied in various fields including medical diagnosis, email filtering, banking, computer vision, financial marketing, image processing, cyber security. The systems inter-connected across the world via internet are attacked by hackers, and it is prevented by cyber security. The optimum solution for cyber-attacks is attained by collaborating ML techniques with cyber security and envisioned issues are designed by cyber machine learning models. In this chapter, an algorithm is proposed to defend data by encoding the text to an unintelligent text and decoding it to original text by applying graph labelling in cryptography. Symmetric key is designed based on the edge label of an odd-even congruence graph to achieve secured communication in CPS. In addition, a program is suggested using Python programming to attain cipher text and its converse.

Quang-Vinh Dang, Industrial University of Ho Chi Minh City, Vietnam

The growth of the internet and network-based services bring to us a lot of new opportunities but also pose many new security threats. The intrusion detection system (IDS) has been studied and developed over the years to cope with external attacks from the internet. The task of an IDS is to classify and stop the malicious traffic from outside to enter the computer system. In recent years, machine learning-based IDS has attracted a lot of attention from the industry and academia. The IDS based on state-of-the-art machine learning algorithms usually achieves a very high predictive performance than traditional approaches. On the other hand, several open datasets have been introduced for the researchers to evaluate and compare their algorithms. This chapter reviews the classification techniques used in IDS, mostly the machine learning algorithms and the published datasets. The authors discuss the achievements and some open problems and suggest a few research directions in the future.

The reason trends in prevalent detection of EEG seizure help in analyzing the various features of EEG signals to customize and to remove visual inspection in reading the EEG signals. Epilepsy is a disorder and is identified by baseless seizures that have been associated with unexpected improper neural discharges which result in various health issues and also result in death. One of the most common methods in detecting contraction seizures is an electroencephalogram. By using machine learning methods, it is easy to extract the features of EEG signals that help in detecting seizures. Convolutional neural network (CNN) includes both inputs as well as output layers that help in training the data acquired since it helps in analyzing the large set of high dimensional data. The performance analysis is done under multiple classifiers such as random forest, gradient boosting, and decision tree, which are used in feature extraction. Among them, random forest proves to be the best classifier in achieving a high degree of accuracy.

Currently the world is experiencing the global digital transformation of the fourth generation revolution for industry in the field of cyber physical systems (CPS) and artificial intelligence. Moreover, by utilizing artificial intelligence, cyber physical systems will be able to perform more proficiently, collaboratively, and spiritedly. Agriculture crop control is a process to protect the crop as much as possible so the crop is not infected by the different kinds of pests. Pests are any living organisms including insects, animals, weeds, pathogens, and other creatures that can harm the agriculture crop. Pests and other diseases cause an average of 20-30% global potential loss of crop production in every year. So, crop protection is required to reduce these losses. This chapter explores CPS concept to improve crop production to protect the crop from wild animals using machine learning and cyber physical systems. The smart agriculture process under CPS includes crop suggestion, irrigation and fertilization automation, crop protection, plant monitoring, and harvesting.

Kuldeep Singh Chouhan, Engineering College Ajmer, India
Jyoti Gajrani, Engineering College Ajmer, India
Bhavna Sharma, JECRC University, Jaipur, India
Satya Narayan Tazi, Engineering College Ajmer, India

As cardiovascular diseases (CVDs) are a serious concern to modern medical science to diagnose at an early stage, it is vital to build a classification model that can effectively reduce mortality rates by treating millions of people in a timely manner. An electrocardiogram (ECG) is a specialized instrument that measures the heart's physiological responses. To accurately diagnose a patient's acute and chronic heart problems, an in-depth examination of these ECG signals is essential. The proposed model consists of a convolutional neural network having three convolutional, two pooling, and two dense layers. The proposed model is trained and evaluated on the MIT-BIH arrhythmia and PTB diagnostic datasets. The classification accuracy is 99.16%, which is higher than state-of-the-art studies on similar arrhythmias. Recall, precision, and F1 score of the proposed model are 96.53%, 95.15%, and 99.17%, respectively. The proposed model can aid doctors explicitly for the detection and classification of arrhythmias.

Apinaya Prethi K. N., Department of CSE, Coimbatore Institute of
        Technology, India
Sangeetha M., Coimbatore Institute of Technology, India
Nithya S., Coimbatore Institute of Technology, India

Cyber space became inevitable in today's world. It needs a security technology to safeguard the whole system from outsiders. An intrusion detection system acts as a strong barrier and screens the vulnerability. There is an upgraded amount of network attacks such as DoS (denial of service), R2L (remote to local) attack, U2R (user to root), and probe attack. These network attacks lead to prohibited usage of data from various applications like medical, bank, car maintenance, and achieve activities. This will result in financial gain and prevent authorized persons from accessing the network. Intrusion detection systems were implemented in systems where security is desirable. The conventional system makes use of machine learning techniques such as random forest and decision trees that entail many computational resources and higher time complexity. To overcome this, a DNN-based intrusion detection system is proposed. This IDS not only detects the abnormalities but also results in higher accuracy compared to existing systems. This also improves the speed, accuracy, and stability of the system.

The people are affected by retinal vascular disease. This research automates the prediction of such disease using retinal image acquisition. The condition of the retinal blood vessels is manifested as the mirror of the vascular disease of the human body. Human retinal images of the eye give extensive data on diagnostic changes caused by local optical sickness that reveal some of the vascular diseases such as diabetes, cardiovascular disease, hypertension, vascular irritation, and stroke. The infinite perimeter active contour with hybrid region information (IPACHI) model is used to segment and calculate perimeter of the blood vessels. The next stage is classification of affected retinal vessels by using support vector model (SVM) and artificial neural network (ANN) models. After classification, the arterio venous ratio (ANR) is computed to identify the exact type of retinal disease. The work is done in MATLAB software, and it proves the accuracy of 95% in prediction of the retinal disease.

Data types and amounts in human society are growing at an amazing speed, which is caused by emerging new services such as cloud computing and internet of things (IoT). As data has been a fundamental resource, research on big data has attracted much attention. An optimized cluster storage method for big data in IoT is proposed. First, weights of data blocks in each historical accessing period are calculated by temporal locality of data access, and the access frequencies of the data block in next period are predicted by the weights. Second, the hot spot of a data block is determined with a threshold that is calculated by previous data access. In this work, big data is divided into multiple segments based on semantic connectivity-based convolutional neural networks. Each segment will be stored in the different nodes by adapting the blockchain distributed-based local regenerative code technology called BCDLR.

Experimental results demonstrate the efficiency of the proposed model in terms of packet delivery ratio, end-to-end delay, energy consumption, and throughput.

Chapter 14

Suganthi K., Vellore Institue of Technology, India
Apratim Shukla, Vellore Institue of Technology, India
Mayank K. Tolani, Vellore Institue of Technology, India
Swapnil Vinod Mishra, Vellore Institue of Technology, India
Abhishek Thazhethe Kalathil, Vellore Institute of Technology, India
Manojkumar R., Vellore Institute of Technology, India

Blockchain technology generally is associated with financial applications where it serves the role of maintaining records. However, such a tamper-resistant distributed ledger can be used for fashioning applications in the healthcare domain. Harnessing the potential of blockchain as a data store for health records would ensure that they would be secure as multiple copies of them are preserved in a decentralized manner to ensure data redundancy and security. With this technology in effect, the medical sector could leverage blockchain tech to allow any authorized hospitals to securely communicate, share information/records independent from a central figure. Information shared would only contain relevant data related to the query between stakeholders with appropriate permission attached to their roles. This chapter delineates the architecture of such a system explaining its benefits and limitations as a medical data-storage architecture.

Chapter 15

Sharanya S., SRM Institute of Science and Technology, India

The rampant developments in the field of predictive analytics, artificial intelligence, big data, along with information and communication technologies have opened new ventures in cyber physical systems (CPS). The wide range of opportunities presented by CPS facilitated massive transformation of industrial processes that converged to building smart systems under the umbrella of Industry 4.0. The manufacturing and energy sector are now shifting their focus on predictive maintenance to pre plan their maintenance activities to reduce the downtime at optimized costs. This proactive maintenance planning involves the integration of multiple technologies like big data analytics, machine learning, and internet of things to build a complete, comprehensive framework that predicts the onset of failure from the early warning signs. The primal focus of this work is to develop a generic CPS framework for predictive maintenance (PdM) in industries from the condition monitored data.

Foreword

"Data is a precious thing and will last longer than the systems themselves" - Tim Berners-Lee, Inventor of the World Wide Web.

As we live and experience the digital age, many people are overwhelmed with a vast sum of data in all aspects of our social and professional lives. Such a vital role for data management has recently been reflected in Google's CEO, Mr. Sundar Pichai's statement that "Artificial Intelligence (AI) and Machine Learning (ML) are the most important things humanity is working on".

Cyber-Physical Systems (CPS) are a new research paradigm in embedded systems. Cyber-Physical systems are a collaboration of physical and computational processes. Different technologies such as sensing, communication, computation, control, and cognition are used to create new technology. CPS have diversified applications include smart grid, autonomous automotive systems, medical monitoring, process control systems, distributed robotics, and automatic pilot avionics. CPS is quite popular because of Integration and Interaction with humans and systems. ML is the backbone of CPS Real-time applications like Green Buildings, Smart Grid, Healthcare, and Humanoid Robots.

This book takes an efficient and practical approach to various real-time problems in CPS. The focus of the first part of the book is to enable student and faculty researchers in academic institutions, researchers in industrial labs, and practitioners to understand what CPS is, how it works, and what tools and frameworks are available to develop applications based on it. Most of the State-of-the-art frameworks in machine learning for CPS were empowered with Google Colab, Jupiter notebook, and APIs like Keras, PyTorch, TensorFlow. The second part of the book covers several real-life Machine learning applications.

Each application area is thoroughly covered, including domain-specific data samples, Machine learning model development, and their actionable insights. From my teaching experience, we have found the approach taken in this book to be efficient.

Machine Learning is a set of algorithms and models typically mathematical in nature. In addition to a walkthrough of mathematical concepts clearly and concisely, it is critical to introduce hands-on tools and real-life success stories.

We are confident that the collective efforts of Editors and authors of this book towards real-time applications on Machine learning in cyber-physical Systems will be precious for booklovers and researchers. We unswervingly recommend this book for those thirsty about Machine learning and cyber-physical systems.

Patrick Acheampong
Ghana Communication Technology University, Accra, Ghana

Preface

Cyber-Physical Systems (CPS) are the intelligent system that combines hardware and software in today's digital age. They are connected through a network as the physical world merges with the virtual world into cyberspace. Applications of CPS are penetrating every domain and reaching their limits. CPS can change and improve lives and address many critical challenges.

One of the most exciting tools entered in recent years is Machine and deep learning. There are several real-time applications of the machine and deep learning in healthcare, manufacturing, marketing, finance, and particularly for making predictions; machine and deep learning algorithms are used in many places in exciting ways. This collection of statistical methods and the availability of large datasets combined with the improvement in algorithms has already proved to be capable of considerably speeding up both fundamental and applied research and led to an unprecedented surge of interest in the topic of machine learning. Machine Learning paradigms are defined in two types, namely supervised learning (SL) and unsupervised learning (UL). In Supervised Learning, objects in each collection are classified using a set of attributes or features. The classification process is a set of rules that prescribe assignments or allocations of things to unique classes based on values of elements. Supervised learning aims to design a reliable system that can precisely predict the class group membership of new objects based on the available attributes or features. Whereas in unsupervised learning (UL), all the data are unlabeled, and the learning process consists of defining the labels and associating objects with them. Deep learning paradigms are defined in different ways of apprehension. Deep learning is an advanced technique for classifying data patterns with higher-order multiple layers neural networks.

This book aims to introduce a relevant theoretical framework and the most recent empirical findings on the various real-time applications of machine learning in cyber-physical systems. In particular, the book investigates the use of Machine Learning techniques and Artificial Intelligence to model different technical solutions on real-time CPS.

ORGANIZATION OF THE BOOK

The book is organized into 15 chapters contributed by researchers, scholars, and professors from prestigious laboratories and educational institutions across the globe. A brief description of each of the chapters in this section is given below.

Chapter 1, "A Survey on Automotive Cyber-Physical Systems: A Machine Learning-Based Approach," briefs a survey about automotive CPS in various domains especially in the development of autonomous cars with different sensors. Further, briefs about the role of machine learning models in the construction of CPS.

Chapter 2, "Cyber Physical Systems Emergence With Reference to Manpower Development: An International Scenario With Indian Potentialities," describes CPS and its role in building human capacity through different levels of the degree program from graduate to research. A comparison of the Indian system with international scenario.

Chapter 3, "Machine Learning in Cyber Physical Systems for Agriculture: Crop Yield Prediction Using Cyber Physical System and Machine Learning," describes CPS and its role in building human capacity through different levels of the degree program from graduate to research. A comparison of the Indian system with the international scenario.

Chapter 4, "Differential Privacy Techniques-Based Information Security for Cyber Physical System Applications: A Overview," aims to introduce various security and privacy issues in CPS and how differential privacy techniques enable to secure information. Different asymmetric and symmetric crypto models were discussed to secure CPS from different level of threats.

Chapter 5, "Machine Learning in Cyber Physical Systems for Healthcare: Brain Tumor Classification From MRI Using Transfer Learning Framework (TLF)," presents Convolution Neural Network (CNN) model for classification of MRI images using TLF for the prediction of early stage brain tumor with improved results. Segmentation is done using Fuzzy c means, texture and shape feature extraction using Support Vector Machines and DNN.

Chapter 6, "Application of Odd-Even Congruence Graph Labeling in Secured Cyber Physical System," aims to address data and control security issues in sensors with cryptography using odd-even congruence graph labeling method. Proposed algorithm is implemented using python programming.

Chapter 7, "Machine Learning for Intrusion Detection Systems: Recent Developments and Future Challenges," presents a review on Intrusion Detection System (IDS) and discussed various machine learning models like K-Nearest neighborhood, Clustering, Logistic Regression, Support Vector Machines, Naïve base, Decision Tree and Random Forest for IDS.

Chapter 8, "Estimating the Efficiency of Machine Learning Algorithm in Predicting Seizure With Convolutional Neural Network Architecture," discussed the problem of epilepsy a neural disorder that occurs in brain which is characterized by seizures. Efficiency of different Machine learning algorithms was analyzed with the EEG sigil data obtained from kaggle repository.

Chapter 9, "Crop Protection Using Cyber-Physical System and Machine Learning for Smart Agriculture," presents CPS and ML model to control agricultural crops control from pests, weeds and diseases and to demonstrate how AI supports to improve crop yields.

Chapter 10, "Arrhythmia Classification Using Deep Learning Architecture," introduces deep learning models for the classification of arrhythmia using EGC signals. Discussed various cardiovascular abnormalities, the proposed model was experimented and tested with MIT-BIH, PTB data set with state-of- art models with better results.

Chapter 11, "Comparing Machine Learning Algorithm and DNN for Anomaly Detection," shows the role of machine learning models for intrusion detection system. The existing Machine learning models having higher timing and computational complexity, to overcome a novel DNN based model has introduced and experimented with better results.

Chapter 12, "Vascular Disease Prediction Using Retinal Image Acquisition Algorithm," presents the machine learning methods for analyzing the vessels patterns to analyze vessel in retinal image to predict vascular disease. CNN and SVM methods are used to classify the artery and veins in retina and experimental results were compared with the state of art models with better accuracy.

Chapter 13, "Convolutional Neural Network-Based Secured Data Storage Mechanism for Big Data Environment," demonstrates a high-performance cluster storage method for big data in IoT. Furthermore, it demonstrates how big data is divided into multiple segments using a semantic connectivity-based convolutional neural network, and how each segment is stored in different nodes by adapting the Blockchain Distributed based Local Regenerative code technology known as BCDLR, with experimented results.

Chapter 14, "Cluniac Chain: Blockchain and ML-Based Healthcare System," presents how Blockchain technology could be used in the medical sector to allow any authorized hospital to securely communicate and share information/records without relying on a central figure. Outline the architecture of such a system, explaining its advantages and disadvantages as a medical data-storage architecture.

Chapter 15, "A Cyber Physical System Framework for Industrial Predictive Maintenance Using Machine Learning," presented a global approach for CPS predictive maintenance in healthcare and Business Processing.

Acknowledgment

It is essential to recognize the unwavering support and innumerable contributions of many people in completing this task. This book would not have been possible without the assistance of IGI Global, USA. We are grateful to the IGI Global team, particularly Gianna Walker, Angelina Olivas, and Jan Travers, for providing this fantastic opportunity and for being exceptionally cooperative throughout the production process from the beginning to the end of this book. Their unique contributions, suggestions, knowledge, and promptness were vital in making this book a reality.

With earnest gratitude and profound thanks, we would like to acknowledge the continuous guidance and encouragements of Prof. Kingston Nyamapfene, Vice-Chancellor, Prof. Francis Sikoki, Dean (Faculty of Basic and Applied Sciences), Prof. Mansi El Mansi, Director, Research, Dr Jackson Akpojaro, Head of the Department of Mathematics and Computer Science, University of Africa, Bayelsa State, Nigeria. Special thanks to Prof. Anders Henten, Prof. Kund Erik Skouby, Prof. Reza Tadayoni, Lene Tolstrup Sørensen, Engineer, Ph.D., Anette Bysøe (Aalborg University, Copenhagen, Denmark) and VDV Singh Sir, Prof. Shrihari Prakash Honwad, Dr. Mukesh Kalla, Dr. Manish Dadhich (Sir Padampat Singhania University, Udaipur, India) and Dr. Ricardo Saavedra (Universidad Azteca, Mexico) for providing in-depth scientific knowledge, guidance, and support.

Our sincere thank goes to our organizations, University of Africa (UAT), Bayelsa State, Nigeria and Sir Padampat Singhania University (SPSU), Udaipur, Rajasthan, India and Aalborg University, Copenhagen, Denmark and Universidad Azteca, Mexico for providing a healthy academic and research environment during our work.

We also wish to thank all reviewers, and authors for their prompt response, dedication, and high standard contributions in the area of Real-Time Applications of Machine Learning in Cyber-Physical Systems.

Acknowledgment

Last but not least, the editorial team wish to express their gratitude to their respective families for their understanding and support throughout.

Balamurugan Easwaran
University of Africa, Toru-Orua, Nigeria

Kamal Kant Hiran
Sir Padampat Singhania University, India

Sangeetha Krishnan
University of Africa, Tora-Orua, Nigeria

Ruchi Doshi
Azteca University, Mexico

Chapter 1
A Survey on Automotive Cyber–Physical Systems:
A Machine Learning–Based Approach

Sujith Jayaprakash
NIIT, Ghana

Shanmugapriya N.
Dr. S. N. S. Rajalakshmi College of Arts and Science, India

Chitra K.
Rathnavel Subramanian College of Arts and Science, India

Kathiresan V.
Dr. S. N. S. Rajalakshmi College of Arts and Science, India

ABSTRACT

The cyber-physical system encompasses physics and cyber systems, which are highly interconnected and networked. Considered to be one of the fascinating inventions of today's world, CPS applications include autonomous vehicles, industrial control systems, medical monitoring, automatic pilot avionics, etc. Autonomous or semi-autonomous vehicles, also known as self-driving or driverless vehicles, are automobiles that require less or no human intervention for operating or controlling them. CPS has brought in several advancements in the automobile industry by providing a seamless human interaction with physical and cyber systems, which includes IoT, artificial intelligence, machine learning, etc. Machine learning algorithms play a major role in enhancing autonomous vehicle models. This chapter focuses on the various machine learning algorithms that are used commonly in building robust autonomous vehicles. This chapter also focuses on the evolution of autonomous vehicles and the backed cyber advancements.

DOI: 10.4018/978-1-7998-9308-0.ch001

1. BACKGROUND

The way humans think and absorb information has changed dramatically as they progressed from Dryopithecus to Homo Sapiens. New technologies and revolutionary ideas opened the path for social and economic progress. The first industrial revolution occurred in the eighteenth century when agrarian civilizations became more industrialized. Electricity, railroads and a slew of other technologies shifted society's outlook dramatically. The three main drivers of the first industrial revolution were land, capital, and labor. Machines, metals, and richer fuels all contributed to the first revolution, which enabled humans to expand their output of agricultural products, textiles, and machinery, among other things. Water, coal, and steam were used as power sources during this time.

The Second Industrial Revolution built on the first, but it was more concerned with minimizing human labour and increasing automation. Electricity and petroleum were the primary sources of energy for this revolution. In 1947, the third industrial revolution began as a digital revolution, with new technologies such as computers, mobile phones, the internet, renewable energy, and a few other forms of technology establishing the groundwork. When studying the history of the industrial revolution, it is evident that these advancements arose from the need to increase automation and production.

Figure 1. Evolution of Industrial Revolution and its major power source

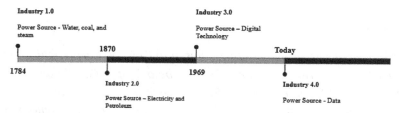

Since Prof. Klaus Schwab, the creator of the World Economic Forum popularized the term "fourth industrial revolution," there has been a rising interest among scholars, academics, and business leaders in learning more about it. Humankind is now surrounded by technological advancements. Everything around us is undergoing a digital revolution, from the alarm clock to automated coolers/heaters, computerized kitchen appliances, and automated automobiles. These digital devices not only save time and effort for humans, but they also capture a massive quantity of data on each individual.

The Fourth Industrial Revolution's main source of power is data. The Fourth Industrial Revolution, often known as Industry 4.0, intends to create a collaborative atmosphere across different divisions within a firm through better communication and the distribution of relevant information. Helen Gil of the National Science Foundation in the United States created the phrase "cyber physical systems," which combines computer and physical processes.

Figure 2. Cyber Physical Systems

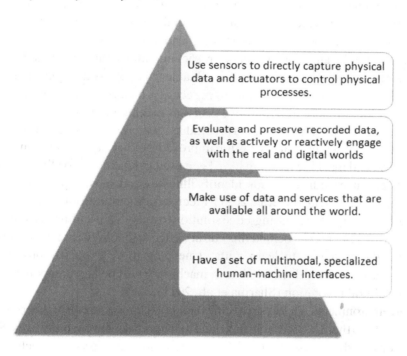

CPS, on the other hand, is a combination of physical and computational processes. Systems having embedded software are known as cyber-physical systems (as part of devices, buildings, means of transport, transport routes, production systems, medical processes, logistic processes, coordination processes, and management processes) (Arcot, 2021). Artificial intelligence, the Internet of Things, and machine learning algorithms are heavily used in autonomous or semi-autonomous cars (Fulton & Platzer, 2018). This chapter deals with the various machine learning algorithms recommended and used in the Automotive Cyber-Physical systems space.

2. MACHINE LEARNING

Machine learning is a field of computer science and artificial intelligence that focuses on using data and algorithms to mimic the way people learn while continuously improving its accuracy. Machine learning has provided us with useful voice recognition, powerful online search, self-driving automobiles, and a comprehensive understanding of the human genome. Machine learning is now so common that you probably use it on a daily basis without even realizing it.

Machine learning is an important component of data science, which is still in its early stages. Algorithms are trained to produce predictions or classifications using statistical approaches, providing significant insights in data mining initiatives (Hiran, Jain, Lakhwani et al, 2021). For retrieving information from the Internet of Things (IoT) data, machine learning is a valuable technique (Lakhwani et al., 2020). In a number of sectors, such as education, security, business, and healthcare, these hybrid solutions significantly improve decision-making processes.

Machine learning is used to interpret hidden patterns in vast quantities of data in the Internet of Things, allowing for improved prediction and recommendation systems. IoT and machine learning have been used in healthcare to allow automated devices to produce medical records, identify illnesses, and, most importantly, monitor patients in real time (Aldahiri et al., 2021). Precision agriculture, often known as smart farming, has emerged as a cutting-edge solution to today's agricultural sustainability issues. The driving reason behind this cutting-edge technology is machine learning. It enables the computer to learn without needing to be explicitly programmed. Machine learning and IoT-enabled farm machinery will be key components of the next agricultural revolution (Sharma et al., 2021).

Smart environments, such as smart cities and smart houses, are also Cyber-Physical-Systems (CPSs) that are becoming more and more prevalent in our daily lives. Several applications in these systems use Machine Learning as a practical technique for extracting valuable knowledge from raw data, such as energy management through home appliance identification or activity recognition. (Khamesi et al., 2020)

Cyber-Physical Systems are made up of a number of sophisticated multi-tasking components that work together to integrate cyber portions into the physical environment. As a result of the massive expansion of cyber-physical systems and the widespread use of smart features and communication tools, new difficulties have emerged. (Mohammadi Rouzbahani et al., 2020)

Figure 3. ML Models

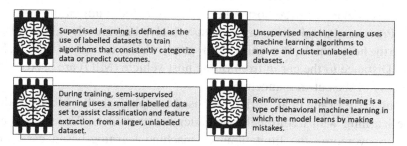

3. ROLE OF MACHINE LEARNING IN CPS

Machine learning algorithms have revolutionized almost every field (Hiran, Khazanchi, Vyas et al, 2021). Businesses all across the globe have increased their efficiency by predicting future occurrences or forecasting based on historical data. The use of machine learning algorithms is growing in every sector of business. Industry 4.0 will concentrate on a wide range of digital applications, such as intelligent control of automated and semi-automated vehicles, health monitoring, analytics, and process optimization. By allowing self-learning and decision-making applications, machine learning algorithms will play a crucial role in achieving the goals of Industry 4.0. The backbone of autonomous or semi-automated cars is machine learning algorithms. To conduct futuristic actions, the models acquire data from various cameras and sensors. Typically, these models are created to improve security, efficiently manoeuvre, or predict road objects. Several researchers and academics have collaborated on and proposed models to improve the capabilities of self-driving or autonomous cars. Here are a few publications that focus on machine learning methods for autonomous cars. N. Motamedidehkordi et al. (Motamedidehkordi et al., 2017) presented a model to analyze human drivers' tactical behaviour during lane-changing manoeuvres. Vehicle ID, Frame ID, Lane ID, Local X, Local Y, Mean Speed, Mean Acceleration, Vehicle Class ID, Vehicle length, Follower ID, and Leader ID are the recognized features used to mimic driving behaviour. Naive Bayes, Support Vector Machine, Linear Regression, KNearestNeighbourhood, Decision Tree, and Random Forest were used to create several models. Decision tree classifiers beat the rest of the models in the study. F. Remmenet.al.,(Remmen et al., 2018) recommended a model to predict the cut-in manoeuvre of a vehicle based on fixed parameters. Truck platooning is gaining more and more interest and thanks to the benefits of improved traffic efficiency, reduced fuel consumption and emissions. In this paper, the researchers have tried to predict the cut-in manoevur of the vehicle based on fixed parameters like Longitudinal distance to host vehicle,

Lateral distance to host vehicle, Longitudinal speed, relative to the host vehicle, Lateral speed, relative to the host vehicle, Previous longitudinal distance to host vehicle, Previous lateral distance to host vehicle, Previous longitudinal speed, relative to the host vehicle, Previous lateral speed, relative to the host vehicle, Matrix location, Distance to the car in front of the host vehicle (MIO) are used to predict the accuracy of the cut-in manoeuvre.

D. Yang et al. (Yang et al., 2019) proposed an approach that blends traditional machine learning with traditional kinematics-based models. The researchers are working to overcome the limitations of machine learning-based car-following algorithms. The combination car-following model is a unique car-following model that combines machine learning-based car-following models and classical kinematics-based car-following models. A hybrid model is built using Random Forest and Back Propagation models. Hengrui Chen et al.(Chen et al., 2021) proposed a model that studies the mechanism of AV-related accidents and assesses the impact of each characteristic on the accident severity. The AV-involved crash reports dataset is balanced using a synthetic minority oversampling approach. For accident mechanism analysis, the Apriori method and classification models are utilized. To investigate the mechanism of crashes, the Apriori method is utilized to find the causal link between numerous variables. The crash severity is assessed using the support vector machine (SVM), classification and regression tree (CART), and eXtreme Gradient Boosting (XGBoost) methods.

Because pedestrian identification has been regarded as one of the most essential jobs for autonomous cars, Navarro PJ et al.(Navarro et al., 2017) proposed a machine learning technique that employs high-definition 3D range data to identify pedestrians in autonomous vehicles. The sensor's cloud of data is processed to detect pedestrians by choosing cubic shapes and projecting the points in the cube using machine vision and machine learning techniques. For pedestrian detection, the k-Nearest Neighbors, Naive Bayes, and Support Vector Machine methods are utilized.SVM was tested with linear and quadratic functions with data normalization; kNN was tested with Euclidean and Mahalanobis distances with data normalization; NBC was tested with Gaussian and Kernel Smoothing Functions (KSF) without data normalization, and NBC was tested with Gaussian and Kernel Smoothing Functions (KSF) without data normalization.

4. COMPONENTS OF CPS

CPS is the most secure, dependable, and efficient computer system available. CPS applications are used in a variety of industries, including healthcare, military, transportation, energy, and infrastructure. RFID & IoT, The Internet, Embedded

Systems, Wireless Sensor Networks, Mobile Networks, and Satellite Networks are all essential components of a Cyber-Physical System. The CPS serves as a link between the actual and virtual worlds. The wireless sensor network, which provides smooth communication between physical devices, is one of the most important components of CPS.(Gunes et al., 2014)

Figure 4. Components of CPS

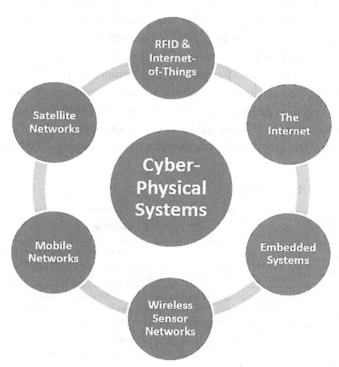

5. JOURNEY OF AUTONOMOUS CARS AND LEVEL OF AUTOMATION

Self-driving automobiles are primarily concerned with dependable mobility, safety, and affordability. Top businesses such as Tesla, Apple, Uber, Amazon, and a slew of others focusing on cutting-edge technology are working to improve the characteristics of self-driving cars. Though the notion of self-driving vehicles was proposed in the 1930s, it was only in the first decade of the twenty-first century that it became a reality. (Wolmar, 2020). Many groundbreaking inventions, such as da Vinci's Self-Propelled Cart (1500), Robert Whitehead's underwater-propelled Torpedo (1868), Mechanical

Mike aircraft autopilot (1933), Teetor Cruise Control (1945), Stanford Cart (1961), and many others, paved the way for today's autonomous vehicle revolution. Since 2004, the US Department of Defense's research arm (DARPA) has hosted a series of competitions aimed at advancing autonomous technology. Cars are challenged to self-navigate through desert highways and metropolitan settings in these events. Six automobiles out of 11 contenders accomplished the challenge covering roughly 55 miles in less than 6 hours in 2007. The six finalist robots offered the first views of a very different future among abandoned military housing and ghostly streets. (Voelcker, 2017). The Navlab group at Carnegie Mellon University has been a pioneer in developing computer-controlled cars for autonomous and semi-autonomous vehicles. Since 1984, robot cars, vans, SUVs, and buses have been produced (The Carnegie Mellon University Autonomous Land Vehicle Project (NAVLAB), 2021). The United Kingdom is the first country to allow autonomous automobiles to travel at a low speed on public roads. Twenty-nine (29) states in the United States have enacted legislation allowing self-driving automobiles. Apart from these two countries, Australia, Germany, South Korea, Canada, Hungary, Turkey, China, and

Table 1. Levels of Automation

Level	Name of the Level	Explanation
0	No Automation	The driver is solely responsible for the vehicle's control, including steering, braking, accelerating, and slowing down. Backup cameras, blind-spot alerts, and collision warnings are all available on Level 0 cars.
1	Driver Assistance	The automated systems start to take control of the vehicle in specific situations but do not fully take over. An example of Level 1 automation is adaptive cruise control, which controls acceleration and braking, typically in highway driving.
2	Partial Automation	Because of its increased awareness of its environment, the vehicle can execute more complicated activities that combine steering (lateral control) with accelerating and braking (longitudinal control).
3	Conditional Automation	Drivers can detach from the task of driving in certain circumstances. Certain vehicle speeds, road types, and weather circumstances may be restricted. Nevertheless, the driver is expected to take over when the system requests it.
4	High Automation	The autonomous driving system of the vehicle is completely capable of monitoring the driving environment and performing all driving operations for routine routes and circumstances described within its operational design scope (ODD). If there is an environmental situation that demands human management, such as thick snow, the vehicle may notify the driver that it is approaching its operating limits. If the driver does not reply, the car will be automatically secured.
5	Full Automation	Vehicles are completely self-contained. There is no requirement for a driver to be present behind the wheel. In fact, Level 5 cars may lack a steering wheel as well as gas and brake pedals. Passengers in Level 5 cars may be able to use voice commands to select a location or control interior settings such as temperature and media selection.

Poland all contribute significantly to the advancement of technology (Global Guide to Autonomous Vehicles, 2021). The classification of automated vehicles is done by separating them into categories based on the degree of automation. The National Highway Traffic Safety Administration (NHTSA) of the United States issued the first categorization in 2013. In 2016, SAE introduced its six degrees of automation, which became the worldwide standard for all automated cars. Table 1 shows the different levels of automation in self-driving cars.

6. SENSORS IN AUTONOMOUS CARS

Sensors are used in autonomous cars. It's difficult to conceive self-driving cars without sensors. They enable the car to see and sense everything on the road, as well as collect the data required for safe driving. This data is collected and evaluated in order to create a pathway from one location to another and deliver the necessary steering, acceleration, and braking commands to the automobile.

The information gathered by sensors in autonomous vehicles, such as the real path, traffic congestion, and any road impediments, may also be exchanged between automobiles linked via M2M technology. Vehicle-to-vehicle communication is what it's called, and it may be a huge assist when it comes to driving automation.

The majority of today's automotive manufacturers most commonly use the following three types of sensors in autonomous vehicles

- Cameras,
- Radars, and
- Lidars.

a. Camera Sensors

Video cameras and sensors are commonly used in autonomous vehicles to detect and interpret things on the road, just like human drivers do with their eyes. By equipping automobiles with these cameras from every angle, they would be able to retain a 360° view of their exterior surroundings, giving them a more comprehensive image of traffic situations. 3D cameras are now available and may be used to display very detailed and lifelike visuals. These image sensors detect, categorize, and calculate distances between objects and the vehicle automatically. Other automobiles, pedestrians, bicycles, traffic signs and signals, road markings, bridges, and guardrails, for example, are all easily identifiable by the cameras.

b. Radar Sensors

Radar (Radio Detection and Ranging) sensors are critical to autonomous driving's general function: they send out radio waves that detect objects and calculate their distance and speed in real-time in relation to the vehicle. Short- and long-range radar sensors are often distributed throughout the vehicle, each with its own set of tasks. While short-range (24 GHz) radar applications allow for blind-spot monitoring, optimum lane-keeping assistance, and parking aids, long-range (77 GHz) radar sensors are responsible for automated distance control and braking assistance. Radar devices, unlike camera sensors, generally have no problem detecting objects in fog or rain.

c. Lidar Sensors

Lidar (Light Detection and Ranging) sensors function similarly to radar systems, with the exception that instead of radio waves, they utilize lasers. Lidar can create 3D pictures of identified items and map the surroundings in addition to measuring distances to various things on the route. Furthermore, rather than relying on a restricted field of vision, lidar may be set to produce a full 360-degree map surrounding the vehicle. Lidar systems are preferred by autonomous car makers such as Google, Uber, and Toyota because of these two benefits.

d. ADAS (Advanced Driver Assistance Systems)

The majority of car collisions are caused by human mistakes, which may be reduced or eliminated using Advanced Driver Assistance Systems (ADAS). The goal of ADAS is to reduce the frequency of automobile accidents and the severity of those that cannot be prevented, thereby preventing fatalities and injuries.

Figure 5. ADAS Applications

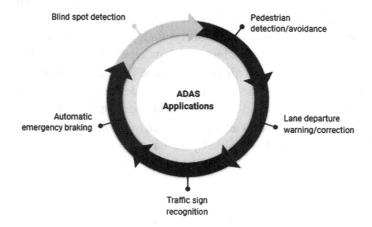

Table 2. Features of ADAS

ADAS Features	Sensors Used
ACC	Camera/LiDAR/RADAR
Park Assistant	Ultrasonic/Camera
Blind Spot	Camera/RADAR
AEB	Camera/LiDAR/RADAR
Drowsiness	Camera
Pedestrian	Camera
Traffic Sign Recognition	Camera
Lane Control Assist	Camera
Night Vision	Camera/Bolometer
High auto beam	Camera

7. CHALLENGES AND OPPORTUNITIES IN AUTONOMOUS VEHICLES

Several automobile companies, investors and tech companies are trying to bring autonomous vehicles to the day to day lives (Khvoynitskaya, 2020). However, the full adoption of these automated vehicles is impossible unless the key issues and challenges are addressed. One of the most pressing issues in this advancing field is the safety of passengers. Many researchers have tried to address safety related issue

Figure 6. Key Challenges

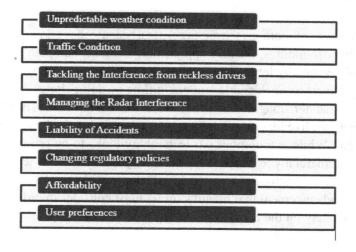

using machine learning models by analyzing the data received from the sensors. Few other researchers have recommended ways to enhance the experience of the passengers in the driverless vehicles by analyzing the user behavior using machine learning algorithms.

a. Challenges

The camera sensors, unfortunately, are still far from ideal. Rain, fog, or snow can obscure the obstructions in the road, increasing the risk of an accident. In addition, there are times when the pictures from the cameras are just insufficient for a computer to make an informed judgement on what the automobile should do. The driving algorithms may fail in circumstances where the colors of objects are very similar to those of the backdrop or when the contrast between them is minimal.

The pedestrian detection algorithm is in desperate need of improvement, given that today's automobile radar sensors only accurately identify between 90 and 95 percent of pedestrians, which is insufficient to assure road safety. Furthermore, because the sensors only scan horizontally, 2D radars cannot correctly detect an object's height, which can pose a number of issues while driving beneath bridges or road signs. To address these difficulties, a broader range of 3D radar sensors is now being developed. Lidar sensors are significantly costlier than radar sensors used in autonomous vehicles because rare earth metals are required to build sufficient lidar sensors. The equipment needed for autonomous driving may cost well over $10,000, with Google and Uber's top sensor costing up to $80,000. Another issue is that snow or fog can occasionally obstruct lidar sensors, making it difficult for them to detect things in the road.

b. Opportunities

In automated driving, autonomous sensors are critical because they allow automobiles to monitor their surroundings, identify approaching hazards, and plan their routes safely. They will eventually let the automation system to assume full control of the vehicle, saving drivers a considerable amount of time by doing duties in a far more efficient and safe manner. Imagine how beneficial autonomous vehicles may be in the fast-paced society we live in, given that the average driver spends about 50 minutes each day in a car. While autonomous car technology looks to be progressing at a rapid rate, no commercially available vehicles have yet achieved the level 4 rating necessary for road-safe autonomous vehicles. There is still a significant amount of technological advancement that manufacturers must consider in order to assure autonomous car safety on the roads.

Figure 7. Challenges and Risks in CPS related to Industry 4.0

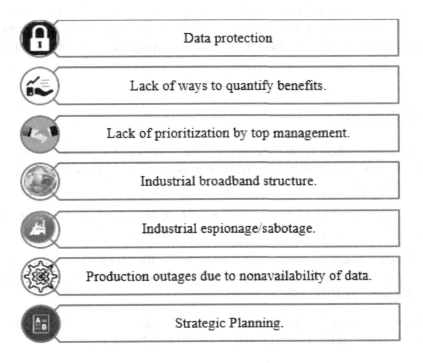

8. CONCLUSION

In the next years, cyber-physical systems will reign supreme. Many innovative ideas will undoubtedly boost productivity and propel companies forward. Unmanned aerial and ground vehicles now have autonomous decision-making skills thanks to a decade of progress in cyber-physical systems with improved sensors, subsystems, and machine-learning algorithms. The degree of autonomy is determined by the vehicle's make-up and sensor sophistication, as well as the vehicle's operational use, which can range from highly expensive military-based combat vehicles to commercially accessible civilian motor vehicles and very low-cost hobby drones. These advancements in the field of Cyber physical systems rely heavily on machine learning techniques. Machine learning algorithms are important for analyzing environments based on observations, learning patterns, building prediction models, clustering related observations, and eventually making choices. Researchers and academics are always attempting to make new changes and fix current difficulties like security and other concerns using machine learning algorithms, thus development in the field of autonomous vehicles will continue. A study is done in this article to determine the machine learning algorithms utilized in autonomous cars and their application. According to the research, there are obstacles and dangers associated with developing completely automated cars; nevertheless, numerous researchers are developing novel ways to reduce these risks and bring the fully automated vehicle to life.

REFERENCES

Aldahiri, A., Alrashed, B., & Hussain, W. (2021). Trends in Using IoT with Machine Learning in Health Prediction System. *Forecasting*, *3*(1), 181–206. doi:10.3390/forecast3010012

Arcot, R. (2021). *Cyber-Physical Systems: The Core of Industry 4.0*. https://blog.isa.org/cyber-physical-systems-the-core-of-industry-4.0

Chen, Chen, Zhou, Liu, & Sun. (2021). Exploring the Mechanism of Crashes with Autonomous Vehicles Using Machine Learning. *Hindawi Mathematical problems in Engineering*. doi:10.1155/2021/5524356

Fulton, N., & Platzer, A. (2018). Safe AI for CPS (Invited Paper). *IEEE International Test Conference (ITC)*, 1-7. 10.1109/TEST.2018.8624774

Global Guide to Autonomous Vehicles. (2021). https://www.dentons.com/en/insights/guides-reports-and-whitepapers/2021/january/28/global-guide-to-autonomous-vehicles-2021

Gunes, V., Peter, S., Givargis, T., & Vahid, F. (2014). A Survey on Concepts, Applications, and Challenges in Cyber-Physical Systems. *Transactions on Internet and Information Systems (Seoul)*, *8*(12), 4242–4268. doi:10.3837/tiis.2014.12.001

Hiran, K. K., Jain, R. K., Lakhwani, K., & Doshi, R. (2021). *Machine Learning: Master Supervised and Unsupervised Learning Algorithms with Real Examples (English Edition)*. BPB Publications.

Hiran, K. K., Khazanchi, D., Vyas, A. K., & Padmanaban, S. (Eds.). (2021). *Machine Learning for Sustainable Development* (Vol. 9). Walter de Gruyter GmbH & Co KG. doi:10.1515/9783110702514

Khamesi, A. R., Shin, E., & Silvestri, S. (2020). Machine Learning in the Wild: The Case of User-Centered Learning in Cyber Physical Systems. *International Conference on COMmunication Systems & NETworkS (COMSNETS)*, 275-281. 10.1109/COMSNETS48256.2020.9027329

Khvoynitskaya, S. (2020, February 11). 3 types of autonomous vehicle sensors in self-driving cars. *Autonomous-vehicle-sensors.* https://www.itransition.com/blog/autonomous-vehicle-sensors

Lakhwani, K., Gianey, H. K., Wireko, J. K., & Hiran, K. K. (2020). *Internet of Things (IoT): Principles, paradigms and applications of IoT.* Bpb Publications.

Mohammadi Rouzbahani, H., Karimipour, H., Rahimnejad, A., Dehghantanha, A., & Srivastava, G. (2020). Anomaly Detection in Cyber-Physical Systems Using Machine Learning. Handbook of Big Data Privacy Springer, 219-235. doi:10.1007/978-3-030-38557-6_10

Motamedidehkordi, N., Amini, S., Hoffmann, S., Busch, F., & Fitriyanti, M. R. (2017). Modeling tactical lane-change behavior for automated vehicles: A supervised machine learning approach. *5th IEEE International Conference on Models and Technologies for Intelligent Transportation Systems (MT-ITS)*, 268-273. 10.1109/MTITS.2017.8005678

Navarro, P., Fernández-Isla, C., Borraz, R., & Alonso, D. (2017). A Machine Learning Approach to Pedestrian Detection for Autonomous Vehicles Using High-Definition 3D Range Data. *Sensors (Basel), 17*(1), 18. doi:10.339017010018 PMID:28025565

Remmen, F., Cara, I., Gelder, E. D., & Willemsen, D. (2018). Cut-in Scenario Prediction for Automated Vehicles. *IEEE International Conference on Vehicular Electronics and Safety (ICVES)*, 1-7. 10.1109/ICVES.2018.8519594

Sharma, A., Jain, A., Gupta, P., & Chowdary, V. (2021). Machine Learning Applications for Precision Agriculture: A Comprehensive Review. *IEEE Access : Practical Innovations, Open Solutions, 9*, 4843–4873. doi:10.1109/ACCESS.2020.3048415

The Carnegie Mellon University Autonomous Land Vehicle Project (NAVLAB). (2021). https://www.cs.cmu.edu/afs/cs/project/alv/www/index.html

Voelcker, J. (2017). *Autonomous Vehicles Complete DARPA Urban Challenge.* https://spectrum.ieee.org/autonomous-vehicles-complete-darpa-urban-challenge

Wolmar, C. (2020). The Long Journey of the Driverless Car. *IntechOpen.* https://www.intechopen.com/online-first/73420 doi:10.5772/intechopen.93856

Yang, D., Zhu, L., Liu, Y., Wu, D., & Ran, B. (2019). A Novel Car-Following Control Model Combining Machine Learning and Kinematics Models for Automated Vehicles. *IEEE Transactions on Intelligent Transportation Systems, 20*(6), 1991–2000. doi:10.1109/TITS.2018.2854827

Chapter 2
Cyber Physical Systems Emergence With Reference to Manpower Development:
An International Scenario With Indian Potentialities

Prantosh Kumar Paul
Raiganj University, India

ABSTRACT

Cyber-physical systems, in short CPS, is a the term coined by Ellen Gill in the year 2006. It is a kind of embedded system. It is a kind of next generation computing systems that comprises the interacting digital, analog, physical components by integrated physics and logic. This CPS is associated and allied with other technologies and concepts such as big data analytics, cloud computing, internet of things (IoT). Furthermore, cyber-physical systems is making smart things by enabling smart grid, smart cities, and other intelligent and smart things, for example, cars, buildings, homes, manufacturing, hospitals, appliances. This chapter discusses the aspects of cyber-physical systems including its basics, features, functions, and emerging and possible roles. Moreover, this chapter also discusses the current trends on educational programs, training programs in the areas of cyber-physical systems internationally with potentiality in Indian context, and it depicts many opportunities in the contemporary scenario.

DOI: 10.4018/978-1-7998-9308-0.ch002

INTRODUCTION

In the year 2006 the term Cyber-Physical Systems was coined by the Ellen Gill. This is known as an important embedded systems and fall under the Next Generation Computing System which is connected with the computational techniques and various computational stakeholders (Agarwal, P., 2007; Chen, G. et.al., 2018). In Cyber-Physical Systems three important means are Computation, Communication and Controls. In CPS, Internet of Things (IoT) plays a leading role due to its connections with the computational and physical units and aspects that leads the advancement in implementations of healthy and sophisticated communication systems. According to some experts 'digital controls' and the 'physical environment' merges and developed Cyber-Physical Systems (Colombo, A. W., et.al., 2014; Paul, P.K. et.al., 2017c). In Cyber-Physical Systems there are two combinations viz. Cyber related elements with physical Components basically results in Cyber-Physical Systems which is simply an information processing computer system, and furthermore embedded into a product and that can also be integrated into the car, plane or any kind of other device. The basic structure is depicted herewith in Fig:1.

Figure 1. Basic Cyber Physical Systems Structure with attributes

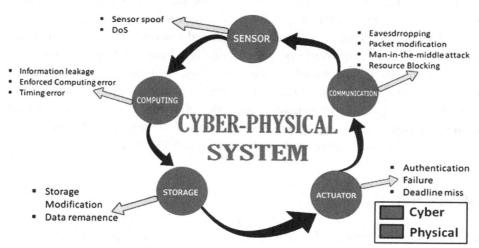

According to the experts in a particular car, the embedded system may be considered as the Anti-lock / Anti-Skid Braking System for controlling the break force. And here the particular systems interact with the physical environment with the uses of Sensors and Actuators (Alguliyev, R. et.al., 2018; Ali, S. et.al., 2015; Paul, P.K., et.al. 2020) Therefore it is important to note that such embedded systems basically no longer standalone and basically they share the contents and data with efficient communication networks like the internet and here cloud computing and similar systems may be used in which data from various embedded systems can be collected and processed. In this regard, CPS can be treated in developing a system of systems, and here decentralized by a computational unit. Here in CPS, the data can be collected and processed by the Human Machine Interface (HMI), (Humayed, A., et.al., 2017; Khaitan, S. K., et.al., 2014). In Cyber-Physical Systems IoT is considered as important and valuable as here devices and systems are effectively connected by internet and do the performances in real time data collection remotely, and furthermore can be processed with other devices. According to the experts, Cyber-Physical Systems can be worked with two computer systems's types viz. Computers (such as Notebooks, Desktop Server and PCs etc), Embedded Computing Systems (i.e. important in the industry, organizations as well as in the invisible part of environment).

Therefore CPS is a kind of intelligent system and mechanism which is merged with the hardware, software and connected with a network and by this 'physical systems & world' properly connected with the 'virtual world'. The innovations of the Cyber-Physical Systems is depends on many skill sets and that requires timely updating as per need and development (Ashibani, Y., 2017; Baheti, R., & Gill, H., 2011; Paul, P.K., 2017b). And as a result many educational institutions worldwide are focused on proper and dedicated manpower development in the field.

Cyber-Physical Systems istherefore associated with the traditional embedded systems, computers, software systems practically where principle mission is not computation. As it is applicable in the cars, toys, medical devices, engineering systems etc and thus it is merged and combines with the physical process with computational systems viz. software, network, modeling, designing and analysis techniques. However Cyber-Physical Systems can be defined and marked its progress during the beginning of cybernetics (Hiran, K. K., & Doshi, R., 2013).

OBJECTIVE

The present paper entitled 'Cyber Physical Systems Emergence with Reference to Manpower Development: An International Scenario with Indian Potentialities' is proposed with mentioned agendas and objectives—

- To know about the Cyber-Physical Systems like its features, nature and characteristics in brief.
- To know about the functions and roles in computation and other activities in brief.

- To learn about the utilizations of the CPS in different sectors and areas in making of Digitalized Systems.
- To know about the basics of the Mobile Cyber-Physical Systems in various systems and computing.
- To dig out the applications, educational opportunities such as training and research opportunities in CPS and allied areas in brief.
- To learn about the potential degrees and educational and training programs of Cyber-Physical Systems in Indian context lies on International market in brief.

CYBER PHYSICAL SYSTEMS (CPS): BASIC CHARACTERISTICS AND COMPONENTS

The CPS or Cyber-Physical Systems is an innovative and intelligent systems lies on devices and electronic and Information Technology and it is deals with following attributes—

- Cyber-Physical Systems is kind of intelligence, adaptive and robustness.
- The Network deal a healthy and potential role in Cyber-Physical Systems for the affairs like communication, cooperation, cloud solutions.
- The Cyber-Physical Systems depends on various Functionalities.
- User friendliness in the Systems and mechanism is must and important in CPS.

Cyber-Physical Systems therefore directly integrated with computational systems and physical processes. And here software is basically embedded with the physical systems and importantly CPS here works on WSN (wireless sensor networks), (Xu, L. D., & Duan, L., 2019; Zanero, S., 2017)

According to the expert, the Cyber-Physical Systems has 5c (five) structure and these include component level, machine level, fleet level, enterprise level etc. and all these are effective in operational level (also refer Fig:2).

Component Level

This level basically keeps virtual twins in the cyber space and moreover it captures different kind of changes that happens in the cloud. The system itself helpful in self awareness related activities properly (Darwish, A., & Hassanien, A. E., 2018; Leitão, P. et.al. 2016)

Machine Level

This level basically dedicated in the information gathered in different layers and component level and therefore it helps in combined machine operations.

Fleet Level

Optimize production process is become possible with the fleet level and further it result in self configuring and self maintenance and has the benefit of maximizing the life span regarding the components of the systems.

Enterprise Level

The Enterprise level of the Cyber Physical System incorporates the outcome of previous level and it is dedicated in producing high performance production (Krämer, B. J., 2014; Kim, K. D., & Kumar, P. R., 2013).

Figure 2. Architecture in Cyber Physical Systems

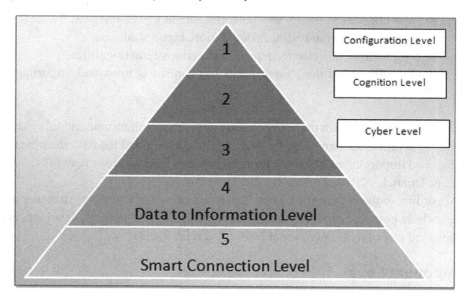

CYBER PHYSICAL SYSTEM: THE IMPORTANCE ABD APPLICATIONS

Cyber-Physical Systems or CPS is emerging and applicable in wide range of areas due to its potential benefits and among these few important are include as depicted bellow. Standards, protocols and test methods used in the cyber physical systems basically dedicated in promoting innovation, and therefore it indirectly improve economic viability and furthermore it is allowing systems more efficient and reduce resource-use and keeps timeliness in the products (Gronau, N., 2016; Iqbal, R. et.al., 2020)

Integration

The Cyber-Physical System or CPS is helpful in the process of the integration of the cloud systems as well as network systems. It offers network integration characteristics like media access control techniques, system dynamics, middleware, network transactions etc.

Healthy Interaction of Human and Computational Systems

The Cyber-Physical Systems keeps healthy benefit in proper and efficient interaction of human and computation systems. Such system is worthy in environmental awareness and decision making systems properly (Guo, Y., 2010; Lee, I. et.al., 2011)

Dealing With Uncertainty

Cyber-Physical System is helpful in developing certain situation and condition and therefore it is beneficial in designing valid and trustworthiness systems.

Effective System Performance

The Cyber-Physical Systems promotes effective system performance due to various benefits regarding feedback and automatic re-designing with proper interaction of the cyber and allied infrastructure.

Flexibility and Suppleness

The flexibility in Cyber-Physical System is another feature than the wireless sensor network and cloud based systems (Alguliyev, R.,et.al, 2014; Huang, Z. et.al., 2014)

Faster Response Timing

One of the important feature of Cyber-Physical System is, it is faster response timing. It offer faster, early detection in timing, proper resource utilizations.

The benefits of the Cyber-Physical System is the cause behind its wider and emerging applications and the areas are increasing viz. manufacturing, water distribution and management systems, smart greenhouse, medical and healthcare systems, transportation systems, building, aeronautics, virtual reality, smart learning and teaching activities and so on. Cyber-Physical System or CPS is a type of sensor based as well as automated communication systems (Rocher, G., 2020; Wan, J., 2011). Here different WSN basically dedicated and monitors some aspect of the environment and connected/ relay with the central node. Among the examples of the Cyber-Physical System are include smart and intelligent grid, autonomous and advanced automotive systems, medical and healthcare monitoring, distributed and healthy robotics etc. There are many real and current examples of the Cyber-Physical System utilizations viz. Distributed Robot Garden at the Campus of Massachusetts Institute of Technology, USA. This is a kind of tomato garden and combines with distributed sensing, navigation, manipulation as well as wireless networking systems (Hehenberger, P. et.al, 2016; Lieu Tran. et.al, 2016). In another example the citation of Idaho National Laboratory can be given which is a prime example of resilient control systems. With this, next generation design with cyber security becomes positively possible. Similar to previous, at Massachusetts Institute of Technology, USA another important example is CarTel project in which taxi is able in data collection that is helpful in real time traffic information management at Boston, USA. Therefore it helps on fastest route management. As far as smartest and advanced electric grids are concerned the Cyber-Physical System is effectively useful and may be able in enhancing the integration of distributed renewable generation (Lu, T.,, 2015; Lun, Y. Z. et. al., 2019). The Cyber-Physical System helpful in empowering Industry 4.0 by the uses of Cloud Technologies, Big Data Applications, IoT Systems etc. There are many projects/ companies engaged in Cyber-Physical System development and activities and among these important are—

- IMC-AESOP Project of European Commission
- SAP
- Honeywell
- Microsoft *etc.*

According to the expert the biggest areas of Cyber-Physical System applications are important in the areas of advanced manufacturing, intelligent water distribution systems, advanced and sophisticated transportation, remote and effective healthcare and smart buildings, etc.

In Manufacturing and Allied Industries

Cyber-Physical System is important in different type of manufacturing related activities it includes the self monitoring of the operations and productions including control. The manufacturing process become easy with Cyber-Physical System applications, it is due to the possible data sharing between machines, supply chain, suppliers, customers, middle mans etc. In smart manufacturing Cyber-Physical System is important in supply chain management and ultimately it helps in traceability and security of goods. The applications of the IoT (Internet of Things) and Big Data Analytics/ Management are important in healthy, sophisticated and advanced manufacturing systems. Here sensors are basically predicted with the equipment wear and diagnose faults and hence here ultimately it is the reason for less maintenance and advanced cost and enhancing operation performance (Marwedel, P., et.al., 2020; Paul, P.K., et.al., 2017a) [25]. As we know that manufacturing is lies on five level of architecture therefore the Cyber-Physical System helps in the following—

Connection

The Cyber-Physical System is helps in building and keeping the connections such as machines, tools as well as the products.

Conversion

This is simply the use of the algorithm that covers the data to information and here is the role of the Cyber-Physical System (Sadiku, M. N., 2017).

Cyber

The sophisticated manufacturing industry lies on sophisticated and advanced manufacturing methods and therefore here deep learning and similar algorithms are play a leading role.

Cognition

The potential problem can be indentified while sending data from different devices and further it helps in monitoring and diagnoses the potential problems and issue.

Configuration

The configuration become an important and worthy tool in managing and deploying the systems as machine can amend their operation based on the malfunctions and workloads (Altbach, P. G., 1993).

In Water Distribution and Management Systems

As far as water distributed systems are concerned Cyber-Physical System is worthy and increasing rapidly. In some of the things it is worthy such as reservoirs, tanks, pumps, well, pipes, water tanks etc. Cyber-Physical System is helpful in monitoring activity viz. sensors for detecting the water level, overflow level, pressure of the water from the pipeline. Moreover the programmable logic controls can automatically open valves, supervision, etc. (Kim, K. D., & Kumar, P. R., 2013; Sanislav, T., & Miclea, L., 2012)

In Agricultural and Promoting Smarter Greenhouse Systems

Cyber-Physical System or CPS is important in enhancing the agriculture systems and it improves the advanced productivity and prevents starvation. And the CPS here is important in healthy temperature, humidity, irrigation system bringing. Here specific computer programs can be used supported by the CPS that may be ensuring better growth and these are helping in greenhouse. Here the feedback and similar systems can be managed using network service using the sensors to collect the data on temperature and humidity, soil moisture as well as light sensors. Therefore, Cyber-Physical System is beneficial in the following—

- To save the money of the farmers and agriculturist including time and effort.
- To offer healthy and better environment including the productivity.
- To control and supply automated water and allied logistics (Paul, P.K., 2017b; Sedjelmaci, H., 2020).

In Health Care and Medical Systems

Cyber-Physical System is basically useful in concerned and different kind of medical and healthcare systems viz. in collecting real time data including in monitoring the patient. Moreover CPS is helpful in gathering data by remote sensing systems and also physical conditions which helps to the patients. Therefore it improves and helps in enhancing healthy and improved treatments for the general patient including for the disabled and elderly patients. As such system will deal with the network closed loop system with a human loop to improve the safety and workflows, therefore the systems towards Cyber-Physical System based healthcare is emerging and gaining potentialities (Guo, Y., et.al., 2017).

In Smarter Transportation

As far as advanced and smarter communication is concerned Cyber-Physical System is important in collecting real time information of different traffic and transportation related affairs such as traffic systems, location management, and therefore CPS here worthy in the following—

- Location and Time Management
- In preventing accident and improving the safety.
- In reduction of the carbon emission also indirectly Cyber-Physical System is worthy.

The developing countries along with the developed countries are now moving towards advanced and intelligent Cyber-Physical System (CPS) in the transportation systems.

In Buildings

Regarding the building management and allied construction related activities as well Cyber-Physical System is important. In smart building developing and advancing CPS is important and this is helpful in improving energy efficiency and also in decreasing energy consumption and that ultimately greenhouse gas emissions. Here Cyber-Physical System is helpful in gathering data related to the temperature, humidity etc. (Baheti, R., & Gill, H., 2011; Serpanos, D., 2018).

In Aeronautic Applications

The applications and utilizations of the Cyber-Physical System in aeronautics and allied activities can be considered as valuable and among the applications few important are flight test instrumentation, pilot crew communications, healthy and structured healthcare monitoring. Moreover in flight related entertainment, wireless cabin systems, landing of the flights etc. too Cyber-Physical System is important and increasing rapidly.

In Virtual Reality

In the context of virtual reality which is technically called Claytronics also an important name in applications of the Cyber-Physical System. IT combines nano scale robots and computer theory is able in making nanometer-scale systems called claytronic atoms / catoms and such offers 3D structure. With claytronic 3 dimensions is easy to create and develop. Here two type of algorithms are being used. Here Cyber-Physical System specially the localization algorithm enables the positioning of catoms in the ensemble.

In Smarter and Enhanced Learning Systems

Cyber-Physical System is important in applications of Advanced and smarter educational Systems and that can be used in gathering data on physical systems and environments, converting measured data, online educational systems, advanced and prompt services for the students, staffs and educational institutions. Cyber-Physical System is helpful in building and developing smart learning environmental systems (SLE).

MOBILE CYBER PHYSICAL SYSTEMS: OVERVIEW

Mobile Cyber-Physical System is a part of Cyber-Physical System where physical system play an important role in which further mobility considered as valuable. Mobile robotics, electronics transported systems are considered as mobile physical systems. The growing mobile uses lead the rise of Cyber-Physical Systems and better to say various Smartphone and allied platforms helps in making of ideal mobile cyber-physical systems for different causes viz.

- Important and Significant computational resources including local storage.
- Various sensor devices which include touch screens, cameras, GPS, speakers, various microphones.
- Various communication platforms like WiFi,G, Bluetooth run by the internet and similar devices.
- Different kind of apps/ applications/ software distribution mechanism like App Store of the Apple or Google.

Network connectivity which links with the mobile systems including server or cloud connectivity is responsible for the enhancing Mobile Cyber Physical Systems (Krämer, B. J., 2014; Törngren, M. et.al, 2017).

MANPOWER AND HUMAN RESOURCE DEVELOPMENT: CYBER PHYSICAL SYSTEMS

Cyber-Physical Systems since become an important technology in the field of computing and information technology therefore this is the high time to introduce this field as an emerging technology within the subject IT and Computing. Even in allied subjects such as Communication Technology, Network Technology also this Cyber-Physical Systems is growing rapidly. Many universities internationally not only included Cyber-Physical Systems as a course or important area within their field of study but also as a specialization and full-fledged subject for making the society smarter, advanced and intelligent (Refer Fig: 3).

Figure 3. Cyber Physical Systems Potential utilizations with proper and adequate manpower

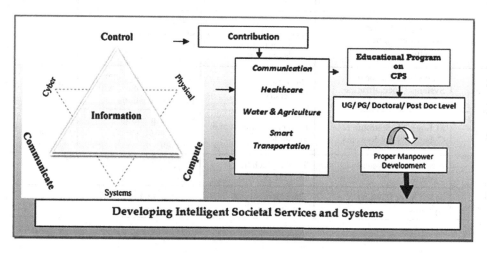

Interestingly even in developing countries also the symptoms on introducing Cyber-Physical Systems is important to note. Cyberphysical systems integrate computation with physical objects such as 'smart' devices, and various other aspects viz. voice assistant devices, driverless vehicles and cars, medical and health monitoring equipment and systems, wearable electronic systems and devices, robotic assistant in different electronic systems etc. therefore in Indian context the field may be introduced as a full-fledged manner in the Departments/ Centres/Units of the following—

• Computer Science

- Computer Science and Engineering (CSE) or Computer Engineering (CE)
- Information Technology (IT) or Information Science & Technology (IST)
- Electronics and Communication Engineering (ECE)
- Telecommunication Systems and so on.

Similar to other emerging fields (Hiran, K. K., 2021) in CPS too there are huge potentialities in introducing starting Cyber-Physical Systems as a major or specialization and this is also been noted as per this study. Table: 1 depicted the result of few programs and educational institutions which are on Cyber-Physical Systems or allied fields.

Table 1. Proposed program of Cyber Physical Systems with ME/MTech

Sl. No.	Degrees Offered	Universities	Remarks	Country
1	MSc-Cyber Physical Systems & Embedded Systems	Advanced Learning and Research Institute	120 ECTS Open to Engineering, Computing, and Pure Science Students	Switzerland
2	MSc-Cyber Physical Systems (Specialization: IoT)	North Eastern University	Offered as Full Time & Part Time basis with multiple locations	USA
3	M.Engg-Mechatronic & Cyber Physical Systems	Deggendorf Institute of Technology	Offered in multiple locations. 3 Semester Progran	Germany
4	MSc Cyber Physical Systems	The Polytechnic Institute of Paris	60 Credit, 2 Semester	France
5	MSc Cyber Physical Systems	The University of Nottingham	2 Years (Graduates with Program or Interest in)	UK

According to this result it is shown that majority of the program are with MSc nomenclature instead of MS and MTech means less offered in the USA and India (and follower countries). As of this five programs, the Cyber-Physical Systems is available as a specialization, full degree. The curriculum of Cyber-Physical Systems should be connected with the telecommunication, computing, Advanced Information Technology and allied Basic Sciences. Here if the The University of Nottingham case, the program is offered with MSc Cyber Physical Systems nomenclature and with total of the credits of 180 and further it is split across 120 credits. And here it is composed with various compulsory and optional modules in addition to 60 credit individual project. This is a two-year course and in the first year coursework are there while in the second year there is a 60 credit research project or similar research related activities leading to the dissertation. If we look into this program of The University of Nottingham then it can be noted that core courses here split into mandatory courses and optional courses, as depicted in Table: 2 and Table: 3.

Table 2. Proposed program of Cyber Physical Systems with ME/MTech

Compulsory Courses
Autonomous Robotics Systems
Designing Sensor based Systems
Topical Trends in Computer Systems
Malware Analysis
Research Methods
Research Project

Cyber-Physical Systems because of interdisciplinary program must be packed with technology and computing including electronics and management related subjects.

Table 3. Proposed program of Cyber Physical Systems with ME/MTech

Optional Courses	
Linear and Discrete Optimization	Advanced Computer Network
Design Ethnography	Advanced Algorithm and Data Structure
Machine Learning	Project in Advanced Algorithm and Data Structure
Human AI Interaction	Data Modeling and Analysis
Fuzzy Logic and Systems	Simulation and Optimization for Decision Making
Mixed Reality Technologies	Games
Software Engineering Management	Programs, Proofs and Types

In India, as of now no institute offers full fledged degrees on the subjects like Cyber-Physical Systems or allied or merged nomenclature but there is a huge potentiality in offering this subject not only in Science degrees but also in Technology/ Engineering degrees. And therefore Table: 4 herewith depicted the list of potential possible degrees with MTech/ ME in Indian context.

Table 4. Proposed program of Cyber Physical Systems with ME/MTech

Proposed Cyber Physical Systems Program Potentiality With MTech/ME Program Level
MTech/ME- Cyber Physical Systems (CPS) MTech/ME- Cyber Physical Systems & Embedded Systems (CPS & ES) MTech/ME- IT with Cyber Physical Systems MTech/ME- Cyber Physical Systems & IoT

Cyber-Physical Systems as proposed here can be merged with allied subjects like embedded systems, IoT even with a broad subject like Information Technology. As far as Science degrees are concerned it may be offered with MSc (which is basically practiced in Asia and Europe), MS (which is practiced in USA and follower countries), and MSc/MS by research degree (which is also emerging globally) nomenclature. Table: 5 here in this regard offered possible and potential degree titles.

Table 5. Proposed program of Cyber Physical Systems with PG Science Degrees

Proposed Cyber Physical Systems Program Potentiality With MSc/ MS/ MS by Research Program Level
MSc/ MS/ MS by Research- Cyber Physical Systems MSc/ MS/ MS by Research- Cyber Physical Systems & Embedded Systems MSc/ MS/ MS by Research- IT with Cyber Physical Systems MSc/ MS/ MS by Research- Cyber Physical Systems & IoT

However here important to look that, in Table: 4 and 5 the potential nomenclature is only with the Cyber-Physical Systems however in Indian context since Computer Applications, Information Technology etc are already established field therefore in such subjects Cyber-Physical Systems and allied fields can be offered and some of the possible programs are depicted in Table:6. Even here degrees are proposed both 'specialization' in the allied program and also in the 'by research degrees' effectively.

Table 6. Proposed program of Cyber Physical Systems with Computer Application & IT nomenclature

Proposed Cyber Physical Systems Program Potentiality With CA/IT Nomenclature
MSc/ MS/ MS by Research (IT/CA) in Cyber Physical Systems MSc/ MS/ MS by Research-(IT/CA) in Cyber Physical Systems & Embedded Systems MSc/ MS/ MS by Research- (IT/CA) in Cyber Physical Systems & IoT

India is a developing country and therefore introducing such degrees and nomenclature can be considered as worthy in developing proper manpower in the field. The programs and subjects can be started similar to the other emerging subjects of the IT and Computing which have been started in recent past viz. Cloud Computing, Big Data and Data Analytics, IoT (Internet of Things, Blockchain Technology, etc. Table: 7 whereas depicted the some of the potential Doctoral Degree programs in Science, Engineering steam. Here importantly Professional Doctorate in Engineering also been proposed.

Table 7. Proposed program of Cyber Physical Systems with Computer Application & IT nomenclature

Proposed Cyber Physical Systems Program Potentiality With CA/IT Nomenclature
PhD (Science)- Cyber Physical Systems PhD (Engineering)-Cyber Physical Systems & Embedded Systems Engg. D.(IT/CA) in Cyber Physical Systems & IoT

Therefore the Cyber-Physical Systems is worthy and important in the context of the preparing intelligent systems and societies and here ready manpower is important in order to fulfill the need and actual requirements of the industry.

CONCLUSION

Cyber-Physical Systems is playing a leading role in developing Information Technology systems in India. Already the subject Cyber-Physical Systems is been introduced in different IT and Computing related program and this is the foremost time to introduced Cyber-Physical Systems and allied field at Masters and Research Degrees leading to Ph.D., MTech by Research, MS by Research etc. Even in future days the subjects can be introduced at Bachelors level with the degrees viz. BSc, BS, BTech and even in research context keeping in mind the research trend. The subject Cyber-Physical Systems is emerging with other latest areas therefore it is important to merge the subject with allied subjects for better and healthy output. Furthermore, the industrial inputs, initiative, awareness along with the Government support is important for healthy and timely introduction of the Cyber-Physical Systems in India. Many countries throughout the world by their councils, ministries, departments and allied stakeholders are engaged in Cyber-Physical Systems related training, education, research and practice/ implementation related initiative and this is the need of hour towards a Digital Society and Economy in real context.

REFERENCES

Agarwal, P. (2007). Higher education in India: Growth, concerns and change agenda. *Higher Education Quarterly, 61*(2), 197–207. doi:10.1111/j.1468-2273.2007.00346.x

Alguliyev, R., Imamverdiyev, Y., & Sukhostat, L. (2018). Cyber-physical systems and their security issues. *Computers in Industry, 100,* 212–223. doi:10.1016/j.compind.2018.04.017

Ali, S., Qaisar, S. B., Saeed, H., Khan, M. F., Naeem, M., & Anpalagan, A. (2015). Network challenges for cyber physical systems with tiny wireless devices: A case study on reliable pipeline condition monitoring. *Sensors (Basel), 15*(4), 7172–7205. doi:10.3390150407172 PMID:25815444

Altbach, P. G. (1993). The dilemma of change in Indian higher education. *Higher Education, 26*(1), 3–20. doi:10.1007/BF01575104

Ashibani, Y., & Mahmoud, Q. H. (2017). Cyber physical systems security: Analysis, challenges and solutions. *Computers & Security, 68,* 81–97. doi:10.1016/j.cose.2017.04.005

Baheti, R., & Gill, H. (2011). Cyber-physical systems. *The Impact of Control Technology, 12*(1), 161-166.

Chen, G., Xu, B., Lu, M., & Chen, N. S. (2018). Exploring blockchain technology and its potential applications for education. *Smart Learning Environments, 5*(1), 1–10. doi:10.118640561-017-0050-x

Colombo, A. W., Bangemann, T., Karnouskos, S., Delsing, J., Stluka, P., Harrison, R., ... Lastra, J. L. (2014). Industrial cloud-based cyber-physical systems. *The Imcaesop Approach, 22,* 4–5.

Darwish, A., & Hassanien, A. E. (2018). Cyber physical systems design, methodology, and integration: The current status and future outlook. *Journal of Ambient Intelligence and Humanized Computing, 9*(5), 1541–1556. doi:10.100712652-017-0575-4

Gronau, N. (2016). Determinants of an appropriate degree of autonomy in a cyber-physical production system. *Procedia CIRP, 52,* 1–5. doi:10.1016/j.procir.2016.07.063

Guo, Y., Hu, X., Hu, B., Cheng, J., Zhou, M., & Kwok, R. Y. (2017). Mobile cyber physical systems: Current challenges and future networking applications. *IEEE Access: Practical Innovations, Open Solutions, 6,* 12360–12368. doi:10.1109/ACCESS.2017.2782881

Hehenberger, P., Vogel-Heuser, B., Bradley, D., Eynard, B., Tomiyama, T., & Achiche, S. (2016). Design, modelling, simulation and integration of cyber physical systems: Methods and applications. *Computers in Industry*, *82*, 273–289. doi:10.1016/j. compind.2016.05.006

Hiran, K. K. (2021). Investigating Factors Influencing the Adoption of IT Cloud Computing Platforms in Higher Education: Case of Sub-Saharan Africa With IT Professionals. *International Journal of Human Capital and Information Technology Professionals*, *12*(3), 21–36. doi:10.4018/IJHCITP.2021070102

Hiran, K. K., & Doshi, R. (2013). An artificial neural network approach for brain tumor detection using digital image segmentation. *Brain*, *2*(5), 227–231.

Huang, Z., Wang, C., Stojmenovic, M., & Nayak, A. (2014). Characterization of cascading failures in interdependent cyber-physical systems. *IEEE Transactions on Computers*, *64*(8), 2158–2168. doi:10.1109/TC.2014.2360537

Humayed, A., Lin, J., Li, F., & Luo, B. (2017). Cyber-physical systems security—A survey. *IEEE Internet of Things Journal*, *4*(6), 1802–1831. doi:10.1109/ JIOT.2017.2703172

Iqbal, R., Doctor, F., More, B., Mahmud, S., & Yousuf, U. (2020). Big Data analytics and Computational Intelligence for Cyber–Physical Systems: Recent trends and state of the art applications. *Future Generation Computer Systems*, *105*, 766–778. doi:10.1016/j.future.2017.10.021

Khaitan, S. K., & McCalley, J. D. (2014). Design techniques and applications of cyberphysical systems: A survey. *IEEE Systems Journal*, *9*(2), 350–365. doi:10.1109/ JSYST.2014.2322503

Kim, K. D., & Kumar, P. R. (2013). An overview and some challenges in cyber-physical systems. *Journal of the Indian Institute of Science*, *93*(3), 341–352.

Krämer, B. J. (2014). Evolution of cyber-physical systems: a brief review. *Applied Cyber-Physical Systems*, 1-3.

Lee, I., Sokolsky, O., Chen, S., Hatcliff, J., Jee, E., Kim, B., ... Venkatasubramanian, K. K. (2011). Challenges and research directions in medical cyber–physical systems. *Proceedings of the IEEE*, *100*(1), 75–90.

Leitão, P., Colombo, A. W., & Karnouskos, S. (2016). Industrial automation based on cyber-physical systems technologies: Prototype implementations and challenges. *Computers in Industry*, *81*, 11–25. doi:10.1016/j.compind.2015.08.004

Lieu Tran, T. B., Törngren, M., Nguyen, H. D., Paulen, R., Gleason, N. W., & Duong, T. H. (2019). Trends in preparing cyber-physical systems engineers. *Cyber-Physical Systems*, *5*(2), 65–91. doi:10.1080/23335777.2019.1600034

Lu, T., Lin, J., Zhao, L., Li, Y., & Peng, Y. (2015). A security architecture in cyber-physical systems: Security theories, analysis, simulation and application fields. *International Journal of Security and Its Applications*, *9*(7), 1–16. doi:10.14257/ijsia.2015.9.7.01

Lun, Y. Z., D'Innocenzo, A., Smarra, F., Malavolta, I., & Di Benedetto, M. D. (2019). State of the art of cyber-physical systems security: An automatic control perspective. *Journal of Systems and Software*, *149*, 174–216. doi:10.1016/j.jss.2018.12.006

Marwedel, P., Mitra, T., Grimheden, M. E., & Andrade, H. A. (2020). Survey on education for cyber-physical systems. *IEEE Design & Test*, *37*(6), 56–70. doi:10.1109/MDAT.2020.3009613

Paul, P. K., Aithal, P. S., Bhuimali, A., & Kumar, K. (2017b). Emerging Degrees and Collaboration: The Context of Engineering Sciences in Computing & IT—An Analysis for Enhanced Policy Formulation in India. *International Journal on Recent Researches in Science, Engineering & Technology*, *5*(12), 13–27.

Paul, P. K., Aithal, P. S., Bhuimali, A., & Kumar, K. (2017c). Emerging Degrees and Collaboration: The Context of Engineering Sciences in Computing & IT—An Analysis for Enhanced Policy Formulation in India. *International Journal on Recent Researches in Science, Engineering & Technology*, *5*(12), 13–27.

Paul, P.K., Aithal, P. S., Saavedra, M. R., Sinha, R. R., Aremu, P. S. B., & Mewada, S. (2020). Information Systems: The Changing Scenario of Concepts, Practice and Importance. *SCHOLEDGE International Journal of Management & Development,* *7*(7), 118-129.

Paul, P. K., Bhuimali, A., & Aithal, P. S. (2017a). Indian higher education: With slant to information technology—a fundamental overview. *International Journal on Recent Researches in Science, Engineering & Technology*, *5*(11), 31–50.

Rocher, G., Tigli, J. Y., Lavirotte, S., & Le Thanh, N. (2020). Effectiveness assessment of cyber-physical systems. *International Journal of Approximate Reasoning*, *118*, 112–132. doi:10.1016/j.ijar.2019.12.002

Sadiku, M. N., Wang, Y., Cui, S., & Musa, S. M. (2017). Cyber-physical systems: A literature review. *European Scientific Journal*, *13*(36), 52–58. doi:10.19044/esj.2017.v13n36p52

Sanislav, T., & Miclea, L. (2012). Cyber-physical systems-concept, challenges and research areas. *Journal of Control Engineering and Applied Informatics*, *14*(2), 28–33.

Sedjelmaci, H., Guenab, F., Senouci, S. M., Moustafa, H., Liu, J., & Han, S. (2020). Cyber security based on artificial intelligence for cyber-physical systems. *IEEE Network*, *34*(3), 6–7. doi:10.1109/MNET.2020.9105926

Serpanos, D. (2018). The cyber-physical systems revolution. *Computer*, *51*(3), 70–73. doi:10.1109/MC.2018.1731058

Törngren, M., Grimheden, M. E., Gustafsson, J., & Birk, W. (2017). Strategies and considerations in shaping cyber-physical systems education. *ACM SIGBED Review*, *14*(1), 53–60. doi:10.1145/3036686.3036693

Wan, J., Yan, H., Suo, H., & Li, F. (2011). Advances in cyber-physical systems research. *Transactions on Internet and Information Systems (Seoul)*, *5*(11), 1891–1908. doi:10.3837/tiis.2011.11.001

Xu, L. D., & Duan, L. (2019). Big data for cyber physical systems in industry 4.0: A survey. *Enterprise Information Systems*, *13*(2), 148–169. doi:10.1080/1751757 5.2018.1442934

Zanero, S. (2017). Cyber-physical systems. *Computer*, *50*(4), 14–16. doi:10.1109/ MC.2017.105

ADDITIONAL READING

Staroverova, N. A., Shustrova, M. L., & Satdarov, M. R. (2020). Development of a cyber-physical system for the specialized on-track machine operators training. In *Cyber-Physical Systems: Industry 4.0 Challenges* (pp. 315–325). Springer. doi:10.1007/978-3-030-32648-7_25

KEY TERMS AND DEFINITION

Human Machine Interface: Human machine interface, in short called as HMI, is a system and mechanism dedicated in proper communication between the machines, humans and contents.

PC: PC stands for Personal Computer run for the computational activities and official activities. Personal Computer is important in multipurpose activities.

WSN: Wireless Sensor Network is the sensor dedicated in collecting the data from different places. Such kind of network is able in working of different physical condition such as temperature, sound, pollution levels, humidity, and wind.

Chapter 3

Machine Learning in Cyber Physical Systems for Agriculture:
Crop Yield Prediction Using Cyber Physical Systems and Machine Learning

Vinay Kumar Yadav
Sir Padampat Singhania University, India

Manish Dadhich
Sir Padampat Singhania University, India

ABSTRACT

The agriculture science system is facing lots of problems from environmental change. Machine learning (ML) and cyber physical systems (CPS) are the best approaches to overcome the problems by building good and effective solutions. Crop yield prediction includes prediction of yield for the crop by analysing the existing data by considering several parameters like weather, soil, water, and temperature. This project addresses and defines the predicting yield of the crop based on the previous year's data using a linear regression algorithm into which you can type your own text.

INTRODUCTION

Industry 4.0, often known as the fourth industrial revolution, is being realized thanks to the advent of cyber-physical systems and precision agriculture (Shubham Tripathi and Manish Gupta, 2021). One of the current concerns in this field is agricultural

DOI: 10.4018/978-1-7998-9308-0.ch003

cyber-physical systems (ACPS), composed of computer systems and the agricultural environment (Tariq Masoodab & Paul Sonntaga, 2020). The growth of systems has created a significant opportunity to improve the food supply chain system (FSC). It is imperative to humans and has a complex cycle that begins and encompasses farm produce. Logistics and distribution, retail, consumer communication, and trash management are all areas that need to be addressed. Furthermore, those cycles encounter various obstacles, mainly when using CPS technology (Goap et al., 2018). Precision agriculture, a management technique that uses conditions and specific information to precisely regulate production inputs such as soil and crop characteristics unique to each field region, is one of the most current problems in this sector (Amami & Smiti, 2017; Chen et al., 2015; Dadhich, Hiran, et al., 2021).

According to (Diale et al., 2019), precision agriculture strives to optimize production inputs in tiny areas of the field in real-time, such as water, fertilizers, herbicides, insecticides, and farm equipment. The Internet of Underground Things has lately enabled precision agricultural technologies (IOUT). IOUT stands for autonomous devices that collect relevant information about the Earth and are linked through communication. Information, transactions from the fields to the farmers, and decision-making systems are all aided by networking technologies (Dusadeerungsikul et al., 2019). IOUT has the advantage of real-time sensing by using deep learning algorithms with CPS (Mahrishi, M., et al.,2020). Sensing has aided in the adoption of precision agriculture technologies while also increasing the efficiency of agricultural production and operations. Essentially, changes in the intrinsic and extrinsic conditions of underground objects such as communication mediums in soil, seasonal changes, and crop growth cycles are caused by product modifications (Goap et al., 2018). The technology should isolate and adjust the conditions to provide farmers with a precise decision-making mechanism promptly. This paper presents an early machine learning approach to handle the adaptation problem. There are five dimensions to the machine learning framework, including data normalization and handling erroneous data for a decision-making system, time-series prediction, information fusion, and a classifier are used (Cui et al., 2021). The researchers tried with a dataset of fifteen sensors to get a more accurate assessment. Several attributes are included in the sensor data, including soil moisture, air temperature, soil temperature, wind velocity, and air pressure. This chapter is organized into five sections. The first section consists of the introduction of green yield prediction. The second part outlines the applications of cyber-Physical Systems for the agriculture domain. The third section explained the related work in the selected domain. The fourth section delineates the conceptual framework based on theories followed by experimental work. The last section assessed the result, analysis, and conclusion.

CYBER-PHYSICAL SYSTEMS FOR AGRICULTRE DOMAIN

In agriculture, mechanization is widespread. However, advances in robotics and autonomous systems will propel agriculture forward as a result of artificial intelligence and embedded systems applications (Tyagi, S.K.S., et al.2020). A drone is a flying robot in and of itself, but when a generation of embedded intelligent CPS robotics systems is deployed, a substantial evolution will occur (Huo & Chaudhry, 2021; Rakesh Kumar Birda & Manish Dadhich, 2019) These systems can be interconnected, interdependent, collaborative, autonomous, and provide computing, communication, checking, and control of physical components and processes in various applications. In other words, by observing how these systems communicate with the physical world (including human users), Typically intended as intelligent sensor networks of (autonomous) systems with unique detecting and actuation capabilities, they play a key role in acquiring data (Jimenez et al., 2020). The cyber and physical worlds cannot be considered separate entities, yet they are inextricably linked with sensor/ actuator integration in so-called cyber systems. By providing real-time control coming from conventional cyber systems, cyber systems become responsive to the physical environment. As a result, the concept of a CPS was born. The "assimilation of computation with physical processes" is what a CPS is. Sensors and actuators, for example, are used to connect computational systems to the real environment. CPS presented significant hurdles, especially because the physical components of such systems introduced safety and dependability; as a result, typical computing abstractions must be altered to meet qualitatively different requirements than those in general-purpose computing (Liao et al., 2021).

Furthermore, physical components differ fundamentally from object-oriented software components, yet concurrency is both inherent. It was a significant advancement in state of the art in computers (Malathi & Padmaja, 2021). The interaction of the "cyber" and "physical" aspects is crucial in CPSs; computation, control, sensing, and networking can be extensively interwoven into every component, and component and system behavior must be safe and interoperable (Myllyaho et al., 2021; Shalendra Singh Rao, n.d.)7, CPSs have been on the model of engineering research agenda in the United States, and since 2010, the European academic and industry community has focused on CPSs as paradigms for the future of systems. The industry as a whole has shown a lot of interest. This is evident when considering that embedded systems, wireless sensor networks, IoT, communication protocols, and their interactions are the most important elements and pillars in CPS (Hiran & Henten, 2020; N. Sharma & Dadhich, 2014) To move forward with CPS's difficulties and prospects, there must be widespread agreement on fundamental principles and shared knowledge of the features and technology that are unique to CPS.

RELATED WORKS

(Nerurkar et al., 2018) studied the technologies based on cyber-physical systems (CPS) created to monitor terrain parameters and make them available on a platform that multiple users can access. (Priyadarshini et al., 2021) studied that CPS can monitor entire agricultural areas and thanks to cellular telephony gateways and information monitoring systems that can display data on a web application. Other options include-Applying and implementing the new and helpful concept of Cyber-Physical Systems (CPSs) in the agriculture industry, which consists of a Zigbee-based network with nodes that function below the ground surface.

(Raza et al., 2018) assessed the mobile devices used in some of the most recent projects, which are advanced, comprehensive systems that monitor environmental factors and employ a closed-cycle control system in which actuators are controlled based on sensor data (Hiran, K. K., 2021) . While it is only a theoretical solution, it still lacks a functional human-machine interaction sub-system. Several studies (Dadhich, Purohit, et al., 2021; Dinesh Setha, Minhaj Ahemad A.Rehman, 2018; Shen et al., 2020) developed Drone-based solutions to obtain picture data at various wavelengths to provide a continual overview of the terrain's physical and chemical state. Different types of camera-equipped drones are already on the market (for example, from Precision Hawk, senseFly, and Agribotix) that take medium-high resolution photographs (up to 20 MP) in various electromagnetic spectrums regions, usually in the visible and Near Infrared (NIR) fields (M. Dadhich, M. S. Pahwa, 2021; Restrepo et al., 2021). Different types of camera-equipped drones are already on the market that take medium-high resolution photographs (up to 20 MP) in various electromagnetic spectrums regions, usually in the visible. The Spanish startup Agroptima is working on another unique system (Kumar Naresh, Dadhich Manish, 2014). This system does not use hardware such as sensors or actuators. Still, it does provide a stunning graphic interface for field cataloguing and management, as well as irrigation and fertilization planning. (R. Sharma et al., 2020) studied agrodron used for parasite control and made it ideal for spraying activities on crops.

PROPOSED FRAMEWORK

Data preprocessing, forecasting, and classifying are the three primary processes in machine learning-based architecture (Manish Dadhich, Manvinder Singh Pahwa, Vipin Jain, 2021; Shubham Tripathi and Manish Gupta, 2021). The data will then be measured using a forecasting algorithm to avoid data shortages or inaccurate data collection for the following sensing cycle. The data classifier uses a Nave Bayes classifier to predict a real-time event using a discretized fusion of forecasted data and prior knowledge (Dadhich, Rao, et al., 2021). In each time cycle, the event prediction is calculated.

Normalizing Data

The best way to overcome this problem is to use normalization to produce data in the same interval. The normalizing method is used to scale each feature element to interval values with a range of [0–1]. In the first equation, the implementation is shown. I denote each source index, and j is a normalized element index in sensor I.

$$\hat{x}_{ij} = \frac{x_{ij} - x_{i\,max}}{x_{i\,max} - x_{i\,min}} \tag{1}$$

Handling Incorrect Data

Due to a variety of variables, data acquired from diverse sources such as sensors can occasionally be incorrect or null. We suggest a novel approach for predicting faulty data rather than discarding all of the data or altering the incorrect value to a random number to address this issue. After that, we estimated the average of proximity between all existing normalized values in all data at the time_ t () and source (i) where the event of the wrong value happens. The process of forecasting inaccurate data is depicted in the second, third, and fourth equations.

$$\phi(i) = \sum_{j=1}^{N-j} (\hat{x}_j - \hat{x}_{(j+1)}) \, for \, \hat{x}_{(j+1)} \neq null \tag{2}$$

$$k_i = \phi_i x_{i\,max} \tag{3}$$

$$xf(i)_j = \frac{\sum_{i=1}^{N} k_{(j+1)} + \sum_{i=1}^{N} k_{(j-1)}}{2} \tag{4}$$

Information Fusion

After that, we estimated the average proximity between all existing normalized values in all the data at the time_t () and source (i) where the wrong value event happens. The process of forecasting inaccurate data is depicted in the second, third, and fourth equations.

$$\hat{x}_t = \frac{\sum_{i=1}^{N} x_i w_i}{N} \tag{5}$$

Prediction Method

To predict the consecutive data at the time, we utilize a single aggressive smoothing forecasting method. The method is selected for the actual value that does not have a significant trend and seasonal behavior at each subsequent time. The exponential smoothing method is defined as the 6th equation.

$$F_t = F_{(t-1)} + \left(A_{(t-1)} - F_{(t-1)} \right) \tag{6}$$

Naïve Bayes Classifier

To choose based on the data sources available at the moment (t). The probabilities or conditional opportunities are expressed as the 7th equation using the Bayesian theorem

$$P\left(H \mid X\right) = \frac{P\left(X \mid H\right) P\left(H\right)}{P\left(X\right)} \tag{7}$$

P(H I X) is the probability of having the correct value of H assumption for true X evidence for H assumption or posterior probability of X with H, where X is a proof and H is an assumption, and P(H I X) is the probability of having the correct value of H assumption for true X evidence for H assumption or posterior probability of X with H, where X is a proof and H is an assumption, and P(H I X) is the probability of having the correct values (H) is the prior probability of evidence X, and P (X) is the preceding hypothesis probability of H. There is a presumption that tuple X is located in class C, and a tuple X or data object usually represents X. In the classification problem, P (H|X) is the probability that the H assumption is accurate for tuple X, or in other words, P (H|X) is the likelihood that tuple X is placed in class C. P (H) is the probability that the H assumption is valid for any tuple regardless of its attribute values, whereas P (X) is the prior of tuple X. The steps below will show you how to utilize the Nave Bayes classifier (Kumar & Dadhich, 2014).

1.   Imagine that Dx is a training set with tuple elements, attributes, and class labels in each attribute. Each n-dimensional tuple can be written as X = (x1, x2,... xN), derived from the characteristics A1, A2, and AN.

2.   2. Assume there are m classes, each containing C1, C2,...Cn. The Naive Bayes classifier would assume that tuple X belongs to the Ci class if and only if the 8th equation is satisfied for the input of tuple X.

$$P(C_i|X) > P(C_j|X) \text{ for } j \leq m, j \neq i \tag{8}$$

The P (Ci | X) value of the Naive Bayes classifier is expanded. Maximum posterior i refers to the class of Ci that forms P (Ci | X) and has the highest value. P(Ci|X) values would be estimated using the Nave Bayes theorem and a 9th equation.

$$P(C_i|X) = P(X|C_i)P(C_i) \tag{9}$$

3.   3. Given that P (X) is the same for all classes, the tuple X has the same chance of being accepted into any class. The only thing that has to be maximized is P (X|Ci) P (Ci). If the prior probability of each class is unknown, the probability of each class can change, and the Naive Bayes classifier must maximize P(X|Ci) P(Ci). Furthermore, when working with data sets with many attributes, it's required to simplify the complexity of P (X|Ci) calculations by assuming that a class has a conditional, such as mutually independent attribute values. As for the tenth equation, this Naive Bayes classifier would maximize the calculation as the 10th equation.

$$P\left(C_i \middle| x\right) = \Pi_k^n = 1^{P\left(x_1 | C_1\right)} \tag{10}$$

Based on the tuples, we can estimate the values of P(X1|Ci) x P(X2|Ci) x... x P(Xn|Ci). P(Xk|Ci) is defined as the number of tuples in the dataset class with an Xk value in the Ak attribute divided by the number of tuples accessible in the dataset Dk class Ci indicated by |Cik| for the categorical value type. Meanwhile, we may use the Gaussian distribution approach as the 11th equation to compute the value of P (Xk | Ci) for characteristics of continuous value.

$$P\left(x_k \middle| C_i\right) = \frac{1}{\sigma\sqrt{2\pi}} \frac{-\left(x - \mu C_i\right)^2}{2\sigma C_i^2}$$ (11)

Finally, for each class of Ci, the probability calculation of P(X|Ci) P(Ci) must be done to forecast the class label of the Dx tuple. The next step is to maximize the probability by selecting the Ci class that produces the highest probability P(X|Ci) P(Ci) as the decision class. Tuples X are mathematically designated as class Ci if and only if they meet the 12th equations.

P(X|C$_i$)P(C$_j$) > P(X|C$_j$)P(C$_j$) for 1≤j≤m and j≠i (12)

EXPERIMENT

Dataset and Tools

Real-time soil moisture and temperature observations for 15 locations in Karnataka were used in this investigation. The network assesses soil moisture in the unsaturated zone for diverse soil textures and land coverings in the area. The five sensors are placed at 5 cm, 10 cm, 20 cm, 40 cm, and 80 cm depths. The time interval for logging is set to 15 minutes.

Prior Knowledge

The researchers used the water sprinkle monitoring system as an example to create the machine learning model. We set a previous knowledge with numerous attributes connected to our dataset to forecast the precise action of the water, sprinkle monitoring system in real-time. Every feature is stored in our knowledge base as an attribute. We use four variables to calculate the likelihood of rain: air temperature, wind speed, air pressure, and air humidity. The rainfall attributes will then be determined as a class attribute. The four qualities are light rain, moderate rain, heavy rain, and no rain. After discovering all the classes, we use rainfall likelihood as an input characteristic to decide the water sprinkler system's action. There are three water attributes and one sprinkle monitoring system attribute. There are four different types of classes:

Table 1. Knowledge Prior of Rainfall Probability

Air Temperature	Wind Speed	Air Pressure	Air Humidity	Rainfall
Low	Slow	Low	Low	Moderate Rain
High	Medium	High	High	Moderate Rain

Table 2. Knowledge Prior of Water Sprinkle Monitoring System

Soil Moisture	Soil Temperature	Water Sprinkle System
Low	Medium	Long Duration
High	High	Not Active

nonactive, short duration, medium duration, and long duration.

Accuracy Measurement

The smallest error number between actual data and anticipated data collected is used to calculate accuracy in the experiment—the less the error value, the better the value. MAE (Mean Absolute Error) is the 13th equation that we use.

$$MAE = \left(\frac{1}{N}\right)\sum_{i=1}^{n}\left|F_t - A_t\right| \tag{13}$$

RESULTS AND ANALYSIS

The researchers used data from fifteen stations. Five soil temperature and soil humidity sensors are installed at each station at various depths, including 5 cm, 10 cm, 20 cm, 40 cm, and 80 cm. A Naive Bayes classifier was used to forecast a rainfall event using a weather sensor consisting of four attributes such as air pressure, wind speed, air temperature, and air humidity. Every fifteen minutes, data is collected.

Meanwhile, our algorithm would adjust the environment attributes to manage faulty data or missing values. Following that, we combined the results of all sources with the same attribute, such as sensor soil humidity and soil temperature. After that, we use forecasting methodologies to predict data and decide what action to take with the water monitoring sprinkler system. The forecasting process is carefully monitored to provide a real-time prediction strategy at all times (t). We could develop procedures to respond to unknown conditions by employing the forecasting method. We receive a better forecasting result for each source, as shown in Table 3.

Table 3. Forecasting Agency

Attributes	MAE (Our Framework)	MAE(Conventional)
Soil Moisture	8.0692890536838E-05	0.01837208
Soil Temperature	0.0157778494	0.018956886
Air Humidity	0.7707157827	0.7707157827
Air Temperature	1.7928824762	1.79528824762
Wind Speed	1.5754473642	1.5754473642
Air Humidity	0.8202079639	0.8202079639

The MAE values in Table 3 represent the mean of the difference between forecasted and actual values. Soil moisture and soil temperature are the two lowest MAE values, indicating little difference in moisture and temperature for 15 minutes. The MAE values in Table 3 represent the mean of the difference between forecasted and actual values. Soil moisture and soil temperature are the two lowest MAE values, indicating little difference in moisture and temperature for 15 minutes. The Nave Bayes classifier is supervised based on our previous technique based on our information. The total number of events predicted is 24.187, with each time phase differing by 15 minutes. Table 4 shows the appropriate outcome for assuming the rainfall and water sprinkle monitoring system activity. The true assumptions are calculated by subtracting the total of the real event from the forecasted event. They observed a clearer contrast between our approach and traditional ones in those tables, particularly regarding precise rainfall forecasts, and the same was in line with previous work (Manrique-silupu et al., 2021; Sujatha et al., 2021). Because the conventional technique cannot manage inaccurate data problems such as -9999, NaN, and Null values produced when sensors are faulty, or the battery is turned off, our framework provides more necessary data to the water sprinkling monitoring system operation. Furthermore, the primitive technique cannot handle information fusion with an accurate weight because the starting weight is only established with static numbers.

Table 4. Naïve Bayes Classifier Accuracy

S.N.	Event	True Prediction (Our Framework)	True Prediction (Our Framework)	%	%
1.	Rainfall Prediction	23,218	21,417	91.85%	88.55%
2.	Water Sprinkle Monitoring System	22,314	21,630	91.51%	89.43%

Table 5. Computational Speed

S. N	Programming Language	Computational Speed(s) (Our Framework)	Computational Speed(s) (Conventional)
1.	C++	0.228	0.117
2.	Python	0.521	0.432
3.	Java	0.627	0.511

The computational speed of these programming languages, which are extensively used for Internet of Things programming and data handling, is shown in Table 5. Measuring computing rate aims to find the optimal tool for real-time situations. The code is built using an exact constant architecture rather than a vector. The computing environment is created on the same system, an Intel-i7 processor and 16 GB of RAM. Overall, the C++ programming language is the fastest due to its sparingly memory and a modest amount of caching. The formulation and simulation of a cyber-physical crop irrigation system based on the intelligent agent concept are presented in this paper. The system allows field data collection via sensors, the application of water-based on a decision system, and control valve activation.

LIMITATIONS OF THE STUDY

Although the suggested cyber-physical infrastructure has these three advantages, it does have some drawbacks. To begin with, the entire infrastructural structure is slightly more complex than earlier approaches. Future work is still needed to balance the infrastructure's functionality and usability. The comprehensiveness is the second limitation. Because this work focuses on sensor-based PA monitoring rather than complete operations, the proposed approach was built to handle agricultural sensors rather than traditional PA data. As a result, if a comprehensive PA solution is desired, the proposed technique must be used in conjunction with other conventional PA information systems to continue providing general PA data and records management. Another limitation is the proposed infrastructure's multi-service registration, query, and management. The integration of amenities will be more efficient if a catalogue service can be added to the business logic.

REFERENCES

Amami, R., & Smiti, A. (2017). An incremental method combining density clustering and support vector machines for voice pathology detection. *Computers & Electrical Engineering*, *57*, 257–265. doi:10.1016/j.compeleceng.2016.08.021

Birda, R. K., & Dadhich, M. (2019). Study of ICT and E-Governance Facilities in Tribal District of Rajasthan. *ZENITH International Journal of Multidisciplinary Research*, *9*(7), 39–49.

Chen, N., Zhang, X., & Hiran, K. K. (2021). Integrated open geospatial web service enabled cyber-physical information infrastructure for precision agriculture monitoring. *Computers and Electronics in Agriculture*, *111*, 78–91. doi:10.1016/j.compag.2014.12.009

Cui, L., Hou, Y., Liu, Y., & Zhang, L. (2021). Text mining to explore the influencing factors of sharing economy driven digital platforms to promote social and economic development. *Information Technology for Development*, *27*(4), 779–801. doi:10.1080/02681102.2020.1815636

Dadhich, Pahwa, S. G., & S. S. R. (2021). Analytical Study of Financial Wellbeing of Selected Public and Private Sector Banks: A CAMEL Approach. *IEEE Explore, Emerging Trends in Industry 4.0 (ETI 4.0)*, 1–6. . doi:10.1109/ETI4.051663.2021.9619424

Dadhich, M., Hiran, K. K., & Rao, S. S. (2021). *Teaching – Learning Perception Toward Blended E-learning Portals During Pandemic Lockdown*. Springer Singapore. doi:10.1007/978-981-16-1696-9

Dadhich, M., Pahwa, M. S., Jain, V., & Doshi, R. (2021). Predictive Models for Stock Market Index Using Stochastic Time Series ARIMA Modeling in Emerging Economy. *Advances in Mechanical Engineering*, 281–290. doi:10.1007/978-981-16-0942-8_26

Dadhich, M., Purohit, H., & Bhasker, A. A. (2021). Determinants of green initiatives and operational performance for manufacturing SMEs. *Materials Today: Proceedings*, *46*(20), 10870–10874. doi:10.1016/j.matpr.2021.01.889

Dadhich, M., Rao, S. S., Sethy, S., & Sharma, R. (2021). Determining the Factors Influencing Cloud Computing Implementation in Library Management System (LMS): A High Order PLS-ANN Approach. *Library Philosophy and Practice*, 6281.

Diale, M., Celik, T., & Van Der Walt, C. (2019). Unsupervised feature learning for spam email filtering. *Computers & Electrical Engineering*, *74*, 89–104. doi:10.1016/j.compeleceng.2019.01.004

Dusadeerungsikul, P. O., Nof, S. Y., Bechar, A., & Tao, Y. (2019). Collaborative control protocol for agricultural cyber-physical system. *Procedia Manufacturing*, *39*, 235–242. doi:10.1016/j.promfg.2020.01.330

Goap, A., Sharma, D., Shukla, A. K., & Rama Krishna, C. (2018). An IoT based smart irrigation management system using Machine learning and open source technologies. *Computers and Electronics in Agriculture*, *155*(September), 41–49. doi:10.1016/j.compag.2018.09.040

Hiran, K. K. (2021). Investigating Factors Influencing the Adoption of IT Cloud Computing Platforms in Higher Education: Case of Sub-Saharan Africa With IT Professionals. *International Journal of Human Capital and Information Technology Professionals*, *12*(3), 21–36. doi:10.4018/IJHCITP.2021070102

Hiran, K. K., & Henten, A. (2020). An integrated TOE – DoI framework for cloud computing adoption in the higher education sector : Case study of Sub-Saharan Africa. *International Journal of System Assurance Engineering and Management*, *11*(2), 441–449. doi:10.100713198-019-00872-z

Huo, D., & Chaudhry, H. R. (2021). Using machine learning for evaluating global expansion location decisions: An analysis of Chinese manufacturing sector. *Technological Forecasting and Social Change*, *163*, 1–15. doi:10.1016/j.techfore.2020.120436

Jimenez, A. F., Cardenas, P. F., Jimenez, F., Canales, A., & López, A. (2020). A cyber-physical intelligent agent for irrigation scheduling in horticultural crops. *Computers and Electronics in Agriculture*, *178*, 1–15. doi:10.1016/j.compag.2020.105777

Kumar, N., & Dadhich, M. (2014). Risk Management for Investors in Stock Market. *EXCEL International Journal of Multidisciplinary Management Studies*, *4*(3), 103–108.

Liao, Y., Ragai, I., Huang, Z., & Kerner, S. (2021). Manufacturing process monitoring using time-frequency representation and transfer learning of deep neural networks. *Journal of Manufacturing Processes*, *68*(PA), 231–248. doi:10.1016/j.jmapro.2021.05.046

Mahrishi, M., Hiran, K. K., Meena, G., & Sharma, P. (Eds.). (2020). *Machine Learning and Deep Learning in Real-Time Applications*. IGI Global. doi:10.4018/978-1-7998-3095-5

Malathi, C., & Padmaja, I. N. (2021). Identification of cyber attacks using machine learning in smart IoT networks. *Materials Today: Proceedings*, *3*. Advance online publication. doi:10.1016/j.matpr.2021.06.400

Manrique-silupu, J., Campos, J. C., Paiva, E., & Ipanaqu, W. (2021). Thrips incidence prediction in organic banana crop with Machine learning. *Heliyon*, *7*(12), 1–27. doi:10.1016/j.heliyon.2021.e08575 PMID:34977405

Masoodab, T., & Sonntaga, P. (2020). Industry 4.0: Adoption challenges and benefits for SMEs. *Computers in Industry*, *121*, 103261. doi:10.1016/j.compind.2020.103261

Myllyaho, L., Raatikainen, M., Männistö, T., Mikkonen, T., & Nurminen, J. K. (2021). Systematic literature review of validation methods for AI systems. *Journal of Systems and Software*, *181*, 111050. doi:10.1016/j.jss.2021.111050

Naresh, K., & Manish, D. (2014). Determinant of Customers' Perception towards RTGS and NEFT Services. *Asian Journal of Research in Banking and Finance*, *4*(9), 253–260. doi:10.5958/2249-7323.2014.00960.2

Nerurkar, P., Shirke, A., Chandane, M., & Bhirud, S. (2018). Empirical Analysis of Data Clustering Algorithms. *Procedia Computer Science*, *125*, 770–779. doi:10.1016/j.procs.2017.12.099

Priyadarshini, I., Kumar, R., Sharma, R., Singh, P. K., & Satapathy, S. C. (2021). Identifying cyber insecurities in trustworthy space and energy sector for smart grids. *Computers and Electrical Engineering*, *93*(July), 107204. doi:10.1016/j.compeleceng.2021.107204

Raza, B., Kumar, Y. J., Malik, A. K., Anjum, A., & Faheem, M. (2018). Performance prediction and adaptation for database management system workload using Case-Based Reasoning approach. *Information Systems*, *76*, 46–58. doi:10.1016/j.is.2018.04.005

Restrepo, L., Aguilar, J., Toro, M., & Suescún, E. (2021). A sustainable-development approach for self-adaptive cyber–physical system's life cycle: A systematic mapping study. *Journal of Systems and Software*, *180*, 111010. doi:10.1016/j.jss.2021.111010

Setha, D., & Minhaj, A. A. (2018). Green manufacturing drivers and their relationships for small and medium(SME) and large industries. *Journal of Cleaner Production*, *198*(10), 1381–1405. doi:10.1016/j.jclepro.2018.07.106

Shalendra Singh Rao, M. D. (n.d.). Impact of Foreign Direct Investment in Indian Capital Market. *International Journal of Research in Economics and Social Sciences*, *7*(6), 172–178.

Sharma, N., & Dadhich, M. (2014). Predictive Business Analytics: The Way Ahead. *Journal of Commerce and Management Thought, 5*(4), 652. doi:10.5958/0976-478X.2014.00012.3

Sharma, R., Kamble, S. S., Gunasekaran, A., Kumar, V., & Kumar, A. (2020). A systematic literature review on machine learning applications for sustainable agriculture supply chain performance. *Computers & Operations Research, 119*, 1–12. doi:10.1016/j.cor.2020.104926

Shen, Z., Shehzad, A., Chen, S., Sun, H., & Liu, J. (2020). Machine Learning Based Approach on Food Recognition and Nutrition Estimation. *Procedia Computer Science, 174*, 448–453. doi:10.1016/j.procs.2020.06.113

Sujatha, R., Chatterjee, J. M., Jhanjhi, N. Z., & Brohi, S. N. (2021). Performance of deep learning vs machine learning in plant leaf disease detection. *Microprocessors and Microsystems, 80*(December). doi:10.1016/j.micpro.2020.103615

Tripathi, S., & Gupta, M. (2021). Identification of challenges and their solution for smart supply chains in Industry 4.0 scenario: A neutrosophic DEMATEL approach. *International Journal of Logistics Systems and Management, 40*(1), 70–94. doi:10.1504/IJLSM.2021.117691

Tyagi, S. K. S., Mukherjee, A., Pokhrel, S. R., & Hiran, K. K. (2020). An intelligent and optimal resource allocation approach in sensor networks for smart agri-IoT. *IEEE Sensors Journal*.

Chapter 4
Differential Privacy Techniques–Based Information Security for Cyber Physical System Applications:
An Overview

A. Kanagaraj
Nallamuthu Gounder Mahalingam College, India

S. Sharmila
Nallamuthu Gounder Mahalingam College, India

A. Finny Belwin
Angappa College of Arts and Science, India

A. Linda Sherin
A. M. Jain College, India

Antony Selvadoss Thanamani
Nallamuthu Gounder Mahalingam College, India

ABSTRACT

A cyber physical system (CPS) is a mechanism that monitors and controls entire devices which are connected together. Secured data transmission in CPS systems is a major problem. To provide information security for CPS applications, certain privacy preservation strategies need to be followed. Encryption and anonymization are existing traditional privacy preservation techniques which are not suitable to provide information security for advanced systems called CPS. Differential techniques is an emerging privacy technique where a required amount of noise is added using various mathematical algorithms with data while sharing information between devices in CPSs. The process of adding noise with data is called data perturbation. There

DOI: 10.4018/978-1-7998-9308-0.ch004

are three major data perturbations mechanisms followed to provide information security. They are exponential mechanism, Laplace mechanism, and Gaussian mechanism. This chapter presents a detailed review about applications of CPSs, significance of implementing differential privacy techniques, challenges, and future research directions of CPSs.

INTRODUCTION

The research on Cyber-Physical Systems (CPS) has recently becomes broad impact on society, economics and the environment. Differential privacy is currently emerging as a future of privacy. Differential privacy safeguards statistical or real-time data by introducing a desired level of noise while maintaining a good balance between privacy and accuracy. In differential privacy, the user can select the level of privacy or distinguishability, resulting in the maximum feasible privacy protection for any individual in the dataset. Over the last ten years, improvements in CPSs have attracted a lot of interest. The dual character of CPSs, by which they blend the dynamic properties of embedded computers with those of information and communication technologies, is the primary reason for this enormous interest (ICT).

To protect data privacy, a number of researchers suggested cryptographic methods. Many cryptographic algorithms are computationally costly because of the users need to maintain large number of encryption keys. When public data sharing is required, maintaining privacy also becomes more difficult. Researchers have also proposed anonymization techniques such as k-anonymity to address privacy concerns. However, because the chance of re-identification increases as the amount of attributes in the dataset grows, this anonymization technique does not ensure perfect security against adversaries. Differential privacy is currently gaining traction as a potential future of privacy. Even though security and privacy are the primary difficulties of modern technology, privacy and security issues influence cyber-physical systems. This chapter provides suggestions and solutions for CPS's security issues.

BACKGROUND

CPS refers to a group of interconnected systems that can monitor and manipulate real-world objects and processes. CPS focuses on the interplay of physical, networking, and compute processes. As a result of their integration with IoT, a new CPS element, the Internet of Cyber-Physical Things, has emerged (IoCPT).In this paper, the main characteristics of CPS, as well as the related applications, technology, and standards, are discussed (Jean-Paul A. Yaacoub, 2020). Furthermore, CPS security vulnerabilities, threats, and attacks are examined, as well as major difficulties and challenges. In addition, existing security methods are given and examined, with their primary weaknesses identified. Finally, based on the lessons learnt throughout this exhaustive examination, various suggestions and recommendations are made. Because of complex cybernetics and the interplay of (independent) CPS domains, the exponential expansion of cyber-physical systems (CPS) has created various security vulnerabilities, particularly in safety-critical applications. (Muhammad Shafique, 2018) presents a concise but thorough overview of current static and adaptive detection and prevention strategies, as well as their inherent shortcomings, such as the inability to detect latent or uncertainty-based runtime security assaults. This study also presents intelligent security methods against many described attacks on different tiers of the CPS stack to meet these problems.

CPS are employed in a variety of industries to provide for process optimization and previously unattainable capabilities (Muhammad Shafique, 2018). The inherent properties of networked digital systems and analogue physical processes influence how security theory is used. As a result, security and privacy are important considerations in the design, development, and operation of CPSs. (Glenn A. Fink, 2018) explain how CPS security and privacy differ from that of pure cyber or physical systems, as well as what may be done to make these systems safer. The purpose is to assist young CPS designers in creating more secure, privacy-enhancing products in the future.CPS are cyber-physical systems that interact in a feedback loop with the help of human intervention, interaction, and utilization. As the foundation for developing and future smart services, these systems will empower the essential infrastructure and have the potential to have a substantial impact on daily life. The rising usage of CPS, on the other hand, introduces new hazards that could have serious ramifications for users. New dangers and cyber-attacks will continue to be exploited, necessitating the development of new strategies to defend CPS.(Yosef Ashibani, 2017) gave an examination of security challenges at various layers of the CPS architecture, risk assessment, and approaches for securing CPS. Finally, the obstacles, prospective study areas, and potential solutions are given and addressed.

A complete study of differential privacy approaches for CPSs is presented in (Muneeb Ul Hassan, 2019). The authors look at how differential privacy is used and implemented in four important CPS applications: energy systems, transportation systems, healthcare and medical systems, and the industrial Internet of things (IIoT). This chapter also discusses unresolved concerns, challenges, and future research directions for CPS differential privacy approaches. This study can be used to help develop new differential privacy strategies that can be used to handle a variety of CPS difficulties and data privacy scenarios. Using the VERIS Community Database, (Steven Walker Roberts, 2020) explores the risk spectrum of a cyber security incident occurring in the cyber-physical-enabled environment. The bulk of known perpetrators were from the United States and Russia, the majority of victims were from western countries, and geographic origin tended to follow global events, according to the research. Information was the most often targeted asset, with the bulk of attack techniques focusing on privilege misuse. This demonstrates the critical necessity for a significant re-evaluation of cyber security's core ideas.

CYBER PHYSICAL SYSTEM

Cyber physical systems are a new type of time-critical and safety-critical real-time embedded systems that have a strong interaction between computing and communication in order to regulate the vast and complicated global world. The challenges of scientific, social, and technical problems have an impact on the cyber physical system. The following sections discuss about cyber physical systems in detail.

CPS Layers

The architecture of CPS systems is made up of various layers and components that communicate with one another using various communication protocols and technologies. The perception layer, transmission layer, and application layer are the three main layers of the CPS architecture. Sensors, actuators, aggregators, Radio-Frequency Identification (RFID) tags, Global Positioning Systems (GPS), and other devices are all part of the perception layer. In order to monitor, track, and understand the physical world, these gadgets acquire real-time data. Between the perception and application levels, the Transmission Layer exchanges and processes data. Local Area Networks (LANs) and communication protocols are used to transmit and interact data over the Internet. This layer also ensures data routing and transmission over cloud computing platforms, routing devices, switching and internet Gateways, firewalls, and intrusion detection and prevention systems (Jean-Paul A. Yaacoub, 2020).The application layer interprets the data received from the data transmission layer and sends commands to the physical devices, such as sensors and actuators. This is accomplished through the use of complex decision-making algorithms based on aggregated data. Furthermore, before deciding the appropriate automated actions, this layer receives and processes information from the perception layer.

Components

CPS components can be used to detect information or regulate signals. Sensing Components (SC) collect and detect data, and Controlling Components (CC) monitor and control signals, are the two basic categories of CPS components.

Sensors capture and record real-world data using a correlation process known as "calibration" to ensure that the data collected is accurate. Data sensing is critical since judgments will be made based on the analysis of this data. Aggregators are typically found at the transmission layer, where they evaluate sensor input before issuing the appropriate decision.

Data aggregation, in reality, is based on the gathered information on a certain goal, which is gathered and summarized after a statistical analysis. Actuators are positioned at the application layer and are responsible for making information visible to the surrounding environment based on the aggregators' judgments. Because actuators are so reliant on other network nodes, each action taken by the CPS is dependent on a previous data aggregation process. Actuators also process electrical signals in terms of operations (Jean-Paul A. Yaacoub, 2020). Signal Controlling Components are used to control signals and play an important role in signal control, monitoring, and management in order to obtain greater levels of accuracy and protection from intentional attacks or accidents, such as signal jamming, noise, and interference.

Characteristics of CPS

CPS is a self-organizing and reconfiguring control system with a high degree of automation, complexity at many spatial and temporal scales, and closed control loops at all scales. Embedded systems, real-time systems, (wired and wireless) networking, and control theory are all represented by CPS. Because many of the computers engaging directly with the real world perform only a few specialized operations, they do not require the general computational capacity of traditional computers or even mobile systems, and hence have limited resources. The time it takes to perform computations in safety-critical systems is critical in ensuring the system's correctness. Developers can use real-time programming languages to specify timing requirements for their systems, and Real-Time Operating Systems guarantee the time it takes for an application to accept and complete a task. Another feature of CPSs is that they communicate with one another, which is increasingly done using IP-compatible networks. Wireless networks are a common feature of CPS as well. The task at hand is to construct networks on top of low-powered, lossy wireless communications. Control theory aims to use differential equations to characterize a physical process and then develop a controller that meets a set of desired properties such as stability and efficiency.

CPSS Security

In the physical layer, an attacker might intervene directly or destroy the physical objects that are being monitored and controlled, such as sensors and controllers, resulting in false sensed measurements, incorrect control decisions, and improper actuator movements. In the sensor or actuator layer, an attacker can use brute force attacks to destroy or hack the sensors or actuators in order to collect critical information and modify them. An attacker can use the power distribution mechanisms of sensors and actuators to drain energy for denial-of-service attacks or to activate malicious circuitry with that energy (Yosef Ashibani, 2017).The network layer of CPS has security vulnerabilities connected to communications. Networking attacks are divided into two categories: replay attacks and denial of service attacks. Because control mechanisms are heavily dependent on timeliness, desynchronization is a common security problem in the control layer of CPS. As a result, even a minor desynchronization in the control signals might be regarded disastrous, as wrong judgments can result in CPS failures. The majority of attacks at the information layer steal information through eavesdropping or analyzing traffic data. Manipulation of key information, on the other hand, can be used to carry out various attacks such as jamming, collision, denial of service, and so on.

Applications of CPS

A cyber physical system can be used in a variety of situations. The following sections describes some of the applications of CPSs. Medical gadgets for patient diagnosis, monitoring, and treatment, such as x-ray machines, magnetic resonance imaging (MRI), surgery, and other medical instruments, have all benefited from technological advancements. With limited computational capability, communication complexity, and battery life, health-care-related CPS in the areas of implantable medical devices, body area networks, and wearable devices necessitates privacy, security, and trust. One of the newer fields of CPSs is intelligent transportation systems (ITSs) (D. Li, Q. Yang. 2017).

ITSs are concerned with the development of traffic systems, automobiles, mass transit, and other comparable variables in order to improve efficiency, congestion, sustainability, and safety (M. Gohar, 2018). Cyber-systems, such as communication networks, control automation systems and centres, and Intelligent Electronic Devices, are installed in power grid components (A. V. Kayem 2017). Smart grids are described as next-generation infrastructure capable of handling all of the energy and environmental needs by supplying with reliable, cost-effective, and environmentally friendly electricity.

Unfortunately, despite its importance, smart house cyber security, which is a key part of smart home system research, is understudied. Security issues in smart homes are addressed at both the system and device levels. Smart city applications are intended to manage urban traffic and provide real-time responses to concerns such as energy efficiency, demand-side response, and energy management. The term "smart city" covers a wide range of topics, including "smart" power, "smart" grid systems, "smart" environment, "smart" transportation, "smart" homes, and "smart" management. (M.-C. Chuang, 2011)

One of the most significant advantages of smart metering is precise bill calculation in a dynamic pricing system (D. Alahakoon, 2016) This pricing strategy necessitates detailed energy consumption data, which, on the other hand, may expose smart meter users' personal information. As a result, researchers face a hurdle in providing differential privacy alongside correct dynamic pricing billing. Many scholars are working on efficient algorithms to overcome this trade-off to the greatest extent possible. Industrial IoT systems have unique needs, including as operation in hostile environments, predictable throughput, maintenance by people other than communication experts, and extremely low downtown. Differential privacy is a new standard for protecting IIoT systems' privacy. Differential privacy defines a detailed attack model, decreases data exposure privacy threats, and ensures data availability at the same time as the query or decision.

CPS THREATS AND ATTACKS

Adversaries are always attempting to breach critical systems in order to gain total or partial access to data. The adversary can recognize the defined list of receivers based on observed traffic in a disclosure attack, which is a traffic pattern analysis attack (Muneeb Ul Hassan, 2019). Adversaries employ this attack approach to identify and compromise a specific receiver's communication. The linking attack is a sort of assault in which external data is coupled with anonymized or protected data in order to derive essential information. To avoid any privacy violations, direct requests regarding any individual are normally banned throughout a query assessment.

A differencing assault is a type of attack like this (Steven Walker-Roberts, 2020). Strong correlation may occur in real-world data, such as shared relationships and family members sharing attributes in various social networking datasets, when using correlation attacks. If an adversary attempts a correlation attack with similar datasets, the existing correlation may result in the revelation of more information than planned. A privacy-preserving system with efficient data handling is necessary to prevent correlation attacks, which decreases the danger of information leaking even in the case of public query evaluation (P. L. Ambassa, 2018).

CPS SECURITY SOLUTIONS AND RECOMMENDATIONS

With the rising use of CPS in many critical domains, security has become a pressing concern, necessitating a thorough risk assessment. With so much reliance on the Internet, the security focus of risk assessment has shifted from computer risk assessment to network risk assessment (enn A. Fink, 2018). The purpose of assessing CPS security is to create a quantifiable risk that can be used to defend future systems. When assessing CPS risk, three factors should be considered: asset identification, threat identification, and vulnerability identification.

Asset identification refers to a resource value that must be preserved, which can be either tangible or immaterial. In truth, the majority of assets are intangible; as a result, assets have a direct value in many daily transactions and services and should be safeguarded. Asset quantification can also be assessed using direct and indirect economic losses and the resulting losses. Threat identification is used to assist in identifying threats that are of high priority concern in the field of CPS, which is a difficult task. Historical data can be utilised to quantify the threat's frequency, whereas sampling records and logs from the Intrusion Detection System (IDS) can be used to determine the risk's frequency, among other things.

DIFFERENTIAL PRIVACY

Differential privacy can save a significant amount of data from both databases and real-time data. The bulk of differential privacy techniques use data disruption. In data perturbation, the amount of noise is determined using differential privacy techniques, then added to the query data to make it secure and unrecognizable to the observer. This disturbance has a direct impact on the data reporting accuracy. The more perturbed data, on the other hand, ensures that privacy is well maintained. As a result, while adopting differential privacy, it's important to strike a balance between accuracy and privacy. Because of this trade-off between privacy and accuracy, implementing differentiated privacy in CPSs is a difficult issue, as many CPSs applications, such as health care and medical systems, require accurate data reporting.

To date, researchers have developed a variety of privacy preservation solutions to combat distinct privacy threats. Because it provides the property of data inaccessibility to unauthorized users, encryption is one of the conventional privacy-preserving techniques employed by the majority of systems to secure data from adversaries and unauthorized users. Because of the sensors' limited computer capacity, encryption can only be used sparingly in current CPSs. The production and distribution of public and private keys in public key cryptography, also known as asymmetric cryptography, is a computationally expensive job that cannot easily be carried out with small devices with minimal resources.

Furthermore, any weakness can utilize multiple methods, such as a brute-force assault, against the encrypted CPS data. Similarly, encryption schemes in a network of numerous sensors necessitate the interconnection of each node for the production and transmission of private keys in the network. As a result, if one node in a network of n nodes fails, decryption and data gathering from CPSs nodes becomes almost impossible due to the lack of keys in the network. Furthermore, by altering the noise addition parameter in differential privacy, CPSs users can control the level of privacy according to their needs. Three major data perturbation mechanisms are the Laplace mechanism, Gaussian mechanism and Exponential mechanism.

FUTURE RESEARCH DIRECTIONS

Because of the dynamic nature of CPSs, differential privacy implementation in cyber physical systems is now confronting a variety of obstacles. Some of the CPS research challenges are:

- The smart grid is the future of energy systems, because it incorporates capabilities of both; traditional energy systems and modern information and communication technologies. This pricing model necessitates thorough energy use data, which, on the other side, may expose smart metre customers' personal information. As a result, researchers face a hurdle in providing differential privacy alongside correct dynamic pricing billing.
- Small wind turbines and solar panels will be used to power most of these energy sources in smart houses. Some smart homes may sell surplus energy to other purchasers; they can auction this energy, and buyers can purchase it based on their needs. The buyer and seller, on the other hand, usually do not want to reveal their identities to each other during this procedure. As a result, preserving this data is critical for the proper operation of the smart grid's auction mechanism.
- Smart meters are often controlled by programming that determines all of their functions. This firmware is often generated by smart meter vendors, who then update it to improve functionality or fix any bugs that are discovered. When only a subset of smart meters needs to be updated rather than all of them, the utility may require case access control. However, specific security and privacy-based methods are required to protect this firmware file.
- Micro-grid resource restricted designs are the best option for a cost-effective supply and power management solution in remote places. Certain lossy

networks are utilized to communicate across these resource restricted systems in order to reduce operational costs. Due to their unstable nature, these lossy networks are vulnerable to a variety of adversaries and privacy assaults. This invasion of privacy can lead to a variety of crimes, such as energy theft.

- A smart city requires a smart transportation system. Route planning applications frequently incorporate real-time traffic data. If the network is open, any intruder can gain access to the live location monitoring of connected cars by hacking the system of these applications. Differential privacy can give real-time location privacy by disrupting location or identity to protect the privacy of drivers.

- V2V (vehicle-to-vehicle) communication is becoming increasingly prevalent. Certain privacy and security concerns with V2V communication have surfaced in recent years. Differential privacy may be the best approach for maintaining privacy in communication between two vehicles.

- In the healthcare and medical system, the trend of integrating the online and physical worlds has exploded. With the evolution of wireless technologies, the use of body sensors for medical applications is becoming more popular. These sensors keep track of your current data and send them to your doctor or trainer. One solution for this type of application is encryption, however it is computationally difficult. Differential privacy-based real-time data reporting, on the other hand, may be a lightweight solution to this challenge.

- Retirement homes and elderly homes demand special attention because the residents require round-the-clock care and attention. Protecting electronic patient records, which contain all useful information, identification, and medical records of persons residing in that home, is one of the potential applications of differentiated privacy in elderly homes.

- Modern IoT technologies have a significant impact on industry advancements. These malicious adversaries can also control machinery, or can even destroy industrial systems. As a result, key IIoT sectors must be secured initially in order for IoT systems in industry to work smoothly.

- One of the most difficult aspects of differentiated privacy is identifying the exact privacy. Even with mathematical proofs and a rigid privacy model in place, differential privacy falls short of providing an intelligible notion of privacy in the context of massive data. The problem of calculating the optimal composition of differential privacy in big data analytics is yet unsolved. Similarly, ensuring privacy protection while also dealing with the issue of dimensionality as a result of enormous data volumes and computing overhead is a major difficulty for researchers in the field of big data.

- Any machine learning algorithm's main goal is to extract useful information from given data. However, one of the most difficult tasks for future machine learning algorithms is maintaining individual privacy while harvesting data.

- The massive volume of data generated by pervasive connection among smart gadgets paved the way for cloud computing, a reliable and secure storage system. Outsourcing this information to a third party may result in privacy concerns. Information redundancy in big data from various sources, multi-tenancy, and ubiquitous access aspects of cloud computing platforms are all factors that contribute to these privacy concerns. Differential privacy is currently gaining traction as a viable solution to the privacy challenges that cloud computing presents. Researchers have begun work on preserving the privacy of cloud computing data by employing differential privacy.

- A substantial amount of private data is stored in wireless edge computing networks and cannot be supplied directly for data prediction and processing. As a result, before evaluating any query, it is necessary to ensure that critical elements of wireless edge computing are protected. To address this problem, researchers propose differential privacy-based techniques as the best approach.

- Block chain has evolved as an unique distributed technique in recent years that provides for the secure storing of transactions or any other sort of data without the requirement for any predetermined centralized data authority. Its feature of public accessible without a centralized authority made it popular among its users, but it also created certain security and privacy concerns.

CONCLUSION

Cyber Physical Systems (CPSs) have become an essential part of daily life. It is a collaboration of computation, communication and control. CPSs is advanced technology to IOT. CPSs basically integrates huge number of sensors and private data. Adversaries can attack in two ways either passive attack or by using active attack. Here passive attack is privacy oriented attack and active attack is security oriented attack. Encryption and anonymization techniques are existing traditional techniques which is not suitable to provide information security for advanced system called CPSs. Since CPSs is an advanced system, implementation of encryption technique based privacy preservation technique cannot provide more accuracy. This technique is not suitable for small devices which have limited resources. In multiple sensors network, sharing and maintaining public, private keys for connections between every node is difficult task. This leads to data loss. So encryption technique provides computationally complex, more expensive, as well as it reduces system speed. Apart from all it is not suitable for public databases. Anonymization is another privacy preservation technique which is used to provide data security. Since it is suitable for work with high dimensional data, lot of drawbacks are there. If size of attributes increased there may be a chance of re-identification of information also increases in this technique. While converting anonymized data to non-anonymized and vice versa there may be a chance of losing 100% original data.

One of the most optimal solutions to overcome these privacy hazards is preserving data by noise addition using differential privacy perturbation mechanisms. In this case users can control level of privacy. This data perturbation has the direct effect with data accuracy. Adding more noise provides more security but less accuracy, where as adding less noise provides low security but more accuracy. So, therefore user needs to concentrate both accuracy as well as security. This technique has the capability to preserve huge amount of data on both real-time and databases. The major objective of this technique is not to provide enough information about any individuals in query output. Exponential mechanism, Laplace mechanism and Gaussian mechanism are the three major data perturbation mechanisms which will provide more information security for CPSs. This chapter presented a detailed and up-to-date survey of CPSs applications security threats, attacks, solutions and recommendations. This chapter concluded the survey article by highlighting challenges, open issues, and future research directions in differential privacy techniques for CPSs.

ACKNOWLEDGMENT

This research received no specific grant from any funding agency in the public, commercial, or not-for-profit sectors.

REFERENCES

Alahakoon, D., & Yu, X. (2016). Smart electricity meter data intelligence for future energy systems: A survey. *IEEE Transactions on Industrial Informatics*, *12*(1), 425–436. doi:10.1109/TII.2015.2414355

Ambassa, P. L., Kayem, A. V. D. M., Wolthusen, S. D., & Meinel, C. (2018). Privacy risks in resource constrained smart micro-grids. *IEEE 32nd International Conference on Advanced Information Networking and Applications Workshops (WAINA)*, 527-532.

Ashibani, Y., & Mahmoud, Q. H. (2017). Cyber physical systems security: Analysis, challenges and solutions. *Computers & Security, ELSEVIER*, *68*, 81–97. doi:10.1016/j.cose.2017.04.005

Chuang, M.-C., & Lee, J.-F. (2011). Ppas: A privacy preservation authentication scheme for vehicle-to-infrastructure communication networks. *IEEE International Conference on Consumer Electronics, Communications and Networks (CECNet)*, 1509-1512. 10.1109/CECNET.2011.5768254

Fink, G. A., Edgar, T. W., Rice, T. R., MacDonald, D. G., & Crawford, C. E. (2018). *Overview of Security and Privacy in Cyber-Physical Systems. Overview of Security and Privacy in Cyber-Physical Systems: Foundations, Principles and Applications.* doi:10.1002/9781119226079.ch1

Gohar, M., Muhammad, M., & Rahman, A. U. (2018). Smart tss: Defining transportation system behavior using big data analytics in smart cities. *Sustainable Cities and Society, 41*, 114–119. doi:10.1016/j.scs.2018.05.008

Hassan, Rehmani, & Chen. (2019). Differential Privacy Techniques for Cyber Physical Systems: A Survey. *IEEE Explore*, 1-44.

Kayem, A. V., Meinel, C., & Wolthusen, S. D. (2017). A smart microgrid architecture for resource constrained environments. *IEEE 31ˢᵗ International Conference on Advanced Information Networking and Applications (AINA)*, 857-864.

Li, D., Yang, Q., Yu, W., An, D., Yang, X., & Zhao, W. (2017). A strategy-proof privacy-preserving double auction mechanism for electrical vehicles demand response in microgrids. *IEEE 36th International Performance Computing and Communications Conference (IPCCC)*, 1–8.

Shafique, M., Khalid, F., & Rehman, S. (2018). Intelligent Security Measures for Smart Cyber-Physical Systems. In *21st Euromicro Conference on Digital System Design.* Conference Publishing Services. 10.1109/DSD.2018.00058

Walker-Roberts, S., Hammoudeh, M., Aldabbas, O., Aydin, M., & Dehghantanha, A. (2020). Threats on the horizon: Understanding security threats in the era of cyber-physical systems. *The Journal of Supercomputing, Springer, 76*(4), 2643–2664. doi:10.100711227-019-03028-9

Yaacoub, J.-P. A., Salman, O., Noura, H. N., Kaaniche, N., Chehab, A., & Malli, M. (2020). Cyber-physical systems security: Limitations, issues and future trends. *Microprocessors and Microsystems, ELSEVIER, 77*, 1–33. doi:10.1016/j.micpro.2020.103201 PMID:32834204

Chapter 5

Machine Learning in Cyber Physical Systems for Healthcare:
Brain Tumor Classification From MRI Using Transfer Learning Framework

Jayaraj Ramasamy
Azteca University, Mexico

Ruchi Doshi
Azteca University, Mexico

ABSTRACT

Brain tumors are prevalent and aggressive disease, with a relatively short life expectancy in their most severe form. Thus, treatment planning is an important element in improving patient quality of life. In general, image techniques such as computed tomography (CT), magnetic resonance imaging (MRI), and ultrasound imaging are used to examine tumors in the brain, lung, liver, and breast. MRI scans are used in this study to diagnose brain tumors. As a result, a reliable and automated classification technique is required to prevent death. Automatic brain tumor detection using convolutional neural networks (CNN) classification is proposed in this chapter. Small kernels are used to conduct the deeper architectural design. In machine learning, brain tumor classification is done by using a binary classifier to detect brain tumors from MRI scan images. In this chapter, transfer learning is used to build the classifier, achieving a good accuracy and visualizing the model's overall performance.

DOI: 10.4018/978-1-7998-9308-0.ch005

INTRODUCTION

A brain tumor is one of the essential organs in the human body, consisting of billions of cells. The aberrant collection of cells is created by the uncontrolled division of cells, which is also known as a tumor. Brain tumors are classified into two types: low grade (grade 1 and grade 2) tumors and high grade (grade 3 and grade 4) tumors (Auzias, 2015). A benign brain tumor is one with a low grade. Similarly, a high grade tumor is sometimes referred to as a malignant tumor. A benign tumor is one that is not cancerous. As a result, it does not spread to other areas of the brain. The malignant tumor, on the other hand, is a cancerous tumor. As a result, it spreads quickly with indeterminate borders to other parts of the body. It results in instant death. The brain MRI picture is primarily used to detect tumors and to simulate tumor progression. Early detection of brain tumors can alter the disease's course and save lives. Computers, on the other hand, can execute complicated tasks in a relatively short amount of time. Computers are utilized in a variety of fields, including health care, since they provide automated, quick, and precise results (Bauer,2015). As a result, computer-aided diagnostic (CAD) systems are now widely employed. The intricate relationships are analyzed using CAD systems. Early diagnosis and categorization of a brain tumor is critical for a patient's successful and timely treatment. The capacity of the human visual cortex to distinguish between distinct shades of gray is known to be limited, as evidenced by magnetic resonance imaging (MRI). This gives rise to computer-aided diagnosis (CAD) or brain tumor classification (BTC) techniques, which can help radiologists, visualize and classify tumor forms. For the categorization of a brain tumor, traditional BTC techniques rely on low-level characteristics and the use of statistical learning methodologies. This group of segmentation methods focuses on estimating the tumor's borders and localization, which includes certain pretreatment processes including contrast enhancement, picture sharpening, and edge detection/refinement. Image capture, preprocessing, ROI segmentation, feature extraction and selection, dimensionality reduction, classification, and performance evaluation are the steps in the fundamental workflow of classic BTC techniques (Fresilli,2020). Deep learning-based methods, in contrast to traditional approaches, rely primarily on training data and require far less preparation. The research on deep learning shows that, notably in the area of BTC the accuracy of a system is strongly reliant on the amount of data. Convolutional neural networks are used in most deep learning approaches in BTC (CNNs). Indeed, the growing use of CNNs for a variety of computer vision issues in many fields encourages their use in BTC, especially for smart health monitoring. These automated brain tumor identification, segmentation, and classification techniques benefit mankind by minimizing the need for surgery (biopsy). These approaches are always available to aid radiologists who are unsure about the type of a tumor or want to visually study it in greater detail. Scientists working in image processing and computer vision are interested in developing precise and efficient techniques for automatically detecting, classifying, and segmenting tumors. This data is mostly utilized in tumor diagnosis and therapy procedures. An MRI picture contains more information about a particular medical imaging than a CT or ultrasound image (Feng,2019). An MRI picture offers precise information on brain anatomy as well as the detection of anomalies in brain tissue. Scholars have really presented unique automated ways for identifying and categorizing brain cancers utilizing brain MRI pictures since the time when it was able to scan and freight medical images to the computer (Hiran, K. K., et al., 2013). In contrast, during the last several years, Neural Networks (NN) and Support Vector Machines (SVM) have been the most utilized approaches for their good implementation. Deep Learning (DL) models (Mahrishi, M., et al.,2020), on the other hand, have recently established a stirring trend in machine learning, as the subterranean architecture can efficiently represent complex relationships without requiring a large number of nodes, as do superficial architectures such as K-Nearest Neighbor (KNN) and Support Vector Machine (SVM). As a result, unlike health informatics, they soon expanded to become the cutting-edge (Hiran, K. K., et al.2021).

MRI IMAGE PREPROCESSING

Image capture, denoising, preprocessing, segmentation, feature extraction, and matching are all phases of the MRI Recognition system. The MRI picture in the detecting machine is considerably distorted by noise. Various disturbances, such as salt and pepper, Gaussian, and speckle noise, damage the MRI picture during acquisition. Denoising the damaged pictures can result in high-quality photographs. In most cases, the machine's traditional procedures eliminate the noise from the signal. The presence of noise reduces the diagnostic efficacy significantly and necessitates a high level of subjectivity in MRI picture interpretation. Each approach for MRI denoising has its own set of benefits and drawbacks. Many approaches for removing sounds based on statistical properties and frequency spectrum distribution have been developed. At every level of the picture capture unit, noise is added. The noises are either Gaussian or non-Gaussian, which can occur for a variety of causes. The signal and the noise are statistically indistinguishable. One of the most essential jobs is to remove noise from an MRI picture. Denoising techniques reduce noise and retain the edges of an MRI to the greatest extent feasible. For eliminating noise from an MRI, there are a variety of filters available, each with its unique set of characteristics. Denoising techniques are divided into two categories: spatial filtering and transform domain filtering. Linear and non-linear filtering are two types of spatial domain filtering. Because of the rapidity with which linear methods remove noise, they are commonly employed (Kumar,2020). However, the linear method has a drawback in that it does not efficiently maintain picture edges. Nonlinear techniques, on the other hand, can handle picture edges considerably better than linear techniques. We are also using non-linear filtering to remove such an impulsive noise.

The arithmetic and geometric filters, which effectively eliminate random noise in the MRI, may be used to remove Gaussian noise. Nonlinear filters such as max-min can be used to eliminate pepper noise, however the dark pixels in the MRI picture that hold important information will be deleted. When there are dark pixels in a picture, nonlinear filters should be avoided. After removing the noise, the tumor edges are sharpened using MRI image enhancement. Edge detection filters, such as spatial filters based on spatial differentiation, Sobel, Gaussian, Prewitt, and Laplacian filters, have been used in the literature to determine the exact position and size of tumors. Edges and discontinuities in the picture will be emphasized. However, because the Laplacian filter output is not an improved picture; the sharpened enhanced image must be removed from the original image. A single technique will not produce a superior outcome, according to the results of the method research. Hybrid approaches are yielding positive results.

Even though previous research has been extensive, picture denoising remains a problem for researchers since the noise reduction process introduces artifacts and causes image blurring. Wavelet transformations, discrete wavelet transforms, biorthogonal wavelet filters, Haar wavelet filters, Coiflet wavelet filters, orthogonal wavelet filters, Symlet wavelet filters, log gobar filters, and other topics are covered. delivers excellent MRI image denoising and is classified as discrete domain transform.

LITERATURE REVIEW

Auzias, G et al.(2015) Proposed between the tumor and non-tumor regions of the brain, Fuzzy C-Means (FCM) segmentation is used. A multilayer Discrete Wavelet Transform is also used to extract wavelet features (DWT). Finally, a Deep Neural Network (DNN) is used to classify brain tumors with great accuracy. This methodology is compared to the classification techniques KNN, Linear Discriminate Analysis (LDA), and Sequential Minimal Optimization (SMO).

Bauer,S et al.(2015) For brain tumor segmentation and classification, the fuzzy based control theory is employed. The Fuzzy Interference System (FIS) is a unique technology that is primarily used to segment the brain. To build a membership function for a fuzzy controller, supervised classification is employed. The performance is excellent, but the precision is poor.

Feng C et al.(2019) The novel Cellular Automata (CA) methodology is used to show a seeded tumor segmentation method that is compared to a graph cut based segmentation method. For effective brain tumor segmentation, the seed selection and Volume Of Interest (VOI) are computed. This research also includes tumor cut segmentation. The level of difficulty is low.

Fresilli et al.(2020) In this article the step-by-step tumor growth of patients, a unique bio-physio mechanical tumor growth simulation is given. It will be used with individual margins for gliomas and solid tumors to prevent the major tumor bulk impact. A tumor growth model is created by combining discrete and continuous techniques. Based on atlas-based registration, the suggested approach provides the likelihood of tacitly segmenting tumor-bearing brain pictures. This method is mostly used to segment brain tissue. However, the computation time is lengthy.

S Kumar et al.(2020) Proposed about the voxel of the brain which is classified using the local independent projection-based classification (LIPC) technique. This technique also extracts the route characteristic. As a result, LIPC does not require explicit regularization.

J Y Jim et al.(2020) The brain tumor is detected and segmented using novel multi-fractal (MultiFD) feature extraction and enhanced AdaBoost classification algorithms. Using the MultiFD feature extraction technique, the texture of brain tumor tissue is retrieved. To determine if a particular brain tissue is tumor or non-neoplastic tissue, enhanced AdaBoost classification techniques are utilized. The level of complexity is great.

PROPOSED SYSTEM

This method's main stages are data collection, pre-processing, and detection via neural network. In general, accurate semi-automatic and automatic detection methods are required. As a result of these factors, a fully automatic segmentation system based on CNN is used.

Data Collection

We acquired our data as MRI pictures because our method is primarily focused on the detection of brain tumors. The dataset obtained included 159 photos with tumors and 99 images without tumors.

Pre-processing

The primary goal is to boost image highlights, which are required for further processing. The input image is transformed to grayscale for the remainder of the preprocessing steps. The image is then thresholded, and the thresholded image is subjected to more erosion and dilation. The contours and extreme points are extracted from this image.

Convolutional Neural Network

CNN is used to improve results. Previous layers are linked together by kernel weights. Back propagation calculation is used to improve the quality of an information image. Since feature maps of all kernel-shared units. It will aid in reducing overfitting. Kernels are used to collect all of the data in the neighborhood. Kernel is a significant source of context information. The activation function is applied to the neural network output.

The human brain is represented via neural network architecture and execution. Vector quantization, approximation, data clustering, pattern matching, optimization functions, and classification algorithms are all common uses for neural networks (Hiran, K. K., et al, 2021). The interconnections of a neural network split it into three categories. There are three types of neural networks: feedback, feed forward, and recurrent. The Feed Forward Neural Network is separated into two types: single layer and multilayer. The hidden layer is not visible in a single layer network (Kim,2020). However, it simply has an input and output layer. The multilayer, on the other hand, is made up of three layers: input, hidden, and output (Liu,2017). The recurrent network is a closed loop based feedback network. Image scalability is not possible in a traditional neural network. However, with a convolution neural network, the picture may be scaled (that is, it can go from a 3D input volume to a 3D output volume) (length, width, height). The input layer, convolution layer, Rectified Linear Unit (ReLU) layer, pooling layer, and fully connected layer make up the Convolution Neural Network (CNN).

The provided input image is divided into tiny areas in the convolution layer. The ReLU layer performs element-by-element activation. The use of a pooling layer is optional. We have the option of using or skipping(Pereira,2016). The pooling layer, on the other hand, is mostly utilized for down sampling. The class score or label score value is generated in the last layer (i.e. fully connected layer) based on the likelihood between 0 and 1.

Figure 1 and Figure 2 shows a block schematic of a convolution neural network-based brain tumor classification system (Pellakuri,2016). The training and testing phases of the CNN-based brain tumor categorization are separated. The number of pictures is split into several categories using labels such as tumor and non-tumor brain imaging and so on. To create a prediction model, preprocessing, feature extraction, and classification using the Loss function are conducted in the training phase. Label the training picture set first. Image resizing is used in preprocessing to modify the image's size. Finally, a convolutional neural network is utilized to classify brain tumors automatically. Image net provided the brain image dataset. One of the pre-trained models is the image net. If you wish to train from the first layer, you must train the full layer (all the way to the finish).

As a result, there is a significant amount of time spent. It will have an impact on the outcome. To overcome this issue, classification stages are performed using a pre-trained model based on a brain dataset. Only the final layer of the proposed CNN will be trained in Python. We don't want to train all of the layers at the same time. As a result, the suggested automated brain tumor classification system has a short calculation time yet a high performance (Liu,2017).The gradient descent technique is used to determine the loss function. Using a scoring function, the raw image pixel is mapped to class scores. The loss function is used to assess the quality of a collection of parameters. It is determined by how closely the induced scores matched the training data's ground truth labels. To increase accuracy, the loss function calculation is crucial. When the precision is low and the loss function is large. Similarly, when the loss function is low, the accuracy is high. To compute the gradient descent algorithm, the gradient value is determined for the loss function (Auzias,2015). To compute the gradient of the loss function, evaluate the gradient value several times.

Figure 1. Training Phase

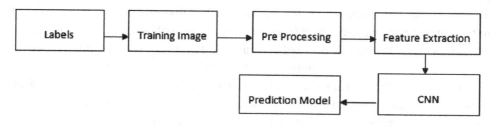

Figure 2. Testing Phase

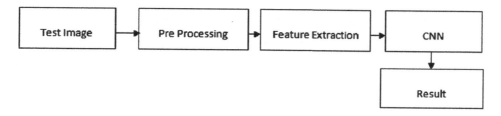

CNN-based classification algorithm:

Step 1. In the first layer, apply a convolution filter.

Step 2. Smoothing the convolution filter (i.e. sub sampling) reduces the sensitivity of the filter.

Step 3. The activation layer regulates signal transmission from one layer to the next.

Step 4. Use a rectified linear unit to shorten the training duration (RELU)

Step 5. Every neuron in the previous layer is linked to every neuron in the following layer.

Step 6. A loss layer is added at the conclusion of the training process to provide feedback to the neural network.

RESULTS AND DISCUSSION

Our Dataset contains tumor and non tumor MRI images and collected from different online resources. In this work, efficient automatic brain tumor detection is performed by using convolution neural network. Simulation is performed by using python language. The accuracy is calculated and compared with the all other state of arts methods. To determine the efficacy of the proposed brain tumor classification method, the training accuracy, validation accuracy, and validation loss are computed. Support Vector Machine (SVM)-based categorization is used in the current approach to detect brain tumors. It necessitates the output of feature extraction. The classification output is created and accuracy is determined based on feature value. In SVM-based tumor and non-tumor identification, the calculation time is long and the accuracy is low. The suggested CNN-based categorization does not need separate feature extraction processes. CNN is used to calculate the feature value. Figure 3 & 4 shows the loss and accuracy of brain tumor categorization. As a result, the complexity and calculation time are minimal, yet the accuracy is good..

Figure 3. Training Loss

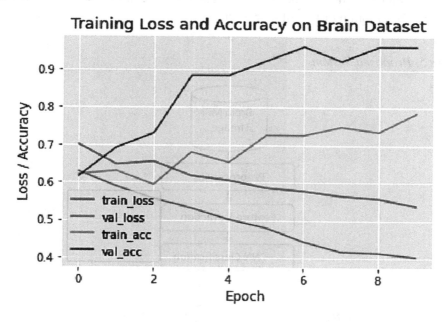

Figure 4. Accuracy

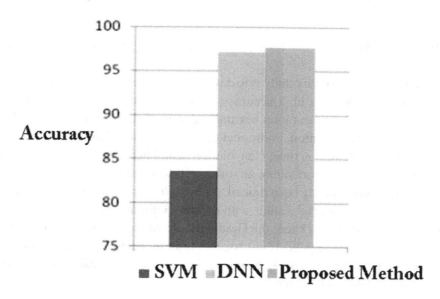

Finally Figure 5, depending on the likelihood score value, the categorization results in Tumor brain or Non-tumor brain.

Figure 5. Proposed System

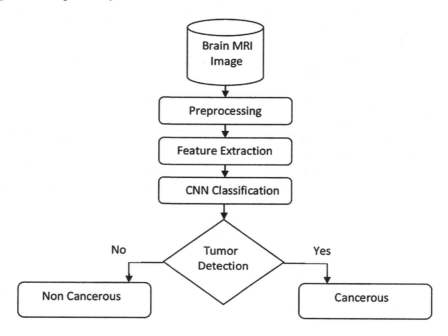

CONCLUSION

The primary objective of this study is to develop an efficient automated brain tumor classification system with high accuracy, speed, and simplicity. Using Fuzzy C Means (FCM) based segmentation, texture and shape feature extraction, and SVM and DNN based classification, traditional brain tumor classification is carried out. To minimize the calculation time, Convolution neural network based classification is incorporated. For categorization, an image net database is employed. It's one of the models that have already been trained. As a result, just the last layer gets trained. CNN also extracts raw pixel values with depth, width, and height feature values. Finally, to obtain high precision, the Gradient descent based loss function is used. The validation accuracy, validation loss, and training accuracy are all computed. The accuracy of the training is 97.5 percent. In the same way, validation accuracy is high and validation loss is minimal.

REFERENCES

Auzias, G., Takerkart, S., & Deruelle, C. (2015). On the influence of confounding factors in multisite brain morphometry studies of developmental pathologies: Application to autism Spectrum disorder. *IEEE Journal of Biomedical and Health Informatics*, 20(3), 810–817. doi:10.1109/JBHI.2015.2460012 PMID:26208373

Bauer, S., Wiest, R., Nolte, L. P., & Reyes, M. (2013). A survey of MRI-based medical image analysis for brain tumor studies. *Physics in Medicine and Biology*, 58(13), R97–R129. doi:10.1088/0031-9155/58/13/R97 PMID:23743802

Feng, C. M., Xu, Y., Liu, J. X., Gao, Y. L., & Zheng, C. H. (2019). Supervised discriminative sparse PCA for com-characteristic gene selection and tumor classification on multiview biological data. *IEEE Transactions on Neural Networks and Learning Systems*, 30(10), 2926–2937. doi:10.1109/TNNLS.2019.2893190 PMID:30802874

Fresilli, D., Grani, G., De Pascali, M. L., Alagna, G., Tassone, E., Ramundo, V., & Cantisani, V. (2020). Computer-aided diagnostic system for thyroid nodule sonographic evaluation outperforms the specificity of less experienced examiners. *Journal of Ultrasound*, 23(2), 169–174. doi:10.100740477-020-00453-y PMID:32246401

Hiran, K. K., & Doshi, R. (2013). An artificial neural network approach for brain tumor detection using digital image segmentation. *Brain*, 2(5), 227–231.

Hiran, K. K., Jain, R. K., Lakhwani, K., & Doshi, R. (2021). *Machine Learning: Master Supervised and Unsupervised Learning Algorithms with Real Examples (English Edition)*. BPB Publications.

Hiran, K. K., Khazanchi, D., Vyas, A. K., & Padmanaban, S. (Eds.). (2021). *Machine Learning for Sustainable Development* (Vol. 9). Walter de Gruyter GmbH & Co KG. doi:10.1515/9783110702514

Kim, J. Y., Kim, J. J., Hwangbo, L., Suh, H. B., Kim, S., Choo, K. S., & Kang, T. (2020). Kinetic heterogeneity of breast cancer determined using computer-aided diagnosis of preoperative MRI scans: Relationship to distant metastasis-free survival. *Radiology*, 295(3), 517–526. doi:10.1148/radiol.2020192039 PMID:32228293

Kumar, S. N., & Ismail, B. M. (2020). Systematic investigation on Multi-Class skin cancer categorization using machine learning approach. *Materials Today: Proceedings*.

Liu, D., & Kumar, S. A. (2017). An exceedingly rare adrenal collision tumor: Adrenal adenoma–metastatic breast cancer–myelolipoma. *Journal of Community Hospital Internal Medicine Perspectives*, 7(4), 241–244. doi:10.1080/20009666.2017.1362 315 PMID:29046752

Mahrishi, M., Hiran, K. K., Meena, G., & Sharma, P. (Eds.). (2020). *Machine Learning and Deep Learning in Real-Time Applications*. IGI Global. doi:10.4018/978-1-7998-3095-5

Pellakuri, V., Rao, D. R., & Murthy, J. V. R. (2016, December). Modeling of supervised ADALINE neural network learning technique. In *2016 2nd International Conference on Contemporary Computing and Informatics (IC3I)* (pp. 17-22). IEEE 10.1109/IC3I.2016.7917928

Pereira, S., Pinto, A., Alves, V., & Silva, C. A. (2016). Brain tumor segmentation using convolutional neural networks in MRI images. *IEEE Transactions on Medical Imaging*, 35(5), 1240–1251. doi:10.1109/TMI.2016.2538465 PMID:26960222

Razmjooy, N., Ashourian, M., Karimifard, M., Estrela, V. V., Loschi, H. J., Do Nascimento, D., & Vishnevski, M. (2020). Computer-aided diagnosis of skin cancer: A review. *Current Medical Imaging, 16*(7), 781-793.

Chapter 6
Application of Odd–Even Congruence Graph Labeling in Secured Cyber Physical Systems

Kanakambika K.
Vellalar College for Women, India

Thamizhendhi G.
Sri Vasavi College, India

ABSTRACT

Technological advancement in the recent decades enhanced the calibre of human life. Contemporary research in machine learning (ML) exhibits a mock-up to make decisions on its own and is applied in various fields including medical diagnosis, email filtering, banking, computer vision, financial marketing, image processing, cyber security. The systems inter-connected across the world via internet are attacked by hackers, and it is prevented by cyber security. The optimum solution for cyber-attacks is attained by collaborating ML techniques with cyber security and envisioned issues are designed by cyber machine learning models. In this chapter, an algorithm is proposed to defend data by encoding the text to an unintelligent text and decoding it to original text by applying graph labelling in cryptography. Symmetric key is designed based on the edge label of an odd-even congruence graph to achieve secured communication in CPS. In addition, a program is suggested using Python programming to attain cipher text and its converse.

DOI: 10.4018/978-1-7998-9308-0.ch006

INTRODUCTION

This chapter aims to design a protected structure for Cyber Physical System(CPS). CPS is necessary for the succeeding generations smart systems, constructed as a network of relation between substantial and virtual model. Its functioning hangs on the concrete process along with feedback loops. Revelation of new concepts revamped the Information Technology every day and one such mandatory system is CPS, introduced in 2006. In late 2006 US National Foundation recognized CPS as a cue field for research and funded for numerous workshop related to CPS. Initially CPS is used in the infrastructure of power grids, home automation system and later in almost all fields. Security challenges of CPS and its security control systems were analysed during 2006 to 2009 (Jairo Giraldo, Esha Sarkar, Alvaro A. Cardenas Michali Maniatakos and Murat Kantarcioglu, 2017). In the succeeding years, CPS transmogrified as a sophisticated domain with countless attributes such as complex systems (Vegh and Miclea, 2014) and acquire data from sensor device machine to carry over in network with or without machine and human interaction (Bhabad and Scholar, 2015). Several security challenges arise, including securing protocols and initialization of certainty among CPS subsystems (Lu et al., 2013). Subsequently safety liability of CPS was investigated and its safety measures were initiated for confidentiality (Jacub Wrm, Yier Jin, Yang Lice and Shiyan Hu, 2016).

Cryptography and Steganagraphy is merged to arrive a new solution for data security, moreover hierarchical approach is employed to the information for universal security (L. Vegh and L. Miclea, 2014). Cryptography is applied to frame secured physical unclonable function using Fuzzy extractors to overwhelm security obstacles, but still it retains the challenges in feedback protocols (Jin C, Herder L, Nguyen P.H, Fuller B, Devadas and Van Dijk M, 2017). To protect the information in sensor communication channel, an event-based cryptographic encryption function is established using non deterministic automation (Publio M. Lima, Lilian K. Carvalho, Marcos V. Moreira, 2020). To reduce the encryption time, a new encryption algorithm is proposed, to separate the sensitive information to be secured in CPS and encrypt it instead of encrypting all communications (Xiaogang Zhu, Gautam Srivastara and Reza M. Parizi, 2019). An advanced cryptographic method is employed to perform the operations directly on encrypted values without decrypting the text, but it occupies more memory space (Junsoo Kim, Chanhwa Lee, Hyungbo Shim, Jung Hee Cheon, Andrey Kim, Miran Kim and Yongsoo Song, 2016). In addition, to enhance security various graph labelling technique such as product mod labelling (Deepa B, Maheswari and Balaji V, 2019), Vertex magic total labelling (Rahul Chawla, Sagar Deshpande, Manas M. N, Saahil Chhabria and Krishnappa H. K, 2019), Inner magic and inner antimagic labelling (Auparajita Krishnaa, 2019), Super magic labelling (Giridaran

M, 2020), Antimagic labelling (Dharmendra Kumar Gurjar, Auparajita Krishnaa, 2021) are utilized to propose the encryption algorithm.

In this chapter, the authors proposed new algorithm to encrypt and decrypt the messages by employing odd-even congruence graph labelling technique in cryptography to ensure confidentiality and security for data in the CPS. It is more secure to manipulate graphs in cryptography, since it is difficult to identify the graph and its labelling technique which is utilized for encryption. Furthermore a Python coding is developed to generate the cipher text in earlier.

CHALLENGES OF CPS AND CRYPTOGRAPHY

Cyber-physical System

Cyber-physical system is a unique network which communicates cyber and physical world. It comprises of sensors, controllers and actuators. Sensors will transfer the physical world data to the cyber world by estimating the existing physical quantities and furnish the estimated facts to controllers. Controllers allocate the commands to actuators depending on the statistics delivered by sensors and the actuators execute the commands. The actuator revamps the cyber solution back to physical solution and transfers it to the sensors. The technology behind the controller is supervisory control and data acquisition system comprises of human interfaces, networking device and workstations.

CPS altered the human life and the substantial world which includes smart grid, transportation, energy system, water supply system, sensor, robotics, traffic control, automobile systems and different fields of worldwide economy. CPS is a methodology employed to combine the sensor tools and the power system. In this procedure information security is essential, since CPS is large complex system, reliability and security is required. The main challenging characteristics of CPS are data confidentiality that is the capacity to securing records during dispatch and storage, to prevent the information from the unaccredited group.

CPS concentrates on the existing mechanism in all fields by accentuating on the lively feedback of the campaign management and interface. The network layer involves many diversified network, various techniques are applied to hold out against safety threat in contrasting ways, so the system has to be constructed to overcome the security threats with network layer compatibility and consistency. To improve the safety, the system is constructed in two ways such as point to point safety and end to end safety. The consistent technique incorporates mutual reliable communication between nodes in end to end reliable communication with concealed confidential key. Confidential key handling mechanism, cryptographic algorithm, hierarchical architecture, port interception are the main components in the construction of secured CPS.

Challenges of CPS

The spiffy CPS comprises of compound structure attracts young researchers and industry for its accomplishment. Since its components are tethered with internet receives threat and it has no literal solution for these attacks, (Teixeira et al, 2012). At the same time, the attackers develop and feed the signals to CPS repeatedly to track the structure of the system to acquire the input and output data. So the security level of CPS is upgraded by encrypting the feedback loop to protect the communication (Junsoo Kim, Chanhwa Lee, Hyungbo Shim, Jung Hee Cheon, Andrey Kim, Miran Kim and Yongsoo Song, 2016). The encrypted data has to be decrypted to operate on the inputs, so the secret key is retained in the interior of the controller and it can be pinched by attacks. Hence the key must be strong and unbreakable to quash the attacks, so it is desired to design a key using edge labels of an odd-even congruence graph.

Cryptography

The fundamental principle of cryptography is to transform the information confidentially by compressing the data to an unintelligent sentence and it can be read only after decoding the compressed one. The cryptographic protection framework resists attacks and mischievous penetration depending on the robustness of the secret key, coherent mechanisms and protocols cognate with the keys. The Major component of cryptographic algorithm is secret key and often large keys are employed to attain improved algorithm. This algorithm alters the data and constructs it as a complicated unreadable text which can be recognized after applying the secret key. This algorithm is implemented to accomplish data confidentiality and message authentication services. The process of transforming the plain text to incomprehensible text is referred as encryption (Sarita Kumari, 2017). Encrypted incomprehensible text is stated as cipher text. The procedure of transforming the incomprehensible text to original text is referred as decryption. A key employed to both encryption and decryption process is identified as symmetric key (Ayushi, 2010). Encryption furnishes confidentiality of data by modifying the ordinary text into cipher text and decryption revamps the cipher text to original text. Cryptography is one of the leading efficient technologies to sustain the recent developed society of internet communications. The cryptography algorithms are assessed as powerful tool based on the secret key, the key will be strong if it is arrived using graph labelling.

Congruence Graph Labelling

Labelling of graphs has been introduced by A. Rosa in 1966. Assignment of natural numbers to vertices and/or integers is referred as graph labelling. Inspired by the ample application of graph labelling technique in real life problems, multifarious labelling strategy was adopted and investigated by many researchers. Congruence Graph Labelling is an allocation of natural numbers as labels for the edges and vertices of a graph based on modular arithmetic property. Odd-even congruence labelling is an allocation of odd integers to vertices and even integers to edges in addition to congruence graph labelling. Congruence Graph labelling performs significant role in numerous sectors and can be implemented in multitudinous discipline including coding theory, X-ray, Psychology, crystallography, circuit design, communication networks, astronomy, radar, data security, secret sharing and data base management. Besides these applications, the labelling technique acts as succour to realm other areas of mathematics. In the recent years all the documents are digitalized and shared via net primarily based on virtual network and at high risk. In order to increase the security, Odd-even congruence labelling technique is applied to generate a powerful and secured key from the edge label value to encrypt and decrypt the content.

Odd-Even Congruence Labelling

Suppose $G = (V,E)$ be a graph with $|V| = p$ and $|E| = q$ is stated as an odd-even congruence graph, if there exist a vertex labelling function f: $V \rightarrow \{1,3,....2k+1\}$ for every v_i in V and induces edge labelling g: $E \rightarrow \{2,4,6,....2k\}$ such that $f(v_i) \equiv f(v_j)$ mod $g(e_i)$ for every $e_i = v_i v_j$, where $k = \min\{2|V|, 2|E|\}$.

A graph which admits odd even congruence labelling is stated as odd even congruence graph.

3. APPLICATION OF ODD-EVEN CONGRUENCE GRAPH IN SECURED CYBER PHYSICAL SYSTEM

Two major threats in CPS are data security and control security, it is essential to guard data during collection, storage, process and transmission. The most crucial one is data security which is gained by encryption. This chapter is devoted to establish data security by fusing cryptography and graph labelling.

Methodology

An encryption and decryption algorithm is proposed focusing on the security of sensor communication channel of CPS. The information received from the sensor nodes are communicated through wire or wireless network using radio signals, which controls the decisional strategy of CPS. So, these communications must be confidential. To achieve this, original message in sensor must be encrypted to cipher text using encryption algorithm before transmitting to the controller. The controller receives the cipher text and decrypts it to the original text using decryption algorithm and perform its necessary operations, then converts its decision as cipher text and send it to actuator. To perform this encryption and decryption algorithm is established in sensors, controllers and actuators to prepare the cipher text before communicating to other channels and to convert the cipher text as original message.

To strengthen the security, secret key is evolved from the edge labels of an odd-even congruence graph to recast the plain text to cypher text and vice versa. In the proposed communication all the data are transmitted as cipher text which cannot be read by the attackers. Even though they trace the security procedure, it will be difficult to recognize the graph implemented and its labelling methods. The flow process is exhibited in figure – 1.

Figure 1. Flow Process

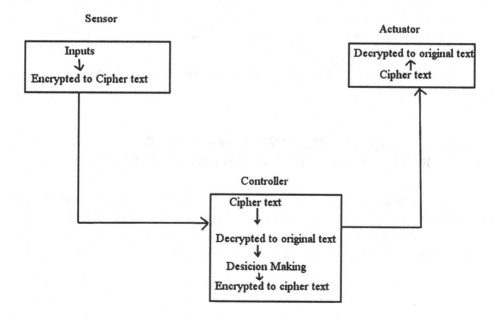

The following algorithm is exploited for encryption and decryption.

Encryption Algorithm

Step 1: Consider any graph G.

Step 2: Label the vertices and edges of G using the definition stated in 2.5

Step 3: The edge weights of G is assigned to alphabets and they are interchanged, for example the first edge in G has 12 as its edge weight then it will be assigned to A, then A is replaced by the 12th alphabet L. Since each edge are labeled distinctly, all the alphabets will be interchanged distinctly.

Step 4: Special characters also encrypted by extending the edges in G.

Decryption Algorithm

Step 1: The graph used in encryption is identified.

Step 2: Using the edge labelling function, edge weights are reckoned and employed to swap the alphabets.

Step 3: Cipher text is interpreted to acquire the earliest text.

Illustration

Consider a graph G, let it be a Comb graph with 28 vertices and 27 edges and it is labeled using odd-even congruence labelling technique. Its edge weights are utilized to allocate dissimilar order for the alphabets to generate cypher text.

Encryption

Step 1: Consider a comb graph $G(V, E) = P_n \odot K_1$, n = 14.

Step 2: Assess the edge weight of G using odd-even congruence labelling function

$g(e_i) = 4(n-i)$, i = 1 to n-1

$g(s_j) = 4(n-i) + 2$, j = 1 to n

where e_i (i = 1, 2, …..,13) are the edges of P_n and s_i (j = 1, 2, …..,14) are edges adjacent to P_n and K_1, it is given in figure - 2.

Step 3: As the edge weights are even numbers it is divided by 2 to arrive the consecutive integers, here edge weights of e_1 is 52, so $(52/2) = 26$ is assigned to 'a' then 'a' is replaced by 'z' and it is continued up to e_{13}, then it is proceeded by s_1 and continued up to the last edge. Here the special character dot '.' is considered and last edge weight is assigned for it.

Step 4: Since each edges are assigned with distinct weights, the alphabets including the special character are rearranged distinctly and it is given in the table - 1.

The odd-even congruence comb graph is depicted in the figure -2.

Figure 2. Odd-even congruence comb graph

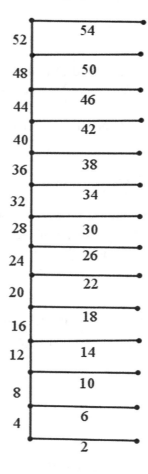

Table 1. Encoded alphabets based on edge weights

Original Alphabet	a	b	c	d	e	f	g	h	i
Assigned edge weight	26	24	22	20	18	16	14	12	10
Encoded alphabet	z	x	v	t	r	p	n	l	j
Original Alphabet	j	k	l	m	n	o	p	q	r
Assigned edge weight	8	6	4	2	27	25	23	21	19
Encoded alphabet	h	f	d	b	.	y	w	u	s
Original Alphabet	s	t	u	v	w	x	y	z	.
Assigned edge weight	17	15	13	11	9	7	5	3	1
Encoded alphabet	q	o	m	k	i	g	e	c	a

Text can be coded manually but it is vague to code enormous content, to reduce time the following Python coding is proposed to encrypt the given text.

```
print("Enter the text: ")
text = input()
text = text.replace("a", "z")
text = text.replace("b", "x")
text = text.replace("c", "v")
text = text.replace("d", "t")
text = text.replace("e", "r")
text = text.replace("f", "p")
text = text.replace("g", "n")
text = text.replace("h", "l")
text = text.replace("i", "j")
text = text.replace("j", "h")
text = text.replace("k", "f")
text = text.replace("l", "d")
text = text.replace("m", "b")
text = text.replace("n", ".")
text = text.replace("o", "y")
text = text.replace("p", "w")
text = text.replace("q", "u")
text = text.replace("r", "s")
text = text.replace("s", "q")
text = text.replace("t", "o")
text = text.replace("u", "m")
text = text.replace("v", "k")
```

```
text = text.replace("w", "i")
text = text.replace("x", "g")
text = text.replace("y", "e")
text = text.replace("z", "c")
text = text.replace(".", "a")
print("\n Cipher text: ")
print(text)
```

Output:
Enter the text:
odd even congruence graph and its applications
Cipher text:
ytt rkr. vy.nsmr.vr nszwl z.t joq zwwdjvzojy.q

Decryption

Step 1: Since the symmetric key method is used, the edge weights of G are computed using odd-even congruence labelling.
Step 2: Cipher text is interpreted to acquire the earliest text.

The following PYTHON coding is employed to decrypt the cipher text and gain the original text automatically.

```
print("Enter the Cipher text: ")
cipher = input()
cipher = cipher.replace("z", "a")
cipher = cipher.replace("x", "b")
cipher = cipher.replace("v", "c")
cipher = cipher.replace("t", "d")
cipher = cipher.replace("r", "e")
cipher = cipher.replace("p", "f")
cipher = cipher.replace("n", "g")
cipher = cipher.replace("l", "h")
cipher = cipher.replace("j", "i")
cipher = cipher.replace("h", "j")
cipher = cipher.replace("f", "k")
cipher = cipher.replace("d", "l")
cipher = cipher.replace("b", "m")
cipher = cipher.replace(".", "n")
cipher = cipher.replace("y", "o")
```

```
cipher = cipher.replace("w", "p")
cipher = cipher.replace("u", "q")
cipher = cipher.replace("s", "r")
cipher = cipher.replace("q", "s")
cipher = cipher.replace("o", "t")
cipher = cipher.replace("m", "u")
cipher = cipher.replace("k", "v")
cipher = cipher.replace("i", "w")
cipher = cipher.replace("g", "x")
cipher = cipher.replace("e", "y")
cipher = cipher.replace("c", "z")
cipher = cipher.replace("a", ".")
print("\n Original text: ")
print(cipher)
```

Output:
Enter the Cipher text:
ytt rkr. vy.nsmr.vr nszwl z.t joq zwwdjvzojy.q
Original text:
odd even congruence graph and its applications

Discussion

CPS are manipulated to solve more challenging problems in day to day life, this proclaims that it is mandatory to strengthen the operating procedure effectively for the current and future scenario. These algorithms are under threat since all the features of CPS are connected through internet and there is no permanent solution for cyber-attacks. To achieve safety for the sensitive information in CPS, the data can be encrypted using cryptography for secured communications.

Cryptography is a technique focussed to attain secure communication between two parties. Cryptographic protection confide on the solidity of the secret key. The communications are compressed to an unintelligent text by coding and it will be realized after decoding. Since the information's are traced by hackers, preserving data is salient.

In the proposed communication all the data are transmitted as cipher text before communicating to other section of CPS. In the above example a Comb graph is considered for encryption, likewise any other graph such as bipartite graph, cycle graph and so on can also be utilized. As one special character is considered for encryption, the graph with 27 edges is employed for encryption. Suppose, if more than one special character is needed to encrypt, and then increase the value of n to achieve the same. Usually alphabets are encrypted, in order to increase the security and strengthen the key authors added the special characters which is unexpected by the attackers and it is difficult to identify the special characters used in encryption. For instance if the dot is replaced for g, even though they hacked the communication and have a study, they will not guess that dot is given instead of an alphabet. So they will try to read the cipher text by rearranging the alphabets and consider dot as end of the sentence, which gives some message other than the original message. The Comb graph with n = 14, receives 52 as edge weight for first edge but it differs for different values of n.

The architecture of CPS includes multiple edge nodes, actuators and so on, the information extracted from data drives the decision policies of CPS. So the secured communication is essential in CPS and it is arrived by generating the secret key from the edge weights of an odd-even congruence graph, it retains reliability and security in CPS communication. This unique concept will develop a new algorithm to guard the communication network.

FUTURE RESEARCH DIRECTIONS

In this chapter an odd-even congruence comb graph is applied to establish the secret key, depending on the situation and to enhance security authors can utilize any odd-even congruence graph to constitute the key, for data authentication, In Comb graph first edge weight is 52 but some other graph will have some different value. Thus secret key will differs for different graph, hence the proposed algorithm can be applied in the construction of numerous types of CPS with secured data. Some additional special characters can also be added for encrypting, the number of edges of the graph can be increased or decreased based on the necessity.

CONCLUSION

It is more crucial to secure the data during the scientific advancement. Cryptosystem is more secured when graphs are utilized to frame the secret key as it is strenuous to recognize the graph assigned for encryption and its edge weights. In the proposed algorithm, the edge weights of an odd-even congruence graph are implemented to construct the secret key for encrypting and decrypting the text. This procedure guard the interaction between the sensor to controller & controller to actuator and it can also be applied for all the communication in CPS. In addition the execution process is explained in detail using Comb graph and furthermore Python coding is developed to convert the original text to cipher text and vice versa to reduce the execution time.

This research received no specific grant from any funding agency in the public, commercial, or not-for-profit sectors.

REFERENCES

Anand, M. (2006). Security challenges in next generation cyber physical systems. *Beyond SCADA: Networked Embedded Control for Cyber Physical Systems.*

Ashibani & Mahmoud. (2017). Cyber physical systems security: Analysis, challenges and solutions. In *Computers & Security.* Elsevier.

Ayushi. (2010). A Symmetric Key Cryptographic Algorithm. *International Journal of Computer Applications.*

Bondy, J. A., & Murty, U. S. R. (2008). *Graph Theory* (International Edition). Springer. doi:10.1007/978-1-84628-970-5

Cardenas, A. (2009). Challenges for securing cyber physical systems. *Workshop Future Directions Cyber-Physical Syst. Secur.*

Cardenas, A. A., Amin, S., & Sastry, S. (2008). Secure control: Towards survivable cyber-physical systems. *IEEE 28th Int. Conf.*

Cardenas, A. A., Amin, S., & Sastry, S. (2008). Research challenges for the security of control systems. *3rd Conf. Hot Topics in Security.*

Chawla, Deshpande, Manas, Chhabria, & Krishnappa. (2019). Vetrtex Magic Labelling and its Application in Cryptography. *Recent Findings in Intelligent Computing Techniques.*

Lima, Carvalho, & Moreira. (2020). Cyber-Physical Systems using Event-Based Cryptography. *IFAC-PapersOnLine.*

Deepa, Maheswari, & Balaji. (2019). Creating Ciphertext and Decipher using Graph Labelling Techniques. *International Journal of Engineering and Advanced Technology.*

Dooley, J. F. (2003). *A Brief History of Cryptology and Cryptographic Algorithms.* Springer.

Gallian, J.A. (2011). #DS6, A dynamic survey of graph labelling. *The Eletronic Journal of Combinatorices.*

Ganesan, V., & Lavanya, S. (2019). Prime labelling of Split Graph of Star $K_{1,n}$. *IOSR Journal of Mathematics*.

Garagad, V. G., & Iyer, N. (2020). A security threat for Internet of Things and Cyber-Physical Systems. *2020 International Conference on Computational Performance Evaluation*. 10.1109/ComPE49325.2020.9200170

Giraldo, Sarkar, Cardenas, Maniatakos, & Kantarcioglu. (2017). Security and Privacy in Cyber–Physical Systems: A Survey of Surveys. *IEEE CEDA, IEEE CASS, IEEE SSCS, and TTTC*.

Giridaran,, M. (2020). Application of Super Magic Labelling in Cryptography. *International Journal of Innovative Research in Science, Engineering and Technology*.

Gurjar. (2021). Lexicographic Labeled Graphs in Cryptography. *Auparajita Krishnaa*, *27*(2), 209–232.

Harary, F. (1969). *Graph Theory*. Addison-Wesley. doi:10.21236/AD0705364

Jin, Herder, Nguyen, & Fuller, Devadas, & Van Dijk. (2017). FPGA Implementation of a Cryptographically – Secure PUF based on Learning Parity with Noise. *Cryptography*, *105*, 1028–1042.

Jirwan, Singh, & Vijay. (2013). Review and Analysis of Cryptography Techniques. *International Journal Scientific & Engineering Research*.

Kim, Lee, Shim, Cheon, Kim, Kim, & Song. (2016). Encryting Controller using Fully Homomorphic Encryption for security of Cyber-Physical Systems. *IFAC-PapersOnLine*.

Krishnaa. (2019). Inner Magic and Inner Antimagic Graphs in Cryptography. *Journal of Discrete Mathematical Sciences and Cryptography*.

Kumari. (2017). A research Paper on Cryptography Encryption and Compression Techniques. *International Journal of Engineering and Computer Science*.

Lee, E. A. (2006) Cyber-physical systems—Are computing foundations adequate. *Workshop on Cyber-Physical Systems: Research Motivation, Techniques and Roadmap*.

Merely & Anto. (2016). Vertex Polynomial for the Splitting Graph of Comd and Crown. *International Journal of Emerging Technologies in Engineering Research*.

Mueller, F. (2006). *Challenges for cyber-physical systems: Security, timing analysis and soft error protection. High-Confidence Softw. Platforms CyberPhysical Syst. (HCSP-CPS) Workshop*.

Neuman, C. (2009). Challenges in security for cyber-physical systems. *DHS Workshop on Future Directions in Cyber-Physical Systems Security*.

Oman, P., Schweitzer, E., & Frincke, D. (2000). Concerns about intrusions into remotely accessible substation controllers and scada systems. *27th Annu. Western Protective Relay Conf.*

Orman, H. (2014). Recent Parables in Cryptography. *IEEE Internet Computing*.

Prasanna, L. (2014). Applications of graph labelling in communication networks. *Oriental Journal of Computer Science & Technology*, *7*(1), 139–145.

Preneel, B. (2010). Understanding Cryptography: A Textbook for Students and Practitioners. Springer.

Ratnadewi, Hutama, & Ahmar, & Setiawan. (2016). Implementation Cryptography Data Encryption Standard and Triple Data Encryption Standard Method in Communication System Based Near Field Communication. *Journal of Physics: Conference Series*.

Rosa, A. (1966). On Certain valuation of the vertices of a graph. *Graph Theory: Int Symp*.

Sadu. (2020). Graph labelling in graph theory. *Malaya Journal of Matematik*.

Sun, M. (2009). Addressing safety and security contradictions in cyber-physical systems. *1st Workshop Future Directions Cyber-Physical Syst. Secur.*

Tang, H., & McMillin, B. M. (2008). Security property violation in cps through timing. *IEEE 28th Int. Conf.*

Teixeira, Shames, Sandberg, & Johansson. (2012). Revealing stealthy attacks in control systems. *Proc. 50th Annu. Allerton Conf. Communication, Control, Computing*.

Vegh & Miclea. (2014). Enhancing Security in Cyber Physical Systems through Cryptographic and Steganographic techniques. *IEEE International Conference on Automation, Quality and Testing, Robotics*.

Wurm. (2017). Introduction to Cyber-Physical System Security: A Cross-Layer Perspective. *IEEE Transactions on Multi Scale Computing Systems*.

Zhu, X., Srivastara, G., & Parizi, R. M. (2019). *An Efficient Encryption Algorithm for the Security of Sensitive Private Information in Cyber Physical System*. MDPI Electronics.

KEY TERMS AND DEFINITIONS

Cipher Text: It is an unreadable output of an encoding algorithm.

Congruence Labelling: Suppose $G = (V,E)$ be a graph with $|V| = p$ and $|E| = q$ is referred as a congruence graph, if there exist a vertex labelling function $f: V \rightarrow \{1,2,....k\}$ for every v_i in V and induces edge labelling $g: E \rightarrow \{1,2,3,....k\}$ such that $f(v_i) \equiv f(v_j) \bmod g(e_i)$ for every $e_i = v_i v_j$, where $k = \min\{2|V|, 2|E|\}$.

Cryptography: Cryptography is a method of protecting information and communications in computer systems through the use of codes.

Encoding: The process of converting data from one form to another form is referred as encoding.

Graph: The graph comprises of vertices and edges to represent the mathematical structures to model pairwise relations between objects.

Graph Labelling: Graph labelling is the assignment of integers to vertices and edges.

Chapter 7

Machine Learning for Intrusion Detection Systems:
Recent Developments and Future Challenges

Quang-Vinh Dang
https://orcid.org/0000-0002-3877-8024
Industrial University of Ho Chi Minh City, Vietnam

ABSTRACT

The growth of the internet and network-based services bring to us a lot of new opportunities but also pose many new security threats. The intrusion detection system (IDS) has been studied and developed over the years to cope with external attacks from the internet. The task of an IDS is to classify and stop the malicious traffic from outside to enter the computer system. In recent years, machine learning-based IDS has attracted a lot of attention from the industry and academia. The IDS based on state-of-the-art machine learning algorithms usually achieves a very high predictive performance than traditional approaches. On the other hand, several open datasets have been introduced for the researchers to evaluate and compare their algorithms. This chapter reviews the classification techniques used in IDS, mostly the machine learning algorithms and the published datasets. The authors discuss the achievements and some open problems and suggest a few research directions in the future.

DOI: 10.4018/978-1-7998-9308-0.ch007

INTRODUCTION

Network security plays a crucial role in our modern world. It helps to secure our communication and information, reduce financial loss and prevent network disruption due to attacks. Particularly, due to the growth of the Internet and its importance, almost every computer in the world is connected hence they are vulnerable to attacks. We can claim that for any computer, attacks will happen sooner or later. Intrusion detection systems (IDSs) are designed to help computer systems deal with external attacks by classifying and stopping any incoming malicious traffic (Tsai et al., 2009). It is worthy to note that the IDS does not deal with internal attacks, i.e. the attacks that started from a computer within the local network. The role of the IDS is visualized in Figure 1.

Figure 1. The IDS in a computer system

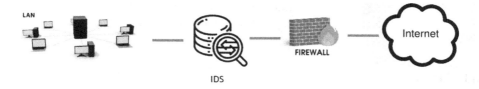

(Tsai et al., 2009) divided the IDSs into two main categories: one relies on anomaly detection and one relies on signature detection. However, regarding the recent development in the research on IDS, we propose to divide the IDSs into three main categories: signature-based approach, anomaly detection approach, and classification approach.

The signature-based IDS relies on the signatures, or rules, defined by the security experts. For instance, the experts might define that any packet with the source IP address that is the same as the destination IP address is malicious. The signature-based IDS is very popular in the early days of the Internet. It is still being used widely in the industry today (Dang, 2020a).

The anomaly detection-based IDS relies on the assumption that the benign data themselves form a common group of traffic, while the malicious traffic is an outlier and does not share their properties. The anomaly detection is visualized in Figure 2. We can see that the majority part of the data is assumed to be normal data (or benign data), and the anomalies are defined as something different from the normal data.

Figure 2. Anomaly detection

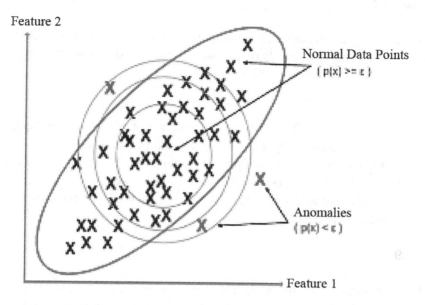

The classification-based IDS rely on one or multiple machine learning classification algorithms (Umadevi and Marseline, 2017). To perform the classification, the algorithms require a labeled dataset (Ring et al., 2019). The required dataset is usually huge and needs to be updated frequently. The difference between anomaly detection and classification is that in the classification setting we know exactly what are attacks, while in the anomaly detection setting we just have a vague definition that the attacks are different from the benign traffic. Hence, the classification algorithms are supervised learning techniques, while the anomaly detection algorithms are unsupervised. The classification algorithms are the dominant algorithms used in the literature recently (Alqahtani et al., 2021).

In recent years, machine learning techniques have achieved a lot of success in empowering IDS (Ahmad et al., 2021). In the rest of the chapter, we will discuss the machine learning algorithms that are studied in the literature and the published datasets for training and testing the models. We then discuss the results and the limitations of the presented approaches. We draw some further research direction and conclude our paper.

DATASETS

In this section, we review some of the most popular published intrusion datasets. These datasets can be used by researchers to train and test intrusion detection algorithms.

DARPA

The dataset DARPA 98/99 (McHugh, 2000) is one of the first intrusion datasets that has been introduced (Ring et al., 2019). The dataset carries two parts: one is for offline evaluation and one is for online evaluation. The dataset is created using an emulated network system. Version 1998 contains seven weeks of data while version 1999 contains the five weeks of data. The data is criticized as containing too much redundancy (McHugh, 2000).

KDD'99

The KDD'99 dataset (Stolfo et al., 2000) is probably the most popular intrusion dataset used in the literature to date. The KDD'99 and its extended version NSL-KDD have been used extensively in the research. The data includes four types of attacks (Table 1).

Table 1. Attack types in NSL-KDD dataset

Attack Type	Description
DOS	denial-of-service, e.g. syn flood
R2L	unauthorized access from a remote machine, e.g. guessing password;
U2R	unauthorized access to local superuser (root) privileges, e.g., various ``buffer overflow" attacks;
Probing	surveillance and another probing, e.g., port scanning.

While the KDD'99 is somehow an out-of-date dataset today (Dang, 2019), the importance of the dataset for cybersecurity research is undeniable. Furthermore, the features designed by the KDD'99 dataset are the fundamentals for many intrusion datasets later on, including the recent CICIDS and InSDN datasets.

Table 2. The basic features of the KDD dataset

Feature Name	Description	Type
duration	length (number of seconds) of the connection	continuous
protocol_type	type of the protocol, e.g. tcp, udp, etc.	discrete
service	network service on the destination, e.g., http, telnet, etc.	discrete
src_bytes	number of data bytes from source to destination	continuous
dst_bytes	number of data bytes from destination to source	continuous
flag	normal or error status of the connection	discrete
land	1 if connection is from/to the same host/port; 0 otherwise	discrete
wrong_fragment	number of ``wrong'' fragments	continuous
urgent	number of urgent packets	continuous

Table 3. Content features of the KDD dataset

Feature Name	Description	Type
hot	number of ``hot'' indicators	continuous
num_failed_logins	number of failed login attempts	continuous
logged_in	1 if successfully logged in; 0 otherwise	discrete
num_compromised	number of ``compromised'' conditions	continuous
root_shell	1 if root shell is obtained; 0 otherwise	discrete
su_attempted	1 if ``su root'' command attempted; 0 otherwise	discrete
num_root	number of ``root'' accesses	continuous
num_file_creations	number of file creation operations	continuous
num_shells	number of shell prompts	continuous
num_access_files	number of operations on access control files	continuous
num_outbound_cmds	number of outbound commands in an ftp session	continuous
is_hot_login	1 if the login belongs to the ``hot'' list; 0 otherwise	discrete
is_guest_login	1 if the login is a ``guest'' login; 0 otherwise	discrete

Table 4. Traffic features of the KDD dataset

Feature Name	Description	Type
count	number of connections to the same host as the current connection in the past two seconds	continuous
	Note: The following features refer to these same-host connections.	
serror_rate	% of connections that have ``SYN'' errors	continuous
rerror_rate	% of connections that have ``REJ'' errors	continuous
same_srv_rate	% of connections to the same service	continuous
diff_srv_rate	% of connections to different services	continuous
srv_count	number of connections to the same service as the current connection in the past two seconds	continuous
	Note: The following features refer to these same-service connections.	
srv_serror_rate	% of connections that have ``SYN'' errors	continuous
srv_rerror_rate	% of connections that have ``REJ'' errors	continuous
srv_diff_host_rate	% of connections to different hosts	continuous

CICIDS

CICIDS is a series of intrusion datasets released by the Canadian Institute of Cybersecurity. As of this writing, there are three versions of the CICIDS that have been introduced which are known as version 2012, 2017, and 2018.

The first version CICIDS 2012 (Shiravi et al., 2012) is collected as the network activity in seven days in 2010 with a total size of 84.4 GB. The dataset consists of several attack types such as HTTP DoS and DDoS using an IRC Botnet, as well as the normal activity.

The second version CICIDS 2017 (Sharafaldin et al., 2018) is introduced to fix some limitations of version 2012. The CICIDS 2017 is collected in five days with a total size of 48GB.

The CICIDS 2018 is the latest intrusion attack dataset as of this writing. The dataset can be considered as an improvement the version 2017.

Figure 3. The network topology to establish the CICIDS 2018 dataset.

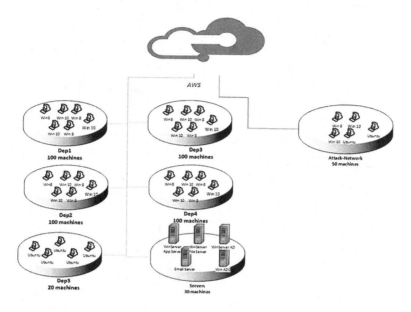

CIDDS

The CIDDS dataset is introduced to present an anomaly-based detection evaluation dataset (Ring et al., 2017). The dataset is created in a simulated environment of a small business.

DoHBRw'2020

The DoHBRw dataset (MontazeriShatoori et al., 2020) is the first attack dataset to the DNS system. The dataset focuses on DNS over HTTPS (DoH), introduced by IETF in RFC8484 which aims to enhance the privacy and protection of DNS.

Figure 4. The network topology to establish the DoHBRw 2020 dataset.

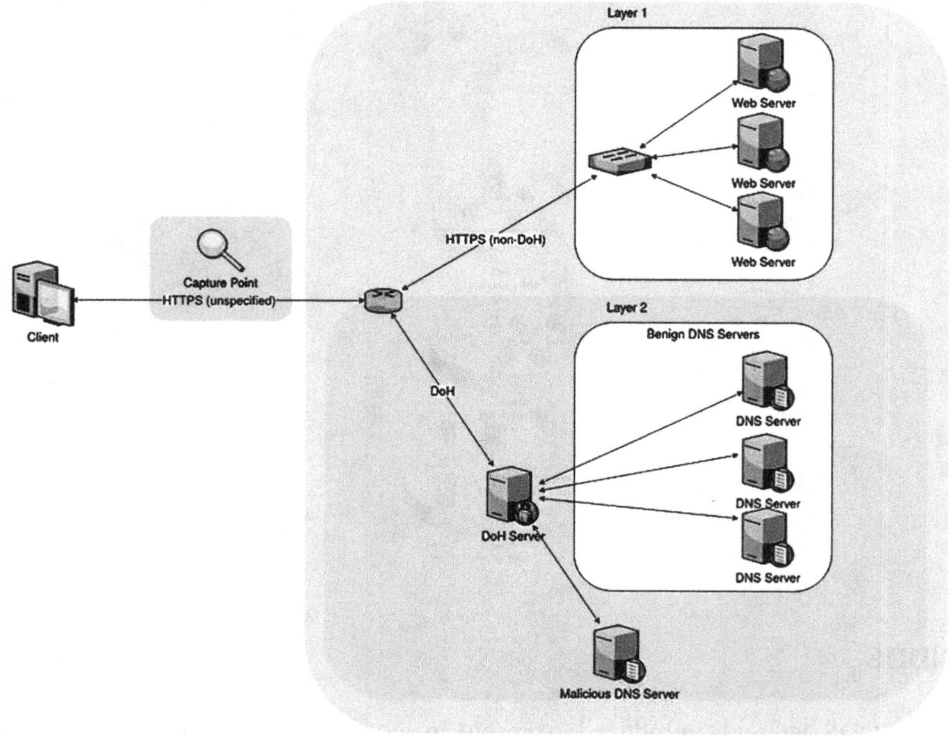

InSDN'2021

The InSDN dataset (Elsayed et al., 2020) is a recent dataset focusing on the attacks on Software-Defined Networking environments.

METRICS

In this section, we discuss the popular metrics used to evaluate intrusion detection algorithms.

The first set of popular metrics is based on the confusion matrix as shown below.

Table 5. Confusion matrix

		Prediction	
		Positive	**Negative**
True Labels	**Positive**	TP	FN
	Negative	FP	TN

The accuracy is calculated as the number of correct predictions divided by the total number of predictions.

$$accuracy = \frac{TP + TN}{TP + FP + FN + TN}$$

The precision metric is calculated as the number of true positive predictions divided by the total number of positive predictions.

$$precision = \frac{TP}{TP + FP}$$

The recall metric is calculated as the number of true positive predictions divided by the total number of actual positives. The recall is also known as the true positive rate (TPR).

$$recall = \frac{TP}{TP + FN}$$

The false-positive rate (FPR) is calculated as:

$$FPR = \frac{FP}{FP + TN}$$

If the accuracy is high, it means that we can correctly predict what traffic is malicious and what is benign. If the precision is high, it means that if we predict traffic is malicious, it is likely that the prediction is correct. If the recall is high, it means that we are unlikely to miss malicious traffic. However, we often need to trade-off between the precision and recall metric: when we try to improve one metric, another metric will be decreased.

Furthermore, to calculate the accuracy, precision, and recall, we need to define the decision threshold. It will limit the flexibility of our model to adapt to the different scenarios. Furthermore, the accuracy is claimed to be biased in the case of an imbalanced dataset: if there is 95% of the traffic is benign, a naïve predictor just needs to predict everything as benign and will achieve an accuracy of 95%.

To overcome the limitation of the hard decision threshold metric, the ROC AUC score is introduced (Fawcett, 2006).

Figure 5. The ROC AUC

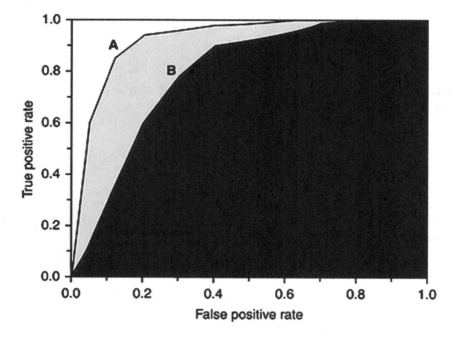

The ROC AUC score is visualized in Figure 4. We draw a line of FPR (False Positive Rate) and TPR (False Negative Rate). When we change the decision threshold, both FPR and TPR will change and they will a curve as we see in Figure 4. The area under the curve (AUC) is considered as the ROC AUC score. For instance, in Figure 4 we can see two ROC of two algorithms A and B, and algorithm A is considered better than algorithm B. From the chart, we can know that, if we accept the FPR of 20% with algorithm A, we can achieve the TPR of around 90%. However, if we accept the FPR of 10% only, the TPR is only about 70%. Hence, the ROC AUC score and ROC line will tell us not only the overall performance but also the detailed performance at each decision threshold.

MACHINE LEARNING ALGORITHMS FOR IDS

k-NN

The algorithm k-nearest neighbors (k-NN) is probably one of the most simple classification algorithms. The idea of k-NN is to classify one data point into a class based on its k nearest neighbors. When a new data point is introduced, we find the most k nearest neighbors of this data point from a labeled dataset, then based on the majority of the neighbors we will decide the class of the new data point.

Figure 6. The visualization of k-NN algorithm. The value of k can be optimized by the hyper-parameter tuning technique.

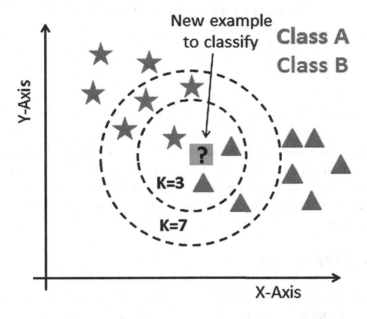

The k-NN algorithm is studied in several early research works (Liao and Vemuri, 2002) with some additions. The pseudo-code proposed by (Liao and Vemuri, 2002) is presented in Figure 5.

Figure 7. The pseudo-code of kNN for the intrusion detection
(Liao and Vemuri, 2002)

```
build the training normal data set D;
for each process X in the test data do
    if X has an unknown system call then
        X is abnormal;
    else then
        for each process Dj in training data do
            calculate sim(X, Dj);
            if sim(X, Dj) equals 1.0 then
                X is normal; exit;
        find k biggest scores of sim(X, D);
        calculate sim_avg for k-nearest neighbors;
        if sim_avg is greater than threshold then
            X is normal;
        else then
            X is abnormal;
```

An issue of the k-NN is the slow processing speed because, for every new data point that needed to be classified, we need to calculate the distance from this data point to every data point in the training set. Hence, the processing time will be correlated with the training data size. (Rao and Swathi, 2017) proposed to use two improved versions of k-NN which are Indexed Partial Distance Search k-Nearest Neighbor (IKPDS), Partial Distance Search k-Nearest Neighbor (KPDS) to speed up the algorithm.

Clustering Algorithms

Clustering algorithms are unsupervised machine learning algorithms that try to group similar items into one group. The clustering algorithms can be divided into two categories: hard-clustering like k-means or fuzzy (Wang et al., 2010) clustering like FCC (Wang and Megalooikonomou, 2005).

Figure 8. Hard and soft clustering

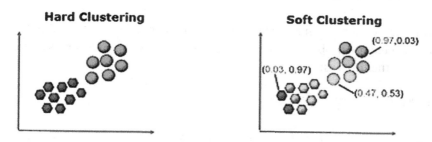

The hard and soft clustering algorithms are visualized in Figure 6. In the hard clustering algorithm, one data point belongs to a single cluster. On the other hand, the soft clustering algorithms allow a data point that belongs to multiple clusters with a weight or *belongness*.

Figure 9. The pseudo-code of k-means

1. Initialize **cluster centroids** $\mu_1, \mu_2, \ldots, \mu_k \in \mathbb{R}^n$ randomly.

2. Repeat until convergence: {

   For every i, set
   $$c^{(i)} := \arg\min_j \|x^{(i)} - \mu_j\|^2.$$

   For each j, set
   $$\mu_j := \frac{\sum_{i=1}^m 1\{c^{(i)} = j\}x^{(i)}}{\sum_{i=1}^m 1\{c^{(i)} = j\}}.$$

   }

The pseudo-code of the k-means algorithm is displayed in Figure 7. We would like to cluster the data into k-clusters. To do that, we first initialize randomly k centroids, then iteratively assign each data points to the closet centroids, then we recompute the centroids as the center points of all the points of a cluster. The algorithm stops when it reaches convergence.

Logistic Regression

Logistic Regression is a linear classification algorithm, hence it is suitable for the intrusion detection problem (Subba et al., 2015). Logistic regression is a predictive function in the form as:

$$f(x) = \theta(wT^x)$$

Where in the X are the input feature matrix and w is the weight vector. The activation function θ can be chosen from several activation families. The most popular activation function is the sigmoid function, defined as:

$$\sigma(s) = \frac{1}{1 + e^{-s}}$$

The logistic regression uses the log-likelihood loss function, defined as:

The logistic regression model can be trained using a stochastic gradient descent algorithm. Today, the logistic regression algorithm is supported by most of the popular data analysis languages. However, the logistic regression algorithm cannot cope with the missing values, hence it is not very useful in practice.

SVM

Support Vector Machine (SVM) is a well-known classification algorithm for intrusion detection (Chen et al.,2005). The idea of the SVM is visualized in Figure 8. In general, the SVM tries to find a hyperplane that separates two classes of data in the way that the margin is maximized. The SVM differs from the logistic regression in that the SVM does care only about the data points that are at the border of the classes, while the logistic regression does care about all the data points in a class.

Figure 10. Binary classification with SVM
(Chen et al., 2005)

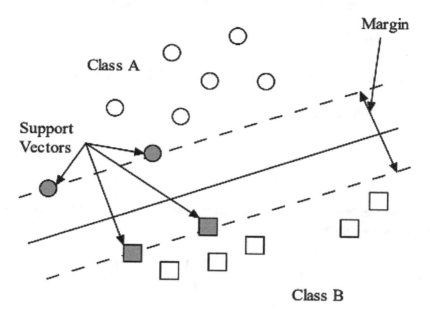

We display the pseudo-code of SVM in Figure 9.

Figure 11. The pseudo-code of SVM
(Chen et al., 2005)

Support vector machine

Problem def:

For a classification problem, we try to estimate a function $f : \Re^n \mapsto \{\pm 1\}$ using training data. So, let us denote two classes – A and B. The class A with $x \in A$, $y = 1$ and the class B with $x \in B$, $y = -1$ $(x_i, y_i) \in \Re^n \times \{\pm 1\}$. If the training data are linearly separable then there exists a pair $(w,b) \in \Re^n \times R$ such that $y(w^T x + b) \geq 1$, for all $x \in A \cup B$.

1. SVM belongs to the type of maximal margin classifier, in which the classification problem can be represented as an optimization problem

$$\underset{w,b}{\text{Minimize }} \Phi(w) = \frac{1}{2}\|w\|^2 \qquad s.t. \ y(w^T x + b) \geq 1$$

2. The dual of the optimization problem: find multipliers λ_i which maxmize

$$W(\Lambda) = \sum_{i=1}^{l} \lambda_i - \frac{1}{2}\|w\|^2 = \sum_{i=1}^{l} \lambda_i - \frac{1}{2}\sum_{i=1}^{l}\sum_{j=1}^{l} \lambda_i \lambda_j y_i y_j x_i^T x_j,$$

and by the Karush-Kuhn-Tuker (KKT) complementary conditions

$$\lambda_i [y_i(w^T x_i + b) - 1] = 0, \qquad i = 1,...,l,$$

In their work, (Chen et al., 2005) achieved an attack detection rate of 99.6% with the false positive rate of 2.87% as the best result using the SVM algorithm.

Naïve Bayes

The Naïve Bayes algorithm is a classification algorithm based on the Bayes rule in probability.

The Bayes rule stated that:

$$P(A \mid B) = \frac{P(B \mid A)P(A)}{P(B)}$$

By using the Naïve Bayes classification, we assume the independence of the features. Then we have:

$$P(y \mid x_1, \ldots, x_n) = \frac{P(y) \prod_{i=1}^{n} P(x_i \mid y)}{\prod_{i=1}^{n} P(x_i)}$$

The advantage of the Naïve Bayes algorithm is that its computation is very fast and suitable for a low-power device. The Naïve Bayes algorithm has been studied for the problem of intrusion detection in the work of (Panda and Patra, 2007). Today, the Naïve Bayes algorithm is considered a weak classification algorithm against the modern dataset and usually is used as a benchmark algorithm (Dang, 2020).

Decision Tree

The decision tree algorithm is one of the most important algorithms in machine learning. The goal of the decision tree algorithm is to build a list of if-else rules automatically, then classify a new data point into a group by applying the rules consequentially. By its nature, the decision tree is suitable for the intrusion detection problem (Amor et al., 2005).

Figure 12. An example of a decision tree implemented in an intrusion detection system (Botes et al., 2017)

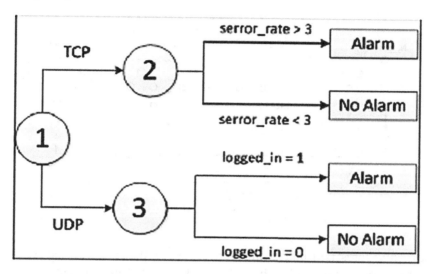

Another advantage of the decision tree is that it is very easy to understand. For instance, Figure 9 shows us an example of a decision tree that is designed for the intrusion detection problem. A typical user can immediately understand the workflow of the tree without any further knowledge.

Similar to the Naïve Bayes algorithm, today the decision tree is considered a weak classifier (Dang, 2019). However, the decision tree is the fundamental block to build more complicated algorithms that are bagging and boosting trees that we will discuss next. These algorithms usually are chosen as the best algorithms in machine learning competitions organized by Kaggle.

Random Forest

Even the decision tree is considered a weak algorithm, ensembling them can make a different story. There are two approaches to ensemble the decision trees: bagging and boosting.

Random forest (Breiman, 2001) is a bagging algorithm. The idea of the random forest is to create multiple decision trees, each differs from the others on the feature and the training data a little. Then the prediction can be treated as a vote between these trees.

Figure 13. The random forest algorithm

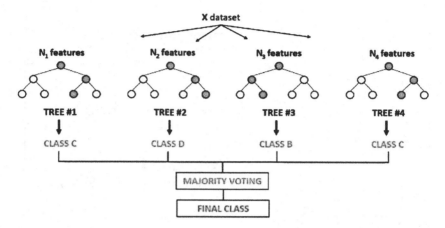

The random forest is visualized in Figure 11. The random forest is used extensively in the literature for the problem of intrusion detection (Resende and Drummond, 2018). However, according to (Dang, 2019), the random forest is outperformed by boosting machines algorithms like xgboost.

Boosting Machines

Boosting is another approach to improve the performance of the decision tree. While in the bagging approach, multiple trees are built simultaneously and independently, the boosting models build multiple decision trees in sequence. The core idea is to let the following tree recover the prediction error made by the previous one.

Figure 14. The boosting trees

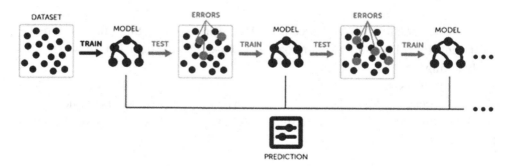

In recent years, several boosting models have been introduced and achieved a lot of success. To name a few of them, we have xgboost (Chen and Guestrin, 2016), lightgbm (Ke et al., 2017), and catboost (Dorogoush et al., 2018). The xgboost model achieved a near-perfect predictive performance in the modern intrusion dataset (Dang, 2019). In recent works (Dang, 2021), the researchers show that catboost might achieve an approximate result as xgboost but with much shorter training and inference time. In some experiments, the catboost algorithm might run faster than xgboost about ten times while the difference in the predictive performance is less than 0.0001%.

Isolation Forest

Isolation Forest (Liu et al., 2008) is an unsupervised machine learning based on the idea of the random forest.

Figure 15. The Isolation Forest

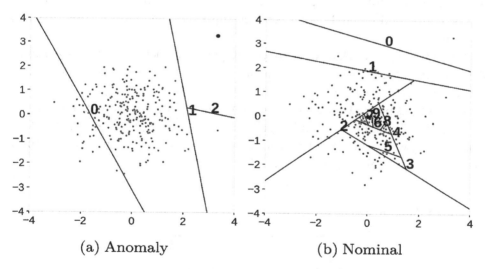

(a) Anomaly (b) Nominal

The idea of the isolation forest is that we will use the random forest to classify each data point from all other data points. The deeper the tree we need to classify a single data point, the more normal it is. Hence, by applying the isolation forest on all the data points we can measure the abnormality of each data point and remove them from the data. The isolation forest can be used to clean data or to detect the intrusion directly (Dang, 2018).

One of the main disadvantages of the Isolation Forest algorithm is its slow processing speed. Furthermore, the algorithm does not support null values which is very popular in practice.

Deep Learning

Deep learning (Goodfellow et al., 2016) is an active research field today with a lot of achievements in recent years. It is no surprise that deep learning techniques are applied for intrusion detection systems. (Vinayakumar et al., 2017) studied multiple convolutional neural networks and their variants to detect the intrusion using the KDD-99 dataset. However, as most of the intrusion datasets are presented in the tabular data, the deep learning techniques do not show any improvement compared to the ensembled learning (Dang, 2021).

Reinforcement Learning

Reinforcement learning (Dang and Vo, 2021) is a branch of machine learning that can be considered a middle point between supervised and unsupervised machine learning.

Instead of requiring a labeled dataset like supervised machine learning algorithms, the reinforcement learning algorithms interact with the environment and observe the response to adapt its policy.

However, as pointed out by many other research studies, reinforcement learning requires the algorithm to learn by trial and error, hence at the beginning of the learning phase, the model must let some malicious packages enter the system. It might not be possible in a real-world cyber system.

Figure 16. Reinforcement Learning

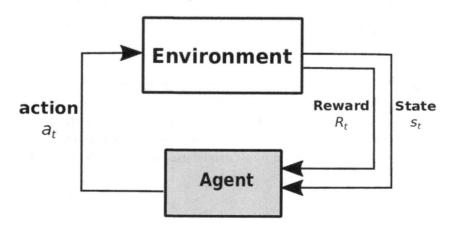

Active Learning

Active learning (Dang, 2020) is a method to actively select the next instance to the training set. By using active learning, we can start the training process with a small subset of the training data then select the next instance from the pool that likely improves the performance of the model. The core idea is that we select some unlabeled data points that we expect if they are labeled and added to the training set, the predictive performance will increase significantly. Some common metrics to determine the data points are entropy or the predictive scores. Then we can ask some experts to manually label these data points. By doing so, we reduce the required effort of the manual labeling task which is expensive.

(Dang, 2020) showed that by using active learning, the computational power is reduced but the predictive performance is maintained.

OPEN PROBLEMS AND FUTURE RESEARCH DIRECTIONS

In recent years, machine learning-based intrusion detection systems have achieved a lot of success. However, there are open problems in the field that we will discuss here.

- How to generate a large realistic labeled dataset? As we discussed in the previous section, many attack datasets have been introduced in recent years. However, most of them are created using a simulated environment. We can use these datasets for educational purposes, but indeed there is a need for the dataset from real-world attacks. However, how to generate the real attacks is not a trivial question. Probably we need cooperation from some retired black-hat hackers.

- How to deal with zero attacks? Dealing with zero attacks is still a crucial challenge for researchers. Even high-performance classifiers like xgboost will fail if it needs to deal with unknown attacks. Reinforcement learning algorithms have a lot of potentials but the state-of-the-art performance does not catch up with other supervised learning techniques. A hybrid method might be a solution: while a supervised learning model deals with known attacks, we train a reinforcement learning algorithm simultaneously to catch the attacks that the first model missed.

- How to train the model using low-power devices? The state-of-the-art models used in the intrusion detection problems are all complicated models, hence requiring a lot of computational power. It is not suitable to put them in low-powered devices such as home routers or IoT devices, particularly if we need to update the models lively. Distributed learning might be a solution: we distribute the training process to multiple devices in the network.

- How to forget the outdated training point? In many cases, if we detect some training data points are outdated or not useful anymore, we need to remove these data points from the training dataset. The naïve approach is to retrain everything from scratch. However, it is not a practical approach (Dang, 2021).

CONCLUSION

In this chapter, we review the intrusion detection problem. The intrusion detection problem is a core problem of many cybersecurity systems today. In this paper, we describe and formulate the problem as the classification task. We review the machine learning algorithms that have been studied for intrusion detection in the literature. We address the open challenges and draw some potential research ideas to solve these challenges.

REFERENCES

Ahmad, Z., Shahid Khan, A., Wai Shiang, C., Abdullah, J., & Ahmad, F. (2021). Network intrusion detection system: A systematic study of machine learning and deep learning approaches. *Transactions on Emerging Telecommunications Technologies*, *32*(1), e4150. doi:10.1002/ett.4150

Alqahtani, H., Sarker, I. H., Kalim, A., Hossain, S. M. M., Ikhlaq, S., & Hossain, S. (2020, March). Cyber intrusion detection using machine learning classification techniques. In *International Conference on Computing Science, Communication and Security* (pp. 121-131). Springer. 10.1007/978-981-15-6648-6_10

Amor, N. B., Benferhat, S., & Elouedi, Z. (2004, March). Naive bayes vs decision trees in intrusion detection systems. In *Proceedings of the 2004 ACM symposium on Applied computing* (pp. 420-424). 10.1145/967900.967989

Botes, F. H., Leenen, L., & De La Harpe, R. (2017, June). Ant colony induced decision trees for intrusion detection. In *16th European Conference on Cyber Warfare and Security* (pp. 53-62). ACPI.

Breiman, L. (2001). Random forests. *Machine Learning*, *45*(1), 5–32. doi:10.1023/A:1010933404324

Chen, T., & Guestrin, C. (2016, August). Xgboost: A scalable tree boosting system. In *Proceedings of the 22nd acm sigkdd international conference on knowledge discovery and data mining* (pp. 785-794). 10.1145/2939672.2939785

Chen, W. H., Hsu, S. H., & Shen, H. P. (2005). Application of SVM and ANN for intrusion detection. *Computers & Operations Research, 32*(10), 2617–2634. doi:10.1016/j.cor.2004.03.019

Dang, Q. V. (2018). *Outlier detection on network flow analysis.* arXiv preprint arXiv:1808.02024.

Dang, Q. V. (2019, November). Studying machine learning techniques for intrusion detection systems. In *International Conference on Future Data and Security Engineering* (pp. 411-426). Springer. 10.1007/978-3-030-35653-8_28

Dang, Q. V. (2020, November). Understanding the Decision of Machine Learning Based Intrusion Detection Systems. In *International Conference on Future Data and Security Engineering* (pp. 379-396). Springer. 10.1007/978-3-030-63924-2_22

Dang, Q. V. (2020, October). Active learning for intrusion detection systems. In *2020 RIVF International Conference on Computing and Communication Technologies (RIVF)* (pp. 1-3). IEEE.

Dang, Q. V. (2021, July). Studying the Fuzzy clustering algorithm for intrusion detection on the attacks to the Domain Name System. In *2021 Fifth World Conference on Smart Trends in Systems Security and Sustainability (WorldS4)* (pp. 271-274). IEEE. 10.1109/WorldS451998.2021.9514038

Dang, Q. V. (2021). Improving the performance of the intrusion detection systems by the machine learning explainability. *International Journal of Web Information Systems.*

Dang, Q. V. (2021, February). Right to Be Forgotten in the Age of Machine Learning. In *International Conference on Advances in Digital Science* (pp. 403-411). Springer. 10.1007/978-3-030-71782-7_35

Dang, Q. V., & Vo, T. H. (2021, May). Studying the Reinforcement Learning techniques for the problem of intrusion detection. In *2021 4th International Conference on Artificial Intelligence and Big Data (ICAIBD)* (pp. 87-91). IEEE. 10.1109/ICAIBD51990.2021.9459006

Dorogush, A. V., Ershov, V., & Gulin, A. (2018). *CatBoost: gradient boosting with categorical features support.* arXiv preprint arXiv:1810.11363.

Elsayed, M. S., Le-Khac, N. A., & Jurcut, A. D. (2020). InSDN: A novel SDN intrusion dataset. *IEEE Access: Practical Innovations, Open Solutions*, 8, 165263–165284. doi:10.1109/ACCESS.2020.3022633

Fawcett, T. (2006). An introduction to ROC analysis. *Pattern Recognition Letters*, 27(8), 861–874. doi:10.1016/j.patrec.2005.10.010

Goodfellow, I., Bengio, Y., & Courville, A. (2016). *Deep learning*. MIT press.

Huai-bin, W., Hong-liang, Y., Zhi-Jian, X. U., & Zheng, Y. (2010, May). A clustering algorithm use SOM and k-means in intrusion detection. In *2010 International Conference on E-Business and E-Government* (pp. 1281-1284). IEEE. 10.1109/ICEE.2010.327

Ke, G., Meng, Q., Finley, T., Wang, T., Chen, W., Ma, W., ... Liu, T. Y. (2017). Lightgbm: A highly efficient gradient boosting decision tree. *Advances in Neural Information Processing Systems*, 30, 3146–3154.

Liao, Y., & Vemuri, V. R. (2002). Use of k-nearest neighbor classifier for intrusion detection. *Computers & Security*, 21(5), 439–448. doi:10.1016/S0167-4048(02)00514-X

Liu, F. T., Ting, K. M., & Zhou, Z. H. (2008, December). Isolation forest. In *2008 eighth IEEE international conference on data mining* (pp. 413-422). IEEE. 10.1109/ICDM.2008.17

Maseer, Z. K., Yusof, R., Bahaman, N., Mostafa, S. A., & Foozy, C. F. M. (2021). Benchmarking of machine learning for anomaly based intrusion detection systems in the CICIDS2017 dataset. *IEEE Access: Practical Innovations, Open Solutions*, 9, 22351–22370. doi:10.1109/ACCESS.2021.3056614

McHugh, J. (2000). Testing intrusion detection systems: A critique of the 1998 and 1999 darpa intrusion detection system evaluations as performed by lincoln laboratory. *ACM Transactions on Information and System Security*, 3(4), 262–294. doi:10.1145/382912.382923

Panda, M., & Patra, M. R. (2007). Network intrusion detection using naive bayes. *International Journal of Computer Science and Network Security, 7*(12), 258-263.

Rao, B. B., & Swathi, K. (2017). Fast kNN classifiers for network intrusion detection system. *Indian Journal of Science and Technology*, 10(14), 1–10. doi:10.17485/ijst/2017/v10i29/109053

Resende, P. A. A., & Drummond, A. C. (2018). A survey of random forest based methods for intrusion detection systems. *ACM Computing Surveys*, *51*(3), 1–36. doi:10.1145/3178582

Ring, M., Wunderlich, S., Grüdl, D., Landes, D., & Hotho, A. (2017, June). Flow-based benchmark data sets for intrusion detection. In *Proceedings of the 16th European Conference on Cyber Warfare and Security* (pp. 361-369). ACPI.

Ring, M., Wunderlich, S., Scheuring, D., Landes, D., & Hotho, A. (2019). A survey of network-based intrusion detection data sets. *Computers & Security*, *86*, 147–167. doi:10.1016/j.cose.2019.06.005

Shahraki, A., Abbasi, M., Taherkordi, A., & Jurcut, A. D. (2021). *Active Learning for Network Traffic Classification: A Technical Survey*. arXiv preprint arXiv:2106.06933.

Sharafaldin, I., Lashkari, A. H., & Ghorbani, A. A. (2018). Toward generating a new intrusion detection dataset and intrusion traffic characterization. *ICISSp*, *1*, 108–116. doi:10.5220/0006639801080116

Shatoori, M., Davidson, L., Kaur, G., & Lashkari, A. H. (2020, August). Detection of doh tunnels using time-series classification of encrypted traffic. In 2020 IEEE Intl Conf on Dependable, Autonomic and Secure Computing, Intl Conf on Pervasive Intelligence and Computing, Intl Conf on Cloud and Big Data Computing, Intl Conf on Cyber Science and Technology Congress (DASC/PiCom/CBDCom/CyberSciTech) (pp. 63-70). IEEE.

Shiravi, A., Shiravi, H., Tavallaee, M., & Ghorbani, A. A. (2012). Toward developing a systematic approach to generate benchmark datasets for intrusion detection. *Computers & Security, 31*(3), 357-374.

Stolfo, J., Fan, W., Lee, W., Prodromidis, A., & Chan, P. K. (2000). Cost-based modeling and evaluation for data mining with application to fraud and intrusion detection. *Results from the JAM Project by Salvatore*, 1-15.

Subba, B., Biswas, S., & Karmakar, S. (2015, December). Intrusion detection systems using linear discriminant analysis and logistic regression. In *2015 Annual IEEE India Conference (INDICON)* (pp. 1-6). IEEE. 10.1109/INDICON.2015.7443533

Tsai, C. F., Hsu, Y. F., Lin, C. Y., & Lin, W. Y. (2009). Intrusion detection by machine learning: A review. *Expert Systems With Applications, 36*(10), 11994-12000.

Umadevi, S., & Marseline, K. J. (2017, July). A survey on data mining classification algorithms. In *2017 International Conference on Signal Processing and Communication (ICSPC)* (pp. 264-268). IEEE. 10.1109/CSPC.2017.8305851

Vinayakumar, R., Soman, K. P., & Poornachandran, P. (2017, September). Applying convolutional neural network for network intrusion detection. In *2017 International Conference on Advances in Computing, Communications and Informatics (ICACCI)* (pp. 1222-1228). IEEE. 10.1109/ICACCI.2017.8126009

Wang, Q., & Megalooikonomou, V. (2005, March). A clustering algorithm for intrusion detection. In Data Mining, Intrusion Detection, Information Assurance, and Data Networks Security 2005 (Vol. 5812, pp. 31-38). International Society for Optics and Photonics. doi:10.1117/12.603567

ADDITIONAL READING

Agarwal, A., & Gupta, N. (2021). *Comparison of Outlier Detection Techniques for Structured Data.* arXiv preprint arXiv:2106.08779.

Kuhn, M., & Johnson, K. (2019). *Feature engineering and selection: A practical approach for predictive models.* CRC Press. doi:10.1201/9781315108230

Zhou, Z. H. (2013). *Ensemble methods: foundations and algorithms.* Chapman and Hall/CRC.

Chapter 8

Estimating the Efficiency of Machine Learning Algorithms in Predicting Seizure With Convolutional Neural Network Architecture:
Classification of Machine Learning Algorithms

Jamunadevi C.
Kongu Engineering College, Perundurai, India

Arul P.
Government Arts College (Trichy), Bharathidasan University, India

ABSTRACT

The reason trends in prevalent detection of EEG seizure help in analyzing the various features of EEG signals to customize and to remove visual inspection in reading the EEG signals. Epilepsy is a disorder and is identified by baseless seizures that have been associated with unexpected improper neural discharges which result in various health issues and also result in death. One of the most common methods in detecting contraction seizures is an electroencephalogram. By using machine learning methods, it is easy to extract the features of EEG signals that help in detecting seizures. Convolutional neural network (CNN) includes both inputs as well as output layers that help in training the data acquired since it helps in analyzing

DOI: 10.4018/978-1-7998-9308-0.ch008

the large set of high dimensional data. The performance analysis is done under multiple classifiers such as random forest, gradient boosting, and decision tree, which are used in feature extraction. Among them, random forest proves to be the best classifier in achieving a high degree of accuracy.

INTRODUCTION

Epilepsy is neural disorder that occurs in the brain which is characterized by the baseless seizures. More than 50 million people around the world are severely affected by this neurological disorder. These patients suffer from neurobiological disorders including the social and psychological impairments. If it is identified in earlier stage it could save the patient's life. EEG signals include two kinds of activities stated, interictal and ictal. The time gap between the EEG seizures is termed as interictal. The time gap between the EEG seizure offset and onset is termed as ictal. But, most of the common studies in seizure detection states to use the scalp EEG because it is easily obtained from non-invasive methods (T. N. Alotaiby, 2014). The visual review of EEG reading is really a time consuming process and also results in trained physicians in identifying the characteristic features of EEG seizures from the multi-channels (L. J. Greenfield, 2012). The hand-crafted features in detecting the EEG signals fall into two broad classifications: they include temporal and spectral features (M. Ahmad, 2016). Recently, many deep learning techniques has given a best results in signal processing due to increasing level in accuracy (Y. Bengio, 2013).The features extracted using Convolution Neural Network (CNN) proved to be the best in detection evaluation where the layers in CNN which support for accurate classification and prediction (Z. Mei, 2018). Despite, the results which are stated by the existing deep learning techniques in seizure detection, there are a few numerous challenges required to be spotted. One among them is presence of irrelevant channels and multiple information due to the extraction of features from multi-channels (A. Temko, 2012), (E. Keogh, 2011).To handle these challenges in the existing methodology (Y. Yuan, 2017), deep learning model is designed to concern the abnormalities in the brain that has been associated with EEG seizures. The demonstration of this proposed model is evaluated under various classification methods in governing the performance of the models. Electroencephalography (EEG) plays major parts in observing the brain movement of patients with epilepsy and makes a difference to analyze epilepsy.

LITERATURE SURVEY

Various researchers have proposed a methodology in combining the handcrafted features using Support Vector Machine (SVM) classifier (C. Cortes, 2015) or Neural Networks (Y.-H. Shih, 2012) (NN) in building a multi-stage seizure detection system. Numerous highlights have been recognized within the time space that experiences the stage (B. Erem, 2015), statistical measures (Q. Lin, 2016) and entropy (H. R. Mohseni, 2016). Wavelet transform (V. Srinivasan, 2014) and Fourier transform (P. E. McSharry, 2003) could be consider for feature extraction purpose. There may be some growing trends in stating the time frequency descriptors mainly concerning the image in detecting seizure from EEG signals along with this precision and recall can be added for accuracy (A. S¸ engur, 2016). EEG system consists of multi electrode channels along with the growing features with increasing number of channels (N. D. Truong, 2017). To remove this dimensionality problem, a lot number of feature selection mechanisms have been identified in eradicating the irrelevant and redundant features before the classifier has been trained, so that effective prediction of epilepsy will be predicted. Enormous methods have been keep on exploiting the ideology that has been imposed on the detection of multi-channel EEG seizure detection that includes PCA (Principal Component Analysis) (U. R. Acharya, 2012), ICA (Individual Component Analysis) (Y.H. Shih, 2012) and Laplacian Eigen maps (B. Erem, 2015). Also, many stacked auto-encoders have been proved to be better methodology in feature extraction than handcrafted extraction (Q. Lin, 2016). The above literature review identifies the limitations that's are

- The existing classifiers found multiple local minimum rather than finding a distinct global minimum.
- Requires more training time.
- Keeps the number of features extracted EEG signals to be small.
- Requires concentrated computing and may not be supported for real time seizure detecting system.
- Very less in accuracy
- Number of parameters taken to estimate the efficiency is very less in number.
- Predicting of inter ictal stage in epileptic seizure is quite complicated.

DATA COLLECTION

The dataset has been obtained from the Kaggle repository. Since the data are collected from open source, it contains irrelevant, null and redundant features. The pre-processing is done to normalize the dataset. The features are extracted from the pre-processed dataset. The extraction of time frequency and wavelet features are trained under CNN (Convolution Neural Network). The metrics are formulated for the trained set of data using Decision tree algorithm and Support Vector Machine. The accuracy, confusion matrix, average precision and ROC is calculated for analyzing the performance measure of the trained dataset. Dataset are classified as test, trained, overall trained and validation. Then classification algorithms such as Random Forest, Gradient boosting, Decision tree are implemented for the comparing the best suited classifier for extracting the features. Random Forest is considered to be the better suited for the classifying whether the pattern of seizure is epileptic or not. Applying (ICFS) Improved Correlation based Feature Selection in selecting the prominent features from the wavelet and time frequency.

ARCHITECTURE

The following are the steps involved in analyzing the machine learning algorithms used in improving the clarity of predicting seizure attacks in elliptic patience,

1. Data collection
2. Data pre-processing
3. Implementation of CNN
4. Classification using Machine Learning Algorithms

Figure 1.

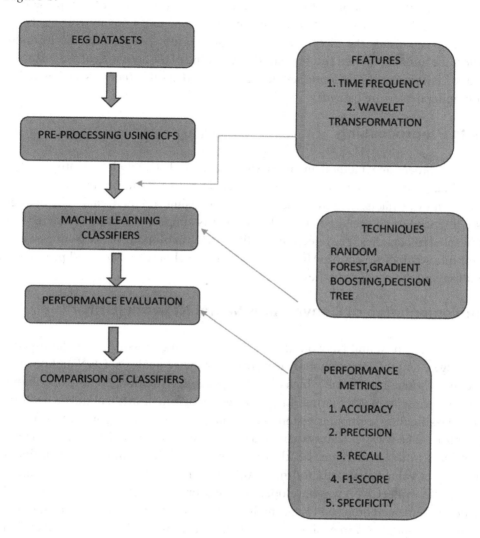

EEG Data Set

The data is obtained from Kaggle repository. The EEG signals of various patients are collected as data values. The original data file extracted from the open source contains 5 set of different folders. Each file contains the recording of the activities of the brain for 23.6 seconds. The supporting time series data is sampled to 4097 points of data. Further, the data points are partitioned into 23 chunks that includes 178 data points that accounts for a second. The explanatory variable values x1, x2, x3....x178 that represents the 178 dimensional input values. And more importantly, y represents the operation of the eye in certain amount of time. It has represented in class {1, 2, 3, 4, 5} where 5 means eye has been opened, 4 means eyes has been closed, 3 represents the identification of tumor region, 2 represents the location where the tumor is spotted and 1 means the recording of the activities of the seizures. Class 1 falls under the epileptic seizure category and all the other classes fall under non-epileptic seizure category.

Data Preprocessing

The pre-processing method involves various steps that includes identifying the individual trail set from the extracted dataset. Then, it is followed by filtering and rejection of artifacts. The identification is done using trigger signal. The dataset is referenced to an averaged channel. Filtering is supposed to do in removing the unwanted frequencies. The rejection of artifacts such as blinking of eyes is done using Multiple Artifact Rejection Algorithm and the signal power is checked proceeded with saving the changes in the same csv file.

Implementation of Convolution Neural Network (CNN)

CNN is a Deep Neural Network that can recognize and classify particular aspects in images, and they're commonly employed for image analysis. CNN architecture is computationally efficient which involves special convolution, pooling operations and perform parameter sharing. Image, video recognition, medical image analysis and classification, computer vision, natural language processing are only a few of their uses. The wavelet feature extracted was trained in order to detect any epileptic transients in the data values of EEG signals. The CNN is employed for training the dataset values especially for the wavelet features concerned. The Convolution Neural Network (CNN) was developed from tenser flow. The parameters supposed to be implemented are used in optimizing the model and prevents over-fitting that includes dropout, 1 dimensional layer, balanced training, batch processing and cross-validation in determining the stopping criteria. In dropout layer, the percentage concerned for the fully connected layer has been dropped out to prevent data values over-fitting. The trained dataset value is further evaluated using Decision tree and Support Vector Machine (SVM). The dataset is classified into trained, tested, overall trained value and validation. The input feature provided for SVM and decision tree is given as the output that has been extracted from the spike detection based on CNN. The metrics obtained for the model are Accuracy, confusion matrix, average precision, recall, support and F1 score.

Machine Learning Algorithms

Machine learning centers on the improvement of computer programs that can get to information and utilize it to memorize for themselves. Machine learning has played an essential role in big data systems due to its ability to efficiently discover hidden information and valuable knowledge. Appreciations to the advanced technology of machine learning and medical imaging for the rapid development of undergone computerized healthcare. Machine Learning is a data analysis of application belongs to build a model that desired predicted output for available data by predictive and statistical features.

Classification Using Machine Learning Algorithms

The classifiers are used in extracting the features from the data values of EEG signals. Among the various machine learning algorithms, Random Forest, Gradient Boosting and Decision tree is implied in the recognizing the variation from the extracted data values. Random forest is a learning algorithm that is supervised. It makes a "forest" out of an gathering of decision trees, which are commonly prepared using the "bagging" method. The bagging method's basic premise is that combining several learning models improves the overall result. Mainly, the feature is concerned with time frequency and wavelet transformations. Since random forest is supervised learning algorithm concerned, it proves to be the better suited and also reduces the complexity. Random Forest is a tree-based machine learning system that leverages by combining the control of several decision trees. A random amount of trained data is used for classification purpose. D represents the dimension of extracted input features. The dimension of the subset features which are selected is represented as d. The d value is seen to be leaser than D. Among the three classifiers, performance proves to be given better for Random Forest (RF). The error rate is found on two aspects. One, the correlation between the tress formed form extracting the valuable feature set from EEG dataset in constructing the forest. Other, is the strength of the particular tree in the selected forest. When the strength is increased, the error rate is highly reduced. The another algorithm which is taken is gradient boosting technique. In machine learning algorithm faults can be partitioned into two categories: bias error and variance error. Gradient boosting is one of the boosting strategies that is used to reduce the model's bias error. For classification and regression, Decision Trees (DTs) are a non-parametric supervised learning method. The decision tree algorithm can be used for solving regression and classification problems; the goal is to learn simple decision rules from data attributes to develop a model that predicts the value of a target variable. Random forest is very effective in classification that helps in constructed at the training time and the output of the class can be either classification

125

or regression. Random Forest Classifiers help to reduce model overfitting, and in some circumstances, they are more accurate than decision trees.

RESULTS AND DISCUSSION

This research concluded new approaches based on the EEG signals detecting the epileptic seizure. Electrical activity is a brain EEG, this paper is used to analyze brain detects seizure problems. The spatial representing of electrodes the wavelet signals of EEG data utilize for analyzing seizure.The trained model is analyzed under various performance metrics. The measures chosen in evaluating the model are accuracy, average precision, support, recall, confusion metrics and F1 score. The random forest chooses features randomly during the training process. Therefore, it does not depend highly on any specific set of features. This is a special characteristic of random forest over bagging trees. When comparing the trained and validated data values under the implied classification algorithm, Random Forest (RF) gives the best accuracy when compared to Decision tree and Gradient Boosting. Specificity determines the ratio of classified seizure activity that has been captured accurately to the total count of labeled data values. The parameters taken for evaluation are accuracy, precision, recall, F1 score and specificity which support accurate prediction of epileptic seizure detection.

Figure 2. Confusion matrix for trained dataset using Random Forest Classifier

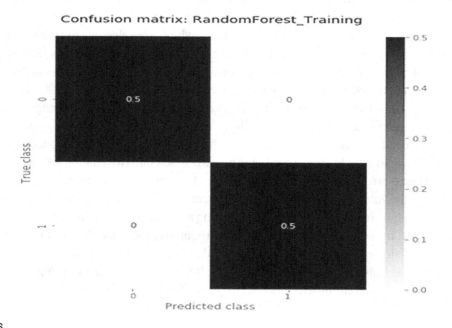

Figure 3. Confusion matrix for validated dataset using Random Forest Classifier

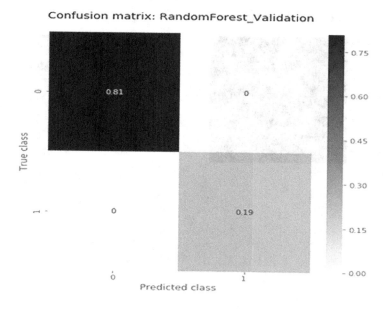

Figure 4. Confusion matrix for trained dataset using Gradient Boosting Classifier

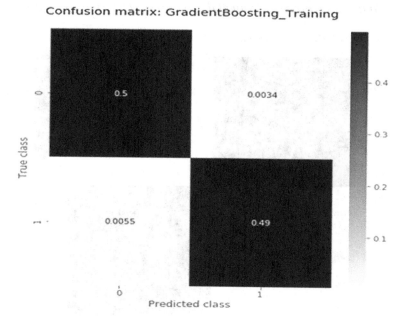

Figure 5. Confusion matrix for validated dataset using Gradient Boosting Classifier

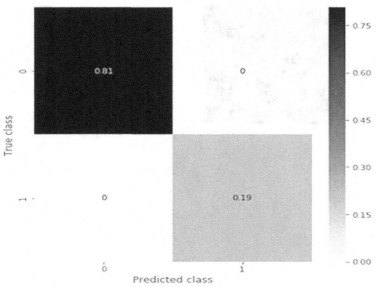

Figure 6. Confusion matrix for trained dataset using Decision tree Classifier

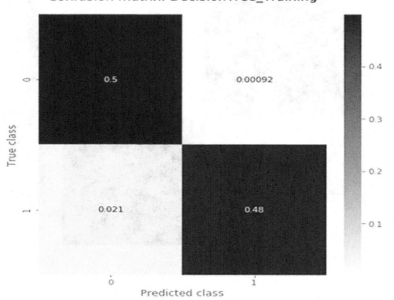

Figure 7. Confusion matrix for validated dataset using Decision tree Classifier

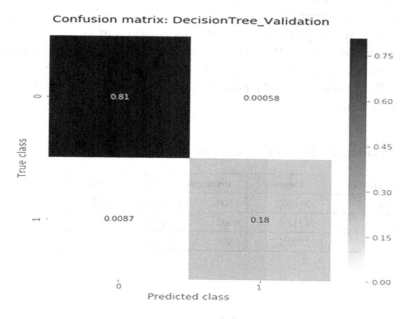

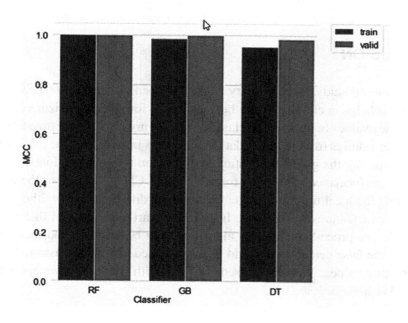

Figure 8. Comparison of classifiers (Random Forest, Gradient Boosting and Decision tree) with trained and validation dataset

The trained values from implementing the CNN architecture is validated under various performance analysis measure. The CNN model helps in achieving ROC of 91.85% and average precision of 83.16% for a specificity of 90%. The various study of seizure detection in the literature available exert various datasets and also provide enormous number of evaluation measures. The performance measure for three classifiers is discussed in the given table which helps in detecting the epileptic activity in the brain.

Table 1. Performance metrics for trained dataset

Type of Classifier	Accuracy	Precision	Recall	F1Score	Specificity
Random Forest	100.000%	1.000	1.000	1.000	1.000
Gradient Boosting	99.111%	0.993	0.989	0.991	0.993
Decision tree	97.793%	0.998	0.958	0..977	0.998

Table 2. Performance metrics for validation dataset

Type of Classifier	Accuracy	Precision	Recall	F1Score	Specificity
Random Forest	100.000%	1.000	1.000	1.000	1.000
Gradient Boosting	100.000%	1.000	1.000	1.000	1.000
Decision tree	99.072%	0.997	0.955	0.975	0.999

CONCLUSION

In this proposed study, a preliminary result has been automated for EEG seizure detection. It helps in classifying the best algorithm for epileptic seizure detection. The accuracy value obtained for the classifier chosen in extracting the time frequency and wavelet features from the EEG data values helps in analyzing the performance. When comparing the gradient boosting and decision tree random forest classifier have good performance metrics for trained dataset. CNN over comes the problem of choosing the local minimum value by involving different layers without setting the number of features to be small. In future, for artifact rejection that has been imposed in pre-processing, various algorithms can be imposed and incorporated to remove the false detection. It could be also implied in medical tasks using same data structure values, particular in sensing the health where the awareness is still identified as a major issue.

REFERENCES

Acharya, U. R., Fujita, H., Sudarshan, V. K., Bhat, S., & Koh, J. E. (2015). Application of entropies for automated diagnosis of epilepsy using eeg signals: A review. *Knowledge-Based Systems, 88*, 85–96. doi:10.1016/j.knosys.2015.08.004

Acharya, U. R., Sree, S. V., Alvin, A. P. C., & Suri, J. S. (2012). Use of principal component analysis for automatic classification of epileptic eeg activities in wavelet framework. *Expert Systems with Applications, 39*(10), 9072–9078. doi:10.1016/j.eswa.2012.02.040

Ahmad, M., Saeed, M., Saleem, S., & Kamboh, A. M. (2016). Seizure detection using eeg: A survey of different techniques. In *Emerging Technologies (ICET), International Conference on.* IEEE. 10.1109/ICET.2016.7813209

Alotaiby, T. N., Alshebeili, S. A., Alshawi, T., Ahmad, I., & El-Samie, F. E. A. (2014). Eeg seizure detection and prediction algorithms: A survey. *EURASIP Journal on Advances in Signal Processing, 2014*(1), 183. doi:10.1186/1687-6180-2014-183

Bengio, Y., Courville, A., & Vincent, P. (2013). Representation learning: A review and new perspectives. *IEEE Transactions on Pattern Analysis and Machine Intelligence, 35*(8), 1798–1828. doi:10.1109/TPAMI.2013.50 PMID:23787338

Bhattacharyya, A., & Pachori, R. B. (2017). A multivariate approach for patient-specific EEG seizure detection using empirical wavelet transform. *IEEE Transactions on Biomedical Engineering, 64*(9), 2003–2015. doi:10.1109/TBME.2017.2650259 PMID:28092514

Cortes, C., & Vapnik, V. (2015). Support-vector networks. *Machine Learning, 20*(3), 273–297. doi:10.1007/BF00994018

Dalton, A., Patel, S., Chowdhury, A. R., Welsh, M., Pang, T., Schachter, S., Olaighin, G., & Bonato, P. (2012). G. OLaighin, and P. Bonato, "Development of a body sensor network to detect motor patterns of epileptic seizures. *IEEE Transactions on Biomedical Engineering, 59*(11), 3204–3211. doi:10.1109/TBME.2012.2204990 PMID:22717505

Engur, Guo, & Akbulut. (2016). Time–frequency texture descriptors of EEG signals for efficient detection of epileptic seizure. *Brain Informatics, 3*(2), 101–108. doi:10.100740708-015-0029-8 PMID:27747603

Erem, B., Hyde, D. E., Peters, J. M., Duffy, F. H., Brooks, D. H., & Warfield, S. K. (2015). Combined delay and graph embedding of epileptic discharges in eeg reveals complex and recurrent nonlinear dynamics. In *Biomedical Imaging (ISBI), 2015 IEEE 12th International Symposium on*. IEEE. 10.1109/ISBI.2015.7163884

Greenfield, L. J., Geyer, J. D., & Carney, P. R. (2012). *Reading EEGs: a practical approach*. Lippincott Williams & Wilkins.

Keogh, E., & Mueen, A. (2011). *Curse of dimensionality. In Encyclopedia of machine learning*. Springer.

Lin, Q., Ye, S.-q., Huang, X.-m., Li, S.-y., Zhang, M.-z., Xue, Y., & Chen, W.-S. (2016). Classification of epileptic eeg signals with stacked sparse autoencoder based on deep learning. In *International Conference on Intelligent Computing*. Springer. 10.1007/978-3-319-42297-8_74

McCulloch, W. S., & Pitts, W. (2012). A logical calculus of the ideas immanent in nervous activity. *The Bulletin of Mathematical Biophysics*, *5*(4), 115–133. doi:10.1007/BF02478259

McSharry, P. E., Smith, L. A., & Tarassenko, L. (2003). Prediction of epileptic seizures: Are nonlinear methods relevant? *Nature Medicine*, *9*(3), 241–242. doi:10.1038/nm0303-241 PMID:12612550

Mei, Z., Zhao, X., Chen, H., & Chen, W. (2018). Bio-signal complexity analysis in epileptic seizure monitoring: A topic review. *Sensors (Basel)*, *18*(6), 1720. doi:10.339018061720 PMID:29861451

Mohseni, H. R., Maghsoudi, A., & Shamsollahi, M. B. (2016). Seizure detection in EEG signals: A comparison of different approaches. *Proc. of the 28th IEEE EMBS Int. Conf.*

Shih, Chen, Yang, & Chiueh. (2012). Hardware-efficient evd processor architecture in fastica for epileptic seizure detection. *APSIPA*, 1–4.

Song, J.-L., Hu, W., & Zhang, R. (2016). Automated detection of epileptic eegs using a novel fusion feature and extreme learning machine. *Neurocomputing*, *175*, 383–391. doi:10.1016/j.neucom.2015.10.070

Srinivasan, V., Eswaran, C., & Sriraam, N. (2014). Epileptic detection using artificial neural networks. *Int. Conf. on Signal Processing & Communications (SPCOM)*.

Temko, A., Lightbody, G., Thomas, E. M., Boylan, G. B., & Marnane, W. (2012). Instantaneous measure of eeg channel importance for improved patientadaptive neonatal seizure detection. *IEEE Transactions on Biomedical Engineering, 59*(3), 717–727. doi:10.1109/TBME.2011.2178411 PMID:22156948

Truong, N. D., Kuhlmann, L., Bonyadi, M. R., Yang, J., Faulks, A., & Kavehei, O. (2017). Supervised learning in automatic channel selection for epileptic seizure detection. *Expert Systems with Applications, 86*, 199–207. doi:10.1016/j. eswa.2017.05.055

Yuan, Y., Xun, G., Jia, K., & Zhang, A. (2017). A multi-view deep learning method for epileptic seizure detection using short-time fourier transform. In *Proceedings of the 8th ACM International Conference on Bioinformatics, Computational Biology, and Health Informatics*. ACM. 10.1145/3107411.3107419

Chapter 9
Crop Protection Using Cyber Physical Systems and Machine Learning for Smart Agriculture

Manish Choubisa
Poornima College of Engineering, Jaipur, India

Ruchi Doshi
Azteca University, Mexico

ABSTRACT

Currently the world is experiencing the global digital transformation of the fourth generation revolution for industry in the field of cyber physical systems (CPS) and artificial intelligence. Moreover, by utilizing artificial intelligence, cyber physical systems will be able to perform more proficiently, collaboratively, and spiritedly. Agriculture crop control is a process to protect the crop as much as possible so the crop is not infected by the different kinds of pests. Pests are any living organisms including insects, animals, weeds, pathogens, and other creatures that can harm the agriculture crop. Pests and other diseases cause an average of 20-30% global potential loss of crop production in every year. So, crop protection is required to reduce these losses. This chapter explores CPS concept to improve crop production to protect the crop from wild animals using machine learning and cyber physical systems. The smart agriculture process under CPS includes crop suggestion, irrigation and fertilization automation, crop protection, plant monitoring, and harvesting.

DOI: 10.4018/978-1-7998-9308-0.ch009

INTRODUCTION

In this digital era, embedding the biotechnology, informational technology and physical space has directed to the 4th revolution in industry i.e. industry 4.0. These revolution in industry has change the life style of human being. The main feature of revolution is transition from semi-adapted fabrication to mass, fully-adapted manufacturing. The emerging technologies for such revolution are embedded system, Internet of Things (IoT), Artificial Intelligence and Machine Learning and many cloud services with next generation internet technology. In basic level of the production line, actuators, sensors devices armed with wired or wireless communication networks are combined and convert the designing of embedded system in to CPS. The major processing units used to monitor and control the CPS in physical space.

The crop protection method are presented in terms of (i) brief introduction new resolution in industry 4.0 and cyber physical system (ii) Smart Agriculture process (iii) prototype designing for crop protection using Machine learning and (iv) pest identification using different sensor techniques.

This chapter explore the brief introduction to new resolution in industry 4.0 and application of cyber physical systems in technology. In order to introduces Cyber Physical system applications in Smart Agriculture, definitions and characteristics of Cyber Physical System (CPS) are explained and define with model architecture for system. In CPS, mostly embedded system and computer network control over all processing environment to protect the crop production in real time. Implementing this type of CPS system, requires the knowledge of network, software, embedded system and physical process. Advance Research and applications are outlined to highlight the latest advancement in the field.

Lastly the crop production will improve by applying the right amount of resources in the accurate period at the exact location.

In this section the brief introduction of industry 4.0 and cyber physical system are presented.

Industry 4.0

The term industrial revolution is define as the process of changing from handcraft to machine manufacturing. The new industrial revolution is called Industry 4.0. In industry 4.0 the automation and information exchange in manufacturing industries using emerging trends such as Cyber Physical System (CPS) (Gil et all., 2019), smart agriculture (Tyagi, Sumarga Kumar Sah, et al.2020), Internet of Things (Lakhwani, Kamlesh, et al., 2020), Machine Learning (Hiran, Kamal Kant, et al.2021), Cloud Computing, Artificial Intelligence, Block chain technology and many more.

When we talk about the first industrial revolution, it used the steam engine power and mechanical installation. This was followed by the electricity for mass manufacturing and assembly line in second categories industrial insurrection. Third time industrial revolution lead by the electronic chip and information technology. Now the Industry 4.0 is associated with CPS.

Industry 4.0 introduces new principles for manufacture industries including:

- Virtualization of assembling methods by connecting sensor generated signal with virtual plant and recreation models.
- Expanded interoperability between assembling through expanded availability.
- Distributed and smart decision-making plan.
- Real-time data collection.

Cyber-Physical Systems

Cyber-Physical system integrated two word "Cyber" and "Physical", the term cyber is used to describe a person or thing as part of the computer and Physical refers to the physical devices. So the Cyber Physical Devices combine cyber capabilities with physical capabilities.

Helen Gill, first introduce the word Cyber-Physical Systems (CPS) in 2006, at US (National Science Foundation). The word CPS are older and related with embedded system design. The Designing the computerized control algorithms is more challenging due to their tight coupling behavior with physical system and need to work properly in real time system. CPS also related with latest advance technology like Industry 4.0, IoT, Wireless Sensor Network (WSN) Automation, and the cloud computing (Hiran, K. K., et al., 2019). The autonomous automobile system, health monitoring system, smart agriculture system, robotics manufacturing etc. are the example of CPS (Feeney et al., 2017).

Figure 1. Cyber Physical System Communication Model

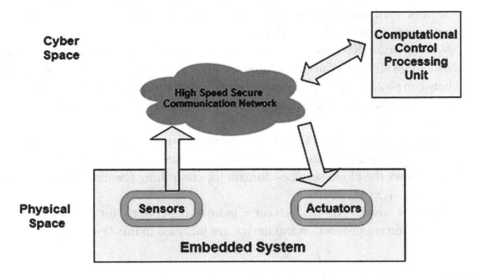

Figure 1 details a block diagram of basic communication between cyber space and physical space in cyber-physical system (Ghobakhloo, 2018). Sensors converted the physical parameter to an electrical signal and this signals transferred to actuator that convert an electrical signal to a physical output. The transformation of information between sensor and actuators is done by the high speed secure internet.

GENERAL REFERENCE ARCHITECTURE MODEL

In this section the architecture prototypical model for Industry 4.0 and cyber-physical system are presented. This architecture model can be used to develop strategy plan and valuation of any other organizational strategies for manufacturing process.

Industry 4.0 Architectures

B. Chen and J. Wan introduces a layered global architecture for industry 4.0, presented in figure 2. The Industrial 4.0 architecture used a mixed wired/wireless communication technologies. The layered architecture composed of four layers as describe as follows (Schweichhart et all., 2016):

1. *Physical resource layer:* This is the bottom layer that include all the physical devices used for industry like robotic arms, automatic vehicles, sensors, unmanned aerial vehicle (UAV) etc.
2. *Network layer:* Network layer is worked above the physical resources layer and it includes all types of networking devices that used for the transfer information between physical resource layer and cloud application layer. These networking devices include the high speed internet i.e. 5G technology (Ordonez-Lucena et al., 2019).
3. *Cloud application layer:* Cloud application layer used to improve its above layer i.e. the terminal layer using data mining and analysis technology. This layer also shows the cloud services domain for controlling the data base services (Yeboah, T.,et al., 2015).
4. *Terminal layer:* All the advance industrial services for improving the manufacturing production and design are included in this layer.

Figure 2. Layered Architecture of Industry 4.0

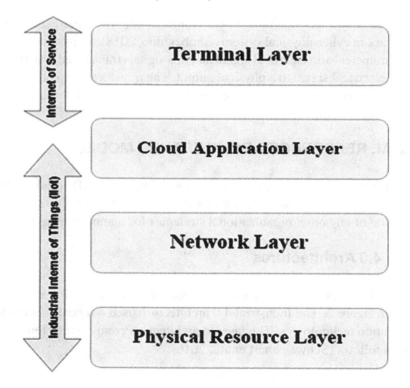

Cyber-Physical System Architecture

Al-Ali introduces a layered architecture for the cyber physical system. This architecture be made up of 5 layers namely, physical layer, network layer, data storage layer, process - analytic layer and last application layers.

1. Physical layer: Physical layer consists all the physical system component including sensors, actuators, System on Chip (SOC), tracking devices (GPS and RFID) and microcontroller computing elements. Sensors capture all the real date and send to the cloud service for further processing.
2. Network layer: The Network Layer consists all the networking devices and protocol for communication with cloud services including protocols such as Wireless Fidelity (IEEE 802.11), Worldwide Interoperability for Microwave Access (IEEE 802.16), General Packet Radio Service and 5G technology. These protocol are differentiate according to their properties according to scalability, bandwidth, speed, reliability, latency and security. Cyber physical system used these protocol in many applications such as hydropower plant monitoring system, Health monitoring system, smart agriculture, smart cities, driverless car, and wind power plant.
3. Data storage layer: The physical layer collect lot of data from the physical objects and this data may be stored in a cloud domain of CPS. Data Storage layer consists the data management services in cloud domain such as Hadoop and the replica of stored data are distributed in different slave machines that are manage by replica management techniques.
4. Processing and Analytic Layer: In this fourth layer different simulation model use processing on stored information with the help of dimensional modeling algorithms. Machine learning approaches for supervised and unsupervised learning including classification, clustering, and regression models are implemented to predict the final output value (Mahrishi, Mehul, et al.,2020).
5. Application layer: Application layer consists of all the consumers level interface used in smart agriculture, green building, Intelligent Transportation Systems, health monitoring and robotics field.

CHARACTERISTICS OF CYBER PHYSICAL SYSTEM

Cyber-physical system have several characteristics for its quick decision making process for empower the manufacturing techniques to increase flexibility and efficiency. Cyber-physical systems should likewise be synchronized with the outer world to share data and trigger activities. Different characteristics of CPS are listed in following Table 1.

Table 1. Cyber Physical System Characteristics

S. No.	Characteristics	Description
1	Complexity	CPSs are complex because all the used elements are different in nature
2	Interoperability	Interoperability allows CPSs to interchange intelligible data.
3	Networking Capability	CPSs should to be made out of interconnected groups of handling components and physical components in enormous scope wired and remote organizations through an assortment of sensors and actuators, targeting developing insight across various fields.
4	Service orientation	CPSs used service oriented model to provide digital services.
5	Modularity	CPSs components may be separated and recombined for achieving the modularity so that CPS to be flexibly as per consumer requirement.
6	Autonomy	CPSs Autonomy is the capacity of individually learn and adjust to the system environment.
7	decentralization	It is the transfer of control command and decision rule in CPS so that it work as independent entity.
8	Integration	CPSs integrated all the new advance technologies so that the design process is faster and accurate.
9	Virtualization	Virtualization in manufacturing consists a copy of actual physical manufacturing process application.
10	real-time capability	CPSs have capabilities to work in a real time environment with sophisticated performance in good predictable manners.
11	Computational capability	CPSs have various numerical computation capability and provide robust accuracy for real-world physical computation.
12	Intelligence	CPSs are able to incorporate intelligent functionalities for fault tolerance, sensing behavior identification and decision making capabilities.

LATEST ADVANCEMENT APPLICATION OF CYBER PHYSICAL SYSTEMS

In this section the latest advancement application of CPS are presented.

Green Buildings

A physical building that eliminates negative influences, and can create positive impacts, on our climate and natural environment are considered as a Green Building. CPS play a vigorous protagonist in the arena of green building infrastructure. It expands the construction process and save time of human efforts. CPS major focuses on the environment parameter such as humidity, temperature, water level, light etc, for constructing a green building. The environmental data collected by various sensors that sense real-time hotness, moisture, and activate actuators is implanted within the construction to sense environmental variations. Overall, the functionality enhances vigor effectiveness and reduces energy feeding and emissions of conservatory gases.

Medical CPS

Medical cyber-physical systems (MCPS) are the network of different medical care devices for critical healthcare management. To achieve quality in large hospital MCPS are used. MCPS contains WSN to collect the diagnostic data, and for health monitoring and drug administration of patient's.

CPS in medical field or MCPS used in many health industries such as hospital, pharma industries, diagnosis centers, patient live assistant system etc. The complexity of MCPS are depends on the particular used application for health monitoring environment. CPS architecture required large number of data to maintain the health of patient such as patient diseases history, historic data, and categories of diseases etc (Kritzinger et al., 2018).

Smart Grid Structure

The simple word 'grid' represent an electric grid, transmission lines network, power substations, transformers and other electricity supplier device. A smart grid structure is an electric system which will depend on data acquisition method. Smart grid contains advance part of cyber physical system. Electrical grid controls will be part of the Smart Grid, along with automation technology and a cyber-physical system that can respond digitally to quickly changing energy demand (Al-Ali, et al., 2018).

Remote Humanoid –Robots

Humanoid Robots are used to help human being in many field such as Entertainment, Education, Healthcare, manufacturing, agriculture etc. The present scenario nevertheless calls for human involvement in self-reliant environment in order to complete tasks which might be higher accomplished with human-in-the-loop. Humans, machines, and software program structures are required to have interaction and apprehend each other which will paintings together in an effective and sturdy way (Kim et al., 2021).

Intelligent Transportation Systems (ITS)

ITS not only for controlling the road traffic but also provide the safety mechanism for road accident and productive infrastructure utilization. An intelligent transportation system (ITS) is an advance technology in transportation area that increase the quality of transportation management and monitor the movement of all vehicle using Global Positioning System (GPS) system. Apart from smart traffic monitoring, the intelligent transportation system is also use in serval area such as Real-time parking management, E-toll collection, Ambulance notification, vehicle speed tracker and alert, real time traffic light management, Collision avoidance systems etc.

Aeronautic Applications

The major and critical application of CPS in the field of aeronautic. Aeronautic presentations include the real time air traffic management, autopilot management, behavior of aircraft, system health monitoring and aircraft landing etc.

Manufacturing

In manufacturing environment, cyber physical system used to auto-nursing the manufacture process and regulate the whole manufacturing process. So that the producing procedures id stepped forward and the better facts communicate between suppliers and clients Smart production gives extraordinary perceptibility controls at the supply chain, resulting in improved goods traceability and security The significance of IoT and CPS on the manufacturing industry is rapidly growing. Sensors are used to be expecting device put on and analyze burdens. The analytics reduces the renovation fee and growths procedure overall enactment (Grassi et al., 2020).

SECURITY ISSUES OF CYBER PHYSICAL SYSTEM

In digital transformation of industries revolution, a major challenge is security which is face by the cyber physical system and the most important element in this digital era is the modern cyber space. CPS security system need to balance the three characteristics named confidentiality, availability and integrity. The primary goal of confidentiality is to protect data by preventing information from being improperly disclosed. Availability is the contention that an authentic system is accessible by an authorized computer user at whatever time. Integrity is the protection of system data from unauthorized modification of information (Bakirtzis et al., 2021).

Cyber security can be achieved by a sound structured of information and specialized experts in the field of cyber physical system (Gupta et al., 2020). In this unit we describe vulnerabilities of cyber physical system in Industry4.0 by classifying attacks according to following two target categories:

1. Vulnerabilities in Physical Devices and
2. Vulnerabilities in intermediate Network.

Vulnerabilities in Physical Devices

Cyber-physical system integrated with serval physical devices with computation and communication. Physical devices includes robotic arm, wireless sensors, robotic vehicles, automated machine, monitoring devices etc. Several types of internal or external attacks could be affected these physical devices such as:

1. Physical attack: In a **physical attack,** an unauthorized employer gain physical access in physical devices to attack its structure in order to steal information or destroy all infrastructure.
2. Data injection attack: A malicious program is injected in computer network by an attacker which corrupt all the device information or send the confidential information to attacker through network. This type of attacks are major problem of security in cyber physical system.
3. Side-Channel attacks (SCAs): Side-Channel attacks steal the confidential information from integrated circuit (ICs) or devices through analyzing the physical parameter such as processing time, apply voltage, current flow etc.
4. Time Delay attack: A Time Delay separate the two event occurrence in mechanical and electronic devices. The Time Delay attack is identification of vulnerabilities in the physical devices by analyzing how long it takes the system to respond to different inputs.
5. Application layer attacks: Application layer attacks also called DDoS attack (Distributed Denial of Service Attacks). This type of attack are specially designed to break the services of application so a particular device application not being able to deliver it services to the user.
6. Zero-day attacks: Zero day attack is a software related vulnerabilities that recently exposed by an attacker to exploits a fault in system which was unknown by developer. The name is derived from the number of days that a software developer has been aware of the issue.

Vulnerabilities in Intermediate Network

Cyber-physical system also integrate the communication network capabilities to connect the cyberspace with physical space. The vulnerabilities also affected the manufacturing industries (You et al., 2020). It also increase the vulnerabilities in communication network. Generally network attacks are classify in to two categories: Active attacks and passive attack. In Active attack, the attacker modify, encrypt or damaging the information in communication channel. In passive attack, the attacker only access the unauthorized network and steal the personal information. The attacker not change the original information flow in network in passive attack.

Types of Network Attacks:

1.   Man-in-the-Middle Attacks: As a name, this type of attacks are access information between any communication networks to access the private keys. A person or attacker who stands in between two communicating parties are known as man in middle. Middle attacker read, monitor or access the controls of communication and can change the flow of information between any two parties. Man in the middle attacks is hard to identify. It is a type of Active attacks in network.

2.   IP spoofing: In IP spoofing, an attacker change the source address in the Internet Protocol (IP) header packet to make a user think the packet is from a trusted source. Using IP spoofing, thousands of computers send message using same source IP address to a large numbers of destination. IP Spoofing is normally a type of Denial-of-Service (DoS) attacks, which increase the network traffic. IP spoofing also known as Packet modification attacks.

3.   Eavesdropping: Generally Eavesdropping is the act of listening to the personal conversation of others without their consent. In eavesdropping attacks, the attacker monito the network packets and steal the personal information in weak network.

4.   Jamming attack: In Jamming attack, attacker send the several radio signals in wireless network to disrupt the communication by minimizing the Signal-to-Inference-plus-Noise ratio. Wireless signal jamming devices are most often used to interfere with wireless networks, a type of denial of service (DoS) attack.

5.   Collision attack: In Collision attack, the attacker change the checksum bit in sent packet and retransmitted this modify packet to receiver.

6.   Wormhole attack: In wormhole attack, two attackers locate strategically in the network and keep track the network and record wireless information.

7.   Sinkhole attack: In Sinkhole attack, a compromised node attract the network traffic by sending it fake information to its neighbors.

CONCLUSION

It is clearly visible that the growth of Industry 4.0 is influencing by the Cyber–physical systems (CPS) in terms of automation and manufacturing. Through a brief introduction on Industry 4.0 and cyber physical system with machine learning, this chapter discussed the general architectural model for different layers in physical and cyber space with complexity, interoperability and networking capabilities of CPS. To be more specific, the chapter focused on security related issues and application of cyber physical system. The impact of cyber physical system on Industry 4.0 was explored, respectively. Now it's time to focus on the next industrial revolution i.e. Industry 5.0 in order to achieve more security in cyber physical to improve productivity and efficiency in manufacturing process.

ACKNOWLEDGMENT

We declare that the work described in this chapter is original and no part of it has been copied or taken from other sources without necessary permissions and this work is not published anywhere in any form of publication (in any language) and not presently under consideration for publication/ presentation anywhere in form of publication. This research received no specific grant from any funding agency in the public, commercial, or not-for-profit sectors.

REFERENCES

Aheleroff, S., Xu, X., Zhong, R. Y., & Lu, Y. (2021). Digital twin as a service (DTaaS) in industry 4.0: An architecture reference model. *Advanced Engineering Informatics*, *47*, 101225. doi:10.1016/j.aei.2020.101225

Al-Ali, A. R., Gupta, R., & Nabulsi, A. A. (2018, April). Cyber physical systems role in manufacturing technologies. In AIP Conference Proceedings (Vol. 1957, No. 1, p. 050007). AIP Publishing LLC. doi:10.1063/1.5034337

Bakirtzis, G., Sherburne, T., Adams, S., Horowitz, B. M., Beling, P. A., & Fleming, C. H. (2021). An ontological metamodel for cyber-physical system safety, security, and resilience coengineering. *Software & Systems Modeling*, 1–25. doi:10.100710270-021-00892-z

Feeney, A. B., Frechette, S., & Srinivasan, V. (2017). Cyber-physical systems engineering for manufacturing. In *Industrial internet of things* (pp. 81–110). Springer. doi:10.1007/978-3-319-42559-7_4

Ghobakhloo, M. (2018). The future of manufacturing industry: A strategic roadmap toward Industry 4.0. *Journal of Manufacturing Technology Management*, *29*(6), 910–936. doi:10.1108/JMTM-02-2018-0057

Gil, S., Zapata-Madrigal, G. D., & García-Sierra, R. (2019, October). Electrical Internet of Things-EIoT: A Platform for the Data Management in Electrical Systems. In *Proceedings of the Future Technologies Conference* (pp. 49-65). Springer.

Grassi, A., Guizzi, G., Santillo, L. C., & Vespoli, S. (2020). A semi-heterarchical production control architecture for industry 4.0-based manufacturing systems. *Manufacturing Letters*, *24*, 43–46. doi:10.1016/j.mfglet.2020.03.007

Gupta, N., Tiwari, A., Bukkapatnam, S. T., & Karri, R. (2020). Additive manufacturing cyber-physical system: Supply chain cybersecurity and risks. *IEEE Access: Practical Innovations, Open Solutions*, *8*, 47322–47333. doi:10.1109/ACCESS.2020.2978815

Hiran, K. K., Doshi, R., Fagbola, T., & Mahrishi, M. (2019). *Cloud computing: Master the concepts, architecture and applications with real-world examples and case studies*. BPB Publications.

Hiran, K. K., Jain, R. K., Lakhwani, K., & Doshi, R. (2021). *Machine Learning: Master Supervised and Unsupervised Learning Algorithms with Real Examples (English Edition)*. BPB Publications.

Kim, J., & Lee, J. Y. (2021). Server-Edge dualized closed-loop data analytics system for cyber-physical system application. *Robotics and Computer-integrated Manufacturing*, *67*, 102040. doi:10.1016/j.rcim.2020.102040

Kritzinger, W., Karner, M., Traar, G., Henjes, J., & Sihn, W. (2018). Digital twin in manufacturing: a categorical literature review and classification. *16th IFAC Symposium on Information Control Problems in Manufacturing INCOM*. 10.1016/j.ifacol.2018.08.474

Lakhwani, K., Gianey, H. K., Wireko, J. K., & Hiran, K. K. (2020). *Internet of Things (IoT): Principles, paradigms and applications of IoT*. BPB Publications.

Li, N., Liu, K., Chen, Z., & Jiao, W. (2020). Environmental-Perception Modeling and Reference Architecture for Cyber Physical Systems. *IEEE Access: Practical Innovations, Open Solutions*, *8*, 200322–200337. doi:10.1109/ACCESS.2020.3034390

Mahrishi, M., Hiran, K. K., Meena, G., & Sharma, P. (Eds.). (2020). *Machine Learning and Deep Learning in Real-Time Applications*. IGI Global. doi:10.4018/978-1-7998-3095-5

Ordonez-Lucena, J., Chavarria, J. F., Contreras, L. M., & Pastor, A. (2019, October). The use of 5G Non-Public Networks to support Industry 4.0 scenarios. In *2019 IEEE Conference on Standards for Communications and Networking (CSCN)* (pp. 1-7). IEEE. 10.1109/CSCN.2019.8931325

Schweichhart, K. (2016). *Reference architectural model industrie 4.0 (rami 4.0). An Introduction*. Available online: https://www. plattform-i40. deI

Tyagi, S. K. S., Mukherjee, A., Pokhrel, S. R., & Hiran, K. K. (2020). An intelligent and optimal resource allocation approach in sensor networks for smart agri-IoT. *IEEE Sensors Journal*.

Yeboah, T., Odabi, I., & Hiran, K. K. (2015, April). An integration of round robin with shortest job first algorithm for cloud computing environment. In International Conference On Management. *Tongxin Jishu, 3*(1), 1–5.

You, Z., & Feng, L. (2020). Integration of industry 4.0 related technologies in construction industry: A framework of cyber-physical system. *IEEE Access: Practical Innovations, Open Solutions, 8*, 122908–122922. doi:10.1109/ACCESS.2020.3007206

Chapter 10
Arrhythmia Classification Using Deep Learning Architecture

Kuldeep Singh Chouhan
Engineering College Ajmer, India

Jyoti Gajrani
Engineering College Ajmer, India

Bhavna Sharma
JECRC University, Jaipur, India

Satya Narayan Tazi
Engineering College Ajmer, India

ABSTRACT

As cardiovascular diseases (CVDs) are a serious concern to modern medical science to diagnose at an early stage, it is vital to build a classification model that can effectively reduce mortality rates by treating millions of people in a timely manner. An electrocardiogram (ECG) is a specialized instrument that measures the heart's physiological responses. To accurately diagnose a patient's acute and chronic heart problems, an in-depth examination of these ECG signals is essential. The proposed model consists of a convolutional neural network having three convolutional, two pooling, and two dense layers. The proposed model is trained and evaluated on the MIT-BIH arrhythmia and PTB diagnostic datasets. The classification accuracy is 99.16%, which is higher than state-of-the-art studies on similar arrhythmias. Recall, precision, and F1 score of the proposed model are 96.53%, 95.15%, and 99.17%, respectively. The proposed model can aid doctors explicitly for the detection and classification of arrhythmias.

DOI: 10.4018/978-1-7998-9308-0.ch010

INTRODUCTION

Cardiovascular diseases (CVDs) are a severe menace to people. They are also the cause of rising global mortality rates. Among all fatalities worldwide, CVDs is the reason of 31% fatalities (Sahoo et al., 2019). The main causes of CVDs include hypertension, unhealthy diet, smoking, unhealthy lifestyle.

According to World Health Organization (WHO) statistics, heart attacks claimed the lives of 17.9 million people in 2019, with the majority of these deaths occur in countries with a low to average income (Gupta, 2016; "CVDs," 2021). The death rate from cardiovascular diseases is approximately 0.27% in India (Prabhakaran et al., 2016). It is suggested that adopting a healthy lifestyle can prevent 90% of CVDs (McGill et al., 2008).

This paper proposes a model based on deep learning to classify different arrhythmias on the electrocardiogram (ECG). The organization of paper is as follows. Section 2 describes the background of the field. Section 3 presents the state-of-the-art. Proposed approach including classification, model configuration, and dataset used is described in Section 4. Section 5 describes the experimental results. Finally, Section 6 shows the findings of our proposed model.

BACKGROUND

This section describes, heart, ECG signal, various cardiovascular abnormalities, and a comparison of various approaches used for the classification of arrhythmias.

Heart, a muscular organ, is responsible for the supply of the blood to all other human body parts (Aje, 2009). As seen in Fig. 1, a blockage in a coronary artery, which feeds blood and oxygen to the heart, causes a heart attack, which is a major health risk.

Figure 1. Heart attack or Myocardial ischemia
(Sahoo et al., 2019).

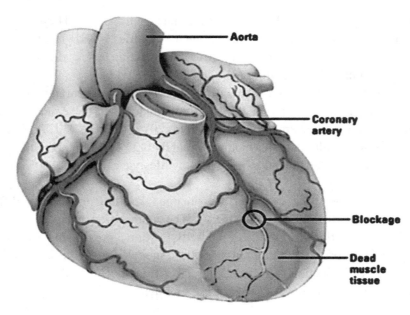

Figure 2. The standard Electrocardiogram (ECG) signal.

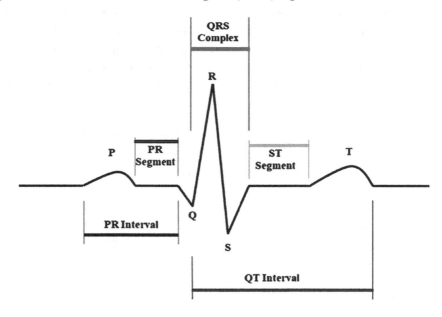

The characteristics of a normal ECG signal are depicted in Figure 2. Where the P-wave and QRS-complex represent depolarization/contraction of the atrium and ventricles, respectively, while the T-wave represents ventricle repolarization. The ECG signal is derived from an electrocardiogram (ECG), a device that records the heart's physiological activities for a time interval. ECG data is used to diagnose various cardiovascular abnormalities, such as premature atrial contractions (PAC), myocardial infarction (MI), atrial fibrillation (AF), premature ventricular contractions (PVC), congestive heart failure (CHF) and supraventricular tachycardias (SVT). A rapid development of portable devices such as Holter monitor (Nikolic et al., 1982), Apple watch etc., are developed to detect the ECG signal in recent years, which resulted in a big datasets for the researchers and human cardiologists to analyse the ECG data more accurately. As a consequence, automatically and reliably analysing ECG data has become a popular research topic. ECG data can also be used in innovative ways such as sleep staging and biometric human identification. To manage the large datasets, we need an efficient approach for the analysis. As a result, the datasets are subjected to machine and deep learning algorithms (Hiran, K. K.et al.2021). Figures 3 and 4 shows the basics of machine and deep learning approaches respectively (Xia et al., 2018). Traditional machine learning approach requires experts (human cardiologists) to extract characteristics from raw data and then generate final outputs using machine learning models or decision rules, whereas deep learning uses deep neural networks and extracts features automatically (Mahrishi, M.,et al.,2020). Here, expert features are a) Statistical features (heart rate variability, density histograms, sample entropy etc.), b) Frequency-domain features (Romero et al., 2001), c) Medical features (P, Q, R, S, and T wave parameters).

Figure 3. Traditional machine learning.

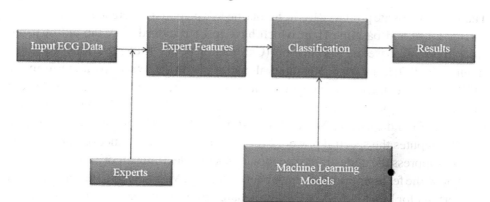

Figure 4. Deep learning Approach.

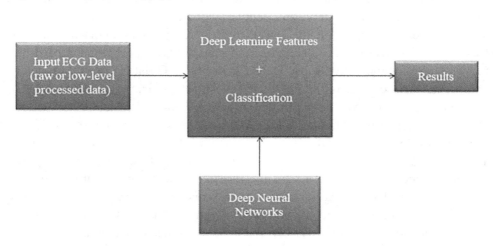

Deep learning features of ECG data have been shown to yield more information than expert features in several studies (Huang et al., 2019). On a number of ECG analysis tasks such as sleep staging (Wei et al., 2019) and disease diagnosis (Li et al., 2019). Traditional image identification methods require stretching image matrices to one-dimensional vectors, which leads to loss of adjoining data in images and omission of some crucial features. Our proposed approach has the inclusion of CNN architecture.

RELATED WORK

The ECG signals are produced by the human heart's potential difference. It additionally carries noise and baseline float which have to be removed with the aid of using smoothing and baseline elimination (Caroubalos et al., 1988). Various functions (inclusive of QRS interval, RR interval, and Beats in step with minutes) from the ECG sign are extracted to categorise diverse arrhythmias with the aid of feature extraction strategies inclusive of Principal Component Analysis (PCA) (Caroubalos et al., 1988) and Discrete Wavelet Transform (DWT) (Caroubalos et al., 1988). DWT computes the spectral power of the sign, and generates functions and PCA is used to suppress the undesirable functions. Machine learning algorithms are used to categorise the features after they have been extracted. Various classifiers inclusive of Support Vector Machine (SVM), Least Square Support Vector Machine (LS-SVM), Convolutional Neural Network (CNN), Artificial Neural Network (ANN), Recurring Neural Network (RNN) have been applied for the classification.

(Acharya et al., 2017) uses deep learning technique for automatically detection of five distinct groups of heartbeats in ECG signals. Authors used 1D ECG signals as input and designed a 9 layer 1-dimentional CNN model. Proposed approach achieved a classification accuracy of 94.03% with 109,449 beats. Model's generalisation capacity improves as they perform filtration on input signals to filter-out high-frequency noise and then used the model to identify and classify noisy and non-noisy ECG signals.

(Abayaratne et al., 2019) proposed two methods where the first method is a rule based abnormality identification which uses Hamilton-Tompkins algorithm for the calculation of R peaks which achieves 97.55% accuracy with 705,000 beats. Second method uses RNN and LSTM models and classifies 15 classes of cardiac arrhythmias with 94.7% average accuracy with 96,265 beats.

(Kommireddy et al., 2020) proposed a four layered hybrid of CNN with LSTM associated ANN with ReLU and Sigmoid operate with inside the final layer and bought accuracy of 98.64% on MIT-BIH cardiac arrhythmia dataset with 107,620 beats. (Hasan et al., 2020) provides an methodology with a CNN of sixteen layers with SoftMax activation function withinside the very last layer that classify five arrhythmia sorts (N, F, V, Q, S) of MIT-BIH arrhythmia dataset with 98.28% mean accuracy. (Izci et al., 2019) proposed a CNN version of 5 layers with ReLU in convolution layers and Softmax within the final layer that performed associate accuracy of 97.42% on comparable dataset with 27,789 beats. (Ullah et al., 2020) proposed a CNN version of 10 layers which classify eight varieties of cardiac arrhythmias of MIT-BIH arrhythmia dataset with an accuracy of 99.11%. (Oh et al., 2018) proposed a mix of CNN and LSTM layers with input as one-dimensional ECG signals. By inserting the waveforms within the processing phase, ECG data was separated into several ECG data segments of varying durations, and each data segment was likewise extended to the same length. The designed architecture classifies ECG signals into 5 categories: N (Normal), LBBB (Left Bundle Branch Block), VPC (Ventricular Premature Contraction), RBBB (Right Bundle Branch Block), and APC (Atrial Premature Contraction). The authors used 16,499 ECG beats from MIT-BIH dataset and obtained 98.10% accuracy.

(Mondéjar-Guerra et al., 2019) developed a method that incorporates a number of different types of Support Vector Machines (SVMs). The approach relies on R-R intervals, wavelets, and the HOS (Higher Order Statistics) of the ECG signal. Each sort of feature has its own SVM model (Hiran, K. K.,et.al.). Using the MIT-BIH arrhythmia dataset with 49,691 beats in total, the approach categorised four categories of normal and abnormal beats (N, F, V, and S) with 94.50% accuracy.

(Subramanian et al., 2020) proposed a SVM classifier based model to classify ECG beats with an accuracy of 91% and F1 score of 90.65% with training data and testing data for of 15 and 23 beats respectively. Two types of comparison, beat to beat and beat to bat is performed which depends on QRS variation and P axis respectively.

PROPOSED APPROACH

This section comprises Section 4.1 which describes the data transformation process from raw ECG signals. Section 4.2 describes the necessary modification on the input data to increase the model performance. Section 4.3 describes the architecture of the proposed model. Section 4.4 describes activation function used in proposed model. Section 4.5 describes a technique to optimize the model. Section 4.6 describes a technique to overcome over-fitting of the model which yield improved accuracy as compared to state of the art. Finally, Section 4.7 describes a detailed overview of the datasets used by our model.

In broad, the proposed model consists of following four steps as depicted in Figure 5.

Step 1: Data transformation step in which ECG beats are extracted from raw ECG signals.

Step 2: After the Data Transformation step, the signals are further pre-processed.

Step 3: After Pre-processing step, the data is sent as input to the Proposed Model (CNN in this research work). Here, training and validation set are provided to the fit the model according to the input data and finally, our model is trained on the given input data and is ready to be tested.

Step 4: Finally, the developed model is used for the classification of six types of arrhythmias, and a fresh set of dataset i.e., Test Set is provided to the model for the classification process.

Figure 5. Classification procedure of an ECG signal by proposed model.

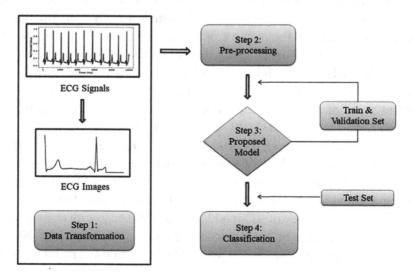

Data Transformation

Data transformation is the first step in which raw ECG signals are being transformed to ECG images to extract relevant features as shown below in Figure 6. It improves the data by suppressing undesired distortions and enhancing some aspects that are required for the model to train accurately. The input ECG image dataset taken from the kaggle open-source dataset, which was converted by (Kachuee et al., 2018) from raw ECG signals to two-dimensional RGB images of size 432x288 pixels. Some research works used time series data as input to the model; however, the proposed approach uses two-dimensional images as input as machine learning approaches are outperformed by deep learning methods. Machine learning approaches are designed to work with one-dimensional vector data, which requires stretching the image matrices to one-dimensional vectors, which leads to loss of adjoining information in images and the omission of some crucial features. Therefore, instead of using one-dimensional signals, we use images for better performance with convolutional neural networks. It can be used with real-time arrhythmia classification, which can aid doctors (Ying, 2019), as well as smart devices and medical devices to automatically classify arrhythmias by providing image data as input to the device.

Figure 6. ECG beat extraction from an ECG signal.

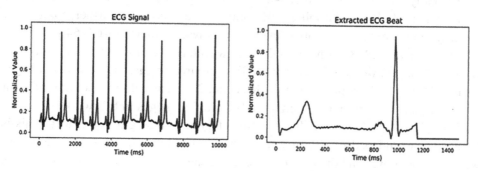

Following steps are performed for the extraction of ECG beats from ECG signal:

1. A split of 10s is performed on continuous ECG signals.
2. Amplitude of ECG signal is normalized to zero and one range.
3. All local maximums are determined through zero-crossings of first derivative.
4. Using a 0.9 criterion on the normalised local maximum value, set of ECG R-peak values are calculated.

5. The nominal heartbeat of the relevant window is calculated using the median values of R-R intervals (T).
6. A signal component with a length of 1.2T for each R-peak is selected.
7. According to a preset fixed length, the corresponding selected part padded with zeroes.

The proposed beat extraction approach is easy and efficient in performing the extraction of R-R intervals from ECG signals with various morphologies. Furthermore, all of the retrieved beats have the same length, which is necessary for them to be utilised as inputs to the following processing steps.

Pre-Processing

The model's performance has to be improved, thus ECG images were further pre-processed in the proposed approach. Using *ImageDataGenerator* library ("IDP," 2021), pre-processing is performed by implementing firstly, rescale = 1./255. Rescale is a multiplier that will be applied to the data before any additional processing. Since the original images include RGB coefficients in the range of 0-255, but such values would be too high for the model to handle (given a normal learning rate), we scale using a 1./255 factor to target values between 0 and 1.

Secondly, shear-range = 0.2, which shears the image by 20% and we added zoom-range = 0.2, which implies 20% zoom-in and zoom-out. Further, color mode = "grayscale" converts the input image to a grayscale image of 64x64 pixels. As (Kachuee et al., 2018) transformed ECG waveforms from raw ECG signals to coloured images, we have to convert RGB (coloured images) to grayscale images for the CNN model's input (Hiran, K. K., et al., 2013), as colour is not a significant feature in distinguishing arrhythmia kinds from the images in this work.

ImageDataGenerator also has the advantage of utilising less memory. This is because we would load all of the images at once if we didn't utilise this class. However, when we use it, we load the images in batches, saving a significant memory space. When trained on new, slightly changed images, the model becomes more resilient.

Model Architecture

Deep learning (Deng et al., 2013) is a relatively recent method in the domain of artificial intelligence and pattern identification that has quickly proved popular. A novel approach for identifying six different forms of ECG signal arrhythmias is created in this work. Our proposed CNN model comprises of three convolutional, two pooling, a flatten and two dense layers as shown in Figure 7, to automatically classify the arrhythmia into six different categories using the MITBIH and PTB arrhythmia diagnostic records. The ECG dataset used includes labels that identify the type of arrhythmia. Expert cardiologists are the ones who assign these labels. The weights of the model are statistically initialised with kernel initializers. This will create and distribute the weights, and it may be used as a starting point. The extracted beats are utilised as inputs, as indicated in Section 4.1. All convolution layers use 2-D convolution and contain 32 kernels of size 3 with kernel initializer = 'he-uniform,' where he-uniform is a variance scaling initializer, which selects values from the range of [-limit, limit], where limit equals sqrt(6/fan-in), and fan-in is the weight tensor's input unit count. As we are working with ReLU activation function he-uniform performs better with ReLU activation function as compared to other kernel-initializers i.e., Glorot/Xavier initializer etc. ("LWI," 2021). All the three convolution layers and the second last fully-connected layer uses ReLU activation function. ReLU is used in our model as it is more computationally efficient as compared to sigmoid and tanh functions because it only activates a limited number of neurons and sets all negative values to zero.

Figure 7. Architecture of proposed approach.

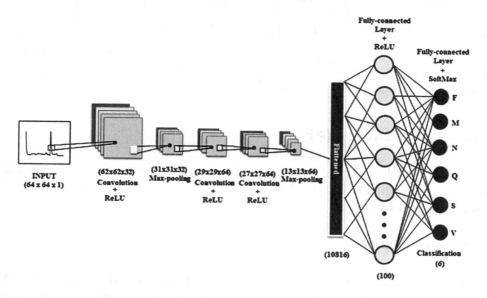

In addition, we employ max pooling layers of size 2 and stride 2. Finally, the last convolution layer is used to represent the input beats. For classification, this representation is fed into a network of two fully linked layers with 100 and 6 neurons on each layer. As it performs multi-class classification, the final fully linked layer employs the Softmax activation function.

By adjusting the optimizer and learning rate, the model's training phases may be enhanced. Therefore, We used a 0.01 learning rate and optimised with SGD (Stochastic Gradient Optimizer) with momentum value equal to 0.9. Further, Early Stopping technique used to prevent over-fitting of the model.

An in-depth look of proposed architecture is given in Table 1.

Table 1. An in-depth look of the proposed approach.

Layer		Type	Activation Function	Output Shapes	No. of Filters	Parameters
0		Input	-	64x64x1	-	-
1		Convolution (Conv2D)	ReLU	62x62x32	32	320
2		Max-pooling	-	31x31x32	-	0
3		Convolution (Conv2D)	ReLU	29x29x64	64	18496
4		Convolution (Conv2D)	ReLU	27x27x64	64	36928
5		Max-pooling	-	13x13x64	-	0
6		Flatten	-	10816	-	0
7		Fully-connected	ReLU	100	100	1081700
8	Fully-connected		Softmax	6	6	606

Activation Function (AF)

Our model employs the ReLU activation function in three convolution layers and one fully-connected layer and Softmax function in the final fully-connected layer as indicated in Section 4.3.

Softmax Function

The Softmax function has application in computing the probability distribution of a set of real numbers (Goodfellow et al., 2016). The Softmax function generates a set of values ranging from 0 to 1, with a probability total of 1. In a multi-class model, Softmax algorithm returns the probabilities of each class with highest probability value corresponds to target class. Almost all deep learning systems employ the Softmax function in their output layers. The two activation function Sigmoid and Softmax are used for binary and multivariate classification respectively.

The standard Softmax function σ: $RK^{\rightarrow}[0,1]K$ is defind by following equation:

$$\sigma\left(z\right)_i = \frac{e^{z_i}}{\sum_{j=1}^{K} e^{z_j}} \text{ for i=1, ..., K and } z = (z_1,...,z_k) \in R^K \tag{1}$$

Where z is the input vector.

Rectified Linear Unit Function

Nair and Hinton created rectified linear unit (ReLU) activation function in 2010 (Nair et al., 2010). In terms of performance and generalisation, it leads the Sigmoid and Tanh activation functions in deep learning. As it is a faster learning activation function it is the most widely utilised function. The ReLU resembles to a linear function, keeping the characteristics of linear models that make gradient-descent optimization straightforward.

$$y = f(x) = \max(0,x) \tag{2}$$

Where x represents the input to the ReLU and y is the corresponding output value.

It removes the vanishing gradient problem occurring in the previous activation function by driving the negative input value to zero. Advantage of implementing ReLU units is they results in faster calculations as they don't compute divisions or exponentials which improves overall computation performance.

The ReLU also compresses the values between zero and maximum, resulting in sparsity in the hidden units. Because of its simplicity and dependability, ReLU has been employed in several architectures.

Cost function

The cost function is used to calculate the difference between the estimated and true value of the CNN model's error (Ullah et al., 2020). The error function is minimized using an optimizer function. In neural network theory, various cost functions have been used. We employed the cross-entropy function using the equation as follows:

$$C = \frac{-1}{n}\sum_{c=1}^{N}\left[y_c * \ln\left(a_c\right) + \left(1-y_c\right)\ln\left(1-a_c\right)\right] \tag{3}$$

Where C, y, N, c, a, and n denotes the cost to be reduced, target value, total number of classes, class index, actual value, and number of training points respectively.

The findings are optimised using a gradient descent approach. In our model, we make use of SGD optimizer with 0.9 momentum and 0.01 learning rate. SGD updates the parameters (weights) of each layer using the computed gradient after passing one training sample through the neural network at a time. As a result, a single training sample is sent through the network at a time, and the loss associated with it is calculated. Following each training sample, the parameters of all the network layers are updated. As the network only processes one training sample, it is easier to memorise. It is computationally fast as only one sample is processed at a time. Equation is given by:

$$w = w - \eta \nabla Q(w) = w - \frac{\eta}{n} \sum_{i=1}^{n} \nabla Q_i(w) \tag{4}$$

Where

$$Q(w) = \frac{1}{n} \sum_{i=1}^{n} Q_i(w) \tag{5}$$

Where η is the learning rate, Q is a loss function and w is the network parameter.

In comparison to similar methods like Batch Gradient Descent and Mini Batch Gradient Descent, it can converge faster for bigger datasets since it causes more frequent parameter updates (Bottou et al., 2012).

Early Stopping (Ying, 2019)

This technique is used to prevent the "learning speed slowdown" problem. Because of noise-learning, algorithm accuracy stops increasing or worsens beyond a certain point.

As a result, the goal is to determine the precise point at which training should be discontinued. We were able to get the ideal balance of under-fitting and over-fitting in this manner. The learning process for artificial neural networks aims to identify the ideal weights and biases. Learning process and learning speed of neurons depends on values of the partial derivatives of the cost function i.e., $\frac{\partial C}{\partial w}$ and $\frac{\partial C}{\partial b}$ as described below in equation 6 and 7

respectively:

160

$$\frac{\partial C}{\partial W_j} = \frac{1}{n} \sum_x X_j \left(\sigma(z) - y \right)$$

(6)

$$\frac{1}{n} \sum_x$$

(7)

Where C is the cost, W_j is the jth weight, X_j is the jth input, b is the bias, a is output when inputs values are 1 and y is the output (Ying, 2019).

Dataset Details

ECG image signals derived from publicly accessible MIT-BIH arrhythmia (Moody & Mark, 2001) and PTB diagnostic (Kachuee et al., 2018) datasets. The MIT-BIH arrhythmia dataset has 48 records, each lasting around 30 minutes from ambulatory ECG records obtained between 1975 and 1979 on two channels. 23 records were chosen at random from a set of 4000 24-hour ambulatory ECG recordings with indoor patients accounting for 60% and outdoor patients accounting for 40%. Remaining twenty-five recordings were selected from a similar collection. The selected ECG recordings were digitised at 360 samples per second with an 11-bit resolution over a 10mV range for each channel. Two or more cardiologists independently analysed each record, providing relevant solutions to the concerns in order to provide a computer-readable result. In addition, this dataset contains approximately 110,000 explanations. The PTB Diagnostics dataset contains ECG records from 290 people, with 148 of them having been diagnosed with MI, 52 with a healthy heart, and the remaining with seven other diseases. ECG signals from 12 leads were captured at 1000Hz in each record.

The dataset contains six types of ECG signals; namely, normal beats (N), ventricular ectopic beats (V), fusion beats (F), unclassified beats (Q), supraventricular ectopic beats (S), and myocardial infarction (M).

Table 2, shows a breakdown of ECG beats.

Figure 8, shows the various ECG signals segments used in this work.

Table 2. Breakdown of six classes of beats.

Type	Number of Beats
F	803
M	10,506
N	94,635
Q	8,039
S	2,779
V	7,236
Total	1,23,998

Figure 8. ECG signals segments, namely; normal beats (N), unclassified beats (Q), fusion beats (F), ventricular ectopic beats (V), supraventricular ectopic beats (S), and myocardial infarction (M).

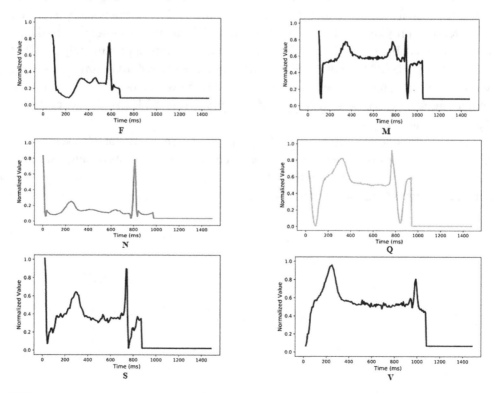

RESULTS AND ANALYSIS

The experimental approach and results of the experiment are described in this section. The experimental data for the proposed model derives from the MIT-BIH and PTB diagnostic databases, which are international standard ECG databases. It is frequently utilised for the development of cardiac arrhythmia research areas as it contains accurate and descriptive expert annotations. The experiment used 64% of the dataset for the training, 16% for validation, and 20% for testing i.e., 79357, 19842, 24799 respectively. In the final model, there were 50 epochs for training. The dataset was split into 32 batches during each epoch.

Two dimensional images were resize to 64x64 grayscale images for the input to CNN model. The proposed CNN model was implemented using Tensorflow (Abadi et al., 2016), a Python package. Hardware specifications for the execution of our models are GPU TITAN XP. Training process took a total of 31448.33 sec.

The optimization parameters of the proposed model are the number of convolution layers, pooling layers, and early stopping technique (a regularization technique to overcome over-fitting (Ying, 2019)). As the proposed model uses a large dataset, more number of convolution operations required to extract features from the training dataset by the proposed model to perform better on the test dataset. Based on the number of convolutional layers and pooling layers present in the model, we evaluated two experimental approaches and performed experimental verification. In Experiment CNN-A, we used a CNN model of five layers with one convolutional, one pooling layer with SGD optimizer having learning rate, momentum, batch size, epochs 0.01, 0.9, 32, and 30 respectively. In Experiment CNN-B, we used a CNN model of eight layers with three convolutional, two pooling layers with SGD optimizer having learning rate, momentum, batch size, epochs 0.01, 0.9, 32, and 50 respectively. The average accuracy improves from 98.04% in CNN-A to 99.16%

Figure 9. Accuracies of two training models CNN-A and CNN-B.

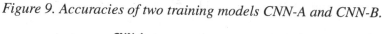

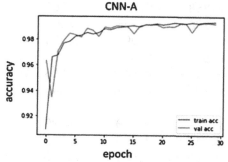
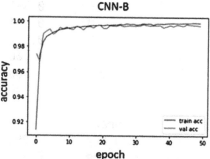

Figure 10. Loss of two training models CNN-A and CNN-B.

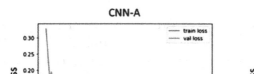

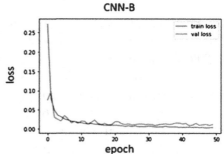

in CNN-B with more number of convolution operations, max-pooling operations, and increased epoch values from 30 to 50 respectively.

Figures 9 and 10 represents the accuracy and loss curves for training and validation for the CNN-A and CNN-B models, respectively.

To further comprehend the trained model's learning, we included a classification report and a confusion matrix for the trained model CNN-A, which explain the trained model's actual prediction on the test data in Fig. 11 and Table 3, respectively.

A low precision value in the prediction of F reflects overfitting and incorrect classification of the model. So by appending more convolutional layers and max-polling layers in CNN-B model we are able to improve the classification report and the confusion matrix as shown below in Fig. 12 and Table 5 respectively.

Classification report presents the overall performance measures such as accuracy, precision, recall, and F1 score of the proposed model as described in the following equations:

Figure 11. Classification Report of CNN-A model.

	precision	recall	f1-score	support
F	0.596	0.888	0.713	161
M	0.934	0.998	0.965	2101
N	0.994	0.996	0.995	18926
Q	1.000	0.930	0.964	1608
S	0.908	0.797	0.849	556
V	0.940	0.895	0.917	1447
accuracy			0.980	24799
macro avg	0.895	0.917	0.900	24799
weighted avg	0.982	0.980	0.981	24799

Table 3. Confusion matrix of CNN-A model.

Predicted/True	F	M	N	Q	S	V
F	143	17	0	0	0	1
M	4	2097	0	0	0	0
N	0	0	18842	0	28	56
Q	0	0	113	1495	0	0
S	19	69	0	0	443	25
V	74	61	0	0	17	1295

$$Accuracy = \frac{TP+TN}{TP+TN+FP+FN} \tag{8}$$

$$Precision = \frac{TP}{TP+FP} \tag{9}$$

$$Recall = \frac{TP}{TP+FN} \tag{10}$$

$$F1_{score} = \frac{2 * Recall * Precision}{Recall + Precision} \tag{11}$$

True positive, false positive, true negative, and false negative predictions are denoted by TP, FP, TN, and FN, respectively. TP denotes the classification of normal ECG data to normal, whereas TN denotes the classification of outlier data to abnormal categories. FP denotes the classification of abnormal ECG data to normal, whereas FN denotes for classifying normal data to abnormal categories. Further, TP and TN denotes correct classification, whereas FP and FN denotes an error in classification. The evaluation indicators from the two experiments were also compared. Table 4 compares the outcomes of the two experimental approaches. With less number of convolutional and pooling layers as compared to CNN-B, CNN-A results in overfitting and low accuracy.

As shown in Fig. 12, overall performance of all the classes i.e., F, M, N, Q, S, V improved.

Table 4. Average classification performances of CNN-A and CNN-B.

Experiment	Scheme	Accuracy	Recall	Precision	F1score
CNN-A	One Conv2D layer	98.04%	91.72%	89.54%	98.06%
CNN-B	Three Conv2D layers	99.16%	96.53%	95.15%	99.17%

Figure 12. Classification Report of CNN-B model.

```
              precision    recall  f1-score    support

         F       0.840     0.882     0.861        161
         M       0.985     1.000     0.992       2101
         N       1.000     0.994     0.997      18926
         Q       1.000     0.994     0.997       1608
         S       0.964     0.955     0.959        556
         V       0.922     0.966     0.943       1447

  accuracy                           0.992      24799
 macro avg       0.952     0.965     0.958      24799
weighted avg     0.992     0.992     0.992      24799
```

Table 5 below depicts the final CNN-B model's confusion matrix. The model performed much better on M, N, Q, and S, whereas the classification of kinds F was mediocre. This might have been produced by the waveforms' slight morphological variations throughout the learning process.

Table 5. CNN-B model's confusion matrix.

Predicted/True	F	M	N	Q	S	V
F	142	19	0	0	0	0
M	0	2101	0	0	0	0
N	0	0	18820	0	4	102
Q	0	0	9	1599	0	0
S	4	4	0	0	531	17
V	23	10	0	0	16	1398

Figure 13. Normalized Confusion Matrix of CNN-B.

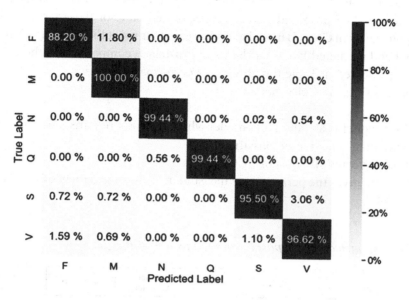

Fig. 13, shows a normalized confusion matrix of the final CNN-B model with true and predicted label. Similar to the proposed approach numerous feature extraction based tasks may incorporated using the application of convolutional computing due to the advancement of deep learning technology (Lai, 2019).

DISCUSSION

In this section, our model is compared to current ECG classification approaches. Deep learning techniques have been used in recent research works to establish a more accurate and reliable way for cardiac arrhythmia classification, with the MIT-BIH arrhythmias dataset being used by the majority of the researchers. In our proposed approach if we have chosen a machine learning model then we need to extract the features by ourselves in a csv file. Here, in our approach we have directly given images as input to the CNN model which automatically extracts features from the input images. The proposed model outperformed state-of-the-art research. The confusion matrix of CNN-B model gives insight of the model's performance in terms of actual and predicted label. Further, a performance comparison of the proposed model is presented in Table 6 with various performance metrics.

The benefits of using CNN model:

1. CNN model is an automatic model which does not require additional feature extraction, selection or classification.
2. It outperforms all types of ECG signals.
3. F1 score gives the performance measure in terms of accuracy of the proposed model.

Table 6. Comparison of proposed work with state-of-the-art.

Author	Classes	Classifier	Average Accuracy	Sensitivity	ECG Beats/ Dataset
Machine Learning Methods					
(Mondéjar-Guerra et al., 2019)	4	Combination of Multiple SVM	94.50%	70.3%	49,691
(Subramanian et al., 2020)	3	SVM	91% F1-90.65%	-	Train = 15, test = 23
Deep Learning Methods					
(Acharya et al., 2017)	5	CNN	94.03%	96.71%	109,449
(Oh et al., 2018)	5	CNN+ LSTM	98.10%	-	16,499
(Abayaratne et al., 2019)	15	Combined RNN-LSTM	94.7% P-98.3% F1-94.1%	98.34%	96,265
(Izci et al., 2019)	5	CNN	97.25%	-	27,789
(Kommireddy et al., 2020)	4	CNN+ LSTM and ANN	98.64%	-	107,620
(Hasan et al., 2020)	5	CNN	98.28%	-	MIT-BIH
(Ullah et al., 2020)	8	CNN	99.11% P-98.59% F1-98.00%	99.61%	MIT-BIH
Proposed model (CNN-A)	6	CNN	98.04% P-89.54% F1-98.06%	91.72%	1,23,998
Proposed model (CNN-B)	6	CNN	99.16% P-95.15% F1-99.17%	96.53%	1,23,998

P: Precision, F1: F1 score

The proposed deep learning model outperformed the competition in terms of average accuracy, precision, recall, and F1 score i.e., 99.16%, 95.15%, 96.53%, and 99.17% respectively in six class classification types of ECG signals; normal beats (N), unclassified beats (Q), fusion beats (F), ventricular ectopic beats (V), supraventricular ectopic beats (S), and myocardial infarction (M) performed on 1,23,998 ECG beats than the others. Our approach has the inclusion of Stochastic Gradient Descent optimizer and Early Stopping technique which improves the performance of the proposed approach. Stochastic Gradient Descent optimizer allows deep neural networks to be trained more efficiently by letting each layer of the network to learn more independently. On the other hand, Early Stopping technique used to prevent over-fitting. Our proposed model can aid doctors explicitly for the detection and classification of arrhythmias.

CONCLUSION

This research work proposes a CNN-based classification model for automatic categorization of arrhythmias using ECG signals. Two-dimensional images are taken as input from the MIT-BIH and PTB dataset. This model classifies six types of ECG with 99.16% classification accuracy that is higher than state-of-the-art studies on similar arrhythmias. This research resulted in a more efficient way for ECG arrhythmias classification with CNN deep learning method. This would aid doctors to better diagnose cardiovascular disease and eventually improves the rate of detection and identification of symptoms at early stage.

REFERENCES

Abadi, M., Agarwal, A., Barham, P., Brevdo, E., Chen, Z., Citro, C., . . . Devin, M. (2016). *Tensorflow: Large-scale machine learning on heterogeneous distributed systems*. arXiv 2016, arXiv:1603.04467.

Abayaratne, H., Perera, S., De Silva, E., Atapattu, P., & Wijesundara, M. (2019). A Real-Time Cardiac Arrhythmia Classifier. *2019 National Information Technology Conference (NITC)*. 10.1109/NITC48475.2019.9114464

Acharya, U., Oh, S., Hagiwara, Y., Tan, J., Adam, M., Gertych, A., & Tan, R. (2017). A deep convolutional neural network model to classify heartbeats. *Computers in Biology and Medicine*, *89*, 389–396. doi:10.1016/j.compbiomed.2017.08.022 PMID:28869899

Aje, T. (2009). Cardiovascular disease: A global problem extending into the developing world. *World Journal of Cardiology*, *1*(1), 3. doi:10.4330/wjc.v1.i1.3 PMID:21160570

Bottou, L., & Bousquet, O. (2012). The Tradeoffs of Large Scale Learning. In Optimization for Machine Learning. MIT Press.

Cardiovascular Diseases (CVDs). (n.d.). *WHO*. Retrieved 15 April 2021, from https://www.who.int/news-room/fact-sheets/detail/cardiovascular-diseases-(cvds)

Caroubalos, C., Perche, C., Metaxaki-Kossionides, C., Sangriotis, E., & Maroulis, D. (1988, July). Method for automatic analysis of the ECG. *Journal of Biomedical Engineering*, *10*(4), 343–347. doi:10.1016/0141-5425(88)90065-9 PMID:3236854

Deng, L., Abdel-Hamid, O., & Yu, D. (2013). A deep convolutional neural network using heterogeneous pooling for trading acoustic invariance. *Proceedings of the IEEE International Conference on Acoustics, Speech and Signal Processing (ICASSP)*. 10.1109/ICASSP.2013.6638952

Goodfellow, I., Bengio, Y., & Courville, A. (2016). 6.2.2.3 Softmax Units for Multinoulli Output Distributions. In Deep Learning. MIT Press.

Gupta, R., Mohan, I., & Narula, J. (2016). Trends in Coronary Heart Disease Epidemiology in India. *Annals of Global Health*, *82*(2), 307. doi:10.1016/j.aogh.2016.04.002 PMID:27372534

Hasan, M. A., Munia, E. J., Pritom, S. K., Setu, M. H., Ali, M. T., & Fahim, S. C. (2020). Cardiac Arrhythmia Detection in an ECG Beat Signal Using 1D Convolution Neural Network. *2020 IEEE Region 10 Symposium (TENSYMP)*. doi:.923058110.1109/tensymp50017.2020

Hiran, K. K., & Doshi, R. (2013). An artificial neural network approach for brain tumor detection using digital image segmentation. *Brain*, *2*(5), 227–231.

Hiran, K. K., Jain, R. K., Lakhwani, K., & Doshi, R. (2021). *Machine Learning: Master Supervised and Unsupervised Learning Algorithms with Real Examples (English Edition)*. BPB Publications.

Hiran, K. K., Khazanchi, D., Vyas, A. K., & Padmanaban, S. (Eds.). (2021). *Machine Learning for Sustainable Development* (Vol. 9). Walter de Gruyter GmbH & Co KG. doi:10.1515/9783110702514

Huang, J., Chen, B., Yao, B., & He, W. (2019). ECG Arrhythmia Classification Using STFT-Based Spectrogram and Convolutional Neural Network. *IEEE Access: Practical Innovations, Open Solutions*, *7*, 92871–92880. doi:10.1109/ACCESS.2019.2928017

Image Data Preprocessing (IDP). (n.d.). *Keras documentation: Image data preprocessing (IDP)*. Keras.io. Retrieved 15 April 2021, from https://keras.io/api/preprocessing/image/

Izci, E., Ozdemir, M. A., Degirmenci, M., & Akan, A. (2019). Cardiac Arrhythmia Detection from 2D ECG Images by Using Deep Learning Technique. In *Proceedings of the 2019 Medical Technologies Congress (TIPTEKNO)*. IEEE. 10.1109/TIPTEKNO.2019.8895011

Kachuee, M., Fazeli, S., & Sarrafzadeh, M. (2018). ECG Heartbeat Classification: A Deep Transferable Representation. *2018 IEEE International Conference on Healthcare Informatics (ICHI)*, 443-444. 10.1109/ICHI.2018.00092

Kommireddy, S., Pandey, P. R., & Kishore NeeliSetti, R. (2020). Detection of Heart Arrhythmia Using Hybrid Neural Networks. *2020 IEEE Region 10 Conference (TENCON)*. . doi:10.1109/TENCON50793.2020.9293831

Lai, Y. (2019). A Comparison of Traditional Machine Learning and Deep Learning in Image Recognition. *Journal of Physics: Conference Series*, *1314*(1), 012148. doi:10.1088/1742-6596/1314/1/012148

Layer Weight Initializers (LWI). (n.d.). *Keras documentation: Layer weight initializers (LWI)*. Keras.io. Retrieved 25 April 2021, from https://keras.io/api/layers/initializers/

Mahrishi, M., Hiran, K. K., Meena, G., & Sharma, P. (Eds.). (2020). *Machine Learning and Deep Learning in Real-Time Applications*. IGI Global. doi:10.4018/978-1-7998-3095-5

McGill, H. Jr, McMahan, C., & Gidding, S. (2008). Preventing Heart Disease in the 21st Century. *Circulation*, *117*(9), 1216–1227. doi:10.1161/CIRCULATIONAHA.107.717033 PMID:18316498

Mondéjar-Guerra, V., Novo, J., Rouco, J., Penedo, M., & Ortega, M. (2019). Heartbeat classification fusing temporal and morphological information of ECGs via ensemble of classifiers. *Biomedical Signal Processing and Control*, *47*, 41–48. doi:10.1016/j.bspc.2018.08.007

Moody, G., & Mark, R. (2001). The impact of the MIT-BIH Arrhythmia Database. *IEEE Engineering in Medicine and Biology Magazine*, *20*(3), 45–50. doi:10.1109/51.932724 PMID:11446209

Nair, V., & Hinton, G. E. (2010). Rectified Linear Units Improve Restricted Boltzmann Machines. *27th International Conference on International Conference on Machine Learning*, 807–814.

Nikolic, G., Bishop, R., & Singh, J. (1982). Sudden death recorded during Holter monitoring. *Circulation, 66*(1), 218–225. doi:10.1161/01.CIR.66.1.218 PMID:7083510

Oh, S., Ng, E., Tan, R., & Acharya, U. (2018). Automated diagnosis of arrhythmia using combination of CNN and LSTM techniques with variable length heart beats. *Computers in Biology and Medicine, 102*, 278–287. doi:10.1016/j.compbiomed.2018.06.002 PMID:29903630

Prabhakaran, D., Jeemon, P., & Roy, A. (2016). Cardiovascular Diseases in India. *Circulation, 133*(16), 1605–1620. doi:10.1161/CIRCULATIONAHA.114.008729 PMID:27142605

Romero, I., & Serrano, L. (2001). ECG frequency domain features extraction: A new characteristic for arrhythmias classification. In *2001 Conference Proceedings of the 23rd Annual International Conference of the IEEE Engineering in Medicine and Biology Society*. IEEE.

Sahoo, S., Dash, M., Behera, S., & Sabut, S. (2019). Machine Learning Approach to Detect Cardiac Arrhythmias in ECG Signals: A Survey. *IRBM, 41*(4), 185–194. doi:10.1016/j.irbm.2019.12.001

Subramanian, K., & Prakash, N. K. (2020). Machine Learning based Cardiac Arrhythmia detection from ECG signal. *2020 Third International Conference on Smart Systems and Inventive Technology (ICSSIT)*. .921407710.1109/ICSSIT48917.2020.9214077

Ullah, A., Anwar, S. M., Bilal, M., & Mehmood, R. M. (2020). Classification of Arrhythmia by Using Deep Learning with 2-D ECG Spectral Image Representation. *Remote Sensing, 12*(10), 1685. doi:10.3390/rs12101685

Wei, Y., Qi, X., Wang, H., Liu, Z., Wang, G., & Yan, X. (2019). A Multi-Class Automatic Sleep Staging Method Based on Long Short-Term Memory Network Using Single-Lead Electrocardiogram Signals. *IEEE Access: Practical Innovations, Open Solutions, 7*, 85959–85970. doi:10.1109/ACCESS.2019.2924980

Xia, Y., Zhang, H., Xu, L., Gao, Z., Zhang, H., Liu, H., & Li, S. (2018). An Automatic Cardiac Arrhythmia Classification System With Wearable Electrocardiogram. *IEEE Access: Practical Innovations, Open Solutions, 6*, 16529–16538. doi:10.1109/ACCESS.2018.2807700

Ying, X. (2019). An Overview of Overfitting and its Solutions. *Journal of Physics: Conference Series, 1168*, 022022. doi:10.1088/1742-6596/1168/2/022022

Chapter 11
Comparing Machine Learning Algorithms and DNN for Anomaly Detection

Apinaya Prethi K. N.
Department of CSE, Coimbatore Institute of Technology, India

Sangeetha M.
Coimbatore Institute of Technology, India

Nithya S.
Coimbatore Institute of Technology, India

ABSTRACT

Cyber space became inevitable in today's world. It needs a security technology to safeguard the whole system from outsiders. An intrusion detection system acts as a strong barrier and screens the vulnerability. There is an upgraded amount of network attacks such as DoS (denial of service), R2L (remote to local) attack, U2R (user to root), and probe attack. These network attacks lead to prohibited usage of data from various applications like medical, bank, car maintenance, and achieve activities. This will result in financial gain and prevent authorized persons from accessing the network. Intrusion detection systems were implemented in systems where security is desirable. The conventional system makes use of machine learning techniques such as random forest and decision trees that entail many computational resources and higher time complexity. To overcome this, a DNN-based intrusion detection system is proposed. This IDS not only detects the abnormalities but also results in higher accuracy compared to existing systems. This also improves the speed, accuracy, and stability of the system.

DOI: 10.4018/978-1-7998-9308-0.ch011

INTRODUCTION

Intrusion Detection system is used to protect systems from intruders. It is a modern security technology to prevent exploitation. In Internet, security can be compromised through numerous ways. More IoT network, Internet usage and data transfer leads to more anomaly problems. Thus researchers need to focus on self-adaptive intrusion detection systems without any human interaction (Jabez & Muthukumar, 2015). IDS monitor, detect any malicious activity and policy violation in the network. Security systems like firewall, an anti-virus software, etc are also used to protect the system. When an enterprise grows larger, existing security measures is not enough to protect the entire system from intruder. Many times anti-virus software's also gets cooperated by the invaders and leads to false alarm (Aung & Min, 2017). A secured network has Intrusion Management System (IMS) which consists of Intrusion Detection System (IDS) and Intrusion Prevention System (IPS). An IDS detects the malicious activity whereas IPS prevents the network from any malicious activity. Intrusion Detection system will monitor the regular activities in network and classify the normal and abnormal events. It will not make any changes in the event occurred. The difficult part is to identify the malicious event which is very similar to normal activity (Mustafa, Jae, Muhammad & Sugwon, 2021). Intrusion Prevention System controls the entire system and stops the packet proactively if it is a risky. It finds and drops the hazardous packet before it reaches the target. If any malicious activity detected, then IDS sends the alarm to the administrator. Then administrator takes necessary actions depends on the anomaly detected in the system. Anyway a human intervention is needed in IDS to prevent the entire system from any type of hazard. After the evolution of modern technologies like machine learning algorithms, human intervention is not essential in IDS interaction (Jabez & Muthukumar, 2015). Machine Learning algorithms detect the anomaly in the system and take the essential actions based on the database it have. In the database, all types of anomaly and its behavior are stored. By comparing the activities of the system with the database, IDS senses the anomaly if any and proceeds the required actions which make the system secure.

Types of IDS

There are two types of IDS namely: Network Intrusion Detection System (NIDS) and Host Intrusion Detection System (HIDS). NIDS works at network level. It's installed at strategic points of network to monitor threats or anomaly. NIDS analyze whether large amount of traffic happens in the network. If traffic occurs, then the chance of attack also will be high. For an example, Firewall configured at network to find good and bad sender. HIDS installed in all network devices with internet connectivity. This intrusion detection system works as a second line in defense against the malicious attack. HIDS role comes into performance only when NIDS failed to detect the attack in the network. When attacker enters the network NIDS should able to detect it, otherwise intruder intrudes into network devices. Then HIDS installed in devices must detect the attack to provide security. For example, monitors the local system and alerts the administrator if any unauthorized person attempts to make any changes in the local file system or about missing files (Cuelogic Technologies,2019).

Cloud Computing and Edge Computing

Cloud computing handles big data and suffers due to security issues. In cloud computing, all data stored at centralized cloud data center and sent to requester when needed. This centralized data center always under a threat and have a chance of compromise. To overcome this, edge computing were introduced, in which data are distributed and stored at small data center located nearer to the user. Edge computing lies between cloud and the user. Edge computing can also be called as Fog Computing. A small distributed and localized data center is called Edge devices. Edge devices can be gateway, router and any network devices. For example, Amazon Prime Video uses edge computing technology in which data centers are placed at different localized zone nearer to the consumer. When a user requests a page, request sent to nearer data center and processed. If it is found, video started playing on the requester screen. If it is not found in nearer data center, then request is forwarded to centralized i.e cloud data center. From centralized cloud, requested video copied to user's nearest data center and started playing on the requester screen. When you play most popular videos, streaming of data will be less comparatively because popular videos are distributed to all small data centers in order to avoid buffering. All videos cannot be stored in edge data center due to limitations in size.

Artificial Intelligence

Artificial Intelligence, Machine Learning and Deep Learning are interconnected and aim to achieve the same. Machine Learning and Deep Learning is a classification of Artificial Intelligence. AI makes the system to perform with human intelligence. In other words, machine which acts like a human. Artificial Intelligence and Machine Learning carries most of the organizations to the topmost level.

Figure 1.

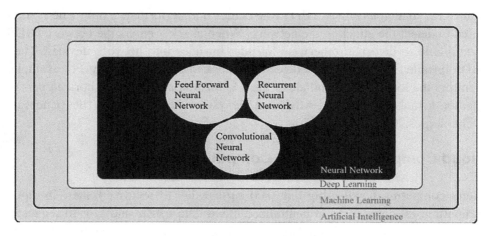

Figure 1 shows the relationship between Artificial Intelligence, Machine Learning Algorithms and Deep Learning. In AI, partial dataset is used to train and remaining to find the output with the trained system. Smart environment became possible in these days by using AI in all applications. Smart Applications can be found in a car, home appliances and in many enterprises. System became an expert system by using human intellectuality. It's able to do all functionality of applications without any human interference.

Machine Learning

Machine Learning became essential in today's machine world. Huge amount of data were created by IoT devices and social network like Watsapp, Facebook etc. Intrusion detection system is unable to handle dynamic and complex cyber-attacks hence efficient adaptive system using machine learning is needed (Anish & Sundarakantham, 2019). Billions of data were created, can be processed, discovered and used for future prediction by ML Algorithms. Machine learning can be classified as supervised, unsupervised and Reinforcement learning. Supervised learning has a set of rules to decide the outcome whereas unsupervised learning will not have any strategies to follow. Reinforcement learning increase the reward by allowing the agent to decide the action based on the current state. Unsupervised algorithm can easily detect anomalies in intrusion system but it is easily disposed to false positive alarms. To reduce the false positive alarm, supervised algorithm can be used. In supervised algorithm, intrusion detection system will be trained with normal and abnormal activities. Supervised machine learning algorithms like Random Forest, Decision Tree were implemented in IDS.

ML Algorithms monitors and learn the network behavior to classify the normal and abnormal activity (Mustafa, Jae, Muhammad & Sugwon, 2021). If any attack (abnormal activity) detected, then the algorithm take the essential actions as programmed. In machine learning algorithms, feature extraction and classification process need to be done separately. In deep learning, neural networks itself extracts the necessary features and do the classification. Internet of Things (IoT) network is enlarging tremendously and became essential thing in day today life. IoT devices can be used in all type of applications like medical, insurance, military etc (Zhenhai, Haoran & Chenglong, 2020). Intrusion detection became mandatory in all fields to prevent intruders. The main challenge is to preventing the false alarm from misleading the system (Alif & Tohari, 2020).SVM with Random Forest in which classification process works with high speed. Parameter variation is not done in the proposal and used as such(Chang, Li &Yang, 2017). Using RF with k-means improves the performance of system and reduces the processing time (Iftikhar, Mohammad, Muhammad & Aneel, 2018).

Decision Tree

Decision tree is one of the supervised machine learning techniques. It is constructed based on ID3 algorithm (He & Runjing, 2017). In ID3 algorithm, for every single attribute Entropy and Information Gain will be considered as given in (1) and (2) respectively. Entropy calculates the disorder in target feature. Entropy value will either 0 or 1 since binary classification is used in our proposed model. Information Gain measures the features which properly classifies the target classes. The feature which has high information gain is designated as best result (Ahmed, Leandros, Mohamed, Makhlouf & Helge, 2019)

$$Entropy(S) = - å\ p_i * log_2(p_i) \qquad (1)$$

where $i = 1$ to n, n is the total number of classes in the target output and p_i is the probability of class 'i'

$$IG(S, A) = Entropy(S) - å((|S_v| / |S|) * Entropy(S_v)) \qquad (2)$$

where S_v is the set of rows in S, $S_v|$ is the number of rows in S_v and $S|$ is the number of rows in S.

Random Forest

It is a grouping of DTree. This gives high accurateness than a single tree and less disposed to over-fitting. This method can be used for both classification and regression algorithm (Chang, Li & Yang, 2017). In this proposed system, it is used for classification in intrusion detection system. Data gets preprocessed then fed for classification. After classification data will be constructed into n number of tress. Depending on the majority vote, each tree gets categorized and generates the result (Ibrahim, Ali, Essam, Raed & 2016).

Deep Learning

Deep Learning is one of the machine learning and it uses programmable neural networks. It learns from processing the training dataset and uses it to learn the characteristics of test dataset. Deep Learning uses multi - layered structure of Artificial Neural network as architecture, which is called as Deep Neural Network. DNN develops a self-adaptive system with better analysis and pattern matching. This network helps to achieve artificial intelligence by implementing machine learning algorithms. Languages like Python, R are mostly used to develop a neural network. Deep Learning is used in many real time applications like Driverless car, Medical field, Recommendation systems etc. It is believed that deep learning, an advancement of ML will rule the future world.DNN can be classified into three types based on its architecture namely: Feed Forward Neural Network (FFNN), Recurrent Neural Network (RNN) and Convolutional Neural Network (CNN).

i) Feed Forward Neural Network

Generally DNN is a Feed Forward Neural Network (FFNN) in which data is unidirectional from input to output layer. Link connects the neurons in all layers in a forward direction. Supervised learning in FFNN uses back propagation to end up with best accuracy.

ii) Recurrent Neural Network

RNN looks like a directed graph, information flows to next layer and next layer to previous layer also. It has memory in internal state to remember the information. In RNN, data flows forward and backward of the layer to work depending on the current input and past output values. RNN became smarter by using Long Short Term Memory (LSTM), which is a special kind of RNN. LSTM has one input gate, forget gate and output gate.

iii) Convolutional Neural Network

Convolutional Neural Network commonly applied to visual applications like object detection, image classification and natural language processing. CNN takes images as input whereas DNN and RNN have values as input. CNN also uses LSTM to achieve good performance. Output of CNN will be extraction of particular region of an image. Region exhibits the desired feature which is called feature map. To overcome this problem, DNN based intrusion detection system is built. IDS are experimented by evaluating DNN in terms of different number of hidden layers to obtain high accuracy for dataset KDD-99.

DNN Architecture

DNN is a collection of neurons and it contains one input layer, hidden layers and one output layer. Input layer has neurons to get input and forward it into hidden layer. Neurons in hidden layer get activated based on the activation function. Activated neurons forward the information to the following layer. This continues and reaches the output layer. In output layer, neurons exists depends on the type of output. If it's a binary classification, then output layer will have only two neurons one for true and one for false. Propagation function plays an important role in neural network to achieve high exactness. Forward and Back propagation are two types of propagation function used in neural network. Forward propagation will deliver "predicted value" whereas back propagation delivers "error rate". Neural network groups the unlabeled data based on its similarities and label the training data based on it. It mechanically adjusts to changing input and results in best output. This technique of adjusting the weight of neurons according to the error value helps DNN to achieve high precision than ML Algorithms. Adjusting the weight of neurons quickly or slowly defined as learning rate of a model. Irrespective of neural network types whether FFNN or RNN, back propagation used as problem solving method. This makes neural network more applicable for speech recognition, text classification, language processing, intrusion detection system and semantic analyzing. In this proposal, DNN with various hidden layers were built and trained. Training and testing of dataset can be split as 80% and 20% or 70% and 30% respectively. In this proposal, 80% of dataset used for training and 20% of input dataset used for test set. Three different DNN with single layer perceptron and multi-layer perceptron (one hidden layer, two hidden layers, and three hidden layers) are trained (80% of dataset) and tested (20% of dataset). After training, test data given as input for all three DNN and results were compared. Performances of all three DNN were analyzed using accuracy, precision, recall and F1-score. It should be noted that this module of predicting the possibility of attack will help the organization to take necessary precautions. Figure 2 describes the workflow of the proposed system.

Figure 2.

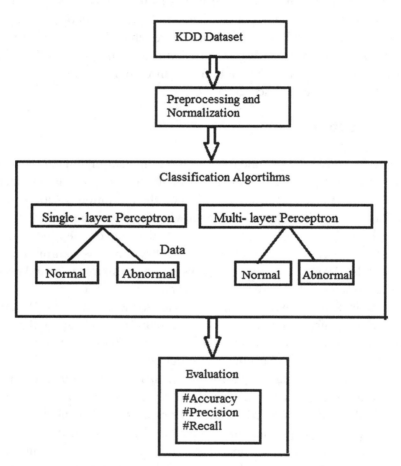

The workings of DNN were explained as follows. The proposed model executed in classification process to categorize normal and abnormal data. Abnormal data might be created by attackers or there is also a chance of a system getting cooperated. This type of data is a fake data which can prevent the system from doing its functionalities. Initially, KDD dataset get preprocessed by cleaning, filling the missed values and removing the noise. During classification process, DNN with different layers were trained and tested.

i) Input and Hidden Layers

The input layer consists of 41 neurons. The outputs of input layer are served into the hidden layers. A hidden layer uses ReLU as the non-linear activation function. Rectified Linear Unit is most popular activation function because of its simplicity and fastness. During training, weights are adjusted and fed into the next upcoming layer. Reducing the count of neurons from first layer to last, results in output with high accuracy.

ii) Regularization

To regularize the neural network, dropout is used in DNN. Dropout is also called as dilution. Dilution used in neural network to avoid over-fitting problem. To make the whole process efficient and time-saving, Dropout (0.01) is used. Accuracy of neural network increased gradually when dropout value is less.

iii) Output Layer and Classification

The output layer is the last layer in neural network. It involves only two neurons namely: Compromised and Uncompromised since it make use of binary classification. The hidden layer has 1024 neurons and its output fed into output layer. The mapping from hidden layer to last layer done by, a sigmoid activation function. The value of sigmoid function lies within the range 0 to 1.

iv) Prediction Phase

In this phase, the data is fed into the proposed system to forecast the input data whether it is an attack or not. The system relates the input data and the weights with the expected output, and makes the prediction. At this phase, the accuracy, precision and recall of the system is considered for benchmarking purposes.

Performance Evaluation

Neural network gets trained and then tested. After training and test phase, three DNN were associated in term of accuracy and confusion matrix. Accuracy is the percentage of correctly categorized data and all categorized data. Confusion matrix is used to identify normal and abnormal data. Correctly classified data is called as True Positive (TP). Correctly classified normal data is called as True Negative (TN). Wrongly identified abnormal data is called as False Positive (FP). Wrongly identified normal data is called as False Negative (FN).

Figure 3.

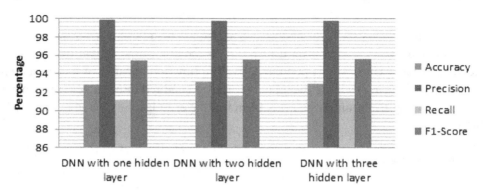

Figure 3 shows the evaluation of the accuracy, precision, recall, f1 score of DNN with different number of layers. Accuracy can be found in the context of total number of correct prediction to the total number of dataset. Precision can be found in the context of total number of correct positive prediction to total number of positive prediction. Recall can be found in the context of total number of correctly classified positive prediction to the total number of correctly classified data. F1-score provides the degree of incorrectly classified data. This proposed model was executed using Tensor flow and Python programming. The outcome of proposed model was measured using accuracy, precision, recall and f1-score as given in (3), (4), (5) and (6) respectively.

Accuracy= (TP+TN) / (TP+TN+FP+FN)   (3)

Precision = (TP) / (TP+FP)   (4)

Recall = (TP) / (TP + FN)   (5)

F1-score = 2*((Precision * Recall) / (Precision + Recall))   (6)

CONCLUSION

Internet became an essential and a part of daily life. Internet application plays a vital role in many fields like medical, transportation etc. Nowadays, Internet of Things (IoT) based Smart city, Smart Agriculture, Smart transportation started empowering the smart world. Big data generated by IoT devices under a severe threat. Security is a major concern which brings the need of detecting abnormal activities. Intrusion detection system senses the variance occurrence in all types of applications and provides security. In the community where internet technologies are used, IDS became an unavoidable one. Implementing DNN in intrusion detection finds anomaly and prevent it with high exactness. The DNN consists of two hidden layers achieves accuracy is 93.1%. The DNN with one hidden layer attains precision of 99.9%. The DNN consists of two hidden layers achieves 91.6% as highest recall value. The DNN with two hidden layers reaches 95.6% of F1 Score. When compared single layer and multi layers perceptron, we conclude that DNN with multi layers perceptron (two hidden layers) perform better. Thus it is determined, DNN with two hidden layers gives high accuracy of 93.1% for the KDD - 99 dataset (80% of training set and 20% of test dataset).

REFERENCES

Ahmad, I., Basheri, M., Iqbal, M. J., & Rahim, A. (2018). Performance Comparison of Support Vector Machine, Random Forest, and Extreme Learning Machine for Intrusion Detection. *Computers & Electrical Engineering*, 274–282. doi:10.1109/ACCESS.2018.2841987

Ahmim, A., Maglaras, L., Ferrag, M. A., Derdour, M., & Janicke, H. (2019). A Novel Hierarchical Intrusion Detection System based on Decision Tree and Rules-based Models. *15th International Conference on Distributed Computing in Sensor Systems*. 10.1109/DCOSS.2019.00059

Alrashdi, I., Alqazzaz, A., Aloufi, E., & Alharthi, R. (2016). AD-IoT: Anomaly Detection of IoT Cyber Attacks in Smart City Using Machine Learning. In *International Conference On Medical Imaging Understanding and Analysis*. MIUA. 10.1109/CCWC.2019.8666450

Altaha, M., Lee, J.-M., Aslam, M., & Hong, S. (2021). An Autoencoder-Based Network Intrusion Detection System for the SCADA System. *Journal of Communication*, *16*(6), 889–905. doi:10.12720/jcm.16.6.210-216

Aung, Y. Y., & Min, M. M. (2017). An analysis of random forest algorithm based network intrusion detection system. *18th IEEE/ACIS International Conference on Software Engineering, Artificial Intelligence, Networking and Parallel/Distributed Computing*, 127-132. 10.1109/SNPD.2017.8022711

Chang, Y., Li, W., & Yang, Z. (2017). Network intrusion detection based on random forest and support vector machine. *Proceedings - 2017 IEEE International Conference on Computational Science and Engineering and IEEE/IFIP International Conference on Embedded and Ubiquitous Computing, CSE and EUC*, 635–638. 10.1109/CSE-EUC.2017.118

Evaluation of Machine Learning Algorithms for Intrusion Detection System. (2019). *Cuelogic Technologies*. https://medium.com/cuelogic-technologies/evaluation-of-machine-learning-algorithms-for-intrusion-detection-system-6854645f9211

Halimaa & Sundarakantham. (2019). *Machine Learning Based Intrusion Detection System. Third International Conference on Trends in Electronics and Informatics*. 10.1109/ICOEI.2019.8862784

Iman, A. N., & Ahmad, T. (2020). Improving Intrusion Detection System by Estimating Parameters of Random Forest in Boruta. *International Conference on Smart Technology and Applications*. 10.1109/ICoSTA48221.2020.1570609975

Jabez, J., & Muthukumar, B. (2015). Intrusion Detection System (IDS): Anomaly Detection using Outlier Detection Approach. *Procedia Computer Science*, *48*, 338–346. doi:10.1016/j.procs.2015.04.191

Mu, Z., Liu, H., & Liu, C. (2020). Design and Implementation of Network Intrusion Detection System. *International Conference on Intelligent Transportation, Big Data & Smart City (ICITBS)*. 10.1109/ICITBS49701.2020.00107

Zhang, H., & Zhou, R. (2017). The Analysis and Optimization of Decision Tree Based on ID3 Algorithm. *9th International Conference on Modelling, Identification and Control*. 10.1109/ICMIC.2017.8321588

Chapter 12
Vascular Disease Prediction Using Retinal Image Acquisition Algorithm

Deepa S.
Kongu Engineering College, India

Suguna R.
Bannari Amman Institute of Technology, India

Sathishkumar P.
Bannari Amman Institute of Technology, India

Vivek D.
SRM Institute of Science and Technology, India

Arunkumar M. S.
Veltech Rangarajan Dr. Sagunthala R&D Institute of Science and Technology, India

ABSTRACT

The people are affected by retinal vascular disease. This research automates the prediction of such disease using retinal image acquisition. The condition of the retinal blood vessels is manifested as the mirror of the vascular disease of the human body. Human retinal images of the eye give extensive data on diagnostic changes caused by local optical sickness that reveal some of the vascular diseases such as diabetes, cardiovascular disease, hypertension, vascular irritation, and stroke. The infinite perimeter active contour with hybrid region information (IPACHI) model is used to segment and calculate perimeter of the blood vessels. The next stage is classification of affected retinal vessels by using support vector model (SVM) and artificial neural network (ANN) models. After classification, the arterio venous ratio (ANR) is computed to identify the exact type of retinal disease. The work is done in MATLAB software, and it proves the accuracy of 95% in prediction of the retinal disease.

DOI: 10.4018/978-1-7998-9308-0.ch012

INTRODUCTION

Image processing leads to image analysis that involves the study of feature extraction from the pre-processed images, segmentation based on vessel and perform classification on the preprocessed images. This technique analyzes the patterns using the vessel retinal image. Diabetic retinopathy is the major problematical disease that distresses the human retina and the result is blindness. Segmentation recognizes the indeed portions of each pixels in the input image in order to invent out the correspondence with various entities. A proposed system is focused mainly with the segmentation which is well automated that avoids all the hand crafty tools and the blood vessels emerging from the retina are inspected repeatedly. Finally, it is permitted to initial vision screen tests, for the identification of various diseases related to retina. This enables us to prevent and minimize vision impairments also many diseases related to age and much vascular sickness. Also, it reduces the cost of the screening.

The retina is interior part of the human eye. The optic disk which is a oval shaped disk located at the center of the retina. The interior position that helps in radiating the major blood vessels will be the optic nerve. The retinal blood vessels are well observed that helps in diagnosing the disease which was compared to the existing technology. The most important step is the extraction of blood vessels in computerized diagnosis and treatment of various vascular disease including diabetic retinopathy, arteriosclerosis, glaucoma, retinal artery occlusion, stroke and hypertension. In inclusion to fovea and optic disc, the blood vessels donates from a wide features of a retinal vessels captured from fundus camera and most of its properties are commonly associated with disease such as diabetes, stroke, arteriosclerosis and hypertension. Also, the most popular eye illness mainly retinal artery occlusion and choroidal neovascularization implies a wide changes in the vasculature network of retina. The blood vessels segmentation in the retinal fundus images proves to be helpful for the diabetic retinopathy detection and glaucoma diagnosis. While taking Cyber Physical System into the account, it mainly focuses on the ability to interpret the data based on the information available on the outer world. Now a days, most of the researchers are involved in the attack detection using CPS. Some of the machine learning algorithms, when approached using CPS resulted in better outcome compared to some of the traditional machine learning models.

LITERATURE SURVEY

In this paper (Timo Hellsted et al., 1996) the author proposed the evaluation of a microaneurysms (MA), fluorescein angiogram (FAG) and conversely time which is in red dot captured in a colored photograph. Wide new varieties of automated segmentation of retinal blood vessels in coplanar color images of the human retina (Joes Staal et al., 2004). The automated method can be worn in computerized analysis of retinal vessels images. The main aim of the research is to classify and categorize each and every pixel in an image as vessel or no vessels. The major causes of blindness in the commercial world that includes many reasons for instance diabetic retinopathy, hypertension, stroke, age-related maculation degeneration, and glaucoma. The methodology for coplanar fundus image processing techniques for concrete Optical Coherence Tomography (OCT) has also been evaluated. Distinct concern is provided to perceptible techniques for the scrutiny of retinal fundus photographs (Michael D.Abràmoff et al., 2010) embedded with a pivot on clinically associated assessment of human retinal vasculature network, recognition of lesions in the retina, evaluation of a particular Optic Nerve Head (ONH) region, and to computerize techniques for the identification of retinal disorders.

The aim of this proposed system is to analyze, review and classify the various vessel extraction algorithms by giving a brief description, marking the necessary points and also mainly the performance measures (M.Fraz et al., 2012). The intent is to provide structural design for the existing exploration and to initiate the wide range of segmentation algorithms (Annunziata et al., 2016). The conduct of algorithms is almost collated and examined on publicly available datasets (DRIVE and STARE) of enormous retinal images using a wide number of measures which include positive rate for both true and false matches. It also accounts for accuracy, sensitivity rate, specificity rate and sector under receiver operating characteristic (ROC) curve. It has been found that the multiple vessel segmentations of a similar image so as to strengthen the detection of confluent points (M. V. Usha, Vidyashree et al., 2015). The concept behind the research is the convergence ought which is a detectable victimization vessel segmentations at completely different scales. DR is that the leading reason for visual defect within the accounting for ninety nine of cases in Asian country (N. Otsu, 1979). Asian country and China currently quite ninety million individuals with polygenic disease pass though polygenic disease. A procedure for vessel extraction in retinal vessels has been projected (S. Roy chowdhury et al., 2016). The most steps are to use associate isotropous diffusion filtration within the original vasculature to revive sure vascular structure lines and take away evaporated lines. At the secondary stage, the four-dimensional line pursuit section permits all vessels to search out the specified volume. Hard a map for a selected image needs many steps.

The development in many tissue engineering technologies (Abdulhannan P et al., 2012) promises in producing some of the matching patency graphs for autologous substances. The elucidation is required in atherosclerosis pathophysiology in providing exclusive targeted material that is well suited for pharmacotherapy.

The main focus on the laser treatments (Raval et al., 2020) in other words, photocoagulation in combination with the growth factor of the anti-vascular tissues helps in measuring the appropriate changing status of the visual acuity and also the IOP (Intra Ocular Pressure) control. The role of sensors plays important functionalities in the increasing growth of Cyber Physical Systems (CPSs) (Iarovyi S et al., 2016). These works not only guarantees reliable work but also provides desirable performances indicating the design and deployment. The emerging of such machine learning techniques and algorithms will be relied most only CPS that it assures promising results when compared with the values obtained from the linear models in calculating the width of the blood vessels.

PROPOSED SYSTEM

The proposed system is to implement automatic process and analyzed model distinct deep learning models. The green channel is first selected from the image that is colored which helps in the contrast enhancement by modifying the color range standards using CLAHE (Contrast Limited Adaptive Histogram Equivalent) algorithm. It uses the active contours for enhancement, remove background noise, mark the edges of the retinal vessels, and compute the width of vessels that helps to recognize diseases. A machine learning concept using deep neural network algorithm including Support Vector Classification Model and Artificial Neural Network is used to segment the blood vessels. Finally, this automated proposed methodology provides segmenting the vessels with higher performance ratio that is used in predicting the vascular disease and the ratio in which the vessels are affected after comparing with the trained sets.

DEEP LEARNING MODELS

Convolution Neural Network

Since large amount of workloads and complexity is involved in pre-processing of data, CNN is the well suited method for classification problems especially in image processing methods. Not only with the images the result goes well but also promises in bringing the excellent results in non-imaging data too. The data after importing into the model, the convolution neural network is built using 4 different parts:-

- **Convolution** – The input data are used in creating the feature maps which is further applied in filtered maps.

- **Max pooling** – It enables the CNN model in detecting whether it encounters any modifications or not.
- **Flattening** – The data is further converted to array by flattening method which makes easier for the data to be read by CNN.
- **Full Connection** – The calculation of loss function for the CNN model will be done by the hidden layer.

Support Vector Machine (SVM)

The kernel function used in SVM will take input in low dimensional space that will be transformed into higher dimensional. It is well suited for non-linear problem that does large complex data transformations. The data here is separated based on the label criteria or the user defined outputs. The two main classes that is positive and negative rates are made separable via linear plane i.e. hyperplane. A technique known as the kernel trick is used in separation of these classes by adding some of the features manually in creating a hyperplane. The algorithm is especially applicable for increasing the mathematical function in respective to the collection of data used. The hidden patterns is well recognized in the huge amount of clinical datasets is SVM techniques in comparison with the other deep learning models.

RETINAL IMAGE ACQUISITION

Image acquisition allows getting retinal image from datasets and setting as input for further processing. The image given as input is stored as Tagged Image File Format in the datasets. Both test dataset (Fig.1) and trained set images (Fig.2) are acquired for predicting the vascular disease.

Figure 1. Test dataset

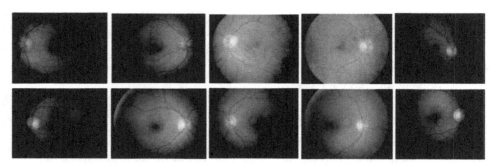

Figure 2. Trained dataset

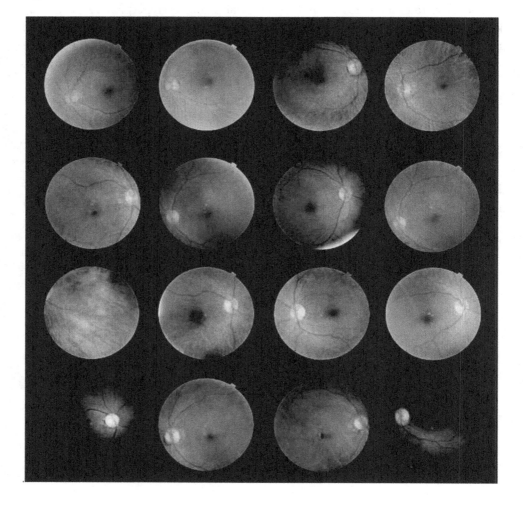

PRE-PROCESSING

The image pre-processing commonly involves eliminating the low-frequency background noise, removing reflections, rationalizing the intensity of the solitary particle images, applying filters and masking undesired portions of images. Gaussian filter has been applied for the entire image in order to reduce the (S P Meshram et al., 2013) contrast and wavelet filter to blur the edges and also extracts the features of the vessels (Fig.3).

Figure 3. Feature Extraction

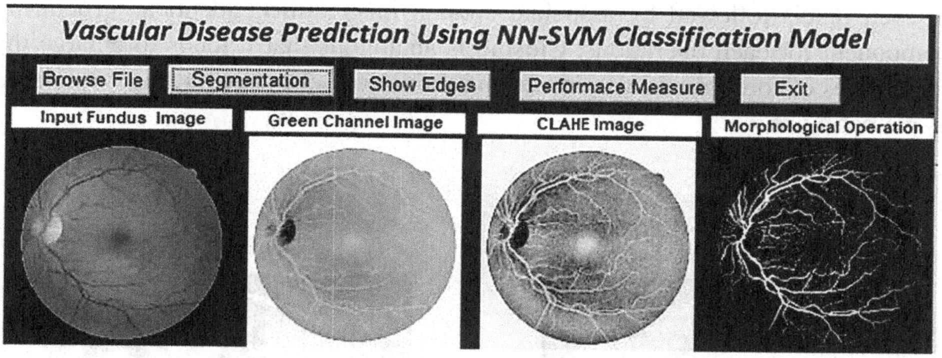

FILTERING

Morphological filters such as dilate, erode, close and open which can be applied by filtering the image in order to shrinking or enlarging the image spaces, which process the tiny spaces in the input image supported the certain detailed characteristics are encoded within the particular structuring element, are reported (Fig.4).

DILATE AND ERODE

Dilation and Erosion are the two essential operators in considering the region of extracting mathematical morphology. As some crucial areas of fore-ground pixels that enlarge in size, some of the spotted holes within the inner regions turn out smaller. The main effect of abrasion on the image is to make erosion in the outer boundaries foreground pixels, typically including the white pixels. While in the case of foreground pixels that diminish in size, holes become enlarged.

OPEN

Mainly, opening springs from the elemental morphological operations of abrasion and dilation. The opening operation basically resembles erosion; it tries to get rid of relatively number of the foreground image pixels from various sides. In general, it is slightly levelling than erosion.

CLOSE

The closing methodology is gap that has been done in reverse, is outlined as dilation in each pixels followed by associate erosion mistreatment identical structuring component for each operations. Closing is analogous that it tends to enlarge the boundaries of fore-ground regions during retinal vessel image backup considered as pepper noise.

Figure 4. Filtering

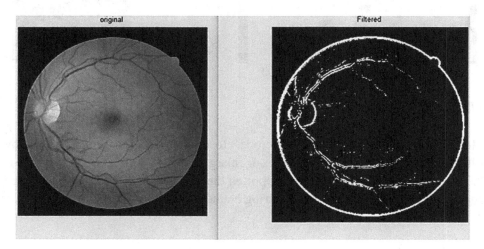

RETINAL VESSELS SEGMENTATION

In Segmentation (N. Patton et al., 2006) of blood vessels neural network mechanism of image processing is implemented. The initial vessel values are tracked and pointed along with the features of the vessels. Bases on the values that has been for the respective feature, subsequent algorithm is implemented. The separation of input values from the retinal image from its integral part is performed. The deep neural network model is implemented for segmentation and feature extraction of the retinal blood vessels. It creates vascular network that has been traced using neural active color contour that has been measured with neighbourhood function. It can extract the vascular network that has been mapped, where every node denotes a convergence point in the vascular tree. Binary mask in the segmentation process is originated by finding the vessels, edges from sharpened image. Finally provide the segmentation mask for pre-processed retinal images (Fig.5).

Figure 5. Segmentation of Retinal Blood Vessel

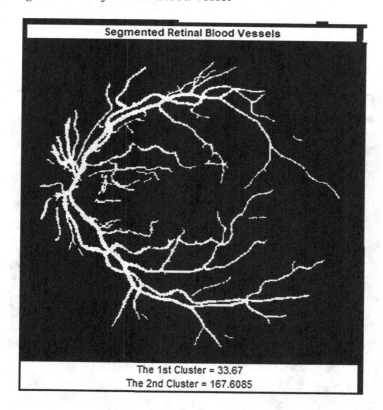

RETINAL VESSELS CLASSIFICATION

The vessels are tracked via vessel classification method and the calculation is done considering the width of every blood vessels. The arteries and veins classification is done based on the width values, and are represented using NN model and Support Vector Machine Model.

After vessel extraction, feature vector is mapped involving the properties of artery and veins. This is adopted for the line extracted image and a label name which is appointed to every line, representing the artery and vein picture element. Supported these labeling section, the ultimate aim is currently to allot one in every of the labels to the respective artery category (A), also the alternative with vein category (V). So as to authorize the final classification between A/V categories at the side of vessel potency data the structural data and also are used (Fig.6). This could be done for the exploitation of SVM classification. The brightness (Naik, S. K et al., 2003) level improvement enhances the exploitation of 'adaptive gamma correction' (AGC) technique is not the suitable gray level varies, so this technique not causes the 'gamut-problem'.

Figure 6. Edge Detection

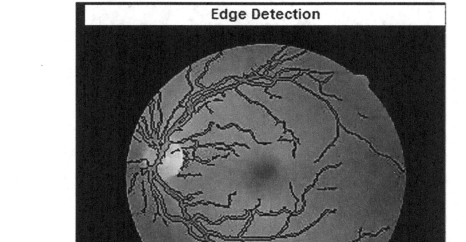

DISEASE DIAGNOSIS

In diagnosis phase, the measurement of testing and training retinal image dataset. The positive and negative matches including True and False Rate, sensitivity, specificity and accuracy is used which in turn used in the calculation of AVR ratio to predict the disease. The disease has been diagnosed using Arteria Ventricular ratio based on the vessel measurements of both arteries and veins mainly Central Retinal Ventricular Equivalent (**CRVE**) and Central Retinal Arteriolar Equivalent (**CRAE**) is found which to be associated with risks factors of vascular diseases and found as a positive real numbers (Fig.7 & Fig.8).

Figure 7. Performance Measure for Normal Image

Performance Measure

True Positive = 0

True Negative = 295875

False Positive = 4645

False Negative = 0

False Positive Rate = 0.015457

Sensitivity = NaN

Figure 8. Performance Measure for Affected Image

Performance Measure

True Positive = 21359

True Negative = 294987

False Positive = 4418

False Negative = 9196

False Positive Rate = 0.014756

Sensitivity = 0.69903

RESULTS AND DISCUSSION

Our fundus retinal image data that has been obtained from the database provided by Kaggle contests are about 90,000 images. We have separated 1500 images from the training dataset in order to provide them to the validation dataset. The probability distribution provides a feature with higher dimensionality. The features have been listed below:-

- The averages of Red, Green, and Blue channel values within 50 percentage cropped image of the human retina.
- Moreover, the overall standard deviation of the original image has been 50 percentages centered cropped image.
- In total, there includes twelve features for one retinal fundus image.
- The feature vectors obtained by the probability distribution of dimensionality are used as vector input of SVM classification.

The Automatic prediction of diabetic retinopathy may reduce the high risk of vision impairment for those who suffer from retinal diabetics. In this study, Fuzzy C Means clustering and ANN has been proposed with a final accuracy rate of 88.03% for more than 2500 test images and proved to be a fitter solution. The result shows that SVM classifier pooling AUC fits the prediction fit value along with the reduced error rate calculation.

The outcome helps in analysing the AUC value obtained those shares a common hike value in addressing the basic clinical queries. Among the boosting algorithm, Support Vector seems to the better working since it deals with most of the linear data and also the data fitting comes with a improved generalized feature using a subsequent non-linear kernel value.

CONCLUSION

The difficulty in segmenting noise image is eliminated by using this application. It reduces the calculation overhead in segmentation. The interface assists in analyzing the photographs effectively. The system is tested well and satisfaction of users is found to be a lot of. A node integrated with Simulation tool structure put in will execute the appliance and identifies the most effective website. The spectral consistency gains better quality than existing for classification functions. It appears higher to aim for better spatial quality as feasible, providing the spectral quality of feature extraction stays higher than acceptable minimum. The system eliminates the difficulties within the existing system. The proposed method is extremely quick in applying segmentation rule and also very particular in reducing the overall difficulties in segmentation algorithms. Enhancement results (Zhou et al., 2018) of CLAHE$_{RGB}$ and CLAHE$_{Lab}$ measure raises the visibility within the processed image.

FUTURE WORK

The new system is developed when the future enhancements are quite often consolidated with the existing current modules with minimum amount of integrated work. The adverse system proves to be helpful if below further enhancements are included in future. The algorithm will be applied to all or reasonably image formats like tiff (Tagged Image File Format) and alternative. The factors employed in the classification algorithms will be generalized in order that default values turn out the generic segmentation. The segmentation rule is used to section only single image at a time. In future, multiple segmenting algorithms including Convolution Neural Networks (CNN) and its layers can be used for sectioning of the multiple retinal images at same time. In future, pattern recognition algorithms that suits for exact matches in the given input data with former patterns. For distinctive, the similar pattern with efficiency.

In analyzing the pattern values and also the correlation obtained from the linear and predictive models, CPS (Cyber Physical System) can also be taken into consideration such that they have the capability to adapt and learn the characterized models. This type of predictive learning can be easily helpful when large amount of test inputs are taken and processed. It also involves high monitoring, along with the continuous maintenance of the predictive models. Hence, Machine learning can be evaluated as the innovative that plays a key role in such kind of development models.

REFERENCES

Abdulhannan, P., Russell, D. A., & Homer-Vanniasinkam, S. (2012). Peripheral arterial disease: A literature review. *British Medical Bulletin, 104*(1), 21–39. doi:10.1093/bmb/lds027 PMID:23080419

Abràmoff, Garvin, & Sonka. (2010). Retinal Imaging and Image Analysis Clinical Applications. *IEEE Reviews in Biomedical Engineering.*

Annunziata, R. (2016). Leveraging multi-scale hessian-based enhancement with a novel exudate inpainting technique for retinal vessel segmentation. *IEEE Journal of Biomedical and Health Informatics.*

Fraz, M., Remagnino, P., Hoppe, A., Uyyanonvara, B., Rudnicka, A., Owen, C., & Barman, S. (2012). *Blood vessel segmentation methodologies in retinal images.* IEEE Publication.

Hellsted, Vesti, & Immonen. (1996). *Identification of individual microaneurysms: A comparison between fluorescein angiograms and red-free and color photographs.* IEEE Publication.

Iarovyi, S., Mohammed, W. M., Lobov, A., Ferrer, B. R., & Lastra, J. L. M. (2016). Cyber-Physical Systems for Open-Knowledge-Driven Manufacturing Execution Systems. *Proceedings of the IEEE, 104*(5), 1142–1154. doi:10.1109/JPROC.2015.2509498

Meshram, S. P., & Pawar, M. S. (2013). Extraction of Retinal Blood Vessels from Diabetic Retinopathy Imagery Using Contrast Limited Adaptive Histogram Equalization. *IEEE Journal of Biomedical and Health Informatics, 20*(6), 1562–1574.

Naik, S. K., & Murthy, C. A. (2003). Hue-preserving color image enhancement without gamut problem. *IEEE Transactions on Image Processing, 12*(12), 1591–1598. doi:10.1109/TIP.2003.819231 PMID:18244713

Otsu, N. (1979). A Threshold Selection Method from Gray-Level Histograms. *IEEE Transactions on Systems, Man, and Cybernetics, 9*(1), 62–66. doi:10.1109/TSMC.1979.4310076

Patton, N., Aslamc, T. M., MacGillivrayd, M., Dearye, I. J., Dhillonb, B. R., Eikelboomf, H., Yogesana, K., & Constablea, I. J. (2006). Retinal image analysis: Concepts, applications and potential. *Retinal and EyeResearch, 25,* 99–127. PMID:16154379

Raval, V., Nayak, S., Saldanha, M., Jalali, S., Pappuru, R. R., Narayanan, R., & Das, T. (2020). Combined retinal vascular occlusion. *Indian Journal of Ophthalmology, 68*(10), 2136-2142.

Roy Chowdhury, S., Koozekanani, D. D., Kochanski, S. N., & Parhi, K. K. (2016). Optic disc boundary and vessel origin segmentation of fundus images. *IEEE J. Biomed. Health Inform., 20*(6), 1562–1574.

Staal, Abramoff, & Niemeijer, Viergever, & van Ginnesen. (2004). Ridge-based vessel segmentation in color images of the retina. *IEEE Transactions on Medical Imaging.*

Usha, M. V., & Vidyashree, M. R. (2015). *Locating the optic nerve and blood vessel in a retinal image using graph partition method.* Academic Press.

Zhou, M., Jin, K., Wang, S., Ye, J., & Qian, D. (2018). Color retinal image enhancement based on luminosity and contrast adjustment. *IEEE Transactions on Biomedical Engineering*, *99*(3), 1. doi:10.1109/TBME.2017.2700627 PMID:28475043

Chapter 13

Convolutional Neural Network–Based Secured Data Storage Mechanism for Big Data Environments

Balamurugan Easwaran

 https://orcid.org/0000-0003-2492-9589

University of Africa, Toru-Orua, Nigeria

Sangeetha Krishnan
University of Africa, Toru-Orua, Nigeria

Anitha P. T.
Wollega University, Ethiopia

Jackson Akpojaro
University of Africa, Toru-Orua, Nigeria

Kirubanand V. B.
CHRIST University (Deemed), India

ABSTRACT

Data types and amounts in human society are growing at an amazing speed, which is caused by emerging new services such as cloud computing and internet of things (IoT). As data has been a fundamental resource, research on big data has attracted much attention. An optimized cluster storage method for big data in IoT is proposed. First, weights of data blocks in each historical accessing period are calculated by temporal locality of data access, and the access frequencies of the data block in next period are predicted by the weights. Second, the hot spot of a data block is determined with a threshold that is calculated by previous data access. In this work, big data is

DOI: 10.4018/978-1-7998-9308-0.ch013

divided into multiple segments based on semantic connectivity-based convolutional neural networks. Each segment will be stored in the different nodes by adapting the blockchain distributed-based local regenerative code technology called BCDLR. Experimental results demonstrate the efficiency of the proposed model in terms of packet delivery ratio, end-to-end delay, energy consumption, and throughput.

1. INTRODUCTION

IoTs have grown more popular in the development of corporate applications. Since these dispersed sensors have generated massive volumes of data, gathering, integrating, storing, processing, and utilizing this data has become a critical issue for businesses. Bothe researchers and engineers are faced with the challenge of processing this voluminous heterogeneous data stored in widely distributed systems like CCSs (Sezer et al., 2017). IoT-based Data Storage Systems in CCSs is attempting to balance distributed executions on three parameters namely unified infrastructure resource managements, multi-tenant storages with isolated performances, and flexible scalability of systems (Ding, Z. et al, 2013)

Transfers, processes, and integrations of IoTs are demanded massive, real-time, and unstructured data processes with hierarchical levels like data storage and analysis (Borthakur, D, et al, 2017). These issues are addressed in traditional data storage systems by fault-tolerant mechanisms (data copies) resulting in redundancy owing to poor utilization and increased data storage costs though only certain portions of information are accessed (Zhang, Q., et al, 2017 and Zhang, Q., et al, 2013).

Current researches have proposed effective cluster storage solutions for these voluminous data from IoTs which are based on temporal localization of data accesses and establishment of weights for data blocks based on access histories and anticipated/forecasted weights of the block's access frequencies (Barik, R.K., et al., 2018). Subsequently, threshold values determined from previous data accesses identify a data block's hot (Marjani, M., et al, 2017 and Jan, B., et al, 2019).

Data balances are maintained by altering copies of data blocks and storing them as distinct groups in high-performing low load nodes for improving access efficiencies and resource utilizations while lowering storage costs (Kumari, A., et al, 2018). Clustering techniques adapted to store data reliably and storing copies of frequently accessed data in multiple nodes ensures data availability at all times. However, storage overheads become very high when duplicate data is more (Ding, Z., et al, 2013).

To overcome those issues, an improved framework is introduced in this chapter. The main goal of the proposed work is to ensure optimal and reliable data storage with reduced storage overhead and ensured data integrity. In this work, big data is divided into multiple segments based on semantic connectivity-based convolutional neural networks. Each segment will be stored in the different nodes by adapting the blockchain distributed-based local regenerative code technology. This work ensures data integrity and as well as ensures data recovery by adapting the regenerative code technology.

Section I of this research work examines the significance of big data storage in IOT networks, Section II provides an overview of the classical approaches used for big data storage, Section III compares research strategies and their benefits and drawbacks, and Section IV discusses simulation results. Section V discusses the conclusion and future direction for work.

2. LITERATURE REVIEW

This section reviews methods used for secure storage of IOTs in big data. Ding (Ding et al, 2013) proposed generic Statistical Database Clustering for Big Data Analysis in IOTs data. The study used statistical functions within DBMS kernels where complex statistical queries were transformed into conventional SQL queries. Moreover, statistics based analyses using distributed/parallel servers, resulted in increased performances in experimentations.

Tripathi (Tripathi et al, 2020) suggested metaheuristic-based clustering for handling massive data based on the power of MapReduce. The study's suggested approach used the searching power of military dog squads to identify the best centroids where MapReduce handled voluminous data. The study tested their proposed schema against 17 benchmark functions for their efficiency in optimizations while comparing experimental results with 5 contemporary algorithms namely BOAs (bat optimization algorithms), PSOs (particle swarm optimizations), ABCs (Artificial Bee Colonies), MVOs (Multi-Verse Optimizations) and WOAs (Whale Optimization Algorithms). Moreover, the study's parallel version used MapReduce [MapReduce-based MDBO (MR-MDBO)] for clustering large datasets of industrial IoTs.

Hosseini (Hosseini et al., 2017) suggested in their study, a new method for predicting and pinpointing epileptic episodes followed by the use of deep learning structures including Stacked Auto-encoders, CNNs, enhanced optimizations based on PCAs (Principal Component Analyses), ICAs (Independent Component Analyse), and DSAs (Differential Search Algorithms). The study's CCS solution for IoTs established recommended architectures for real-time processes, autonomous computations, and massive data storages.

Wu (Wu et al., 2019) suggested a log fusion approach for tuning logs of components into structured data by removing noises, adding timestamps, and labeling data. The study introduced prediction models for voluminous data and improved sequence-to-sequence (seq2seq) approaches by the addition of attention mechanisms and changing global data distributions with adjustors. Their findings showed that trained NNs (neural networks) performed well on real-world data and in comparison to prior prediction techniques, their RMSEs (root mean square errors) were reduced by 46.65%, while their R2s (R-squared) fitting degrees increased by 14.28%.

Chervyakov (Chervyakov et al., 2019) in their study used distributed data storage systems for encryptions and governance of data. Their RRNSs (Redundant Residue Number Systems) included a revolutionary strategy for error correction codes and mechanisms for secret sharing. The study while decoding from RNS to binary formats AR (approximated rank) values of numbers for minimizing computational complexities and size of coefficients. The study's AR-RRNS approach, detected errors while controlling computations based on approximate values and arithmetic properties of RNSs. Their theoretical foundations for configuring information losses, data redundancies, and encode/decode speeds could be adapted to preferred workloads and storage. Their theoretical study demonstrated proper selections of RRNs parameters could not only increase security and dependability but also reduce storage overheads with the processing ability of encrypted data.

Mohammed (Mohammed et al., 2014) generated healthcare infrastructures with IOIO microcontrollers, signals, communication protocols, secure and efficient mechanisms for large file transfers, database management systems, and centralized clouds. Their research focused on system/software architectural design needed for developing IoTs CCS medical applications. Their proposed infrastructures could be used by other sectors of healthcare where they concluded on recommendations and extensions of identified healthcare solutions.

Guo (Guo et al., 2017) proposed CSFs (Crowdsourcing Semantic Fusions), leveraging on social users' pooled expertise and blended crowd computations to semantic fusions. They first mined cross-modal semantics correlations and standardized semantic objects for their fusions. Subsequently, dimension reductions and relevance feedbacks were employed to eliminate non-primary components and noises. In examining storages and distributions, their results illustrated the effectiveness and accuracy of their proposed approach as it was an effective and practical cross-modal semantic fusion and distribution mechanism for heterogeneous social media data in a novel social media semantic processing. The study used interactive visualization frameworks for mining social media information which enhanced semantic knowledge and representations of data.

3. PROPOSED METHODOLOGY

This section stages the proposed model data storage of big data in detail in the first stage big data is divided into multiple segments based on semantic connectivity using a convolution neural network and then in the second stage, each segment will be stored in the different nodes by adapting the blockchain distributed based local regenerative code technology (Li, J., et al, 2017). The overall architecture of the proposed model is shown in figure: 1.

Figure 1. Overall architecture of the proposed model

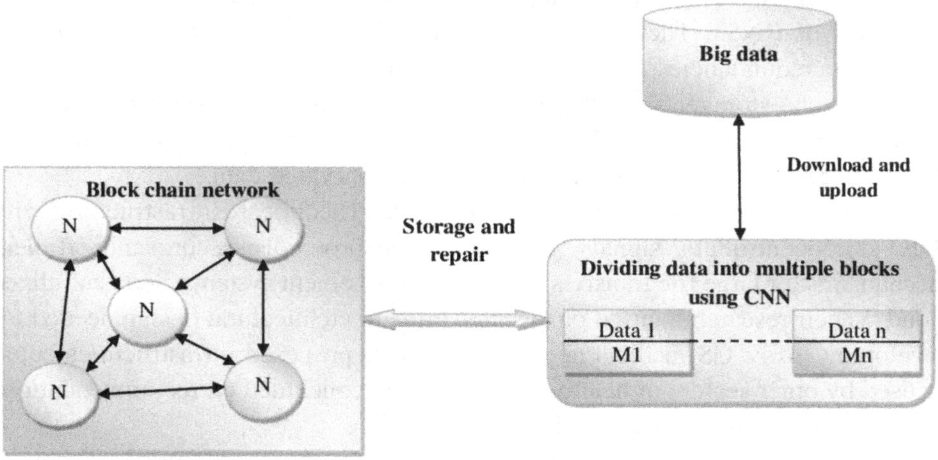

3.1. Dividing Big Data Into Multiple Blocks Using Semantic Segmentation Based CNN

Big data create storage overhead to reduce this problem it requires dividing into small segments. This work using semantic connectivity based segmentation using CNN (Eggert, C., et al, 2017).

- **Input:** It accepts large amounts of data as input. Perform a normalization before passing information to the first convolution layers.
- **Convolution Layer:** Convolution layers (Abbas, S.M. and Singh, S.N., 2018) are composite convolutions followed by batch normalizations for non-linearity with ReLUs (Rectified Linear Units) and where normalizations eliminate covariance, allow quicker learning rates with improved generalizations

(Pandey, A. and Wang, D., 2019). ReLUs are well-suited for deep learning techniques and avoid information losses by zero padding of convolution layers (Nguyen, K., et al., 2017 and Biswas, A. and Chandrakasan, A.P., 2018)

- **Residual Separable Bottleneck**: To achieve faster processing and preserving receptive fields, principal building blocks of networks are based on residual connections, bottlenecks, and separating convolutions where parameters of corresponding layers of [5 x 5] convolutions with 16 kernels are reduced from 6 to 896 for designs (Zhang, Q., et al, 2020)

- **Unpooling with Shared Indexes**: These procedures in decoders share pooling indices of symmetrical pooling operations of encoders and thus enable networks to keep track of maximal activation spatial placements on encoders without transposed convolutions and are costly(Kim, T.Y. and Cho, S.B., 2019). As a result, unpooling operations produce sparse feature maps that subsequent convolutions use for learning and increasing densities. Pooling layers are [2 x 2] convolutions with stride 2.

- **Output:** The last layer uses linear operations followed by softmax activations that predict pseudo probability vectors and where elements represent likelihood of features belonging to classes for divisions into segments.

Figure 2. Structure of CNN

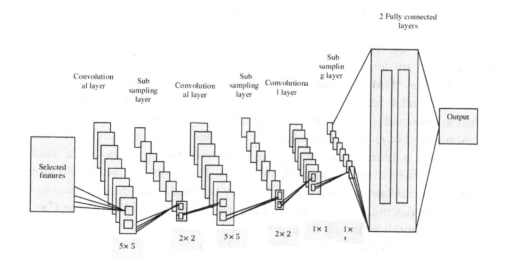

3.2. Block Chain Distributed Based Local Regenerative Code Technology for Data Storage in Different Nodes

After the data is divided, it must be stored in a safe location, such as separate nodes. This is accomplished through the use of Block chain distributed based local regenerative code technology.

The distributed storage fault-tolerant structure of industrial blockchain consists of high fault-tolerant local code block namespaces, index records, and mappings from code blocks to storage nodes. Perception modules assess storage node's loss of data and communicate the loss to metadata information management modules. When clients read files, they first acquire file encoding block's offset information from storage servers. Original terminal data is then retrieved directly from block chain storage nodes by using system's local codes which are high fault-tolerant local codes. To improve the overall reliability and resilience of industrial block chain storage systems, cache servers are configured for storage servers and fault-tolerant local code encoded data are transmitted and cached on storage servers. Cache servers are in charge of file backup caches and when storage servers are physically destroyed, cache servers assume control and begin operation thus reducing latency overheads of data file reconstructions but by increasing the storage overhead (Sajjad, M., et al., 2019).

Fault-Tolerant Distributed Storage Algorithm

Because of the massive number of nodes in block chain cloud storage systems, many storage nodes are destroyed and local codes that can effectively repair failed nodes need to be created (Md. Shahidul Hasan, et al, 2020). This study selects appropriate values of n and k based on the number of cloud storage system nodes in block chains to construct a local code with locality of (n, k). The usage of vector codes in development of single local codes with localities (n, k) is investigated as vector codes include n discrete repair groups and numerous failing nodes can be patched concurrently from k discrete local repair groups. The number of local repair groups specifies the number of failed nodes that may be fixed concurrently, whereas the number of nodes in the repair group determines the repair locality. Using Cauchy matrix and multidimensional linear vector codes, a local code with the locality of (n, k) may be created (Balamurugan E et al, 2020).

First, the source file M is divided into n data blocks $\{X_1, X_2, \ldots, X_n\}$ and stored in nodes in which each node contains three blocks. The first block is a data block X_i the second block is a check block $Y_i = X_1A_{i1} + X_2A_{i2} + \cdots X_kA_{in}$, and the third block is a timestamp block T_i, combined as a coding vector $B_i = \{X_i, Y_i, Ti\}$, $1 \leq i \leq n$, so that fault-tolerant local regeneration code is constructed. Whenever one node fails, it is assumed that node 1 fails, so the sources file M can be restored by (14) that fastly locate the node other than node 1 and download its first block $\{X_2, X_3, \ldots$., $X_n\}$, and downloading next its second block Y_j by any surviving node j ($j \neq 1$). Whenever i ($i \leq \lceil n \rceil$) nodes fail, the source file M can be recovered by quickly locating the other $n - i$ nodes and download the first block $\{X_{i1}, X_{i2}, \ldots, X_{in-1}\}$, and then download the second block $Y_{j1}, Y_{j2}, \ldots Y_{ji}$ from any i surviving nodes $j_1, j_2, \ldots$., j_i ($j_l > i$, $l = 1, 2, \ldots, i$). Each regeneration code has three parts, namely, data domain X_i, check domain Y_i, and timestamp T_i, as. As shown in Algorithm 1, the design of distributed storage regeneration code, when one node fails, the source file can be restored by other surviving nodes.

Creation of matching flow graph information for block chain networks (Fig. 4), comprehend structure of fault-tolerant local regenerative codes in block chain networks as neighbouring local codes in fault-tolerant local regeneration codes recover from faulty local codes. Industrial block chain networks have nodes that upload data to the network and damages in network's node data triggers data recoveries that completely restore nodes' data by downloading relevant data Xi, Yi, Ti from surviving nodes.

Algorithm 1.

```
Input:
Source file M, non-singular matrix U, V ;
Output:
Coding matrix G;
1: Divide souce file M into n data blocks
Xᵢ = xᵢ₁, xᵢ₂,    . . .,    xᵢₙ, i = 1, 2, . . ., n;
2: for i ≤ i, j ≤ n do
3: Compute Aᵢⱼ = (Vi)ᵀUⱼ + cᵢⱼE;
4: end for
5: Compute Yᵢ = X₁Aᵢ₁ + X₂Aᵢ₂ + . . . + XₖAᵢₙ;
6: Record Tᵢ to get coding vector Bᵢ = Xᵢ, Yᵢ, Tᵢ;
7: Generate code B = B₁, B₂, . . ., Bₙ;
8: return Coding matrix G.
```

Figure 3. Blockchain-based fault-tolerant distributed storage structure

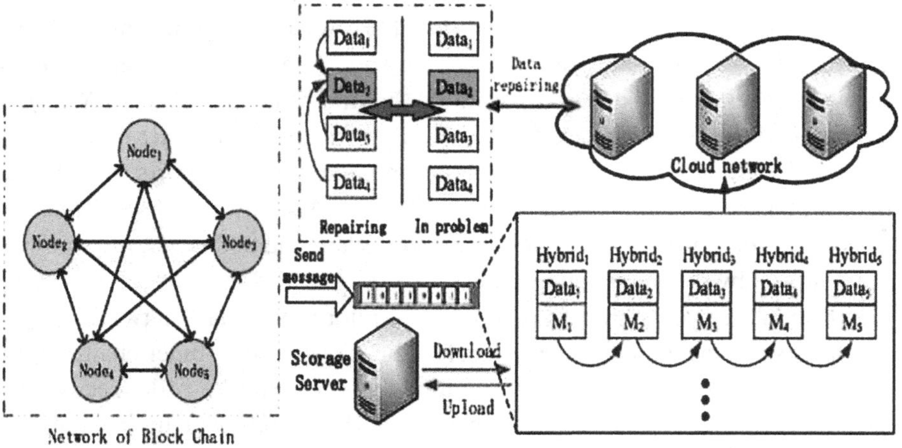

Efficient Blockchain-Based Recovery Algorithm

1. Data Recovery for Single Node Failure

When developing regenerative codes, data storage and node repair are often segregated but not exposed. When mending data in nodes, no encoding and decoding operations are required to download data, and a single failing node in the system may be precisely repaired using a simple XOR operation. It was discovered that by adjusting the current basic regenerative codes, it is possible to extract the encoding form that can properly repair several failing at the same time, nodes repairing methods, and bandwidths are detailed. This proposed unique regenerative code's coding approach is simple to implement with storage capacity closer to theoretical minimum node storage. Because of improved local repair capacity and low overheads of disc input/ output, several nodes in the connection system can quickly repair multiple failed nodes when specific conditions are satisfied, resulting in a high practical application value.

When a new storage node is added to the blockchain cloud storage system, it is supposed to distribute evenly to local codes, as well as ensure the construction of high fault-tolerant local regenerative codes while keeping the count of local codes a constant as lengths of local codes increase. If l storage nodes are added to the local code, the bandwidth cost of creating high fault-tolerant local regenerative code is reduced and the expanded code, the system's information bits are preserved but the check bits are increased to $1/2$. The enhanced code $(n_L + 1/2, k, d'min + 1/2)$ corresponding to the local code $(n_L, k, d'min)$ is being built. At present time, the system's minimum distance for expanded code is $d'min + 1/2$.

Furthermore, the system's improved code is capable of fixing failed nodes more effectively. The additional codes ($n_L + 1/2$, k, d'min + $1/2$) are based on system extended codes, and network coding is utilized to produce a set of high fault-tolerant local regenerative codes to develop the distributed local check of local codes. At this point, the distributed local check adds $1/2$ bits, and the local codes add 1 bits altogether.

When a single node, such as node 1, is damaged, the following procedure is used: Find the injured node 1 through the blockchain network and undamaged nodes, then use all data in the network except node 1 to construct a checking domain $Y_i (i \neq 2)$ and any other node can recover node 1's data. Algorithm 2 depicts this as pseudo-code.

Algorithm 2.

```
Input:
Coding matrix G, failure node 1 ;
Output:
First block X₁ stored in node 1 ;
1: Locate other n - 1 nodes other than node 1 by the third
block of storage nodes quickly;
2: Download its first block X₂,X₃, . . ., Xₙ;
3: Select any surviving node j(j ≠1) to download its second
block Yⱼ ;
4: Use formula (14) to recover the first block X₁ in node 1;
5: return First block X₁ in node 1.
```

2. Data Recovery for Multiple Nodes Failure

Appropriate selection of repair nodes from surviving nodes and transmission channels of repair nodes to new nodes are explored for fault-tolerant local regeneration codes for lowering regeneration time and bandwidth overheads during fault node repairs. This figure represents repair methods of failed node counts and includes phases indicated below(Balamurugan E., et al, 2020).

Step 1: Create a mathematical model of repair node selection in a heterogeneous cloud storage system, with the goal of minimizing $\sum_{i=1}^{n} c_i \lambda_i$, in which c_i is the download cost of node I and $\{\lambda_1, \lambda_2, L, \lambda_n\}$ is the download distribution for the chosen repair node. When the problem node is placed in the system local code portion of each local code in the fault-tolerant local regeneration code, many local repair groups may be available for each fault node, and the repair group with the lowest repair cost is considered.

Step 2: Consider all constraints when selecting repair nodes including repairs where regeneration times may be longer data transmission times of repair nodes to new nodes, linking bandwidths may limit transmission rates from repair nodes to new nodes, and flow conservations on heterogeneous network's cloud storage nodes.

Step 3: Find the optimal value of the function Minimize $\sum_{i=1}^{n} c_i \lambda_i$. When the scope of the industrial blockchain cloud storage systems are limited, linear programming techniques optimize the selection of new/repair nodes, and data transmission lines. Computational complexity of linear techniques increases as breadths of industrial blockchain's cloud storage systems expand. Further, heuristic selection techniques including genetic, simulated annealing, and ant colony algorithms are investigated for identifying estimated optimal new/repair nodes, and transmission channels with the aim of reducing fault node repair regeneration times and bandwidth overheads.

When I nodes in the n industrial nodes are damaged, it is best to assume that node 1 to node I fails. can make use of the initial blocks $X_{i+1}, X_{i+2}, \ldots, X_n$ of $n - i$ nodes other than node 1 to node i and the second blocks $Y_{j1}, Y_{j2}, \ldots Y_{ji}$ of any surviving nodes $j_1, j_2, \ldots, j_i$ ($j_i > k$, $l = 1, 2, \ldots, i$) to reconnect node 1 to node 1, Algorithm 3 represents the pseudo code.

Algorithm 3.

```
Input:
Coding matrix G, failure nodes 1 - i;
Output:
First block X₁,X₂, . . ., Xᵢ stored in node 1 to node i ;
1: Locate other n - 1 nodes other than node 1 by the third
block of storage nodes;
2: Download its first block X ᵢ₊₁, X ᵢ₊₂, . . ., Xₙ;
3: Select any surviving nodes
j1, j2, . . ., jᵢ(jₗ > k, l = 1, 2, . . ., i) to download its
```

```
second blocks Y_{j1}, Y_{j2}, . . ., Y_{ji} ;
4: Use formula (15) to recover the first blocks
X_{1},X_{2}, . . ., X_{i} in node 1 to node i;
5: return First blocks X_{1},X_{2}, . . ., X_{i} in node 1 to node i.
```

4. RESULTS AND DISCUSSION

The experimental findings of the proposed model BCDLR are discussed in this section. NS2 is used to implement the proposed model. In terms of data access speed, data consumption, cost, and storage overhead, this suggested model is compared to existing RRNS and CSF. An experiment with six racks is simulated using Ubuntu14.04 as the operating system, installing the Hadoop cloud platform, and employing a computer with an Intel Xeon 4 core CPU, 8G RAM, 1 TB SATA hard drive, and Gigabit NIC configuration for storing cluster data node connection.

Figure 4. Data access speed (Gbps)

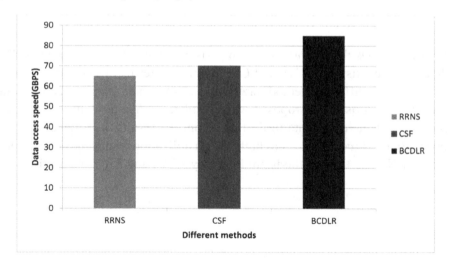

Performance comparison results of the proposed BCDLR method and the existing RRNS and CSF method in terms of Data access speed is shown in the above figure. In the above figure different methods are taken as X-Axis and Data access speed values are taken as Y-Axis. The proposed Model uses blockchain distributed based local regenerative code technology by which access speed increases. From the results, it concludes that the proposed BCDLR model produces higher Data access speed results of 85(Gbps) whereas existing RRNS and CSF methods produces only 65 (Gbps) and 70(Gbps) respectively.

Figure 5. Data utilization (%)

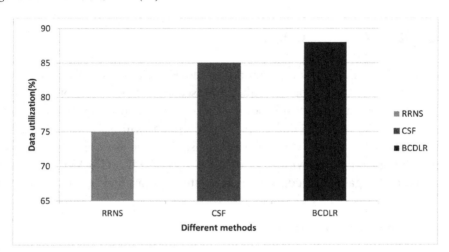

Figure:5.Shows the performance comparison results of the proposed BCDLR method and the existing RRNS and CSF method in terms of Data utilization. In the above figure, different methods are taken as X-Axis and Data utilization values are taken as Y-Axis. The proposed Model utilizes semantic connectivity-based segmentation it increases data utilization. From the results, it concludes that the proposed BCDLR model produces higher Data utilization results of 88(%) whereas existing RRNS and CSF methods produce only 75(%) and 85(%) respectively.

Figure 6. cost ($)

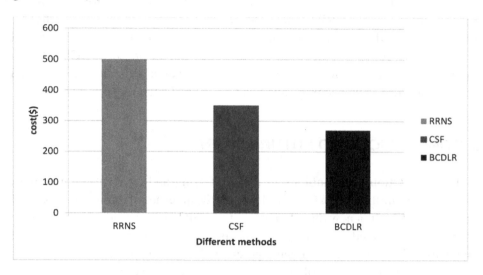

Performance metric cost results of the proposed BCDLR method and the existing RRNS and CSF method in terms of cost are compared in figure.6. In the above figure, different methods are taken as X-Axis, and cost values are taken as Y-Axis. From the results, it concludes that the proposed BCDLR model consumes lower costs 500($) whereas existing RRNS and CSF methods consume higher costs 350 ($) and 270($) respectively.

Figure 7. Storage overhead (bits)

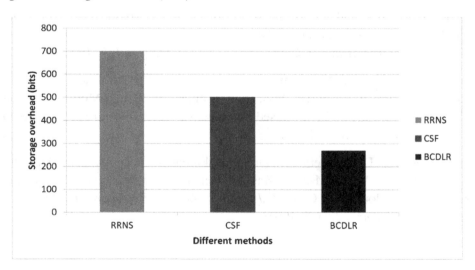

Figure: 7. Shows the performance comparison results of the proposed BCDLR method and the existing RRNS and CSF method in terms of storage overhead. In the above figure, different methods are taken as X-Axis and Storage overhead values are taken as Y-Axis. From the results, it concludes that the proposed BCDLR model produces lower Storage overhead results of 88(%) whereas existing RRNS and CSF methods produce higher Storage overhead 75(%) and 85(%) respectively.

5. CONCLUSION AND FUTURE WORK

With the evolution of technology in data collecting and retrieval, the number of available data in the context of big data and the Internet of Things grows by the minute. As a result, a new data-management architecture is required. In this work, first big data is divided into multiple segments based on semantic connectivity based convolutional neural network. Each segment will be stored in the different nodes by adapting the block chain distributed based local regenerative code technology. This work ensures the data integrity and as well as ensures the data recovery by adapting the regenerative code technology. Experimental results shows that the proposed model provides better results in terms of data access speed, Data utilization, Cost and Storage overhead than other state of art models. However, deep learning increases computational difficulties, necessitating the employment of another machine learning model for data segmentation in the future.

REFERENCES

Abbas, S. M., & Singh, S. N. 2018, February. Region-based object detection and classification using faster R-CNN. In *2018 4th International Conference on Computational Intelligence & Communication Technology (CICT)* (pp. 1-6). IEEE.

Balamurugan, Hasan, Almamun, & Sangeetha. (n.d.). An Energy Efficient And Self Adaptive Resource Allocation Framework Using Modified Clonal Selection Algorithm For Cloud Based Software Services. *Journal of Psychosocial Rehabilitation, 24*(2), 5182-5203.

Balamurugan, E., Dr Sangeetha, K., Dr Sathishkumar, K., & Dr Akpajaro, J. (2020). Modified Support Vector Machine Based Efficient Virtual Machine Consolidation Procedure For Cloud Data Centers. *Journal of Advanced Research in Dynamical and Control Systems, 12*(4), 501-508.

Barik, R. K., Dubey, H., Misra, C., Borthakur, D., Constant, N., Sasane, S. A., Lenka, R. K., Mishra, B. S. P., Das, H., & Mankodiya, K. (2018). Fog assisted cloud computing in era of big data and internet-of-things: systems, architectures, and applications. In *Cloud computing for optimization: foundations, applications, and challenges* (pp. 367–394). Springer.

Biswas, A., & Chandrakasan, A. P. 2018, February. Conv-RAM: An energy-efficient SRAM with embedded convolution computation for low-power CNN-based machine learning applications. In *2018 IEEE International Solid-State Circuits Conference-(ISSCC)* (pp. 488-490). IEEE.

Borthakur, D., Dubey, H., Constant, N., Mahler, L., & Mankodiya, K. 2017, November. Smart fog: Fog computing framework for unsupervised clustering analytics in wearable internet of things. In *2017 IEEE Global Conference on Signal and Information Processing (GlobalSIP)* (pp. 472-476). IEEE.

Chervyakov, N., Babenko, M., Tchernykh, A., Kucherov, N., Miranda-López, V., & Cortés-Mendoza, J. M. (2019). AR-RRNS: Configurable reliable distributed data storage systems for Internet of Things to ensure security. *Future Generation Computer Systems*, *92*, 1080–1092.

Ding, Z., Gao, X., Xu, J., & Wu, H. (2013, August). IOT-StatisticDB: a general statistical database cluster mechanism for big data analysis in the internet of things. In *2013 IEEE International Conference on Green Computing and Communications and IEEE Internet of Things and IEEE Cyber, Physical and Social Computing* (pp. 535-543). IEEE.

Eggert, C., Brehm, S., Winschel, A., Zecha, D., & Lienhart, R. (2017, July). A closer look: Small object detection in faster R-CNN. In 2017 IEEE international conference on multimedia and expo (ICME) (pp. 421-426). IEEE.

Guo, K., Tang, Y., & Zhang, P. (2017). CSF: Crowdsourcing semantic fusion for heterogeneous media big data in the internet of things. *Information Fusion*, *37*, 77–85.

Hasan, Balamurugan, Almamun, & Sangeetha. (2020). An Intelligent Machine Learning And Self Adaptive Resource Allocation Framework For Cloud Computing Environment. *EAI Endorsed Transactions on Cloud Systems*.

Hosseini, M. P., Pompili, D., Elisevich, K., & Soltanian-Zadeh, H. (2017). Optimized deep learning for EEG big data and seizure prediction BCI via internet of things. *IEEE Transactions on Big Data*, *3*(4), 392–404.

Jan, B., Farman, H., Khan, M., Talha, M., & Din, I. U. (2019). Designing a smart transportation system: An internet of things and big data approach. *IEEE Wireless Communications, 26*(4), 73–79.

Kim, T. Y., & Cho, S. B. (2019). Predicting residential energy consumption using CNN-LSTM neural networks. *Energy, 182*, 72–81.

Kumari, A., Tanwar, S., Tyagi, S., Kumar, N., Maasberg, M., & Choo, K. K. R. (2018). Multimedia big data computing and Internet of Things applications: A taxonomy and process model. *Journal of Network and Computer Applications, 124*, 169–195.

Li, J., Qu, C., & Shao, J. (2017, November). Ship detection in SAR images based on an improved faster R-CNN. In 2017 SAR in Big Data Era: Models, Methods and Applications (BIGSARDATA) (pp. 1-6). IEEE.

Marjani, M., Nasaruddin, F., Gani, A., Karim, A., Hashem, I.A.T., Siddiqa, A. and Yaqoob, I., 2017. Big IoT data analytics: architecture, opportunities, and open research challenges. *IEEE Access, 5*, 5247-5261.

Mohammed, J., Lung, C.H., Ocneanu, A., Thakral, A., Jones, C., & Adler, A. (2014, September). Internet of Things: Remote patient monitoring using web services and cloud computing. In *2014 IEEE international conference on internet of things (IThings), and IEEE green computing and communications (GreenCom) and IEEE cyber, physical and social computing (CPSCom)* (pp. 256-263). IEEE.

Nguyen, K., Fookes, C., Ross, A., & Sridharan, S. (2017). Iris recognition with off-the-shelf CNN features: A deep learning perspective. *IEEE Access: Practical Innovations, Open Solutions, 6*, 18848–18855.

Pandey, A., & Wang, D. (2019). A new framework for CNN-based speech enhancement in the time domain. *IEEE/ACM Transactions on Audio, Speech, and Language Processing, 27*(7), 1179–1188.

Sajjad, M., Khan, S., Muhammad, K., Wu, W., Ullah, A., & Baik, S. W. (2019). Multi-grade brain tumor classification using deep CNN with extensive data augmentation. *Journal of Computational Science, 30*, 174–182.

Sezer, O. B., Dogdu, E., & Ozbayoglu, A. M. (2017). Context-aware computing, learning, and big data in internet of things: A survey. *IEEE Internet of Things Journal, 5*(1), 1–27.

Tripathi, A. K., Sharma, K., Bala, M., Kumar, A., Menon, V. G., & Bashir, A. K. (2020). A Parallel Military-Dog-Based Algorithm for Clustering Big Data in Cognitive Industrial Internet of Things. *IEEE Transactions on Industrial Informatics*, *17*(3), 2134–2142.

Wu, P., Lu, Z., Zhou, Q., Lei, Z., Li, X., Qiu, M., & Hung, P. C. (2019). Bigdata logs analysis based on seq2seq networks for cognitive Internet of Things. *Future Generation Computer Systems*, *90*, 477–488.

Zhang, Q., Chen, Z., Lv, A., Zhao, L., Liu, F., & Zou, J. 2013, August. A universal storage architecture for big data in cloud environment. In *2013 IEEE International Conference on Green Computing and Communications and IEEE Internet of Things and IEEE Cyber, Physical and Social Computing* (pp. 476-480). IEEE.

Zhang, Q., Wang, X., Cao, R., Wu, Y. N., Shi, F., & Zhu, S. C. (2020). Extracting an explanatory graph to interpret a CNN. *IEEE Transactions on Pattern Analysis and Machine Intelligence*.

Zhang, Q., Zhu, C., Yang, L. T., Chen, Z., Zhao, L., & Li, P. (2017). An incremental CFS algorithm for clustering large data in industrial internet of things. *IEEE Transactions on Industrial Informatics*, *13*(3), 1193–1201.

Chapter 14
CluniacChain:
Blockchain and ML–Based Healthcare Systems

Suganthi K.

iD https://orcid.org/0000-0003-4064-6394

Vellore Institue of Technology, India

Apratim Shukla

iD https://orcid.org/0000-0002-2356-5333

Vellore Institue of Technology, India

Mayank K. Tolani

Vellore Institue of Technology, India

Swapnil Vinod Mishra

Vellore Institue of Technology, India

Abhishek Thazhethe Kalathil

Vellore Institute of Technology, India

Manojkumar R.

Vellore Institute of Technology, India

ABSTRACT

Blockchain technology generally is associated with financial applications where it serves the role of maintaining records. However, such a tamper-resistant distributed ledger can be used for fashioning applications in the healthcare domain. Harnessing the potential of blockchain as a data store for health records would ensure that they would be secure as multiple copies of them are preserved in a decentralized manner to ensure data redundancy and security. With this technology in effect, the medical sector could leverage blockchain tech to allow any authorized hospitals to securely communicate, share information/records independent from a central figure. Information shared would only contain relevant data related to the query between stakeholders with appropriate permission attached to their roles. This chapter delineates the architecture of such a system explaining its benefits and limitations as a medical data-storage architecture.

DOI: 10.4018/978-1-7998-9308-0.ch014

INTRODUCTION

In the present scenario, bulk Electronic Medical Records (EMRs) handling is dependent on the Health Information Systems (HISs) (Haux, R., 2006). These systems are centralized and provide multiple functionalities such as patient scheduling, admission/discharge/transfer logs, and billing information. The principal disadvantage of this centralized infrastructure is the lack of transparency, increased risk of data leaks, and subsequently higher repair costs (Menachemi, N., & Collum, 2011). The HIS usually handles Electronic Medical Records (EMRs) from a single hospital. It means that the patient's cumulative report from multiple hospitals and doctors is not part of the EMR. This information can be pivotal for providing detailed insight in identifying symptoms and envisaging responses for the patient. An Electronic Health Record (EHR) is, therefore, a better alternative. EHRs give a holistic, long-term view of the patient's health (Heart, T., Ben-Assuli, O., & Shabtai, I. 2017).

The word blockchain seems quite self-explanatory since one would initially think of it as a collection of blocks linked together linearly. But in the real world, blockchains can be intricate. On the ground level, it is just a database storing information. But the structure and the concepts used in this database make it so unique (Pilkington, M., 2016). With the advent of cryptocurrencies in the last decade, blockchain has gained much popularity. It forms the heart of any cryptocurrency or a decentralized system (Eyal, I. 2017). Talking about decentralization, it is the process by which activities of a system are distributed and are not in direct control of a centralized authority.

Our work proposes a Consortium Blockchain (Hasselgren, A., Kralevska, K., Gligoroski, D., Pedersen, S. A., & Faxvaag, A., 2020) to support transparent Electronic Health Records (EHRs) and enhance the disease prediction system. The proposed architecture ensures transparency while maintaining anonymity by utilizing the principle of Smart Contracts. Some key highlights of the proposal include organizing multiple hospitals under Hospital Clusters (HCs). The Hospital Clusters (HCs) aggregate multiple hospitals according to seven parameters. These parameters are specialization, location, threshold rating, average cost of treatment, capacity, fatalities, and recovery rate. The combination of these HCs forms a decentralized network that shares the consortium blockchain. A chatbot tuned according to each Hospital Cluster (HC) is then entwined with the user interface. The architecture encapsulates the following primary objectives:

- Channelized rule-based patient information gathering.
- Transparent and perspicacious Electronic Health Records maintenance.
- Secure storage of appropriate information on the ledger.

Communicating with customers through live chat interfaces has become an increasingly popular means to provide real-time customer service in e-commerce and medical services domains. Customers use these chat services to obtain information, seek assistance, or consult for reservations. The real-time nature of chat services has transformed customer service into two-way communication (Mero, J., 2018). The addition of a chatbot to gather user inputs can further enhance the proposed system.

At least four different structures are the basis of the functioning of a chatbot (Davenport, T., & Kalakota, R., 2019):

- Natural language processing: To make sense of the demands.
- Knowledge management: To process the relevant details and provide an answer.
- Deep learning helps the chatbot improve its response to each interaction.
- Sentiment analysis: To detect the frustration and transfer them to a human.

The idea is that the user enters their symptoms as the input in the input section of the chatbot. Then the chatbot finds the keywords from the given text and updates the state of the dialogue using the state tracking system (Noroozi, V., Zhang, Y., Bakhturina, E., & Kornuta, T., 2020). After the user has provided all their inputs, the chatbot converts the results into a natural language and gives the output back in a form that the user (human) can understand.

Section 2 of the paper explores existing blockchain-based Healthcare Systems available in the literature. Description of the proposed architecture of the system CluniacChain is in Section 3. Section 4 provides the implementation, and Section 5 provides the conclusion, highlighting the benefits of CluniacChain. The blueprint of the database used by the described system is present in the appendix.

LITERATURE SURVEY

Blockchain application extends to pharmaceutical traceability, data sharing, clinical trials, and device tracking (Bell, L., Buchanan, W. J., Cameron, J., & Lo, O. 2018). Passing healthcare data through third parties, insurance, and healthcare providers puts it at substantially high risk. Thus, healthcare data interchange is a problem. Data sharing and interoperability can work together only if the proposed system takes care of privacy. Our system will allow nationwide interoperability by implementing Electronic Health Records (EHRs) (Reisman, & Miriam., 2017) securely.

With the increasing internet usage, people started using it to browse related symptoms out of curiosity which led to the development of Natural language-based chatbots and prediction systems. Based on the text provided, these systems utilize various NLP algorithms to engage with the user and predict the user's disease. The features from the text that are symptoms, in this case, are extracted and analyzed to predict the output (Rajput, A.E., 2019).

However, only a limited number of applications exist that combine these prediction systems with blockchain technology. Many barriers stand in the way of blockchain technology emerging in the field of healthcare. One of the prominent barriers is the inherent resistance to change the current practices and move to blockchain. Our system will help remove this reluctance by keeping the patient at the center and taking care of their privacy. A sublime way of storing data between the patient and the hospital on a consortium blockchain is smart contracts. Prior application of smart contracts in healthcare is limited. Thus, the data storage techniques on the permissions authorities need to be analyzed further.

Some services (HealthCoin, 2019) have expanded their vision towards building a system to construct a global electronic health record system. Other initiatives are combining AI/ML to improve healthcare services. There are existing systems that issue a smartcard to link EHR data with blockchain-based identity. Others manage the permission and authorization for the data in a decentralized manner. These systems (BurstIQ., 2017) see the future of healthcare in blockchain technology because they believe that it keeps the patient at the center.

There is extensive research available on blockchain security and challenges. Some of these research works (Park, J., & Park, J., 2017) proposed contracts through a multi-signature technique ensuring secure transactions. Such a system discards transactions with improper configurations. Additional data security is possible by using encryption algorithms such as AES (Uthayashangar et al., 2021). Systems can combine AES with Attribute-based encryption to store encrypted data securely in untrusted cloud servers (Yadav et al., 2020, p. 2321 - 2336). Healthcare systems can benefit from this and allow secure storage and sharing of patients' data.

Further, combining chatbots with the healthcare system can enhance the application (Athota et al., 2020). The concept of chatbots is not new. Chatbots have evolved over a long period. Limited computation power was the primary reason for the delay in their development. Currently, performance, functionality, and humanity are the metrics used to judge chatbots (Radziwill, & Benton, 2017). Healthcare systems can utilize the chatbots tuned according to these parameters for interactively gathering the patient's data.

Finally, the Healthcare systems can incorporate clustering techniques for grouping hospitals based on similarities and matching the patient to the ideal hospital. Clustering using K-Mean is a simple technique to cluster large datasets. The complexity of a simple K-Mean clustering algorithm depends on the selection of the initial centroids. Basic K-Mean clustering algorithm requires maximum space and processing speed for large datasets. The parallelized K-Mean algorithm is more efficient since the centroid selection process is more optimized than the simple K-Mean. The outcomes of the parallel algorithms are always the same, which improves the cluster quality, number of iterations, and elapsed time. Therefore, the benefits of parallel K-Mean over simple K-Mean make it an ideal candidate for clustering applications and subsequent usage in healthcare systems (Shang et al., 2021, p. 1-20).

PROPOSED METHOD

The proposed architecture known as CluniacChain (CC) comprises several sub-components. The workflow of the proposed architecture is shown in Figure 1 and Figure 2

Figure 1. Workflow of the CluniacChain System

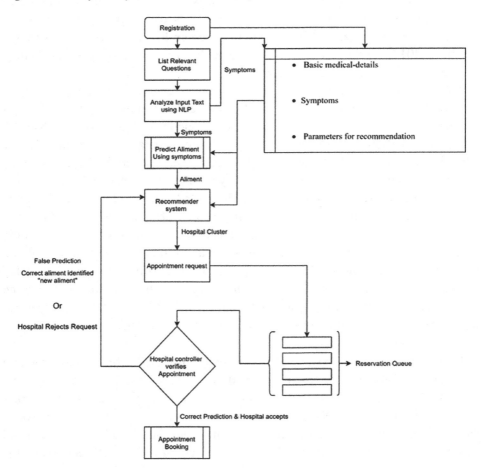

Figure 2. Workflow of the CluniacChain Storage System

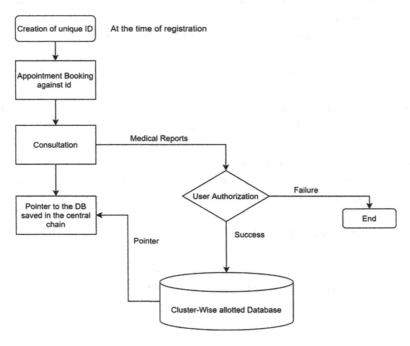

Disease Prediction

The chatbot serves the purpose of getting the user's input in the form of natural language. Wherein the patient describes their feelings. The machine learning model uses the patient's description in Natural language for predicting the disease. The disease gets mapped to a specialization that is one of the parameters considered while recommending a cluster. The dataset used for this purpose is obtained from UCI-The Machine Learning Repository (Drug review dataset, 2018). The model was trained on 27453 data instances and seven attributes, out of which only three are of our interest, these are:

- UniqueId - Unique ID for each data instance
- Condition - Diagnosed disease
- Review - Patient's description of their condition in natural language

The Machine Learning model utilizes the BERT (Devlin et al., 2019) algorithm. It is an NLP-based state-of-the-art model developed by Google. On our test set, it gave an accuracy of 80.37%. For preprocessing, remove the stop words from the user's input to provide only keywords to the model. Removal of unnecessary words like conjunctions and prepositions also occurs in this process.

There is another option of manually choosing the department that the patient wants to go to instead of using the disease prediction system. Some patients that don't have a medical record and are unsure of their condition can utilize the chatbot for disease prediction.

The user also enters his location. It is one of the core parameters responsible for recommending a hospital cluster to the patient. Some other additional inputs are threshold rating which is the minimum hospital rating that the patient desires, and approximate budget that is the patient's budget. After the completion of disease prediction, assign the patient to their respective specialization. Then the next part of the system deals with cluster allocation and hospital selection.

Recommendation System

The recommender system is one of the crucial components of CluniacChain. This system uses a clustering algorithm to categorize hospitals into several clusters, which may then be selected based on several parameters described in Table 1.

Table 1. List of parameters for the CluniacChain Recommender System

Sr No	Parameter	Description
1	Specialization	Specialization of the hospital
2	Location	Lat. Long. of the hospital /geo-tracking
3	Threshold Rating	Feedback from patients
4	Average cost of treatment	Median cost treatment for any procedure
5	Capacity	Availability of seats
6	Fatalities	Fatalities in hospital
7	Recovery rate	Average survival-to-discharge rate

Table 2. Comparison of clustering algorithms ideal for the proposed recommender system

Algorithm	Complexity
K Means	O(n^2)
Mean Shift	O(n^2)
Agglomerative Clustering	O(n^3)
Affinity Propagation	O (n^2 * T), T = no of iterations

Time complexities of each Algorithm (*n is the no of datapoints)

Based on the time complexity as shown in Table 2, K-Means and Mean Shift clustering takes the least time and Agglomerative Clustering has the highest time complexity. Higher time complexity may cause significant delay and require more computation power to be feasible for big chunks of data. The distinguishing power of each algorithm is tested by running it on the 2-D data as shown in Figure 3.

Figure 3. Arbitrary data plotted

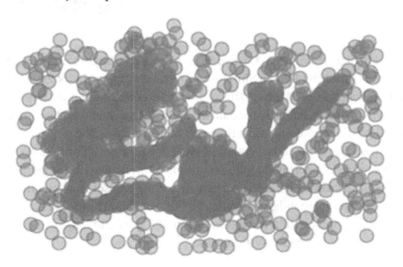

Figure 4. Cluster formation of different algorithms

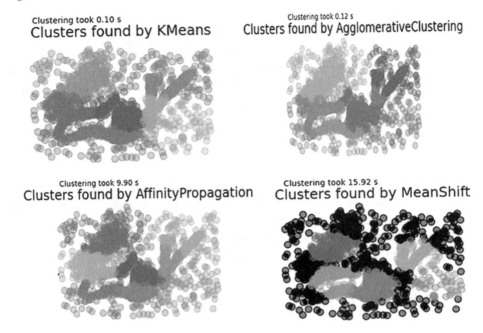

Figure 4 depicts the clusters formed by K-Means and Agglomerative Clustering, Affinity Propagation, and Mean Shift providing the Arbitrary data shown in Figure 3 as input. In conclusion, K-Means, Affinity propagation, and Agglomerative Clustering formed similar clusters on the same dataset, and K-Means took the least time of 0.10 seconds. Mean Shift took the most time of 15.92 seconds. The plots show that the K-Means algorithm is the most versatile in speed vs. cluster identification, followed by Agglomerative Clustering that showed similar clustering with comparable speed.

The algorithms are then tested on a benchmarking dataset created with a varying number of data points to judge the scalability of each algorithm. This mock dataset consists of data points with a fixed dimension of 7 attributes (the same number of factors that the recommender system uses).

Figure 5. Performance Comparison of Clustering Implementations

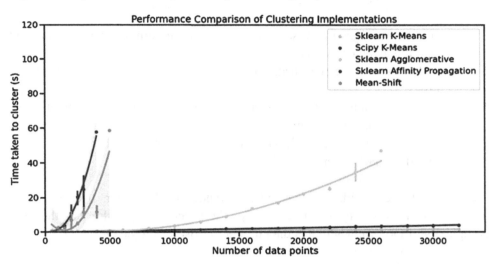

Figure 5 clearly shows that the K-Means algorithm fares well in terms of scalability that is of utmost importance in this application since the number of data points increases rather rapidly. Based on the above results, K-Means clustering is selected as the ideal candidate as the clustering algorithm for the recommender system.

K-Means Algorithm in Hospital Clustering

1. Select k number of clusters.
2. Select k number of centroids at random from the data set of hospitals.
3. 3. Calculate proximity to each of these centroids from the hospital by determining the Euclidean distance d between them.

$$d = \sqrt{((s_1-s_2)^2+(l_1-l_2)^2+(t_1-t_2)^2+(a_1-a_2)^2+(c_1-c_2)^2+(f_1-f_2)^2+(r_1-r_2)^2)} \tag{1}$$

Here the subscripts (1) represent the values of the centroid and subscript (2) represents the value of attributes for the data point that is the hospital to be clustered.

s = Specialization (categorical variable)

l = Location

t = Threshold Rating

a = Average cost of treatment

c = Capacity

f = Fatalities

r = Recovery rate

4. Group the hospitals into k sets based on the minimum distance d calculated around the given centroids.
5. Calculate the average of each attribute within each cluster formed around these centroids.
6. Updated centroids have their attribute value as an average calculated for hospitals assigned to its cluster.
7. Continue performing steps 3, 6 till these centroids cease to update.
8. Obtain the final clusters.

Initially, the centroids are selected in a randomized manner. It ensures that the process of clustering executes quickly. The proposed algorithm has the time complexity of $O(n^2)$, where n is the number of hospitals to be clustered.

If a new hospital enters the CluniacChain system, it gets classified using the K-Means algorithm described above into a cluster in which other hospitals with similar attributes are grouped.

CluniacChain then re-clusters the hospital when the ratio of the number of clustered hospitals to the number of unclustered hospitals is severely disturbed from the preset threshold. For the ratio calculation, the system fetches the value of the number of hospitals clustered since the previous iteration and the number of the new additions/removals of hospitals since the last clustering from the hospital cluster table defined. Once re-clustered, a more accurate cluster is formed with the updated assignment of new hospitals. Now the system reinitializes the number of additions/removals of unclustered hospitals.

The cluster allocation by CluniacChain's recommender system for a new patient is done by calculating the Euclidean distance d as shown in Eq. (1) of the query with details from Table 1. These details are sent to the recommender system and compared to each k centroids to form the clusters. After cluster allocation, a list is presented to the patient, ranking hospitals with the lowest Euclidean distance of the selected cluster. In the following sections, the blockchain specification and schema for databases are explained to store and share the EHR records by the CluniacChain system.

Blockchain Specifications

Consortium blockchain, also known as a federated blockchain, is the blockchain type used in our system. Here the hospital clusters act as the federated entities responsible for pushing data onto the blockchain. The patient needs to provide their consent for the access of medical records by the hospital. Keep the Electronic Health Records in the cluster's database and create pointers to the medical records. Only push these pointers to the blockchain network as Smart Contracts between the hospital and the patient. Because medical records are very data expensive, storing them on the blockchain would make the whole blockchain network very data inefficient. The pointer-based approach helps in overcoming this. Thus, healthcare records will be kept in the cluster's database.

Data stored on the cluster's database is in encrypted form so that in case of a data breach, this ensures that the data can't be misused. The encryption is done based on the attributes issued by the attribute issuers. When the data is encrypted and signed by the patient, enter it into the cluster database. The application's database is managed using firebase, which is a NoSQL cloud-hosted database. It can scale up as per the requirements. It is a platform developed by Google for providing database support to mobile and web applications. Firebase provides CRUD APIs for seamless integration with the application. Since the patient records consist of sensitive data, therefore it is encrypted before being pushed to firebase. The encryption algorithm used is AES, and the secret key used for encryption and decryption of data is the user's document key provided by firebase. The subsequent sections discuss Attribute-based encryption and signing in detail.

Since the system comprises a consortium blockchain, the consensus algorithm used is Proof of Stake (PoS). Due to the prior authorization of the hospital clusters to push data onto the blockchain, using Proof of Work (PoW) consensus would be a waste of computing power and resources (Cao et al., 2020, p. 480-485). For the verification of a block, choose another hospital cluster. It is done based on an age factor of the Hospital Cluster. The older the age, the greater the chance of being selected. After a Hospital Cluster has done its verification task, reset its age to zero to avoid starvation. The hospital that will push fraudulent transactions onto the blockchain would be given a low priority in the recommender system, one of the factors responsible for recommending the hospital. Since no hospital would want its reputation to go down, it ensures that it constantly pushes correct data to the chain. Keep a counter for each hospital that would increase every time a fraudulent transaction is encountered from that hospital. Upon crossing the threshold of fraudulent transactions, that hospital would be removed from the system. Therefore, the CluniacChain penalty system prioritizes valid transactions and incentivizes the hospitals to push correct data to the chain.

Figure 6 shows the performance of the CluniacChain prototype with PoW implementation. It shows how PoW is a time-consuming mechanism. The block size was fixed at 1 KB, and the mathematical puzzle involved finding a number q such that hash(pq) contained leading five zeroes, where p is the previous proof, and q is the new proof. The prototype was tested on Intel(R) Core (TM) i5-7300HQ CPU @ 2.50GHz, 2496 Mhz, 4 Core(s), 4 Logical Processor(s) using Python 3.8.10.

Based on the prior works (Gervais et al., 2016), and (Wu, & Song, & Wang, 2020, p. 1-13), Table 3 shows the comparison between Proof of Work (PoW) and Proof of Stake (PoS) in terms of Consensus, Finality, Latency, Throughput, and Scalability.

Figure 6. Performance analysis for PoW implementation of CluniacChain

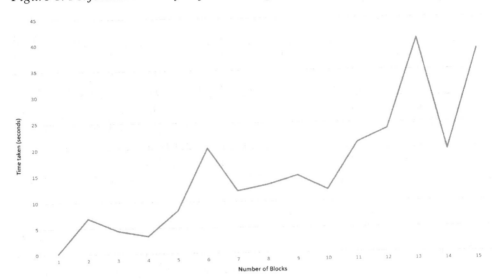

Table 3. Comparison of PoW and PoS

Parameters	PoW	PoS Consortium
Consensus	No supervising permission	Supervising permission required
Finality	Is not ensured	Is ensured
Latency	6 blocks time	Network latency
Throughput	Less no of tx per sec	Huge no tx per sec
Scalability	Large number of miners	Small number of validators

Issuing Attribute Keys for Privileges

Among popular cryptographic hash functions like SHA-1, BLAKE2, SHA-3, and MD5, BLAKE2 seems the ideal candidate for our purpose due to the following factors:

- It is appropriate for distributed systems because it can quickly compute a large amount of secure hash data.
- It is also quite efficient on a single-core CPU.
- It is currently the only hash function with no successful attack performed on it.

According to the reviewed work (Sharma, & Yasmin, 2018), it was concluded that BLAKE2 had no avowed security threats as compared to popular hashing algorithms like MD-5 and SHA-1.

To ensure that only patient-authorized entities are allowed access to their data, encrypt it and sign it, providing data authenticity. For understanding the generation of attribute keys, it is required to define the additional terms.

Generate a secret key to encrypt the patient data. This step involves the AES (Daor et al., 1999) algorithm for encrypting the EHR belonging to the patient and ABE (Attribute-based encryption) to encrypt the secret key.

Let the private key of the patient be denoted as *K1* and the public key as *K2*.

Let the key-issuer be denoted by *KI* (KI is the Hospital Cluster in this system). The cluster generates different keys (Read/Write/Update/Delete) based on permissions granted.

Let the Secret Key be denoted by *Skey*.

Let the Attribute Key Set be denoted by *AKS* which can be called the secret key of the secret key *Skey*.

Let the Electronic Health Record of the patient be denoted by EHR.

Let the Final Signature generated after applying the hashing algorithm BLAKE2b (Aumasson et al., 2013) on the ciphertexts be ζ.

Now, generating the ciphertexts:

$$T = \text{AES} \ (Skey, \text{EHR}) \tag{2}$$

Suppose the user has multiple attribute keys issued by some key issuer *KI*, then the ciphertext would be represented by:

$$U = \{ \text{ABE} \ (AKS_1, \ Skey), \ \text{ABE} \ (AKS_2, \ Skey) \ ..., \ \text{ABE} \ (AKS_n, \ Skey) \} \tag{3}$$

Where *AKS1* might be the secret key for the user's read permission, *AKS2* for the user's write permission, and so on.

Now before storing it into the database, hash these ciphertexts by using an appropriate hashing algorithm. Based on the advantages discussed earlier, the BLAKE2b algorithm for hashing is used here. So, after hashing these two ciphertexts, it can be denoted as:

V = blake2b (T, U) (4)

Finally, a signature will be generated using

ED25519, ζ = Sign $(K1, V)$ (5)

The ciphertexts T in Eq. (2), U in Eq. (3), and the signature ζ in Eq. (5) are ready to be uploaded into the database after the generation of the signature.

If the doctor wants to access the EHR of any patient, then the ciphertexts and the signature ζ in Eq. (5) are downloaded. If the ζ in Eq. (5) is valid, and the doctor possesses the required attributes used as attribute keys while encrypting, then they will be allowed to decrypt the U in Eq. (3) to obtain the *Skey* using which they can decrypt the EHR available in T Eq. (2).

Figure 7, Figure 8, Figure 9 and Figure 10 shows the comparison of the time taken to generate keys after encryption and signatures for different combinations of encryption and hashing algorithms. The Read x-label indicates that only Read permission was provided, based on which the signature was generated after hashing. Similarly, the Read + Write x-label indicates that only Read and Write permissions were provided, and Read + Write + Delete means that all the three permissions were provided. All the values in the y-axis are in seconds.

Figure 7. 3DES and Blake2b combination

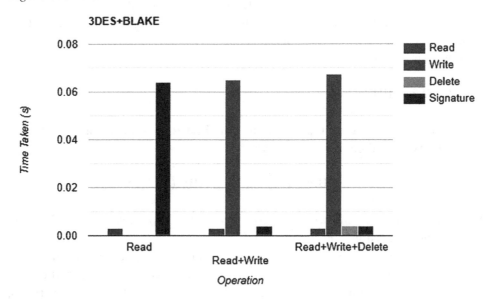

Figure 8. 3DES and SHA256 combination

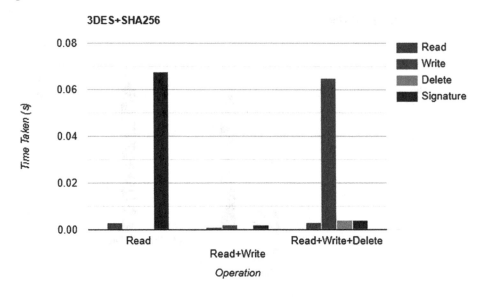

Figure 9. AES and Blake2b combination

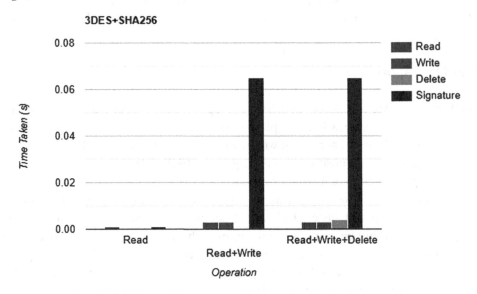

Figure 10. AES and SHA256 combination

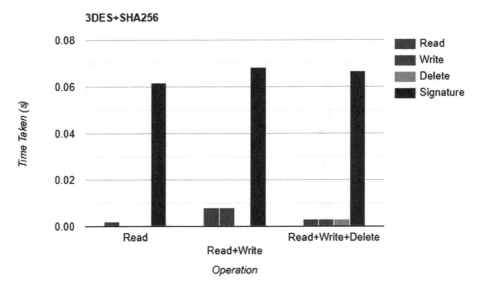

Observing the security and computation time tradeoff, AES with Blake2b proves to be ideal for CluniacChain, as shown in Figure 9. Also, the cluster permissions table stores the Signature (ζ in Eq. (5)), Attribute Keys (U in Eq. (3)), and the list of permissions which includes the Patient Id, Hospital Id, and the Keys issued for every patient.

The Operations

The Electronic Medical Records (EMRs) of a patient are combined with additional information to provide a holistic picture as Electronic Health Records (EHRs). Storing the EHRs after encryption would ensure the security of the data. Similarly, a digital signature will ensure the integrity of the EHR. For future enhancement, a sign-encrypt-sign approach would be ideal.

As discussed in the previous sections, encryption and signing are part of a multistage process. The Hospital Cluster (HC) would act as the attribute issuing authority in the process. It would be responsible for issuing the secret key for the patient. The user authorizes the hospital for specific permissions such as Read, Write, Update and Delete in the next step. Based on the allowed attributes, the Hospital Cluster issues corresponding attribute keys. The four operations, Read, Write, Update and Delete, applied on the EHR are synchronized to the blockchain.

Record Reading and Adding (Read and Write)

The EHR reading and adding operation requires the two attributes Read and Write. In the first step, the patient's secret key encrypts the EHR. Signing the encrypted text by the patient in the next step ensures data integrity. Using a mutually agreed set of attribute keys between the hospital and the patient, the patient's secret key encryption happens simultaneously. In the next step, the user uploads the encrypted EHR to the server. The server sends the information regarding the encrypted data to the blockchain as a Smart Contract. After verification, the addition of the new block into the blockchain occurs. Finally, storing encrypted data in the database happens, and the patient receives information added notification.

If another hospital wants to read the encrypted data, the patient needs to grant the read permission to the hospital through the Hospital Cluster. The creation of a smart contract for information retrieval happens. Then the block for this transaction is verified and added to the chain. Because of the patient's read permission grant, the hospital can use the read attribute key to get the secret key for decrypting the encrypted EHR.

Record Update (Update)

If patients want to update their EHR for a particular hospital, they need the update attribute key. After the permission is granted, the patient can upload their modified EHR to the server. Encryption of the EHR using the patient's secret key and signing by the patient occurs just like the Record Reading and Writing operation. Once again, the server sends information regarding the encrypted EHR to the blockchain as a Smart Contract. After verification, the addition of the new block to the blockchain occurs. Replacement of old EHR with the new EHR occurs through unlinking followed by linking. Finally, deletion of old EHR and addition of new EHR in the database happens. Once successful, the patient receives an information update notification.

Record Deletion (Delete)

If the patient wants to delete their EHR, they need the delete attribute key. After the permission authorization between the patient and hospital to delete the EHR, the delete attribute key comes into the picture. The patient then needs to confirm the deletion operation on the EHR. Then, the server sends information regarding the deletion of the EHR to the blockchain as a Smart Contract. After verification, the addition of the new block to the blockchain occurs. The EHR is then unlinked and deleted from the database. Once successful, the patient receives an information deletion notification.

IMPLEMENTATION

To use the services offered by CluniacChain, a new user should register first before unlocking all the services like Disease predictor, medicine prescription, saving their medical reports safely in the Cluniac database, and requesting appointments with a doctor based on the severity of the disease.

After the user registers, they have to submit their blood group, Date of Birth, Email ID, name, and address which are stored and mapped to a generated unique ID. Let's assume the user wants to identify a particular disease they are suffering from by providing symptoms like headaches, nausea, and sensitivity to light. The CluniacChain Recommender System predicts migraine and prescribes ibuprofen to the user. If the user is satisfied with the medication, their medical record would be stored in CluniacChain through the Record Reading and Adding operation. Otherwise, they can go ahead and book an appointment with a doctor.

For booking an appointment, CluniacChain uses the user's address at the time of registration. The system will search for the nearby hospital clusters containing a list of hospitals and assign a hospital based on the patient's requirements. In this case, the user is assigned to a Neurology hospital in Hospital Cluster A to diagnose migraine further. Then the appointment request is sent to the reservation queue, and the hospital administrator handles them. After the appointment confirmation, the doctor will prescribe medicines and the patient's EHR update occurs through the Record Update operation. Figure 11 shows the described example in a stepwise manner.

Figure 11. Example showing the workflow of real-world implementation of CluniacChain

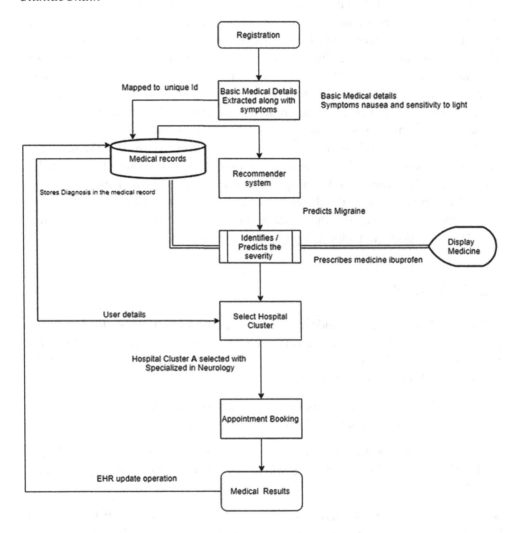

CONCLUSION

The proposed system incorporates blockchain technology to store medical records to harness its potential advantages in the medical sector. The system uses the Attribute-based encryption method to sign the EHR of the user such that only authorized personnel can retrieve the EHR using the designated attribute keys they possess, ensuring that the EHRs are secure and no unauthorized access is allowed.

Users can enter their location, filter hospitals based on ratings and budget. The proposed system will then match them with the best possible Hospital Cluster, and then the user can choose any hospital as per their liking from the list of hospitals. Hospitals trying to access the EHR must be permitted by the user through the sharing of attribute keys. If the user doesn't want to visit the hospital, they can use the chatbot to describe their symptoms. The system will then give the possible disease based on the input using the BERT algorithm. The specialized doctors are suggested to the user based on the prediction. If the user is not satisfied, they can book an appointment to visit the nearest specialized doctor.

The penalty system implemented in the architecture ensures that the privileges are not misused. A penalty score keeps track of the misconduct. If it exceeds a preset threshold value, then that hospital would be banned from using this system. Also, for keeping track of the different clusters, this system uses a Global Cluster Connector. Data security through blockchain is the main advantage of this system. The data stays protected with less possibility of a breach.

REFERENCES

Athota, L., Shukla, V. K., Pandey, N., & Rana, A. (2020). Chatbot for Healthcare System Using Artificial Intelligence. *2020 8th International Conference on Reliability, Infocom Technologies and Optimization (Trends and Future Directions) (ICRITO).* 10.1109/ICRITO48877.2020.9197833

Aumasson, J-P., Neves, S., Wilcox-O'Hearn, Z., & Winnerlein, C. (2013). *BLAKE2: Simpler, smaller, fast as MD5.*. doi:10.1007/978-3-642-38980-1_8

Bell, L., Buchanan, W. J., Cameron, J., & Lo, O. (2018). Applications of Blockchain Within Healthcare. *Blockchain in Healthcare Today, 1.* Advance online publication. doi:10.30953/bhty.v1.8

Burst, I. Q. (2017). *Bringing Health to Life Whitepaper* [White paper]. Retrieved from https://www.burstiq.com/wp-content/uploads/2017/08/BurstIQ-whitepaper_19Jul2017reduced.pdf

Cao, B., Zhang, Z., Feng, D., Zhang, S., Zhang, L., Peng, M., & Li, Y. (2020). Performance analysis and comparison of PoW, PoS and DAG based blockchains. *Digital Communications and Networks, 6*(4), 480–485. doi:10.1016/j.dcan.2019.12.001

Daor, J., Daemen, J., & Rijmen, V. (1999). *AES proposal: rijndael.* Academic Press.

Davenport, T., & Kalakota, R. (2019). The potential for artificial intelligence in healthcare. *Future Healthcare Journal*, *6*(2), 94–98. doi:10.7861/futurehosp.6-2-94 PMID:31363513

Devlin, J., Chang, M., Lee, K., & Toutanova, K. (2019). *BERT: Pre-training of Deep Bidirectional Transformers for Language Understanding.* ArXiv, abs/1810.04805.

Drug Review Dataset (Drugs.com) Data Set. (2018, October 4). *UCI Machine Learning Repository.* https://archive.ics.uci.edu/ml/datasets/ Drug+Review+Dataset+%28Drugs.com%29

Eyal, I. (2017). Blockchain Technology: Transforming Libertarian Cryptocurrency Dreams to Finance and Banking Realities. *Computer*, *50*(9), 38–49. doi:10.1109/ MC.2017.3571042

Gervais, A., Karame, G. O., Wüst, K., Glykantzis, V., Ritzdorf, H., & Capkun, S. (2016). On the Security and Performance of Proof of Work Blockchains. *Proceedings of the 2016 ACM SIGSAC Conference on Computer and Communications Security.* 10.1145/2976749.2978341

Hasselgren, A., Kralevska, K., Gligoroski, D., Pedersen, S. A., & Faxvaag, A. (2020). Blockchain in healthcare and health sciences—A scoping review. *International Journal of Medical Informatics*, *134*, 104040. doi:10.1016/j.ijmedinf.2019.104040 PMID:31865055

Haux, R. (2006). Health information systems – past, present, future. *International Journal of Medical Informatics*, *75*(3–4), 268–281. doi:10.1016/j. ijmedinf.2005.08.002 PMID:16169771

HealthCoin. (2019). *The Health Coin White Paper* [White paper]. Retrieved from https://thehealthcoin.io/wp-content/uploads/2018/04/HEALTHCOIN-WHITE-PAPER.pdf

Heart, T., Ben-Assuli, O., & Shabtai, I. (2017). A review of PHR, EMR and EHR integration: A more personalized healthcare and public health policy. *Health Policy and Technology*, *6*(1), 20–25. doi:10.1016/j.hlpt.2016.08.002

Menachemi, N., & Collum. (2011). Benefits and drawbacks of electronic health record systems. *Risk Management and Healthcare Policy*, *47*, 47. Advance online publication. doi:10.2147/RMHP.S12985 PMID:22312227

Mero, J. (2018). The effects of two-way communication and chat service usage on consumer attitudes in the e-commerce retailing sector. *Electronic Markets*, *28*(2), 205–217. doi:10.100712525-017-0281-2

Noroozi, V., Zhang, Y., Bakhturina, E., & Kornuta, T. (2020). *A Fast and Robust BERT-based Dialogue State Tracker for Schema-Guided Dialogue Dataset.* ArXiv. arXiv:2008.12335

Park, J., & Park, J. (2017). Blockchain Security in Cloud Computing: Use Cases, Challenges, and Solutions. *Symmetry, 9*(8), 164. doi:10.3390ym9080164

Pilkington, M. (2016). Blockchain technology: principles and applications. *Research Handbook on Digital Transformations*, 225–253. doi:10.4337/9781784717766.00019

Radziwill, N., & Benton, M. (2017). *Evaluating Quality of Chatbots and Intelligent Conversational Agents.* arXiv:1704.04579

Rajput, A.E. (2019). *Natural Language Processing, Sentiment Analysis and Clinical Analytics.* ArXiv, abs/1902.00679.

Reisman & Miriam. (2017). EHRs: The Challenge of Making Electronic Data Usable and Interoperable. *P & T: A Peer-Reviewed Journal for Formulary Management, 42*, 572–575.

Shang, R., Ara, B., Zada, I., Nazir, S., Ullah, Z., & Khan, S. U. (2021). Analysis of Simple K-Mean and Parallel K-Mean Clustering for Software Products and Organizational Performance Using Education Sector Dataset. *Scientific Programming, 2021*, 1–20. doi:10.1155/2021/9988318

Sharma, V. & Yasmin, N. (2018). An overview-comparative study of Hash Functions. *International Journal of Engineering Research, 5*(6).

Uthayashangar, S., Dhanya, T., Dharshini, S., & Gayathri, R. (2021). Decentralized Blockchain Based System for Secure Data Storage in Cloud. *2021 International Conference on System, Computation, Automation and Networking (ICSCAN).* 10.1109/ICSCAN53069.2021.9526408

Wu, Y., Song, P., & Wang, F. (2020). Hybrid Consensus Algorithm Optimization: A Mathematical Method Based on POS and PBFT and Its Application in Blockchain. *Mathematical Problems in Engineering, 2020*, 1–13. doi:10.1155/2020/7270624

Yadav, C. (2021). Design Engineering AES-Light Weight CP-ABE Based Privacy Protection Framework with Effective Access Control Mechanism in Cloud Framework. *Design Engineering.*

Chapter 15
A Cyber Physical System Framework for Industrial Predictive Maintenance Using Machine Learning

Sharanya S.
SRM Institute of Science and Technology, India

ABSTRACT

The rampant developments in the field of predictive analytics, artificial intelligence, big data, along with information and communication technologies have opened new ventures in cyber physical systems (CPS). The wide range of opportunities presented by CPS facilitated massive transformation of industrial processes that converged to building smart systems under the umbrella of Industry 4.0. The manufacturing and energy sector are now shifting their focus on predictive maintenance to pre plan their maintenance activities to reduce the downtime at optimized costs. This proactive maintenance planning involves the integration of multiple technologies like big data analytics, machine learning, and internet of things to build a complete, comprehensive framework that predicts the onset of failure from the early warning signs. The primal focus of this work is to develop a generic CPS framework for predictive maintenance (PdM) in industries from the condition monitored data.

DOI: 10.4018/978-1-7998-9308-0.ch015

A BRIEF OVERVIEW OF CONDITION
MONITORING AND INDUSTRY 4.0

Condition Monitoring (CM) is the latest buzzword in the manufacturing sector. CM is defined as the uninterrupted process of monitoring a system, in the context of diagnosing a fault or failure. This process can be fractionated into a sequence of activities such as monitoring, detection of faults, diagnosing the cause of fault and fault prognostics. CM involves closely monitoring the critical parameters that can effectively characterize the health state of the system or equipment under study. Not all the parameters contribute to CM which is followed by fault detection. The domain experts have to delineate the critical variables or parameters whose deviated values can be a direct implication of the occurrence of faults.

CM is broadly bifurcated into reactive and proactive CM. The former diagnoses the causes of the fault after its occurrence while the latter strives to foresee the fault before its occurrence. It is very evident that the world is moving deeper into the era of Artificial Intelligence (AI) and its cognate technologies. The maintenance sector in industries also harness its benefits by embracing Machine Learning (ML), Big Data Analytics (BDA) and Deep Learning (DL) in CM and failure prediction of equipment. Fault prognostics is an integral part of smart manufacturing, which is the pivotal objective of Industry 4.0. Predicting the fault from the early signs offers many fold advantages to the industries:

- Demean the overall equipment maintenance time and downtime
- Accelerate the productivity rate
- Increase the working time
- Mitigate the maintenance costs
- Ensure safety

CM is an effective tool in fault prognostics, since it can avoid mitigating the frequency of unplanned maintenance activities. Predicting the failures has become an inevitable part of any smart infrastructure. The advent of technologies like Internet of Things (IoT), Cloud computing, Digital twins, Edge computing and Edge AI has accelerated the advancements in industries, facilitating the evolution of Industry 4.0.

Evolution of Industry 4.0

The smart transformation of the industries towards embedding intelligence and empowering the workers by using modern control systems is the primary motto of Industry 4.0. The conviction of Industry 4.0 is perceived to achieve the following traits:

- Integrate the physical and digital world
- Secure data transfer
- Intelligent automation
- Increased degree of product customization
- Smart assemble line
- More tightly coupled industry value chain

The metamorphosis to Industry 4.0 is realized as a result of numerous advancements that happened over the years, which are compartmentalized into various generations. Each generation will evolve as a progression in which the legacy systems will be replaced with more powerful modern rendition. The changes in each generation are gradual and incremental. The salient features of each industrial revolution are discussed below.

Industry 1.0

Eighteenth century witnessed the era of the first industrial revolution, which was triggered by steam power. The production line was mechanized thereby capable of producing large volumes of goods. Power looms and steam powered locomotives came into reality. This brought a massive change in human lifestyle and industrial activity. Ford assembly line is a well-known example for mass production with increased productivity.

Industry 2.0

The great breakthrough in the second generation was the generation of electricity. 1870's envisioned massive industrial production driven by electrical energy. This led to stupendous employment of the human workforce. Mammoth conveyor belts and large assembly lines can exist.

Industry 3.0

The third generation was mainly characterized by the advent of electronic products and computers. Usage of computers and data exchange was further increased by the deployment of ARPANET, which is the brainchild of today's internet. These developments further automated the production lines in the manufacturing industries with high end technologies. The memory programmable controls reduced the requirement of human assistance.

Industry 4.0

The main plug of the fourth industrial revolution is the debut of Information and Communication Technologies (ICT), which constitutes the cyber world. This era is actually a constellation of array of technologies like AI, digital twins, 3D printing, additive manufacturing, cloud computing, edge computing, IoT etc. Industry 4.0 is a lattice of all these technologies built with the aim of achieving smart factories, in which the communication between components, systems and people is completely networked (Ricardo, 2018). The projected production line is nearly autonomous with minimal human control. The elementary hallmarks of this era are wholesomeness, speed and pervasive nature. One of the pivotal application areas is predictive maintenance, where the maintenance activities are scheduled by foreseeing the failures.

Thus the modern day industries are transiting to become smarter by imparting the futuristic and state of art technologies to increase the production at declined maintenance and manufacturing costs.

Condition Monitoring

The main goal of CM is to control the adverse effects of equipment failure, thereby reducing its downtime. The term availability focus on the duration of time the machine can operate to its promised performance. This is analogous to the operational time. The maintenance policies of the industries is designed based on the CM strategies adopted by them. There are two types of maintenance policies namely reactive and proactive maintenance. The reactive maintenance policies come into effect after the occurrence of fault in the system. This is relatively cheap. The proactive maintenance policies predicts the occurrence of fault from its early warning signs. Hence these strategies has wider scope to be deployed in smart industries. Proactive strategies are classified into preventive and predictive maintenance. The taxonomy of the maintenance activity is shown in Figure 1.

Preventive Maintenance

This policy plans the maintenance activity in regular time intervals. Maintenance team does their routine checks periodically based on the operational hours or time. The usage or operational based maintenance activities are carried out after the equipment crosses a threshold running time. Time based maintenance is done after a pre-specified amount of time. Both these methods are widely applied in manufacturing industries to save time and costs. The major limitation here is the maintenance activity will be invoked irrespective of the health condition of the machine.

Predictive Maintenance

This proactive maintenance strategy predicts the lifetime of the equipment by analyzing the trends and patterns from the critical variables values. This deploys condition monitoring as a tool to detect the abnormal patterns from the data (Thyago, 2019). This increases the magnitude of proactive nature, thus reducing the frequency of maintenance activity. The ambit of predictive maintenance is further widened by predictive analytics, AI based techniques and IoT.

Differences Between Preventive and Predictive Maintenance

Though both predictive and preventive maintenance fall under the canopy of proactive maintenance strategies, they possess some inherent differences. Preventive maintenance involves periodic inspection of the equipment irrespective of the need. On the other hand predictive maintenance is done only when there is need for maintenance activity. Preventive maintenance does not necessarily require any condition monitoring activity, since they are done periodically without any inspection. Hence they do not incur any additional investment to develop the infrastructure. But predictive maintenance is an on demand strategy which requires initial investments in infrastructure and skill training. Preventive maintenance is bounded on the average lifespan of an equipment whereas predictive maintenance is determined on predetermined health conditions of the machinery. In short preventive maintenance appears to be more economical and simple but the long term benefits of predictive maintenance outmatch the former.

Figure 1. Taxonomy of Maintenance Strategies

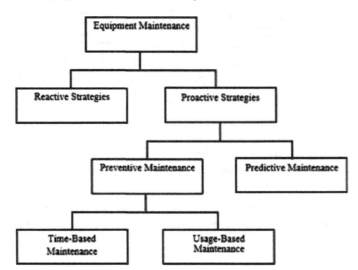

ROLE OF CYBER PHYSICAL SYSTEMS
IN PREDICTIVE MAINTENANCE

The Industry 4.0, swarming sensor deployment, data analytic tools, developments in predictive analytics and BDA has collectively conferred to achieve excellence in the field of smart manufacturing (Saeed, 2019). The notion of Cyber physical Systems (CPS) appears to be an amalgamation of computing entities that connects the physical world with the digital world (Monostori, 2014). Cyber physical systems operate on 3C's namely Connect, Communicate and Control. This makes them best suited for use cases like industrial automation. CPS redesign the outlook of the entire manufacturing sector by transforming the industries into a complete cognitive enterprise. The three major pillars that foster the growth of CPS in industries are:

- Interconnection between various edge devices
- Analytics and visualization of industrial Big Data
- Smart decision systems

Figure 2. CPS connecting the physical and digital world

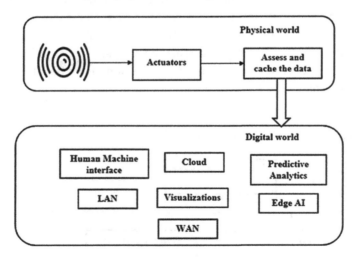

Figure 2 depicts the interconnection of the physical and digital world through CPS. The raw data from the physical entities are recorded through sensors. The actuators operate in reverse direction which realizes the physical process from the sensor values. These data are cached in a storage medium. All these activities ensure that the physical world data is decoded and further processed by the virtual computing systems. The cyber world comprises innumerous advanced technologies for intelligent data analytics such as predictive analytics, Edge AI, Machine Learning, Deep Learning, fog computing etc. The data from the physical world floats in the cyber world through multiple interconnection mediums such as WAN, LAN, Low range communication and wireless medium. The general perspective of CPS is given in Figure 3.

Figure 3. Various perspectives of CPS in the context of Industry 4.0
(Lee, 2015)

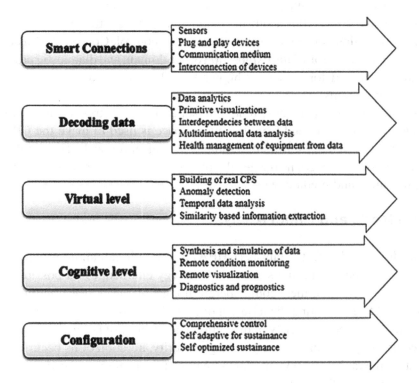

- **Smart Connections at More Granular Level:** Various networking technologies like LAN, WAN, Fibre optic cables and wireless medium are deployed to collect data from the edge devices installed at various geographic locations. Appropriate sensors, actuators, data transfer protocols, data security measures are the key components of the CPS. Inappropriate selection of these entities will heavily penalize the final performance of the CPS system.
- **Decoding data:** The data collected from various sensors actually represent the physical processes. Proper analysis will transform these data into useful

information, which escalates as higher level knowledge. Visualizations and exploring interdependencies among the data will give a detailed understanding on the domain. These results are later converted into valuable business insights.

- **Virtual level:** This is a more complex and advanced level where the acquired information reaches a central repository. CPS systems are built at this level only after extracting useful information from the free floating data. Some of the common ways of uprooting information are similarity analysis, anomaly detection, surprise event detection etc. These form the key constituent of the advanced decision support systems that are built in any CPS.

- **Cognitive level:** After acquiring detailed knowledge, the intelligent decision making is done on site or in remote mode of control. Cognitive data analysis, insights drawn from data, exploration of the domain and diagnostic procedures are considered for achieving higher level knowledge to build the decision support systems.

- **Configuration:** This level holds the supervisory control of the entire CPS. The feedback obtained from the cyber space is used to make the CPS more adaptive, reliable, self-configurable and self-optimized. The implications drawn from the cognitive level are applied to take real time corrective, preventive and predictive decisions.

Failure Mode and Effect Analysis

Failure Modes and Effect Analysis (FMEA) is a traditional failure prognostic tool that is widely adapted in industries. This strategy enumerates all possible failure modes in which an equipment could operate along with the recovery actions (Okoh, 2014). Apart from isolating the failure modes, FMEA also focuses on the effects of faults and the degree of severity of the faults. The severity of failure is gauged based on three primary variables namely damage severity, iteration of its occurrence and delineating the faulty component. All these three factors are integrated to form Risk Priority Number (RPN) as mentioned in equation 1.1.

RPN = Severity x Occurrence x Isolation   (1.1)

The RPN score is considered as an important metric to assess the impact of a specific fault or failure. The value of RPN is a predominant factor in evaluating the impact of the risk. The risks are higher, when the score is high. The historic data and heuristics are also involved in determining the extent of risk occurrence. The complete FMEA chart is given in Figure 4.

Figure 4. Failure Modes and Effect Analysis

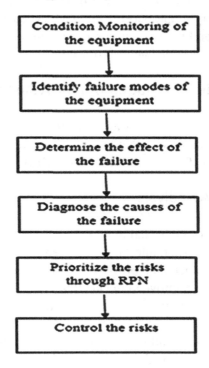

The continuous condition monitoring of the equipment under investigation will help in the process of fault identification. The cause of effect analysis of the fault is done to determine the reason behind the failure. The risk priority is estimated based on the RPN, which holds a primary role in carrying out the maintenance activity. This will greatly reduce the effect of faults and equipment failure in industries. The two common types of FMEA that is widely adopted by manufacturing industries are:

- **Design Failure Mode and Effect Analysis (DFMEA):** This mainly probes into the system to detect design-related failure and its controls. Malfunctioning of finished products, reliability and safety in the context of the product design is assessed by DFMEA. This is very desirable, since the failures are controlled at the design level without causing much damage to assets.
- **Process Failure Mode and Effect Analysis (PFMEA):** This mainly focuses on the faults and failures that are likely to occur in various manufacturing processes of equipment such as assembling, fabricating and mounting. This analysis is very much useful in identifying missing parts, misalignment, inappropriate dimensioning etc.

FMEA is the classical maintenance solution that is widely adopted in manufacturing industries. Though it is very simple but effective, FMEA depends on expert's decision. The rudimentary faults and failures can easily be identified and isolated. This is a more economical predictive fault diagnosis procedure with intensive human activity.

Advantages and Disadvantages of FMEA Analysis

FMEA is a well-structured and logical way of identifying the faults in a cost effective way. This is a proven methodology that highlights the key performance areas that require attention. The benefits and limitations of FMEA are analyzed here:

Advantages of FMEA Analysis

- Early identification of faults and failures
- Easily highlight the system interfacing problems
- Keeps track of product and process failures, whose knowledge will be immensely helpful to improve in the lagging areas.
- Helps the architect or designer about the pitfalls in the product at the design stage
- Proper documentation of failure modes and its mitigation strategies
- Easily designed either through hand drafted sheets or computer software
- Recovery actions can be planned according to the RPN score

Limitations of FMEA Analysis

- One of the traditional methods that requires tedious and human intensive tracking activities.
- When the FMEA is not done on proper time, then it does not serve its purpose
- Detection of multiple failures and propagation of failures to different points is often disregarded
- It is a complete subjective analysis
- FMEA should be built as a dynamic system, where frequent analysis and updates should happen
- Uncertainty in assessing the failure and recovery rates

Rationale of CPS in Predictive Maintenance

Industry 4.0 mainly focuses on imparting smartness at every feasible locale in its spectrum. One of the most lucrative areas is predictive maintenance, where the failure time of the equipment is predicted from the early warning signs. Predictive maintenance is one of the features of Prognostics and Health Management (PHM). ML and DL algorithms used to predict the health state of any equipment by quantitatively monitoring its critical health parameters like dissipated heat/ temperature, process efficiency, auditory signals, pressure, vibration, flow rate of any liquid, and humidity (Shankar Sankararaman, 2015). Any deviation from the normal operational profile of the equipment under study will be considered as an anomaly. This is an early symptom of fault or equipment failure. Literature suggests many instances of deploying CPS in maintenance systems. Some of the notable works are discussed here.

Maxim Shcherbakov proposed a concept based CPS model for proactive maintenance that optimizes the downtime of the equipment (Shcherbakov, 2020) . Two approaches are proposed in this work. The first work focuses on predicting the failure before its onset while the latter aids in automating the decision making process. This acts as an excellent platform for building a CPS system for predictive maintenance. Integration of multiple computing technologies like BDA, IoT and cloud computing for developing a CPS for predictive maintenance is proposed by Fang-Ning Yang (Yang, 2019). The critical variables from the mechanical big data are processed by offline association rules to implement predictive maintenance. The salient feature of this work is that it considers interrelation between various factors that causes faults and equipment failures in industries.

Intense research has been done in positioning the COS in its right place in the industrial maintenance. A holistic and well-structured process with various stages in development of CPS in the perspective of the organization (Sascha Julian Oks, 2018). This framework will greatly help the small and medium scale industries to adapt to setting a CPS. An integrated work that intertwines the modelling and simulation of the physical systems into CPS is proposed under the notion cyber physical modelling and simulation (Sascha Julian Oks, 2019). The reference architecture in the proposed work delineates guidelines and structure for the industrial activities that could mimic the CPS. This system provides a greater degree of scalability, robustness and modularity. This work can be extended to any specific industrial case study, which is a real success for the proposed work.

A tight coupling of CPS with the maintenance principles is described by Santiago Ruiz-Arenas (Santiago Ruiz-Arenas, 2014). This work details that some of the features of CPS cannot be connected with the physical world and some will be partially connected. Some features will be strongly connected with CPS. These principles are implemented with practical examples that provide more detailed insights to develop a complete maintenance advisory system. A complete deployable framework is proposed by Olivier that explores CPS for enabling intelligent decision making (Olivier Sénéchal, 2019). The key constituents are Sustainable Condition based maintenance that guides in the evaluation of Remaining sustainable life or

Remaining Useful Life of any equipment. This framework is very generic and shifted towards building holonic structures.

The 5C way of incremental building of CPS under multi regime conditions is discussed in Behrad Bagheri (Bagheri, 2015). The proposed architecture covers the entire lifecycle of data right from its gathering stage to decision making phase. This makes use of emerging computing technologies like cloud computing to provide efficient data access. Highly adaptive clustering which can detect new operational regimes without human intervention is proposed in the work. CPS finds its application even in the post prognosis. A cloud based framework that uses IoT to connect the physical space and the cyber space is proposed by Sata et. al (Sata, 2018). The cloud services are utilized at PaaS, SaaS and IaaS levels. This framework is implemented to estimate the travel costs by the technicians. The Genetic Algorithm (GA) approach is used to optimize the problem. The shortest distance is calculated using stochastic based searching techniques.

A cloud and IoT based CPS is proposed by Hehenberger that focuses on integration of individual physical components into a comprehensive computational system (Hehenberger, 2016). This work details the requirements of CPS from the industry perspective along with the interaction and integration to form Cyber Physical Production Systems (CPPSs). A fresh approach of combining Unified Modelling Language (UML) and System Modelling Language (SysML) into a new framework termed Concurrent Modeling and Architectural Design (COMET) that aids in creation of prototypes and blueprints for maintenance activities (Rauniyar, 2010). Another methodology of integrating CPS with Digital Twins (DTs) in developing a more efficient, resilient and intensive real time CPS is proposed by Fei Tao (FeiTao, 2019). Though the CPS and DTs are not aligned on same objective, but their correlation will definitely help in building collaborative components. CPS systems are not confined only to mechanical industry. Cyber Physical Energy Systems (CPES) are new flavor of energy management and maintenance system with intelligent co-ordination and communication (Faruque, 2014). This model validates the usage of multitude of technologies to build residential microgrid. Jazdi et al. introduced a new framework for integrating CPS in implementing more reliable and secure development cycle (Jazdi, 2014). This framework addresses the major challenges of CPS in Industry 4.0.

Role of Machine Learning and Deep Learning in Predictive Maintenance

Handcrafting of features to deploy predictive maintenance in industries is a tiresome and challenging task. A weighted long Recurrent Convolutional Long Short Term Memory (LSTM) addresses this challenge by modelling a double layered inner LSTM and double layered outer LSTMs (Zhenyu Wu, 2018) . This model uses under sampling and the objective function used here is weighted cost sensitive loss function. The primary advantage of this model is that it is best suited for highly imbalanced classes, which is more common in fault diagnosis. This model is able to learn from the temporal signals with considerably low overheads. Another CPS based model that detects the Remaining Useful Life (RUL) of rotary components in a motor is proposed by Eva Masero Rúbio et. al (Rúbio, 2019). The health condition of the motor is classified into four classes namely unacceptable, unsatisfactory, satisfactory and good through unsupervised K-Nearest Neighbors (KNN) algorithm. Apart from detecting the fault, this CPS is capable of detecting the severity of the faults also.

A deep learning based architecture to implement the concept of Digital Twin (DT) is proposed by Jay Lee et. al (Lee, 2020). This reference architecture supports the manufacturing industries with necessary guidelines which are extremely cooperative, transparent with a high degree of efficiency and resilience. This proves that fostering the development of AI based approaches like deep learning can contribute to the gradual development in the manufacturing sectors. Apart from learning features from textual or numerical data, visual representations are also very useful in learning features. Rafael Penna et. al proposed an improved 2D/3D visualization tool for intelligent predictive maintenance (Penna, 2014) . The HTTP makes the remote access more plausible. The complete implementation of this tool Toggle makes it possible to create or edit maintenance scenarios. The Blender 2D is used for 2D visualizations.

Erkki Jantunen et. al presented a complete overview of the expectations of Industry 4.0 (Jantunen, 2016). The wear and tear of the equipment are measured through vibration and optical methods. The author has suggested CPS based optimizing solutions to address the issues regarding predictive maintenance. A framework that helps in maintenance based decision making is proposed by Olivier Senechal et. al (Olivier Senechal, 2019). The key elements are sustainable condition based maintenance, remaining useful life prediction and building a prognostic business environment. The framework is implemented in real word use cases.

The challenges and pitfalls in maintenance operations in manufacturing firms are effectively combated by computerized maintenance management systems (CMMS). These systems are lack dynamicity in their operation. Jun Ni et al. proposed a effective decision support tool for predictive maintenance in manufacturing industries (Jun Ni, 2012). This prioritizes maintenance activities based on the heuristics and the real time implementation in automotive industries gave promising results. A novel hybridization of Genetic Algorithm with data envelopment analysis to improve the overall reliability is proposed by Sheikhalishahi et al. (Sheikhalishahi, 2014). This deals with multi-objective solution to determine pareto-optimal solution to find the best maintenance policy by the top management. A flavor of bi objective GA that retains superior selection of maintenance policy augmented with unit-cost cumulative reliability expectation measure is suggested to assess the effect of maintenance cost of individual component (Wang, 2014).

Piero Baraldi et. al used a simple K Nearest Neighbours classification algorithm to detect bearing faults under variable speed and load conditions (Piero Baraldi, 2014). The feature engineering is done by multi objective optimization that is supported by Binary differential evolution technique. This method is very simple but its implementation in real time industrial scenarios can be done only after testing and modifying the method in par with the external conditions. Extreme Learning Machines (ELMs) are gaining significance that smoothen the feature selection process. Ye Tian et. al proposed an ELM that uses Local Mean Decomposition and Single Valued Decomposition to detect failure in bearings (Ye Tian, 2015). This work extracted fault feature vectors to categorise the faulty bearings from healthy bearings and could be extended to rotating components like shafts.

Wavelet function based Auto encoders are deployed with ELM to extract important features from bearing vibration signals (Shao Haidong, 2018). This unsupervised technique was able to characterize the raw signals more effectively and then classify the faults using ELM. The performance of the work, when subjected to multivariate data is not studied. S. S. Udmale et. al proposed application of ELMs using the features extracted through spectral kurtosis of vibration signals (S. S. Udmale, 2019). The hyperparameter tuning of hidden nodes is done by modified bidirectional search, which is the main reason for the development of more concise ELM for bearing fault classification. This method offers the scope for analysis of more evolutionary algorithms for fault classification.

Literature reveals that implementing CPS based frameworks that integrate sensors, actuators and intelligence in predictive maintenance has a long history. Though it is very evident that the benefits of CPS based solutions outweigh the challenges, it is quintessential to develop a comprehensive framework that could be readily deployed in real world industrial scenarios.

PROGNOSTICS AND HEALTH MANAGEMENT TRIANGLE

CPS technology is actually a complex amalgamation of heterogeneous active and passive elements that are capable of defining the dynamic environment. The CPS needs to adapt autonomously to the changing environment in both internal and external aspects. The failures, faults and threats need to be diagnosed and recovery actions must be scheduled to avoid catastrophic disasters. Building CPS based Prognostics and Health Management (PHM) frameworks must inherently inculcate resilience as a vital element. The pivotal elements in CPS are sensors, actuators and intelligent elements. This can be perceived as instilling smartness or intelligent elements in a mechatronics system. A very primitive architecture that uses a legacy network to transfer data is shown in Figure 5. The sensors and actuators are connected through a legacy network, which already exists in the industry.

Figure 5. Primitive CPS connected through legacy network

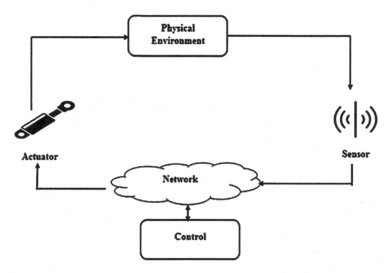

The PHM focuses on degradation of equipment due to fatigue, erosion, wear and tear to manage the maintenance activities by assessing equipment health. The advancements in PHM has triggered the industry to shift its focus to predict the Remaining Useful Life (RUL) of the equipment from the run-to-failure data. RUL of any component is the time duration during which it gives its maximum performance (Shankar Sankararaman, 2015) . RUL prediction plays a key role in planning maintenance activity and mitigating the negative effects of faults with complete cause and effect analysis. Though there are various strategies for predictive maintenance under the umbrella of PHM such as analytical models and physical models, data driven models take precedence over the others (Okoh, 2014) . The real challenge confronted by the PHM domain is the availability of run to failure data, which is very scarce. The PHM in industries is realizable in two flavors:

- Prognostics, which is the prediction process that models the degradation rate by assessing the present health status for prognosis of future health. This also includes estimation of risks

- Health management, which is scheduling maintenance activities and recovery actions based on the prognostic results.

The definition of prognostics presented by the International Organization for Standardization states that the prognosis process in any domain is the actual estimation of risk along with time to failure in one or more fault modes (Tobon-Mejia, 2012). Figure 6 shows a detailed view of the processes happening under the canopy of PHM.

Figure 6. PHM Process in industry

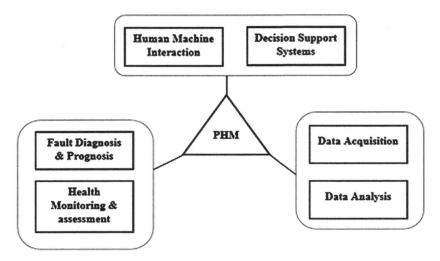

The PHM process envelopes a series of activities that can be grouped under three main categories namely data collection, intelligent decision making and interactions with the outside world. The connectivity between these entities is brought about by recent communication protocols depending on the industrial requirements and standards. The PHM triangle is quintessential to understand the magnitude of activities that is involved in the success of predictive maintenance. Also, the expertise and other associated resources that are required to implant PHM strategy in any industrial sector, can be planned and organized from the PHM triangle.

BUSINESS PROCESSES IN IMPLANTING CPS BASED PHM

All the changes incorporated in the industries has a long lineage of business processes and high-level decisions taken by top management. Determining the right time and right context to introduce PHM in smart manufacturing is very crucial for advanced health monitoring. The considerations and rationale in framing best practices in industrial maintenance demands a strategic business purpose to reduce, access and tract the faults. The domain of PHM uncovers the errors and faults even in smaller subsystems, thus enhancing the performance of the entire manufacturing process in terms of Overall Equipment Effectiveness (OEE). This term is a gold standard and distinct business metric that is set by the manufacturing industries to improve productivity. This metric plays a significant role in isolating losses and tracking the progress of faults. This OEE is governed by three factors namely availability (A), performance (P) and quality (Q). The computation of OEE is done according to Equation 1. This forms a benchmark in estimating the equipment's reliability in operation to achieve the desired quality metrics.

$$OEE = A \times P \times Q \tag{1}$$

This metric is a gold standard for assessing the lifetime and performance of the maintenance tool process or strategy. The cost benefit analysis of the equipment's performance and maintenance measures can be carried out based on the OEE. Incorporating PHM into manufacturing involves decisions taken at various managerial levels. These strategic decisions mainly focus on:

- Isolating the areas with room for improvement in terms of OEE
- Delineating operational profiles and mapping them to costs, environment and safety considerations
- Establishing benchmarks for maintenance practices
- Deploying cost effective condition monitoring strategies
- Drafting top management level maintenance policies

Business Processes in PHM Based CPS

Major changes in the manufacturing industries happen by collaborative effort made by top level management and the skilled workforce. Realizing PHM in industries involves two main phases namely conception phase, which mostly involves top and middle level management personnel. They are responsible for making strategic decisions in the maintenance context. The decision making process is iterative and the decisions are assessed based on the room for optimization and cost benefits. These decisions are accomplished in real time scenarios by the skilled workforce which comprises maintenance engineers. Figure 7 gives a detailed overview.

Figure 7. Business processes in CPS based PHM

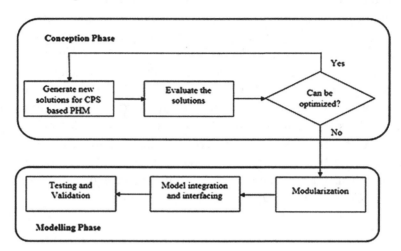

Thus the maintenance engineers are solely responsible for implementing the maintenance policies in the end systems. Proper training and enhancing the skill set will make the implementation of CPS based PHM solutions in industries, a more effective task.

CYCLIC FRAMEWORK OF CPS BASED PREDICTIVE MAINTENANCE

It is evident that CPS transforms the technologies by interfacing the physical and cyber world (Baheti, 2011). The surge in the computational capabilities and affordability of sensors has made the cutting edge technologies like Big Data, AI and IoT recent buzzwords in Industry 4.0. The CPS are physically engineered systems that are integrated with communication and high tech computing technologies (Rajkumar, 2010) . The new modalities of these systems involves amalgamation of multitude of technologies to monitor, assess, control and coordinate various physical processes by means of computations. The smooth handover of physical space to the cyber world for intelligent decisions making and enforcing those decisions back into the physical world is the crux of the CPS.

The era of predictive maintenance has seen a rampant surge after the multidisciplinary researches focused on building intelligent solutions to solve maintenance issues. PHM and predictive maintenance has emerged as a potential candidate to implement many CPS frameworks. As CPS is still in its embryonic stage, there is definitely space for developing new frameworks to aid the deployment of predictive maintenance solutions in manufacturing systems. The detailed framework is presented in Figure 8.

Figure 8. Cyclic framework for CPS based Predictive Maintenance

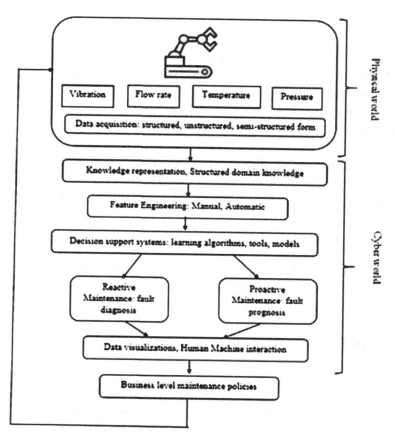

It is apparent that implementation of predictive maintenance solutions in smart manufacturing involves physical condition monitoring of equipment for isolating operational profiles. Not all operational profiles are fruitful in detecting the presence of faults. It is extremely necessary to delineate the fault profiles that could effectively characterize the health condition of the equipment. Thus learning important trends and patterns from the degrading signals are termed as feature extraction. These trends and patterns are then subjected to decision support systems, where learning algorithms are deployed to diagnose or predict the occurrence of faults. As the world is swiftly moving into the era of visualization, the results and detailed analysis are converted to visuals for effective understanding. The maintenance decisions are made of the top management regarding the maintenance activities, which are again consigned into the physical world. A more granular view of the proposed framework is explained here.

Data Acquisition

Data acquisition from sensors is the primary means of collecting the physical properties and its related events in the environment. Predictive maintenance involves the usage of heterogeneous types of sensors like vibration, temperature, oil analysis, flow rate, pressure etc. The observations from the sensors can be any one of the following types:

- **Structured data:** They are clearly defined in some fixed pattern or format. These data can be readily processed by higher levels.
- **Unstructured data:** These data are not organized or could be fitted in some specified format. They are naïve data with large quantities of noise. These data have to undergo intensive preprocessing to convert them into usable forms.
- **Semi structured data:** They are the data elements which are not in specific pattern but carry some inherent organizational structure. Minimum to moderate amount of data cleaning is required to process this data.

Knowledge Representation

The data that is sourced by the sensors is actually a warehouse of information. The process of knowledge representation delves on the raw data to extricate the judgments and beliefs suitable to be processed by intelligent environments. The condition monitored data are transformed into maintenance knowledge space to enable business level knowledge sharing (Guo Jian-wen, 2010). Alternatively ontology based knowledge representation is also done. Apart from these, logical and unambiguous rule representation, semantic network representation, predicate and first order logic, Fuzzy rules, attribute based frame representation and conditional rules are some of the other popular structured knowledge representation forms. The choice of knowledge representation depends on the industrial use case.

Any form of representation must adhere to the following important properties:

- **Accurate representation:** The representation strategy must be capable of characterizing and representing versatile and heterogeneous knowledge with adequate accuracy.

- **Inferential Adequacy**: This refers to the trait of dynamically forming new representational structures from already existing ones.
- **Efficient inferences**: The knowledge representation form must be simple and effective such that drawing inferences from them is easy.
- **Acquisitional efficiency**: This is the ability to automatically attain higher knowledge levels.

Decision Support Systems

Engineering predictive maintenance is strongly supported by decision making algorithms and models. The knowledge obtained from the symbolic reasoning in the previous phase is utilized by learning algorithms and AI based methodologies to diagnose the faults based on the condition monitored data. These algorithms reduce the degree of uncertainty that is widely prevalent in conventional condition based maintenance systems. The intelligent predictive maintenance decision support system complements the conventional maintenance process by including intelligence with a greater amount of predictive prowess based on the degradation trends and patterns. The primal goals of intelligent decision support systems are listed below:

- Identification of loopholes in conventional maintenance systems
- Finding new ventures for innovations
- Assigning priority based maintenance tasks
- Upgrading the maintenance skill set
- Integrating production and maintenance activities

The decision support systems are generally implemented by amalgamating the techniques like big data, fuzzy logic, machine learning models and tools, deep learning techniques, Internet of Things and predictive analytics. Lot of algorithms, frameworks, tools and models are currently surging in as a result of research. The results of decision support systems comes in four flavors:

- Intelligent condition monitoring
- Fault diagnosis
- Fault prognostics
- Prediction of Remaining Useful Life of the equipment

These results can be broadly placed into two categories namely reactive maintenance strategies and proactive maintenance strategies. The maintenance activities that are carried out after the occurrence of faults are termed as reactive strategies. Fault diagnosis is a reactive strategy while fault prognosis is proactive strategy, where faults are predicted from the early warning signs. Prognosis can be either a classifying mechanism which labels the equipment to be in faulty or healthy state; or a regressive algorithm that predicts the time at which the equipment fails completely (RUL).

Data Visualization

Graphical representations of data, information, intermediate results, exploratory data analysis, signal representation are easy ways to understand inherent patterns, trends and even outliers. The visualization helps to extract latent correlations between various physical entities. Visualizations in predictive maintenance serves the following purposes:

- Deeper insights about the various physical quantities can be obtained by drilling into the data
- Higher degree of dynamicity
- Visualizations can effectively portray the results of various pre-processing, signal extraction and predictive models.
- They are time saving approach and are effective communication tools about predictive maintenance

Another notable area that draws attention is Human–machine interaction (HMI), which is actually the communication between a human and a machine through a user interface and is shown in Figure 9. The stages in this interaction process are intention, selection, execution and evaluation [28]. The workflow manager is responsible for the data exchanges and communication between Machine to Machine and Machine to Human in the production process (Ziqiu Kang, 2012).

Figure 9. sequence of HMI

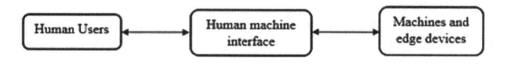

The visualization tools are able to process dynamic scenarios such as prediction of RUL in aircraft engines, health state of nuclear and thermal power plants (Scheifele, 2014). Human machine cooperation is an advanced form of HMI that addresses the new issues emerging in human machine association. Portable and handheld devices,

Model-View-Controller (MVC) and tangible user interfaces are some of the popular HMI techniques.

Business Level Maintenance Policies

The process of maintenance is a continuous activity that involves maintaining the working condition of the equipment at optimal thresholds. Maintenance management involves sequence of related processes by utilizing the resources in an efficient and regulated fashion complying with performance standards. Every company has its own, unique maintenance policy that are dictum to be followed by the workforce at all levels. The salient features of these policies are:

- To assure the reliability of equipment and safety of workers.
- Maintain the equipment in proper calibration to avoid unexpected and frequent failures
- Proper adherence to maintenance policies reduces the likelihood of loss in inventory and equipment
- Negligence to maintenance policies may result in devastating effects such as:
- Underutilization of equipment
- Surge in the maintenance cost and labor costs
- Increase in the cost of procurement of industrial spare parts
- Occupational hazard

Framing business level maintenance policy presupposes detailed planning. Proper planning and scheduling of maintenance activity on demand without any disruption of services and production is an important criterion for any maintenance planning board. It is to be concluded that every manufacturing company is entitled to possess customized, effective and robust maintenance policy in compliance with their business goals.

Implementation of Proposed Solution in Real Time Industrial Scenario

The intermingling of physical world and cyber/digital world is the most distinguishing feature of CPS. The real time deployment of the proposed framework necessitates the usage of variety of computing technologies along with comprehensive data handling mechanisms.

- **Data Acquisition:** This is generally done by installing homogeneous or heterogeneous sensors at the site. Recent years have witnessed many digital sensors that reduces human interventions in measuring the physical world data.

- **Knowledge extraction:** This is a quintessential phase for any CPS. The real-world data are processed and useful information are extracted from the underlying raw data. Data mining tools like Rapid miner, Oracle data miner can be explored to gain insights to the data. Alternatively feature extraction algorithms and Deep Learning algorithms are some of the potential candidates that combines the knowledge extraction and decision making.

- **Maintenance and visualization solutions:** The CPS based maintenance solutions are assisted by AI, ML and DL algorithms that effectively diagnosis and prognose the faults from the historic data. Visualizing the data and outcomes of the prediction is an easier way to convey the machine's health status to the maintenance teams. Tabuleau, Zoho analytics, Sisence are some of the tools that can be considered for visualizing the inner details.

CHALLENGES IN IMPLEMENTING CPS BASED PREDICTIVE MAINTENANCE SYSTEMS IN MANUFACTURING INDUSTRIES

CPS is a fast growing field, which faces challenges in three perspectives namely dynamic reconfiguration, increased productivity and communication & information technology (Dafflon, 2014).

Figure 10. Challenges in implementing CPS based predictive maintenance systems

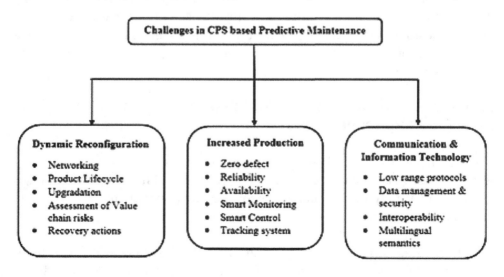

Figure 10 enumerates some of the prominent challenges arrayed under three umbrellas. Besides these, CPS based predictive maintenance in real world industrial scenarios possess some inherent complexities as:

- Integrating the highly volatile customer demands and unsatisfied design dictate frequent modifications in the functional requirements of the maintenance systems.
- Instilling smartness in the factory floors requires a clear and long term business perspective. The acquaintance of CPS based predictive maintenance systems could be realised only in the long run.
- The transition from the classical manual maintenance systems to CPS based systems occurs at a swift pace. This also necessities high initial investments. Hence the top level administrators must integrate the maintenance systems as a part of their strategic business plans.
- Acquiring and mining the right data in its right context is an eventful hurdle in the design of maintenance systems.
- Inseminating smartness in the control and monitoring of equipment warrants the coalescence of a multitude of technologies, which in turn demands upskilling the workforce. Proper training and awareness must be habituated to the skilled workforce, so as to cope up with a highly dynamic environment.
- Security concerns, HCI and M2M interactions are not verifiable by the existing formal methods.
- Availability of run-to-failure data of any equipment is very rare. This makes training and developing predictive maintenance models a difficult task.
- Unpredictable failure modes of fresh products challenges the reliability of the maintenance systems.
- Scaping ambiguous system behaviour and cause-effect analysis requires extensive domain knowledge.

Though the CPS based predictive maintenance systems drop in with a lot of challenges, they are actually perceived as a blessing in disguise. These are some of the elementary research areas that is currently drawing attention.

CONCLUSION

CPS based predictive maintenance systems are steadily gaining momentum in Industry 4.0, as they replace the conventional reactive condition monitoring strategies with AI actuated smart solutions. As CPS based solutions are pristine for real time deployment, it naturally possess space for the evolution of new frameworks and models for efficient real time condition monitoring of equipment. This chapter presents a novel cyclic CPS based predictive maintenance framework that very well establishes the coexistence of the cyber world with the physical world. The consummate result of the proposed framework can act as a diligent driving force for articulating the predictive maintenance policies as a part of the business strategic plan. This is a very generic and robust framework that can be customized to suit any type of equipment or even complex systems. In the near future, this framework will serve as a blueprint for developing and deploying a CPS based predictive maintenance system in a real time industrial environment.

REFERENCES

Bagheri, B., Yang, S., Kao, H.-A., & Lee, J. (2015). Cyber-physical Systems Architecture for Self-Aware Machines in Industry 4.0 Environment. *IFAC-PapersOnLine*, *48*(3), 1622–1627. doi:10.1016/j.ifacol.2015.06.318

Baheti, R., & Gill, H. (2011). *The impact of control technology: Cyber-physical systems*. IEEE Control Systems Society.

Baraldi, P., Cannarile, F., Di Maio, F., & Zio, E. (2016). Hierarchical k-nearest neighbours classification and binary differential evolution for fault diagnostics of automotive bearings operating under variable conditions. *Engineering Applications of Artificial Intelligence*, *56*, 1–13. doi:10.1016/j.engappai.2016.08.011

Dafflon, B., Moalla, N., & Ouzrout, Y. (2021). Ouzrout, "The challenges, approaches, and used techniques of CPS for manufacturing in Industry 4.0: A literature review. *International Journal of Advanced Manufacturing Technology*, *113*(7-8), 2395–2412. doi:10.100700170-020-06572-4

Guo, J., Yu, D., Jian, L., & Xu, C. (2010). Knowledge sharing model for equipment maintenance federation based on knowledge grid. *Jisuanji Jicheng Zhizao Xitong*, *16*(1), 47–56.

Hehenberger, V.-H., Bradley, E., & Tomiyama, A. (2016). Design, modelling, simulation and integration of cyber physical systems: Methods and applications. *Computers in Industry*, *82*, 273–289. doi:10.1016/j.compind.2016.05.006

Jantunen, E., Zurutuza, U., Ferreira, L. L., & Varga, P. (2016). Optimising maintenance: What are the expectations for Cyber Physical Systems. *2016 3rd International Workshop on Emerging Ideas and Trends in Engineering of Cyber-Physical Systems (EITEC)*, 53-58. 10.1109/EITEC.2016.7503697

Jazdi. (2014). Cyber physical systems in the context of Industry 4.0. *2014 IEEE International Conference on Automation, Quality and Testing, Robotics*, 1-4.

Kang, Z., Catal, C., & Tekinerdogan, B. (2021). Remaining Useful Life (RUL) Prediction of Equipment in Production Lines Using Artificial Neural Networks. *Sensors (Basel), 21*(3), 21. doi:10.339021030932 PMID:33573297

Lee, J., Azamfar, M., Singh, J., & Siahpour, S. (2020). Integration of digital twin and deep learning in cyber-physical systems: Towards smart manufacturing. *IET Collaborative Intelligent Manufacturing, 2*(1), 34–36. doi:10.1049/iet-cim.2020.0009

Lee, J., Bagheri, B., & Kao, H.-A. (2015). A cyber-physical systems architecture for industry 4.0-based manufacturing systems. *Manufacturing Letters, 3*, 18–23. doi:10.1016/j.mfglet.2014.12.001

Meraghni, S., Terrissa, L. S., Ayad, S., Zerhouni, N., & Varnier, C. (2018). Post-prognostics decision in cyber-physical systems. *2018 International Conference on Advanced Systems and Electric Technologies (IC_ASET)*, 201-205. 10.1109/ASET.2018.8379859

Monostori, L. (2014). Cyber-physical Production Systems: Roots, Expectations and R&D Challenges. *Procedia CIRP, 17*, 9–13. doi:10.1016/j.procir.2014.03.115

Ni, J., & Jin, X. (2012). Decision support systems for effective maintenance operations. *CIRP Annals, 61*(1), 411–414. doi:10.1016/j.cirp.2012.03.065

Norman, D. A. (1984). Stages and levels in human-machine interaction. *International Journal of Man-Machine Studies, 21*(4), 365–375. doi:10.1016/S0020-7373(84)80054-1

Okoh, C., Roy, R., Mehnen, J., & Redding, L. (2014). Overview of Remaining Useful Life Prediction Techniques in Through-Life Engineering Services. *Procedia CIRP, 16*, 158–163. doi:10.1016/j.procir.2014.02.006

Oks, S. J., Fritzsche, A., & Möslein, K. M. (2018). Engineering industrial cyber-physical systems: An application map based method. *Procedia CIRP, 72*, 456–461. doi:10.1016/j.procir.2018.03.126

Oks, S. J., Jalowski, M., Fritzsche, A., & Möslein, K. M. (2019). Cyber-physical modeling and simulation: A reference architecture for designing demonstrators for industrial cyber-physical systems. *Procedia CIRP, 84*, 257–264. doi:10.1016/j.procir.2019.04.239

Penna. (2014). Visualization tool for cyber-physical maintenance systems. *2014 12th IEEE International Conference on Industrial Informatics (INDIN)*, 566-571. 10.1109/INDIN.2014.6945575

Peres, R. S., Rocha, A. D., Leitao, P., & Barata, J. (2018). IDARTS – Towards intelligent data analysis and real-time supervision for industry 4.0. *Computers in Industry, 101*, 138–146. doi:10.1016/j.compind.2018.07.004

Rajkumar, R., Lee, I., Sha, L., & Stankovic, J. (2010). Cyber-physical systems: The next computing revolution. *Design Automation Conference*, 731-736. 10.1145/1837274.1837461

Rauniyar, T. (2014). Integrated Product Development Approach for Cyber-Physical Systems Utilizing Standardized Modeling Languages and Methodologies. *Journal of Integrated Design & Process Science, 14*(3), 1–11.

Rúbio, E. M., Dionísio, R. P., & Torres, P. M. B. (2019). *Industrial IoT Devices and Cyber-Physical Production Systems: Review and Use Case. In Innovation, Engineering and Entrepreneurship, Lecture Notes in Electrical Engineering* (Vol. 505). Springer. doi:10.1007/978-3-319-91334-6_40

Ruiz-Arenas, S., Horváth, I., Mejía-Gutiérrez, R., & Opiyo, E. Z. (2014). Towards the Maintenance Principles of Cyber-Physical Systems. *Jixie Gongcheng Xuebao, 60*(12), 815–831.

Saber, V., & Venayagamoorthy, G. K. (2010). Efficient Utilization of Renewable Energy Sources by Gridable Vehicles in Cyber-Physical Energy Systems. *IEEE Systems Journal, 4*(3), 285–294. doi:10.1109/JSYST.2010.2059212

Sankararaman, S. (2015). Significance, interpretation, and quantification of uncertainty in prognostics and remaining useful life prediction. *Mechanical Systems and Signal Processing, 52-53*, 228–247. doi:10.1016/j.ymssp.2014.05.029

Scheifele, S., Friedrich, J., Lechler, A., & Verl, A. (2014). Flexible, self-configuring control system for a modular production system. Procedia Technology, 15, 398–405.

Sénéchal, O., & Trentesaux, D. (2019). A framework to help decision makers to be environmentally aware during the maintenance of cyber physical systems. *Environmental Impact Assessment Review, 77*, 11–22. doi:10.1016/j.eiar.2019.02.007

Shao, H., Jiang, H., Li, X., & Wu, S. (2018). Intelligent fault diagnosis of rolling bearing using deep wavelet auto-encoder with extreme learning machine. *Knowledge-Based Systems, 140*, 1–14. doi:10.1016/j.knosys.2017.10.024

Shcherbakov, M. V., Glotov, A. V., & Cheremisinov, S. V. (2020). *Proactive and Predictive Maintenance of Cyber-Physical Systems. In Cyber-Physical Systems: Advances in Design & Modelling, Studies in Systems, Decision and Control, 259.* Springer. doi:10.1007/978-3-030-32579-4_21

Sheikhalishahi, E., Ebrahimipour, V., & Farahani, M. H. (2014). An integrated GA-DEA algorithm for determining the most effective maintenance policy for a k-out-of-n problem. *Journal of Intelligent Manufacturing, 25*(6), 1455–1462. doi:10.100710845-013-0752-z

Tao, F., Qi, Q., Wang, L., & Nee, A. Y. C. (2014). Digital Twins and Cyber–Physical Systems toward Smart Manufacturing and Industry 4.0: Correlation and Comparison. *Engineering, 5*(4), 653–661. doi:10.1016/j.eng.2019.01.014

Thyago, Carvalho, Soaresa, Vita, & Francisco, Basto, & Alcal. (2019). A systematic literature review of machine learning methods applied to predictive maintenance. *Computers & Industrial Engineering, 137.* doi:10.1016/j.cie.2019.106024

Tian, Y., Ma, J., Lu, C., & Wang, Z. (2015). Rolling bearing fault diagnosis under variable conditions using LMD-SVD and extreme learning machine. *Journal of Mechanics and Machine Theory, 90,* 175–186. doi:10.1016/j.mechmachtheory.2015.03.014

Tobon-Mejia, D. A., Medjaher, K., & Zerhouni, N. (2012). CNC machine tool's wear diagnostic and prognostic by using dynamic Bayesian networks. *Mechanical Systems and Signal Processing, 28,* 167–182. doi:10.1016/j.ymssp.2011.10.018

Udmale, S. (2019). Application of Spectral Kurtosis and Improved Extreme Learning Machine for Bearing Fault Classification. *IEEE Transactions on Instrumentation and Measurement, 68*(11), 4222–4233.

Wang, T., & Tsai, S.-W. (2014). Optimizing bi-objective imperfect preventive maintenance model for series-parallel system using established hybrid genetic algorithm. *Journal of Intelligent Manufacturing, 25*(3), 603–616. doi:10.100710845-012-0708-8

Wu, Z., Guo, Y., Lin, W., Yu, S., & Ji, Y. (2018). A Weighted Deep Representation Learning Model for Imbalanced Fault Diagnosis in Cyber-Physical Systems. *Sensors (Basel), 18*(4), 1096. Advance online publication. doi:10.339018041096 PMID:29621131

Yang, F.-N., & Lin, H.-Y. (2019). Development of A Predictive Maintenance Platform for Cyber-Physical Systems. *2019 IEEE International Conference on Industrial Cyber Physical Systems (ICPS),* 331-335, , 2019.10.1109/ICPHYS.2019.8780144

Compilation of References

Abadi, M., Agarwal, A., Barham, P., Brevdo, E., Chen, Z., Citro, C., . . . Devin, M. (2016). *Tensorflow: Large-scale machine learning on heterogeneous distributed systems.* arXiv 2016, arXiv:1603.04467.

Abayaratne, H., Perera, S., De Silva, E., Atapattu, P., & Wijesundara, M. (2019). A Real-Time Cardiac Arrhythmia Classifier. *2019 National Information Technology Conference (NITC).* 10.1109/NITC48475.2019.9114464

Abbas, S. M., & Singh, S. N. 2018, February. Region-based object detection and classification using faster R-CNN. In *2018 4th International Conference on Computational Intelligence & Communication Technology (CICT)* (pp. 1-6). IEEE.

Abdulhannan, P., Russell, D. A., & Homer-Vanniasinkam, S. (2012). Peripheral arterial disease: A literature review. *British Medical Bulletin, 104*(1), 21–39. doi:10.1093/bmb/lds027 PMID:23080419

Abràmoff, Garvin, & Sonka. (2010). Retinal Imaging and Image Analysis Clinical Applications. *IEEE Reviews in Biomedical Engineering.*

Acharya, U. R., Fujita, H., Sudarshan, V. K., Bhat, S., & Koh, J. E. (2015). Application of entropies for automated diagnosis of epilepsy using eeg signals: A review. *Knowledge-Based Systems, 88,* 85–96. doi:10.1016/j.knosys.2015.08.004

Acharya, U. R., Sree, S. V., Alvin, A. P. C., & Suri, J. S. (2012). Use of principal component analysis for automatic classification of epileptic eeg activities in wavelet framework. *Expert Systems with Applications, 39*(10), 9072–9078. doi:10.1016/j.eswa.2012.02.040

Acharya, U., Oh, S., Hagiwara, Y., Tan, J., Adam, M., Gertych, A., & Tan, R. (2017). A deep convolutional neural network model to classify heartbeats. *Computers in Biology and Medicine, 89,* 389–396. doi:10.1016/j.compbiomed.2017.08.022 PMID:28869899

Agarwal, P. (2007). Higher education in India: Growth, concerns and change agenda. *Higher Education Quarterly, 61*(2), 197–207. doi:10.1111/j.1468-2273.2007.00346.x

Aheleroff, S., Xu, X., Zhong, R. Y., & Lu, Y. (2021). Digital twin as a service (DTaaS) in industry 4.0: An architecture reference model. *Advanced Engineering Informatics, 47,* 101225. doi:10.1016/j.aei.2020.101225

Ahmad, M., Saeed, M., Saleem, S., & Kamboh, A. M. (2016). Seizure detection using eeg: A survey of different techniques. In *Emerging Technologies (ICET), International Conference on.* IEEE. 10.1109/ICET.2016.7813209

Ahmad, I., Basheri, M., Iqbal, M. J., & Rahim, A. (2018). Performance Comparison of Support Vector Machine, Random Forest, and Extreme Learning Machine for Intrusion Detection. *Computers & Electrical Engineering,* 274–282. doi:10.1109/ACCESS.2018.2841987

Ahmad, Z., Shahid Khan, A., Wai Shiang, C., Abdullah, J., & Ahmad, F. (2021). Network intrusion detection system: A systematic study of machine learning and deep learning approaches. *Transactions on Emerging Telecommunications Technologies, 32*(1), e4150. doi:10.1002/ett.4150

Ahmim, A., Maglaras, L., Ferrag, M. A., Derdour, M., & Janicke, H. (2019). A Novel Hierarchical Intrusion Detection System based on Decision Tree and Rules-based Models. *15th International Conference on Distributed Computing in Sensor Systems.* 10.1109/DCOSS.2019.00059

Aje, T. (2009). Cardiovascular disease: A global problem extending into the developing world. *World Journal of Cardiology, 1*(1), 3. doi:10.4330/wjc.v1.i1.3 PMID:21160570

Alahakoon, D., & Yu, X. (2016). Smart electricity meter data intelligence for future energy systems: A survey. *IEEE Transactions on Industrial Informatics, 12*(1), 425–436. doi:10.1109/TII.2015.2414355

Al-Ali, A. R., Gupta, R., & Nabulsi, A. A. (2018, April). Cyber physical systems role in manufacturing technologies. In AIP Conference Proceedings (Vol. 1957, No. 1, p. 050007). AIP Publishing LLC. doi:10.1063/1.5034337

Alguliyev, R., Imamverdiyev, Y., & Sukhostat, L. (2018). Cyber-physical systems and their security issues. *Computers in Industry, 100,* 212–223. doi:10.1016/j.compind.2018.04.017

Ali, S., Qaisar, S. B., Saeed, H., Khan, M. F., Naeem, M., & Anpalagan, A. (2015). Network challenges for cyber physical systems with tiny wireless devices: A case study on reliable pipeline condition monitoring. *Sensors (Basel), 15*(4), 7172–7205. doi:10.3390150407172 PMID:25815444

Alotaiby, T. N., Alshebeili, S. A., Alshawi, T., Ahmad, I., & El-Samie, F. E. A. (2014). Eeg seizure detection and prediction algorithms: A survey. *EURASIP Journal on Advances in Signal Processing, 2014*(1), 183. doi:10.1186/1687-6180-2014-183

Alqahtani, H., Sarker, I. H., Kalim, A., Hossain, S. M. M., Ikhlaq, S., & Hossain, S. (2020, March). Cyber intrusion detection using machine learning classification techniques. In *International Conference on Computing Science, Communication and Security* (pp. 121-131). Springer. 10.1007/978-981-15-6648-6_10

Alrashdi, I., Alqazzaz, A., Aloufi, E., & Alharthi, R. (2016). AD-IoT: Anomaly Detection of IoT Cyber Attacks in Smart City Using Machine Learning. In *International Conference On Medical Imaging Understanding and Analysis*. MIUA. 10.1109/CCWC.2019.8666450

Altaha, M., Lee, J.-M., Aslam, M., & Hong, S. (2021). An Autoencoder-Based Network Intrusion Detection System for the SCADA System. *Journal of Communication, 16*(6), 889–905. doi:10.12720/jcm.16.6.210-216

Altbach, P. G. (1993). The dilemma of change in Indian higher education. *Higher Education, 26*(1), 3–20. doi:10.1007/BF01575104

Amami, R., & Smiti, A. (2017). An incremental method combining density clustering and support vector machines for voice pathology detection. *Computers & Electrical Engineering, 57*, 257–265. doi:10.1016/j.compeleceng.2016.08.021

Ambassa, P. L., Kayem, A. V. D. M., Wolthusen, S. D., & Meinel, C. (2018). Privacy risks in resource constrained smart micro-grids. *IEEE 32nd International Conference on Advanced Information Networking and Applications Workshops (WAINA)*, 527-532.

Amor, N. B., Benferhat, S., & Elouedi, Z. (2004, March). Naive bayes vs decision trees in intrusion detection systems. In *Proceedings of the 2004 ACM symposium on Applied computing* (pp. 420-424). 10.1145/967900.967989

Anand, M. (2006). Security challenges in next generation cyber physical systems. *Beyond SCADA: Networked Embedded Control for Cyber Physical Systems*.

Annunziata, R. (2016). Leveraging multi-scale hessian-based enhancement with a novel exudate inpainting technique for retinal vessel segmentation. *IEEE Journal of Biomedical and Health Informatics*.

Ashibani & Mahmoud. (2017). Cyber physical systems security: Analysis, challenges and solutions. In *Computers & Security*. Elsevier.

Ashibani, Y., & Mahmoud, Q. H. (2017). Cyber physical systems security: Analysis, challenges and solutions. *Computers & Security, 68*, 81–97. doi:10.1016/j.cose.2017.04.005

Athota, L., Shukla, V. K., Pandey, N., & Rana, A. (2020). Chatbot for Healthcare System Using Artificial Intelligence. *2020 8th International Conference on Reliability, Infocom Technologies and Optimization (Trends and Future Directions) (ICRITO)*. 10.1109/ICRITO48877.2020.9197833

Aumasson, J-P., Neves, S., Wilcox-O'Hearn, Z., & Winnerlein, C. (2013). *BLAKE2: Simpler, smaller, fast as MD5*. . doi:10.1007/978-3-642-38980-1_8

Aung, Y. Y., & Min, M. M. (2017). An analysis of random forest algorithm based network intrusion detection system. *18th IEEE/ACIS International Conference on Software Engineering, Artificial Intelligence, Networking and Parallel/Distributed Computing*, 127-132. 10.1109/SNPD.2017.8022711

Auzias, G., Takerkart, S., & Deruelle, C. (2015). On the influence of confounding factors in multisite brain morphometry studies of developmental pathologies: Application to autism Spectrum disorder. *IEEE Journal of Biomedical and Health Informatics*, 20(3), 810–817. doi:10.1109/JBHI.2015.2460012 PMID:26208373

Ayushi. (2010). A Symmetric Key Cryptographic Algorithm. *International Journal of Computer Applications*.

Bagheri, B., Yang, S., Kao, H.-A., & Lee, J. (2015). Cyber-physical Systems Architecture for Self-Aware Machines in Industry 4.0 Environment. *IFAC-PapersOnLine*, 48(3), 1622–1627. doi:10.1016/j.ifacol.2015.06.318

Baheti, R., & Gill, H. (2011). Cyber-physical systems. *The Impact of Control Technology, 12*(1), 161-166.

Baheti, R., & Gill, H. (2011). *The impact of control technology: Cyber-physical systems*. IEEE Control Systems Society.

Bakirtzis, G., Sherburne, T., Adams, S., Horowitz, B. M., Beling, P. A., & Fleming, C. H. (2021). An ontological metamodel for cyber-physical system safety, security, and resilience coengineering. *Software & Systems Modeling*, 1–25. doi:10.100710270-021-00892-z

Balamurugan, E., Dr Sangeetha, K., Dr Sathishkumar, K., & Dr Akpajaro, J. (2020). Modified Support Vector Machine Based Efficient Virtual Machine Consolidation Procedure For Cloud Data Centers. *Journal of Advanced Research in Dynamical and Control Systems, 12*(4), 501-508.

Balamurugan, Hasan, Almamun, & Sangeetha. (n.d.). An Energy Efficient And Self Adaptive Resource Allocation Framework Using Modified Clonal Selection Algorithm For Cloud Based Software Services. *Journal of Psychosocial Reha*bilitation, 24(2), 5182-5203.

Baraldi, P., Cannarile, F., Di Maio, F., & Zio, E. (2016). Hierarchical k-nearest neighbours classification and binary differential evolution for fault diagnostics of automotive bearings operating under variable conditions. *Engineering Applications of Artificial Intelligence*, 56, 1–13. doi:10.1016/j.engappai.2016.08.011

Barik, R. K., Dubey, H., Misra, C., Borthakur, D., Constant, N., Sasane, S. A., Lenka, R. K., Mishra, B. S. P., Das, H., & Mankodiya, K. (2018). Fog assisted cloud computing in era of big data and internet-of-things: systems, architectures, and applications. In *Cloud computing for optimization: foundations, applications, and challenges* (pp. 367–394). Springer.

Bauer, S., Wiest, R., Nolte, L. P., & Reyes, M. (2013). A survey of MRI-based medical image analysis for brain tumor studies. *Physics in Medicine and Biology*, 58(13), R97–R129. doi:10.1088/0031-9155/58/13/R97 PMID:23743802

Bell, L., Buchanan, W. J., Cameron, J., & Lo, O. (2018). Applications of Blockchain Within Healthcare. *Blockchain in Healthcare Today, 1*. Advance online publication. doi:10.30953/bhty.v1.8

Bengio, Y., Courville, A., & Vincent, P. (2013). Representation learning: A review and new perspectives. *IEEE Transactions on Pattern Analysis and Machine Intelligence, 35*(8), 1798–1828. doi:10.1109/TPAMI.2013.50 PMID:23787338

Bhattacharyya, A., & Pachori, R. B. (2017). A multivariate approach for patient-specific EEG seizure detection using empirical wavelet transform. *IEEE Transactions on Biomedical Engineering, 64*(9), 2003–2015. doi:10.1109/TBME.2017.2650259 PMID:28092514

Birda, R. K., & Dadhich, M. (2019). Study of ICT and E-Governance Facilities in Tribal District of Rajasthan. *ZENITH International Journal of Multidisciplinary Research, 9*(7), 39–49.

Biswas, A., & Chandrakasan, A. P. 2018, February. Conv-RAM: An energy-efficient SRAM with embedded convolution computation for low-power CNN-based machine learning applications. In *2018 IEEE International Solid-State Circuits Conference-(ISSCC)* (pp. 488-490). IEEE.

Bondy, J. A., & Murty, U. S. R. (2008). *Graph Theory* (International Edition). Springer. doi:10.1007/978-1-84628-970-5

Borthakur, D., Dubey, H., Constant, N., Mahler, L., & Mankodiya, K. 2017, November. Smart fog: Fog computing framework for unsupervised clustering analytics in wearable internet of things. In *2017 IEEE Global Conference on Signal and Information Processing (GlobalSIP)* (pp. 472-476). IEEE.

Botes, F. H., Leenen, L., & De La Harpe, R. (2017, June). Ant colony induced decision trees for intrusion detection. In *16th European Conference on Cyber Warfare and Security* (pp. 53-62). ACPI.

Bottou, L., & Bousquet, O. (2012). The Tradeoffs of Large Scale Learning. In Optimization for Machine Learning. MIT Press.

Breiman, L. (2001). Random forests. *Machine Learning, 45*(1), 5–32. doi:10.1023/A:1010933404324

Burst, I. Q. (2017). *Bringing Health to Life Whitepaper* [White paper]. Retrieved from https://www.burstiq.com/wp-content/uploads/2017/08/BurstIQ-whitepaper_19Jul2017reduced.pdf

Cao, B., Zhang, Z., Feng, D., Zhang, S., Zhang, L., Peng, M., & Li, Y. (2020). Performance analysis and comparison of PoW, PoS and DAG based blockchains. *Digital Communications and Networks, 6*(4), 480–485. doi:10.1016/j.dcan.2019.12.001

Cardenas, A. (2009). Challenges for securing cyber physical systems. *Workshop Future Directions Cyber-Physical Syst. Secur.*

Cardenas, A. A., Amin, S., & Sastry, S. (2008). Research challenges for the security of control systems. *3rd Conf. Hot Topics in Security.*

Cardenas, A. A., Amin, S., & Sastry, S. (2008). Secure control: Towards survivable cyber-physical systems. *IEEE 28th Int. Conf.*

Cardiovascular Diseases (CVDs). (n.d.). *WHO.* Retrieved 15 April 2021, from https://www.who.int/news-room/fact-sheets/detail/cardiovascular-diseases-(cvds)

Caroubalos, C., Perche, C., Metaxaki-Kossionides, C., Sangriotis, E., & Maroulis, D. (1988, July). Method for automatic analysis of the ECG. *Journal of Biomedical Engineering*, *10*(4), 343–347. doi:10.1016/0141-5425(88)90065-9 PMID:3236854

Chang, Y., Li, W., & Yang, Z. (2017). Network intrusion detection based on random forest and support vector machine. *Proceedings - 2017 IEEE International Conference on Computational Science and Engineering and IEEE/IFIP International Conference on Embedded and Ubiquitous Computing, CSE and EUC*, 635–638. 10.1109/CSE-EUC.2017.118

Chawla, Deshpande, Manas, Chhabria, & Krishnappa. (2019). Vetrtex Magic Labelling and its Application in Cryptography. *Recent Findings in Intelligent Computing Techniques.*

Chen, G., Xu, B., Lu, M., & Chen, N. S. (2018). Exploring blockchain technology and its potential applications for education. *Smart Learning Environments*, *5*(1), 1–10. doi:10.118640561-017-0050-x

Chen, N., Zhang, X., & Hiran, K. K. (2021). Integrated open geospatial web service enabled cyber-physical information infrastructure for precision agriculture monitoring. *Computers and Electronics in Agriculture*, *111*, 78–91. doi:10.1016/j.compag.2014.12.009

Chen, T., & Guestrin, C. (2016, August). Xgboost: A scalable tree boosting system. In *Proceedings of the 22nd acm sigkdd international conference on knowledge discovery and data mining* (pp. 785-794). 10.1145/2939672.2939785

Chen, W. H., Hsu, S. H., & Shen, H. P. (2005). Application of SVM and ANN for intrusion detection. *Computers & Operations Research*, *32*(10), 2617–2634. doi:10.1016/j.cor.2004.03.019

Chervyakov, N., Babenko, M., Tchernykh, A., Kucherov, N., Miranda-López, V., & Cortés-Mendoza, J. M. (2019). AR-RRNS: Configurable reliable distributed data storage systems for Internet of Things to ensure security. *Future Generation Computer Systems*, *92*, 1080–1092.

Chuang, M.-C., & Lee, J.-F. (2011). Ppas: A privacy preservation authentication scheme for vehicle-to-infrastructure communication networks. *IEEE International Conference on Consumer Electronics, Communications and Networks (CECNet)*, 1509-1512. 10.1109/CECNET.2011.5768254

Colombo, A. W., Bangemann, T., Karnouskos, S., Delsing, J., Stluka, P., Harrison, R., ... Lastra, J. L. (2014). Industrial cloud-based cyber-physical systems. *The Imc-aesop Approach*, *22*, 4–5.

Cortes, C., & Vapnik, V. (2015). Support-vector networks. *Machine Learning*, *20*(3), 273–297. doi:10.1007/BF00994018

Cui, L., Hou, Y., Liu, Y., & Zhang, L. (2021). Text mining to explore the influencing factors of sharing economy driven digital platforms to promote social and economic development. *Information Technology for Development*, *27*(4), 779–801. doi:10.1080/02681102.2020.1815636

Dadhich, M., Hiran, K. K., & Rao, S. S. (2021). *Teaching – Learning Perception Toward Blended E-learning Portals During Pandemic Lockdown*. Springer Singapore. doi:10.1007/978-981-16-1696-9

Dadhich, M., Rao, S. S., Sethy, S., & Sharma, R. (2021). Determining the Factors Influencing Cloud Computing Implementation in Library Management System (LMS): A High Order PLS-ANN Approach. *Library Philosophy and Practice*, 6281.

Dadhich, Pahwa, S. G., & S. S. R. (2021). Analytical Study of Financial Wellbeing of Selected Public and Private Sector Banks: A CAMEL Approach. *IEEE Explore, Emerging Trends in Industry 4.0 (ETI 4.0)*, 1–6. . doi:10.1109/ETI4.051663.2021.9619424

Dadhich, M., Pahwa, M. S., Jain, V., & Doshi, R. (2021). Predictive Models for Stock Market Index Using Stochastic Time Series ARIMA Modeling in Emerging Economy. *Advances in Mechanical Engineering*, 281–290. doi:10.1007/978-981-16-0942-8_26

Dadhich, M., Purohit, H., & Bhasker, A. A. (2021). Determinants of green initiatives and operational performance for manufacturing SMEs. *Materials Today: Proceedings*, *46*(20), 10870–10874. doi:10.1016/j.matpr.2021.01.889

Dafflon, B., Moalla, N., & Ouzrout, Y. (2021). Ouzrout, "The challenges, approaches, and used techniques of CPS for manufacturing in Industry 4.0: A literature review. *International Journal of Advanced Manufacturing Technology*, *113*(7-8), 2395–2412. doi:10.100700170-020-06572-4

Dalton, A., Patel, S., Chowdhury, A. R., Welsh, M., Pang, T., Schachter, S., Olaighin, G., & Bonato, P. (2012). G. OLaighin, and P. Bonato, "Development of a body sensor network to detect motor patterns of epileptic seizures. *IEEE Transactions on Biomedical Engineering*, *59*(11), 3204–3211. doi:10.1109/TBME.2012.2204990 PMID:22717505

Dang, Q. V. (2018). *Outlier detection on network flow analysis*. arXiv preprint arXiv:1808.02024.

Dang, Q. V. (2021). Improving the performance of the intrusion detection systems by the machine learning explainability. *International Journal of Web Information Systems*.

Dang, Q. V., & Vo, T. H. (2021, May). Studying the Reinforcement Learning techniques for the problem of intrusion detection. In *2021 4th International Conference on Artificial Intelligence and Big Data (ICAIBD)* (pp. 87-91). IEEE. 10.1109/ICAIBD51990.2021.9459006

Dang, Q. V. (2019, November). Studying machine learning techniques for intrusion detection systems. In *International Conference on Future Data and Security Engineering* (pp. 411-426). Springer. 10.1007/978-3-030-35653-8_28

Dang, Q. V. (2020, November). Understanding the Decision of Machine Learning Based Intrusion Detection Systems. In *International Conference on Future Data and Security Engineering* (pp. 379-396). Springer. 10.1007/978-3-030-63924-2_22

Dang, Q. V. (2020, October). Active learning for intrusion detection systems. In *2020 RIVF International Conference on Computing and Communication Technologies (RIVF)* (pp. 1-3). IEEE.

Dang, Q. V. (2021, February). Right to Be Forgotten in the Age of Machine Learning. In *International Conference on Advances in Digital Science* (pp. 403-411). Springer. 10.1007/978-3-030-71782-7_35

Dang, Q. V. (2021, July). Studying the Fuzzy clustering algorithm for intrusion detection on the attacks to the Domain Name System. In *2021 Fifth World Conference on Smart Trends in Systems Security and Sustainability (WorldS4)* (pp. 271-274). IEEE. 10.1109/WorldS451998.2021.9514038

Daor, J., Daemen, J., & Rijmen, V. (1999). *AES proposal: rijndael*. Academic Press.

Darwish, A., & Hassanien, A. E. (2018). Cyber physical systems design, methodology, and integration: The current status and future outlook. *Journal of Ambient Intelligence and Humanized Computing, 9*(5), 1541–1556. doi:10.100712652-017-0575-4

Davenport, T., & Kalakota, R. (2019). The potential for artificial intelligence in healthcare. *Future Healthcare Journal, 6*(2), 94–98. doi:10.7861/futurehosp.6-2-94 PMID:31363513

Deepa, Maheswari, & Balaji. (2019). Creating Ciphertext and Decipher using Graph Labelling Techniques. *International Journal of Engineering and Advanced Technology*.

Deng, L., Abdel-Hamid, O., & Yu, D. (2013). A deep convolutional neural network using heterogeneous pooling for trading acoustic invariance. *Proceedings of the IEEE International Conference on Acoustics, Speech and Signal Processing (ICASSP)*. 10.1109/ICASSP.2013.6638952

Devlin, J., Chang, M., Lee, K., & Toutanova, K. (2019). *BERT: Pre-training of Deep Bidirectional Transformers for Language Understanding*. ArXiv, abs/1810.04805.

Diale, M., Celik, T., & Van Der Walt, C. (2019). Unsupervised feature learning for spam email filtering. *Computers & Electrical Engineering, 74*, 89–104. doi:10.1016/j.compeleceng.2019.01.004

Ding, Z., Gao, X., Xu, J., & Wu, H. (2013, August). IOT-StatisticDB: a general statistical database cluster mechanism for big data analysis in the internet of things. In *2013 IEEE International Conference on Green Computing and Communications and IEEE Internet of Things and IEEE Cyber, Physical and Social Computing* (pp. 535-543). IEEE.

Dooley, J. F. (2003). *A Brief History of Cryptology and Cryptographic Algorithms*. Springer.

Dorogush, A. V., Ershov, V., & Gulin, A. (2018). *CatBoost: gradient boosting with categorical features support*. arXiv preprint arXiv:1810.11363.

Drug Review Dataset (Drugs.com) Data Set. (2018, October 4). *UCI Machine Learning Repository*. https://archive.ics.uci.edu/ml/datasets/Drug+Review+Dataset+%28Drugs.com%29

Dusadeerungsikul, P. O., Nof, S. Y., Bechar, A., & Tao, Y. (2019). Collaborative control protocol for agricultural cyber-physical system. *Procedia Manufacturing, 39*, 235–242. doi:10.1016/j.promfg.2020.01.330

Eggert, C., Brehm, S., Winschel, A., Zecha, D., & Lienhart, R. (2017, July). A closer look: Small object detection in faster R-CNN. In 2017 IEEE international conference on multimedia and expo (ICME) (pp. 421-426). IEEE.

Elsayed, M. S., Le-Khac, N. A., & Jurcut, A. D. (2020). InSDN: A novel SDN intrusion dataset. *IEEE Access: Practical Innovations, Open Solutions, 8*, 165263–165284. doi:10.1109/ACCESS.2020.3022633

Engur, Guo, & Akbulut. (2016). Time–frequency texture descriptors of EEG signals for efficient detection of epileptic seizure. *Brain Informatics, 3*(2), 101–108. doi:10.100740708-015-0029-8 PMID:27747603

Erem, B., Hyde, D. E., Peters, J. M., Duffy, F. H., Brooks, D. H., & Warfield, S. K. (2015). Combined delay and graph embedding of epileptic discharges in eeg reveals complex and recurrent nonlinear dynamics. In *Biomedical Imaging (ISBI), 2015 IEEE 12th International Symposium on.* IEEE. 10.1109/ISBI.2015.7163884

Evaluation of Machine Learning Algorithms for Intrusion Detection System. (2019). *Cuelogic Technologies.* https://medium.com/cuelogic-technologies/evaluation-of-machine-learning-algorithms-for-intrusion-detection-system-6854645f9211

Eyal, I. (2017). Blockchain Technology: Transforming Libertarian Cryptocurrency Dreams to Finance and Banking Realities. *Computer, 50*(9), 38–49. doi:10.1109/MC.2017.3571042

Fawcett, T. (2006). An introduction to ROC analysis. *Pattern Recognition Letters, 27*(8), 861–874. doi:10.1016/j.patrec.2005.10.010

Feeney, A. B., Frechette, S., & Srinivasan, V. (2017). Cyber-physical systems engineering for manufacturing. In *Industrial internet of things* (pp. 81–110). Springer. doi:10.1007/978-3-319-42559-7_4

Feng, C. M., Xu, Y., Liu, J. X., Gao, Y. L., & Zheng, C. H. (2019). Supervised discriminative sparse PCA for com-characteristic gene selection and tumor classification on multiview biological data. *IEEE Transactions on Neural Networks and Learning Systems, 30*(10), 2926–2937. doi:10.1109/TNNLS.2019.2893190 PMID:30802874

Fink, G. A., Edgar, T. W., Rice, T. R., MacDonald, D. G., & Crawford, C. E. (2018). *Overview of Security and Privacy in Cyber-Physical Systems. Overview of Security and Privacy in Cyber-Physical Systems: Foundations, Principles and Applications.* doi:10.1002/9781119226079.ch1

Fraz, M., Remagnino, P., Hoppe, A., Uyyanonvara, B., Rudnicka, A., Owen, C., & Barman, S. (2012). *Blood vessel segmentation methodologies in retinal images.* IEEE Publication.

Fresilli, D., Grani, G., De Pascali, M. L., Alagna, G., Tassone, E., Ramundo, V., & Cantisani, V. (2020). Computer-aided diagnostic system for thyroid nodule sonographic evaluation outperforms the specificity of less experienced examiners. *Journal of Ultrasound, 23*(2), 169–174. doi:10.100740477-020-00453-y PMID:32246401

Gallian, J.A. (2011). #DS6, A dynamic survey of graph labelling. *The Eletronic Journal of Combinatorices.*

Ganesan, V., & Lavanya, S. (2019). Prime labelling of Split Graph of Star $K_{1,n}$. *IOSR Journal of Mathematics.*

Garagad, V. G., & Iyer, N. (2020). A security threat for Internet of Things and Cyber-Physical Systems. *2020 International Conference on Computational Performance Evaluation.* 10.1109/ComPE49325.2020.9200170

Gervais, A., Karame, G. O., Wüst, K., Glykantzis, V., Ritzdorf, H., & Capkun, S. (2016). On the Security and Performance of Proof of Work Blockchains. *Proceedings of the 2016 ACM SIGSAC Conference on Computer and Communications Security.* 10.1145/2976749.2978341

Ghobakhloo, M. (2018). The future of manufacturing industry: A strategic roadmap toward Industry 4.0. *Journal of Manufacturing Technology Management, 29*(6), 910–936. doi:10.1108/JMTM-02-2018-0057

Gil, S., Zapata-Madrigal, G. D., & García-Sierra, R. (2019, October). Electrical Internet of Things-EIoT: A Platform for the Data Management in Electrical Systems. In *Proceedings of the Future Technologies Conference* (pp. 49-65). Springer.

Giraldo, Sarkar, Cardenas, Maniatakos, & Kantarcioglu. (2017). Security and Privacy in Cyber–Physical Systems: A Survey of Surveys. *IEEE CEDA, IEEE CASS, IEEE SSCS, and TTTC.*

Giridaran,, M. (2020). Application of Super Magic Labelling in Cryptography. *International Journal of Innovative Research in Science, Engineering and Technology.*

Goap, A., Sharma, D., Shukla, A. K., & Rama Krishna, C. (2018). An IoT based smart irrigation management system using Machine learning and open source technologies. *Computers and Electronics in Agriculture, 155*(September), 41–49. doi:10.1016/j.compag.2018.09.040

Gohar, M., Muhammad, M., & Rahman, A. U. (2018). Smart tss: Defining transportation system behavior using big data analytics in smart cities. *Sustainable Cities and Society, 41*, 114–119. doi:10.1016/j.scs.2018.05.008

Goodfellow, I., Bengio, Y., & Courville, A. (2016). 6.2.2.3 Softmax Units for Multinoulli Output Distributions. In Deep Learning. MIT Press.

Goodfellow, I., Bengio, Y., & Courville, A. (2016). *Deep learning.* MIT press.

Grassi, A., Guizzi, G., Santillo, L. C., & Vespoli, S. (2020). A semi-heterarchical production control architecture for industry 4.0-based manufacturing systems. *Manufacturing Letters, 24*, 43–46. doi:10.1016/j.mfglet.2020.03.007

Greenfield, L. J., Geyer, J. D., & Carney, P. R. (2012). *Reading EEGs: a practical approach.* Lippincott Williams & Wilkins.

Gronau, N. (2016). Determinants of an appropriate degree of autonomy in a cyber-physical production system. *Procedia CIRP, 52*, 1–5. doi:10.1016/j.procir.2016.07.063

Guo, J., Yu, D., Jian, L., & Xu, C. (2010). Knowledge sharing model for equipment maintenance federation based on knowledge grid. *Jisuanji Jicheng Zhizao Xitong, 16*(1), 47–56.

Guo, K., Tang, Y., & Zhang, P. (2017). CSF: Crowdsourcing semantic fusion for heterogeneous media big data in the internet of things. *Information Fusion, 37,* 77–85.

Guo, Y., Hu, X., Hu, B., Cheng, J., Zhou, M., & Kwok, R. Y. (2017). Mobile cyber physical systems: Current challenges and future networking applications. *IEEE Access: Practical Innovations, Open Solutions, 6,* 12360–12368. doi:10.1109/ACCESS.2017.2782881

Gupta, N., Tiwari, A., Bukkapatnam, S. T., & Karri, R. (2020). Additive manufacturing cyber-physical system: Supply chain cybersecurity and risks. *IEEE Access: Practical Innovations, Open Solutions, 8,* 47322–47333. doi:10.1109/ACCESS.2020.2978815

Gupta, R., Mohan, I., & Narula, J. (2016). Trends in Coronary Heart Disease Epidemiology in India. *Annals of Global Health, 82*(2), 307. doi:10.1016/j.aogh.2016.04.002 PMID:27372534

Gurjar. (2021). Lexicographic Labeled Graphs in Cryptography. *Auparajita Krishnaa, 27*(2), 209–232.

Halimaa & Sundarakantham. (2019). *Machine Learning Based Intrusion Detection System. Third International Conference on Trends in Electronics and Informatics.* 10.1109/ICOEI.2019.8862784

Hasan, Balamurugan, Almamun, & Sangeetha. (2020). An Intelligent Machine Learning And Self Adaptive Resource Allocation Framework For Cloud Computing Environment. *EAI Endorsed Transactions on Cloud Systems.*

Hasan, M. A., Munia, E. J., Pritom, S. K., Setu, M. H., Ali, M. T., & Fahim, S. C. (2020). Cardiac Arrhythmia Detection in an ECG Beat Signal Using 1D Convolution Neural Network. *2020 IEEE Region 10 Symposium (TENSYMP).* doi:.923058110.1109/tensymp50017.2020

Hassan, Rehmani, & Chen. (2019). Differential Privacy Techniques for Cyber Physical Systems: A Survey. *IEEE Explore,* 1-44.

Hasselgren, A., Kralevska, K., Gligoroski, D., Pedersen, S. A., & Faxvaag, A. (2020). Blockchain in healthcare and health sciences—A scoping review. *International Journal of Medical Informatics, 134,* 104040. doi:10.1016/j.ijmedinf.2019.104040 PMID:31865055

Haux, R. (2006). Health information systems – past, present, future. *International Journal of Medical Informatics, 75*(3–4), 268–281. doi:10.1016/j.ijmedinf.2005.08.002 PMID:16169771

HealthCoin. (2019). *The Health Coin White Paper* [White paper]. Retrieved from https://thehealthcoin.io/wp-content/uploads/2018/04/HEALTHCOIN-WHITE-PAPER.pdf

Heart, T., Ben-Assuli, O., & Shabtai, I. (2017). A review of PHR, EMR and EHR integration: A more personalized healthcare and public health policy. *Health Policy and Technology, 6*(1), 20–25. doi:10.1016/j.hlpt.2016.08.002

Hehenberger, P., Vogel-Heuser, B., Bradley, D., Eynard, B., Tomiyama, T., & Achiche, S. (2016). Design, modelling, simulation and integration of cyber physical systems: Methods and applications. *Computers in Industry, 82,* 273–289. doi:10.1016/j.compind.2016.05.006

Hellsted, Vesti, & Immonen. (1996). *Identification of individual microaneurysms: A comparison between fluorescein angiograms and red-free and color photographs.* IEEE Publication.

Hiran, K. K. (2021). Investigating Factors Influencing the Adoption of IT Cloud Computing Platforms in Higher Education: Case of Sub-Saharan Africa With IT Professionals. *International Journal of Human Capital and Information Technology Professionals, 12*(3), 21–36. doi:10.4018/IJHCITP.2021070102

Hiran, K. K., & Doshi, R. (2013). An artificial neural network approach for brain tumor detection using digital image segmentation. *Brain, 2*(5), 227–231.

Hiran, K. K., Doshi, R., Fagbola, T., & Mahrishi, M. (2019). *Cloud computing: Master the concepts, architecture and applications with real-world examples and case studies.* BPB Publications.

Hiran, K. K., & Henten, A. (2020). An integrated TOE – DoI framework for cloud computing adoption in the higher education sector : Case study of Sub-Saharan Africa. *International Journal of System Assurance Engineering and Management, 11*(2), 441–449. doi:10.100713198-019-00872-z

Hiran, K. K., Jain, R. K., Lakhwani, K., & Doshi, R. (2021). *Machine Learning: Master Supervised and Unsupervised Learning Algorithms with Real Examples (English Edition).* BPB Publications.

Hiran, K. K., Khazanchi, D., Vyas, A. K., & Padmanaban, S. (Eds.). (2021). *Machine Learning for Sustainable Development* (Vol. 9). Walter de Gruyter GmbH & Co KG. doi:10.1515/9783110702514

Hosseini, M. P., Pompili, D., Elisevich, K., & Soltanian-Zadeh, H. (2017). Optimized deep learning for EEG big data and seizure prediction BCI via internet of things. *IEEE Transactions on Big Data, 3*(4), 392–404.

Huai-bin, W., Hong-liang, Y., Zhi-Jian, X. U., & Zheng, Y. (2010, May). A clustering algorithm use SOM and k-means in intrusion detection. In *2010 International Conference on E-Business and E-Government* (pp. 1281-1284). IEEE. 10.1109/ICEE.2010.327

Huang, J., Chen, B., Yao, B., & He, W. (2019). ECG Arrhythmia Classification Using STFT-Based Spectrogram and Convolutional Neural Network. *IEEE Access: Practical Innovations, Open Solutions, 7*, 92871–92880. doi:10.1109/ACCESS.2019.2928017

Huang, Z., Wang, C., Stojmenovic, M., & Nayak, A. (2014). Characterization of cascading failures in interdependent cyber-physical systems. *IEEE Transactions on Computers, 64*(8), 2158–2168. doi:10.1109/TC.2014.2360537

Humayed, A., Lin, J., Li, F., & Luo, B. (2017). Cyber-physical systems security—A survey. *IEEE Internet of Things Journal, 4*(6), 1802–1831. doi:10.1109/JIOT.2017.2703172

Huo, D., & Chaudhry, H. R. (2021). Using machine learning for evaluating global expansion location decisions: An analysis of Chinese manufacturing sector. *Technological Forecasting and Social Change, 163*, 1–15. doi:10.1016/j.techfore.2020.120436

Iarovyi, S., Mohammed, W. M., Lobov, A., Ferrer, B. R., & Lastra, J. L. M. (2016). Cyber-Physical Systems for Open-Knowledge-Driven Manufacturing Execution Systems. *Proceedings of the IEEE, 104*(5), 1142–1154. doi:10.1109/JPROC.2015.2509498

Image Data Preprocessing (IDP). (n.d.). *Keras documentation: Image data preprocessing (IDP).* Keras.io. Retrieved 15 April 2021, from https://keras.io/api/preprocessing/image/

Iman, A. N., & Ahmad, T. (2020). Improving Intrusion Detection System by Estimating Parameters of Random Forest in Boruta. *International Conference on Smart Technology and Applications.* 10.1109/ICoSTA48221.2020.1570609975

Iqbal, R., Doctor, F., More, B., Mahmud, S., & Yousuf, U. (2020). Big Data analytics and Computational Intelligence for Cyber–Physical Systems: Recent trends and state of the art applications. *Future Generation Computer Systems, 105*, 766–778. doi:10.1016/j.future.2017.10.021

Izci, E., Ozdemir, M. A., Degirmenci, M., & Akan, A. (2019). Cardiac Arrhythmia Detection from 2D ECG Images by Using Deep Learning Technique. In *Proceedings of the 2019 Medical Technologies Congress (TIPTEKNO).* IEEE. 10.1109/TIPTEKNO.2019.8895011

Jabez, J., & Muthukumar, B. (2015). Intrusion Detection System (IDS): Anomaly Detection using Outlier Detection Approach. *Procedia Computer Science, 48*, 338–346. doi:10.1016/j.procs.2015.04.191

Jan, B., Farman, H., Khan, M., Talha, M., & Din, I. U. (2019). Designing a smart transportation system: An internet of things and big data approach. *IEEE Wireless Communications, 26*(4), 73–79.

Jantunen, E., Zurutuza, U., Ferreira, L. L., & Varga, P. (2016). Optimising maintenance: What are the expectations for Cyber Physical Systems. *2016 3rd International Workshop on Emerging Ideas and Trends in Engineering of Cyber-Physical Systems (EITEC),* 53-58. 10.1109/EITEC.2016.7503697

Jazdi. (2014). Cyber physical systems in the context of Industry 4.0. *2014 IEEE International Conference on Automation, Quality and Testing, Robotics,* 1-4.

Jimenez, A. F., Cardenas, P. F., Jimenez, F., Canales, A., & López, A. (2020). A cyber-physical intelligent agent for irrigation scheduling in horticultural crops. *Computers and Electronics in Agriculture, 178*, 1–15. doi:10.1016/j.compag.2020.105777

Jin, Herder, Nguyen, & Fuller, Devadas, & Van Dijk. (2017). FPGA Implementation of a Cryptographically – Secure PUF based on Learning Parity with Noise. *Cryptography, 105*, 1028–1042.

Jirwan, Singh, & Vijay. (2013). Review and Analysis of Cryptography Techniques. *International Journal Scientific & Engineering Research.*

Kachuee, M., Fazeli, S., & Sarrafzadeh, M. (2018). ECG Heartbeat Classification: A Deep Transferable Representation. *2018 IEEE International Conference on Healthcare Informatics (ICHI),* 443-444. 10.1109/ICHI.2018.00092

Kang, Z., Catal, C., & Tekinerdogan, B. (2021). Remaining Useful Life (RUL) Prediction of Equipment in Production Lines Using Artificial Neural Networks. *Sensors (Basel)*, *21*(3), 21. doi:10.339021030932 PMID:33573297

Kayem, A. V., Meinel, C., & Wolthusen, S. D. (2017). A smart microgrid architecture for resource constrained environments. *IEEE 31st International Conference on Advanced Information Networking and Applications (AINA)*, 857-864.

Ke, G., Meng, Q., Finley, T., Wang, T., Chen, W., Ma, W., ... Liu, T. Y. (2017). Lightgbm: A highly efficient gradient boosting decision tree. *Advances in Neural Information Processing Systems*, *30*, 3146–3154.

Keogh, E., & Mueen, A. (2011). *Curse of dimensionality. In Encyclopedia of machine learning*. Springer.

Khaitan, S. K., & McCalley, J. D. (2014). Design techniques and applications of cyberphysical systems: A survey. *IEEE Systems Journal*, *9*(2), 350–365. doi:10.1109/JSYST.2014.2322503

Kim, J. Y., Kim, J. J., Hwangbo, L., Suh, H. B., Kim, S., Choo, K. S., & Kang, T. (2020). Kinetic heterogeneity of breast cancer determined using computer-aided diagnosis of preoperative MRI scans: Relationship to distant metastasis-free survival. *Radiology*, *295*(3), 517–526. doi:10.1148/radiol.2020192039 PMID:32228293

Kim, J., & Lee, J. Y. (2021). Server-Edge dualized closed-loop data analytics system for cyber-physical system application. *Robotics and Computer-integrated Manufacturing*, *67*, 102040. doi:10.1016/j.rcim.2020.102040

Kim, K. D., & Kumar, P. R. (2013). An overview and some challenges in cyber-physical systems. *Journal of the Indian Institute of Science*, *93*(3), 341–352.

Kim, Lee, Shim, Cheon, Kim, Kim, & Song. (2016). Encryting Controller using Fully Homomorphic Encryption for security of Cyber-Physical Systems. *IFAC-PapersOnLine*.

Kim, T. Y., & Cho, S. B. (2019). Predicting residential energy consumption using CNN-LSTM neural networks. *Energy*, *182*, 72–81.

Kommireddy, S., Pandey, P. R., & Kishore NeeliSetti, R. (2020). Detection of Heart Arrhythmia Using Hybrid Neural Networks. *2020 IEEE Region 10 Conference (TENCON)*. . doi:10.1109/TENCON50793.2020.9293831

Krämer, B. J. (2014). Evolution of cyber-physical systems: a brief review. *Applied Cyber-Physical Systems*, 1-3.

Krishnaa. (2019). Inner Magic and Inner Antimagic Graphs in Cryptography. *Journal of Discrete Mathematical Sciences and Cryptography*.

Kritzinger, W., Karner, M., Traar, G., Henjes, J., & Sihn, W. (2018). Digital twin in manufacturing: a categorical literature review and classification. *16th IFAC Symposium on Information Control Problems in Manufacturing INCOM*. 10.1016/j.ifacol.2018.08.474

Kumari. (2017). A research Paper on Cryptography Encryption and Compression Techniques. *International Journal of Engineering and Computer Science.*

Kumari, A., Tanwar, S., Tyagi, S., Kumar, N., Maasberg, M., & Choo, K. K. R. (2018). Multimedia big data computing and Internet of Things applications: A taxonomy and process model. *Journal of Network and Computer Applications, 124*, 169–195.

Kumar, N., & Dadhich, M. (2014). Risk Management for Investors in Stock Market. *EXCEL International Journal of Multidisciplinary Management Studies, 4*(3), 103–108.

Kumar, S. N., & Ismail, B. M. (2020). Systematic investigation on Multi-Class skin cancer categorization using machine learning approach. *Materials Today: Proceedings.*

Lai, Y. (2019). A Comparison of Traditional Machine Learning and Deep Learning in Image Recognition. *Journal of Physics: Conference Series, 1314*(1), 012148. doi:10.1088/1742-6596/1314/1/012148

Lakhwani, K., Gianey, H. K., Wireko, J. K., & Hiran, K. K. (2020). *Internet of Things (IoT): Principles, paradigms and applications of IoT.* BPB Publications.

Layer Weight Initializers (LWI). (n.d.). *Keras documentation: Layer weight initializers (LWI).* Keras.io. Retrieved 25 April 2021, from https://keras.io/api/layers/initializers/

Lee, E. A. (2006) Cyber-physical systems—Are computing foundations adequate. *Workshop on Cyber-Physical Systems: Research Motivation, Techniques and Roadmap.*

Lee, I., Sokolsky, O., Chen, S., Hatcliff, J., Jee, E., Kim, B., ... Venkatasubramanian, K. K. (2011). Challenges and research directions in medical cyber–physical systems. *Proceedings of the IEEE, 100*(1), 75–90.

Lee, J., Azamfar, M., Singh, J., & Siahpour, S. (2020). Integration of digital twin and deep learning in cyber-physical systems: Towards smart manufacturing. *IET Collaborative Intelligent Manufacturing, 2*(1), 34–36. doi:10.1049/iet-cim.2020.0009

Lee, J., Bagheri, B., & Kao, H.-A. (2015). A cyber-physical systems architecture for industry 4.0-based manufacturing systems. *Manufacturing Letters, 3*, 18–23. doi:10.1016/j.mfglet.2014.12.001

Leitão, P., Colombo, A. W., & Karnouskos, S. (2016). Industrial automation based on cyber-physical systems technologies: Prototype implementations and challenges. *Computers in Industry, 81*, 11–25. doi:10.1016/j.compind.2015.08.004

Li, D., Yang, Q., Yu, W., An, D., Yang, X., & Zhao, W. (2017). A strategy-proof privacy-preserving double auction mechanism for electrical vehicles demand response in microgrids. *IEEE 36th International Performance Computing and Communications Conference (IPCCC)*, 1–8.

Li, J., Qu, C., & Shao, J. (2017, November). Ship detection in SAR images based on an improved faster R-CNN. In 2017 SAR in Big Data Era: Models, Methods and Applications (BIGSARDATA) (pp. 1-6). IEEE.

Liao, Y., Ragai, I., Huang, Z., & Kerner, S. (2021). Manufacturing process monitoring using time-frequency representation and transfer learning of deep neural networks. *Journal of Manufacturing Processes, 68*(PA), 231–248. doi:10.1016/j.jmapro.2021.05.046

Liao, Y., & Vemuri, V. R. (2002). Use of k-nearest neighbor classifier for intrusion detection. *Computers & Security, 21*(5), 439–448. doi:10.1016/S0167-4048(02)00514-X

Lieu Tran, T. B., Törngren, M., Nguyen, H. D., Paulen, R., Gleason, N. W., & Duong, T. H. (2019). Trends in preparing cyber-physical systems engineers. *Cyber-Physical Systems, 5*(2), 65–91. doi:10.1080/23335777.2019.1600034

Lima, Carvalho, & Moreira. (2020). Cyber-Physical Systems using Event-Based Cryptography. *IFAC-PapersOnLine.*

Li, N., Liu, K., Chen, Z., & Jiao, W. (2020). Environmental-Perception Modeling and Reference Architecture for Cyber Physical Systems. *IEEE Access: Practical Innovations, Open Solutions, 8*, 200322–200337. doi:10.1109/ACCESS.2020.3034390

Lin, Q., Ye, S.-q., Huang, X.-m., Li, S.-y., Zhang, M.-z., Xue, Y., & Chen, W.-S. (2016). Classification of epileptic eeg signals with stacked sparse autoencoder based on deep learning. In *International Conference on Intelligent Computing*. Springer. 10.1007/978-3-319-42297-8_74

Liu, F. T., Ting, K. M., & Zhou, Z. H. (2008, December). Isolation forest. In *2008 eighth IEEE international conference on data mining* (pp. 413-422). IEEE. 10.1109/ICDM.2008.17

Liu, D., & Kumar, S. A. (2017). An exceedingly rare adrenal collision tumor: Adrenal adenoma–metastatic breast cancer–myelolipoma. *Journal of Community Hospital Internal Medicine Perspectives, 7*(4), 241–244. doi:10.1080/20009666.2017.1362315 PMID:29046752

Lun, Y. Z., D'Innocenzo, A., Smarra, F., Malavolta, I., & Di Benedetto, M. D. (2019). State of the art of cyber-physical systems security: An automatic control perspective. *Journal of Systems and Software, 149*, 174–216. doi:10.1016/j.jss.2018.12.006

Lu, T., Lin, J., Zhao, L., Li, Y., & Peng, Y. (2015). A security architecture in cyber-physical systems: Security theories, analysis, simulation and application fields. *International Journal of Security and Its Applications, 9*(7), 1–16. doi:10.14257/ijsia.2015.9.7.01

Mahrishi, M., Hiran, K. K., Meena, G., & Sharma, P. (Eds.). (2020). *Machine Learning and Deep Learning in Real-Time Applications*. IGI Global. doi:10.4018/978-1-7998-3095-5

Malathi, C., & Padmaja, I. N. (2021). Identification of cyber attacks using machine learning in smart IoT networks. *Materials Today: Proceedings, 3*. Advance online publication. doi:10.1016/j.matpr.2021.06.400

Manrique-silupu, J., Campos, J. C., Paiva, E., & Ipanaqu, W. (2021). Thrips incidence prediction in organic banana crop with Machine learning. *Heliyon, 7*(12), 1–27. doi:10.1016/j.heliyon.2021.e08575 PMID:34977405

Marjani, M., Nasaruddin, F., Gani, A., Karim, A., Hashem, I.A.T., Siddiqa, A. and Yaqoob, I., 2017. Big IoT data analytics: architecture, opportunities, and open research challenges. *IEEE Access, 5*, 5247-5261.

Marwedel, P., Mitra, T., Grimheden, M. E., & Andrade, H. A. (2020). Survey on education for cyber-physical systems. *IEEE Design & Test, 37*(6), 56–70. doi:10.1109/MDAT.2020.3009613

Maseer, Z. K., Yusof, R., Bahaman, N., Mostafa, S. A., & Foozy, C. F. M. (2021). Benchmarking of machine learning for anomaly based intrusion detection systems in the CICIDS2017 dataset. *IEEE Access: Practical Innovations, Open Solutions, 9*, 22351–22370. doi:10.1109/ACCESS.2021.3056614

Masoodab, T., & Sonntaga, P. (2020). Industry 4.0: Adoption challenges and benefits for SMEs. *Computers in Industry, 121*, 103261. doi:10.1016/j.compind.2020.103261

McCulloch, W. S., & Pitts, W. (2012). A logical calculus of the ideas immanent in nervous activity. *The Bulletin of Mathematical Biophysics, 5*(4), 115–133. doi:10.1007/BF02478259

McGill, H. Jr, McMahan, C., & Gidding, S. (2008). Preventing Heart Disease in the 21st Century. *Circulation, 117*(9), 1216–1227. doi:10.1161/CIRCULATIONAHA.107.717033 PMID:18316498

McHugh, J. (2000). Testing intrusion detection systems: A critique of the 1998 and 1999 darpa intrusion detection system evaluations as performed by lincoln laboratory. *ACM Transactions on Information and System Security, 3*(4), 262–294. doi:10.1145/382912.382923

McSharry, P. E., Smith, L. A., & Tarassenko, L. (2003). Prediction of epileptic seizures: Are nonlinear methods relevant? *Nature Medicine, 9*(3), 241–242. doi:10.1038/nm0303-241 PMID:12612550

Mei, Z., Zhao, X., Chen, H., & Chen, W. (2018). Bio-signal complexity analysis in epileptic seizure monitoring: A topic review. *Sensors (Basel), 18*(6), 1720. doi:10.339018061720 PMID:29861451

Menachemi, N., & Collum. (2011). Benefits and drawbacks of electronic health record systems. *Risk Management and Healthcare Policy, 47*, 47. Advance online publication. doi:10.2147/RMHP.S12985 PMID:22312227

Meraghni, S., Terrissa, L. S., Ayad, S., Zerhouni, N., & Varnier, C. (2018). Post-prognostics decision in cyber-physical systems. *2018 International Conference on Advanced Systems and Electric Technologies (IC_ASET)*, 201-205. 10.1109/ASET.2018.8379859

Merely & Anto. (2016). Vertex Polynomial for the Splitting Graph of Comd and Crown. *International Journal of Emerging Technologies in Engineering Research.*

Mero, J. (2018). The effects of two-way communication and chat service usage on consumer attitudes in the e-commerce retailing sector. *Electronic Markets, 28*(2), 205–217. doi:10.100712525-017-0281-2

Meshram, S. P., & Pawar, M. S. (2013). Extraction of Retinal Blood Vessels from Diabetic Retinopathy Imagery Using Contrast Limited Adaptive Histogram Equalization. *IEEE Journal of Biomedical and Health Informatics*, *20*(6), 1562–1574.

Mohammed, J., Lung, C.H., Ocneanu, A., Thakral, A., Jones, C., & Adler, A. (2014, September). Internet of Things: Remote patient monitoring using web services and cloud computing. In *2014 IEEE international conference on internet of things (IThings), and IEEE green computing and communications (GreenCom) and IEEE cyber, physical and social computing (CPSCom)* (pp. 256-263). IEEE.

Mohseni, H. R., Maghsoudi, A., & Shamsollahi, M. B. (2016). Seizure detection in EEG signals: A comparison of different approaches. *Proc. of the 28th IEEE EMBS Int. Conf.*

Mondéjar-Guerra, V., Novo, J., Rouco, J., Penedo, M., & Ortega, M. (2019). Heartbeat classification fusing temporal and morphological information of ECGs via ensemble of classifiers. *Biomedical Signal Processing and Control*, *47*, 41–48. doi:10.1016/j.bspc.2018.08.007

Monostori, L. (2014). Cyber-physical Production Systems: Roots, Expectations and R&D Challenges. *Procedia CIRP*, *17*, 9–13. doi:10.1016/j.procir.2014.03.115

Moody, G., & Mark, R. (2001). The impact of the MIT-BIH Arrhythmia Database. *IEEE Engineering in Medicine and Biology Magazine*, *20*(3), 45–50. doi:10.1109/51.932724 PMID:11446209

Mueller, F. (2006). *Challenges for cyber-physical systems: Security, timing analysis and soft error protection. High-Confidence Softw. Platforms CyberPhysical Syst. (HCSP-CPS) Workshop.*

Mu, Z., Liu, H., & Liu, C. (2020). Design and Implementation of Network Intrusion Detection System. *International Conference on Intelligent Transportation, Big Data & Smart City (ICITBS)*. 10.1109/ICITBS49701.2020.00107

Myllyaho, L., Raatikainen, M., Männistö, T., Mikkonen, T., & Nurminen, J. K. (2021). Systematic literature review of validation methods for AI systems. *Journal of Systems and Software*, *181*, 111050. doi:10.1016/j.jss.2021.111050

Naik, S. K., & Murthy, C. A. (2003). Hue-preserving color image enhancement without gamut problem. *IEEE Transactions on Image Processing*, *12*(12), 1591–1598. doi:10.1109/TIP.2003.819231 PMID:18244713

Nair, V., & Hinton, G. E. (2010). Rectified Linear Units Improve Restricted Boltzmann Machines. *27th International Conference on International Conference on Machine Learning*, 807–814.

Naresh, K., & Manish, D. (2014). Determinant of Customers' Perception towards RTGS and NEFT Services. *Asian Journal of Research in Banking and Finance*, *4*(9), 253–260. doi:10.5958/2249-7323.2014.00960.2

Nerurkar, P., Shirke, A., Chandane, M., & Bhirud, S. (2018). Empirical Analysis of Data Clustering Algorithms. *Procedia Computer Science*, *125*, 770–779. doi:10.1016/j.procs.2017.12.099

Neuman, C. (2009). Challenges in security for cyber-physical systems. *DHS Workshop on Future Directions in Cyber-Physical Systems Security.*

Nguyen, K., Fookes, C., Ross, A., & Sridharan, S. (2017). Iris recognition with off-the-shelf CNN features: A deep learning perspective. *IEEE Access: Practical Innovations, Open Solutions, 6*, 18848–18855.

Ni, J., & Jin, X. (2012). Decision support systems for effective maintenance operations. *CIRP Annals, 61*(1), 411–414. doi:10.1016/j.cirp.2012.03.065

Nikolic, G., Bishop, R., & Singh, J. (1982). Sudden death recorded during Holter monitoring. *Circulation, 66*(1), 218–225. doi:10.1161/01.CIR.66.1.218 PMID:7083510

Norman, D. A. (1984). Stages and levels in human-machine interaction. *International Journal of Man-Machine Studies, 21*(4), 365–375. doi:10.1016/S0020-7373(84)80054-1

Noroozi, V., Zhang, Y., Bakhturina, E., & Kornuta, T. (2020). *A Fast and Robust BERT-based Dialogue State Tracker for Schema-Guided Dialogue Dataset.* ArXiv.arXiv:2008.12335

Oh, S., Ng, E., Tan, R., & Acharya, U. (2018). Automated diagnosis of arrhythmia using combination of CNN and LSTM techniques with variable length heart beats. *Computers in Biology and Medicine, 102*, 278–287. doi:10.1016/j.compbiomed.2018.06.002 PMID:29903630

Okoh, C., Roy, R., Mehnen, J., & Redding, L. (2014). Overview of Remaining Useful Life Prediction Techniques in Through-Life Engineering Services. *Procedia CIRP, 16*, 158–163. doi:10.1016/j.procir.2014.02.006

Oks, S. J., Fritzsche, A., & Möslein, K. M. (2018). Engineering industrial cyber-physical systems: An application map based method. *Procedia CIRP, 72*, 456–461. doi:10.1016/j.procir.2018.03.126

Oks, S. J., Jalowski, M., Fritzsche, A., & Möslein, K. M. (2019). Cyber-physical modeling and simulation: A reference architecture for designing demonstrators for industrial cyber-physical systems. *Procedia CIRP, 84*, 257–264. doi:10.1016/j.procir.2019.04.239

Oman, P., Schweitzer, E., & Frincke, D. (2000). Concerns about intrusions into remotely accessible substation controllers and scada systems. *27th Annu. Western Protective Relay Conf.*

Ordonez-Lucena, J., Chavarria, J. F., Contreras, L. M., & Pastor, A. (2019, October). The use of 5G Non-Public Networks to support Industry 4.0 scenarios. In *2019 IEEE Conference on Standards for Communications and Networking (CSCN)* (pp. 1-7). IEEE. 10.1109/CSCN.2019.8931325

Orman, H. (2014). Recent Parables in Cryptography. *IEEE Internet Computing.*

Otsu, N. (1979). A Threshold Selection Method from Gray-Level Histograms. *IEEE Transactions on Systems, Man, and Cybernetics, 9*(1), 62–66. doi:10.1109/TSMC.1979.4310076

Panda, M., & Patra, M. R. (2007). Network intrusion detection using naive bayes. *International Journal of Computer Science and Network Security, 7*(12), 258-263.

Pandey, A., & Wang, D. (2019). A new framework for CNN-based speech enhancement in the time domain. *IEEE/ACM Transactions on Audio, Speech, and Language Processing, 27*(7), 1179–1188.

Park, J., & Park, J. (2017). Blockchain Security in Cloud Computing: Use Cases, Challenges, and Solutions. *Symmetry, 9*(8), 164. doi:10.3390ym9080164

Patton, N., Aslamc, T. M., MacGillivrayd, M., Dearye, I. J., Dhillonb, B. R., Eikelboomf, H., Yogesana, K., & Constablea, I. J. (2006). Retinal image analysis: Concepts, applications and potential. *Retinal and EyeResearch, 25*, 99–127. PMID:16154379

Paul, P.K., Aithal, P. S., Saavedra, M. R., Sinha, R. R., Aremu, P. S. B., & Mewada, S. (2020). Information Systems: The Changing Scenario of Concepts, Practice and Importance. *SCHOLEDGE International Journal of Management & Development, 7*(7), 118-129.

Paul, P. K., Aithal, P. S., Bhuimali, A., & Kumar, K. (2017b). Emerging Degrees and Collaboration: The Context of Engineering Sciences in Computing & IT—An Analysis for Enhanced Policy Formulation in India. *International Journal on Recent Researches in Science, Engineering & Technology, 5*(12), 13–27.

Paul, P. K., Bhuimali, A., & Aithal, P. S. (2017a). Indian higher education: With slant to information technology—a fundamental overview. *International Journal on Recent Researches in Science, Engineering & Technology, 5*(11), 31–50.

Pellakuri, V., Rao, D. R., & Murthy, J. V. R. (2016, December). Modeling of supervised ADALINE neural network learning technique. In *2016 2nd International Conference on Contemporary Computing and Informatics (IC3I)* (pp. 17-22). IEEE 10.1109/IC3I.2016.7917928

Penna. (2014). Visualization tool for cyber-physical maintenance systems. *2014 12th IEEE International Conference on Industrial Informatics (INDIN),* 566-571. 10.1109/INDIN.2014.6945575

Pereira, S., Pinto, A., Alves, V., & Silva, C. A. (2016). Brain tumor segmentation using convolutional neural networks in MRI images. *IEEE Transactions on Medical Imaging, 35*(5), 1240–1251. doi:10.1109/TMI.2016.2538465 PMID:26960222

Peres, R. S., Rocha, A. D., Leitao, P., & Barata, J. (2018). IDARTS – Towards intelligent data analysis and real-time supervision for industry 4.0. *Computers in Industry, 101*, 138–146. doi:10.1016/j.compind.2018.07.004

Pilkington, M. (2016). Blockchain technology: principles and applications. *Research Handbook on Digital Transformations*, 225–253. doi:10.4337/9781784717766.00019

Prabhakaran, D., Jeemon, P., & Roy, A. (2016). Cardiovascular Diseases in India. *Circulation, 133*(16), 1605–1620. doi:10.1161/CIRCULATIONAHA.114.008729 PMID:27142605

Prasanna, L. (2014). Applications of graph labelling in communication networks. *Oriental Journal of Computer Science & Technology, 7*(1), 139–145.

Preneel, B. (2010). Understanding Cryptography: A Textbook for Students and Practitioners. Springer.

Priyadarshini, I., Kumar, R., Sharma, R., Singh, P. K., & Satapathy, S. C. (2021). Identifying cyber insecurities in trustworthy space and energy sector for smart grids. *Computers and Electrical Engineering, 93*(July), 107204. doi:10.1016/j.compeleceng.2021.107204

Radziwill, N., & Benton, M. (2017). *Evaluating Quality of Chatbots and Intelligent Conversational Agents.* arXiv:1704.04579

Rajkumar, R., Lee, I., Sha, L., & Stankovic, J. (2010). Cyber-physical systems: The next computing revolution. *Design Automation Conference*, 731-736. 10.1145/1837274.1837461

Rajput, A.E. (2019). *Natural Language Processing, Sentiment Analysis and Clinical Analytics.* ArXiv, abs/1902.00679.

Rao, B. B., & Swathi, K. (2017). Fast kNN classifiers for network intrusion detection system. *Indian Journal of Science and Technology, 10*(14), 1–10. doi:10.17485/ijst/2017/v10i29/109053

Ratnadewi, Hutama, & Ahmar, & Setiawan. (2016). Implementation Cryptography Data Encryption Standard and Triple Data Encryption Standard Method in Communication System Based Near Field Communication. *Journal of Physics: Conference Series.*

Rauniyar, T. (2014). Integrated Product Development Approach for Cyber-Physical Systems Utilizing Standardized Modeling Languages and Methodologies. *Journal of Integrated Design & Process Science, 14*(3), 1–11.

Raval, V., Nayak, S., Saldanha, M., Jalali, S., Pappuru, R. R., Narayanan, R., & Das, T. (2020). Combined retinal vascular occlusion. *Indian Journal of Ophthalmology, 68*(10), 2136-2142.

Raza, B., Kumar, Y. J., Malik, A. K., Anjum, A., & Faheem, M. (2018). Performance prediction and adaptation for database management system workload using Case-Based Reasoning approach. *Information Systems, 76*, 46–58. doi:10.1016/j.is.2018.04.005

Razmjooy, N., Ashourian, M., Karimifard, M., Estrela, V. V., Loschi, H. J., Do Nascimento, D., & Vishnevski, M. (2020). Computer-aided diagnosis of skin cancer: A review. *Current Medical Imaging, 16*(7), 781-793.

Reisman & Miriam. (2017). EHRs: The Challenge of Making Electronic Data Usable and Interoperable. *P & T: A Peer-Reviewed Journal for Formulary Management, 42*, 572–575.

Resende, P. A. A., & Drummond, A. C. (2018). A survey of random forest based methods for intrusion detection systems. *ACM Computing Surveys, 51*(3), 1–36. doi:10.1145/3178582

Restrepo, L., Aguilar, J., Toro, M., & Suescún, E. (2021). A sustainable-development approach for self-adaptive cyber–physical system's life cycle: A systematic mapping study. *Journal of Systems and Software, 180*, 111010. doi:10.1016/j.jss.2021.111010

Ring, M., Wunderlich, S., Grüdl, D., Landes, D., & Hotho, A. (2017, June). Flow-based benchmark data sets for intrusion detection. In *Proceedings of the 16th European Conference on Cyber Warfare and Security* (pp. 361-369). ACPI.

Ring, M., Wunderlich, S., Scheuring, D., Landes, D., & Hotho, A. (2019). A survey of network-based intrusion detection data sets. *Computers & Security, 86*, 147–167. doi:10.1016/j.cose.2019.06.005

Rocher, G., Tigli, J. Y., Lavirotte, S., & Le Thanh, N. (2020). Effectiveness assessment of cyber-physical systems. *International Journal of Approximate Reasoning, 118*, 112–132. doi:10.1016/j.ijar.2019.12.002

Romero, I., & Serrano, L. (2001). ECG frequency domain features extraction: A new characteristic for arrhythmias classification. In *2001 Conference Proceedings of the 23rd Annual International Conference of the IEEE Engineering in Medicine and Biology Society.* IEEE.

Rosa, A. (1966). On Certain valuation of the vertices of a graph. *Graph Theory: Int Symp.*

Roy Chowdhury, S., Koozekanani, D. D., Kochanski, S. N., & Parhi, K. K. (2016). Optic disc boundary and vessel origin segmentation of fundus images. *IEEE J. Biomed. Health Inform., 20*(6), 1562–1574.

Rúbio, E. M., Dionísio, R. P., & Torres, P. M. B. (2019). *Industrial IoT Devices and Cyber-Physical Production Systems: Review and Use Case. In Innovation, Engineering and Entrepreneurship, Lecture Notes in Electrical Engineering* (Vol. 505). Springer. doi:10.1007/978-3-319-91334-6_40

Ruiz-Arenas, S., Horváth, I., Mejía-Gutiérrez, R., & Opiyo, E. Z. (2014). Towards the Maintenance Principles of Cyber-Physical Systems. *Jixie Gongcheng Xuebao, 60*(12), 815–831.

Saber, V., & Venayagamoorthy, G. K. (2010). Efficient Utilization of Renewable Energy Sources by Gridable Vehicles in Cyber-Physical Energy Systems. *IEEE Systems Journal, 4*(3), 285–294. doi:10.1109/JSYST.2010.2059212

Sadiku, M. N., Wang, Y., Cui, S., & Musa, S. M. (2017). Cyber-physical systems: A literature review. *European Scientific Journal, 13*(36), 52–58. doi:10.19044/esj.2017.v13n36p52

Sadu. (2020). Graph labelling in graph theory. *Malaya Journal of Matematik.*

Sahoo, S., Dash, M., Behera, S., & Sabut, S. (2019). Machine Learning Approach to Detect Cardiac Arrhythmias in ECG Signals: A Survey. *IRBM, 41*(4), 185–194. doi:10.1016/j.irbm.2019.12.001

Sajjad, M., Khan, S., Muhammad, K., Wu, W., Ullah, A., & Baik, S. W. (2019). Multi-grade brain tumor classification using deep CNN with extensive data augmentation. *Journal of Computational Science, 30*, 174–182.

Sanislav, T., & Miclea, L. (2012). Cyber-physical systems-concept, challenges and research areas. *Journal of Control Engineering and Applied Informatics, 14*(2), 28–33.

Sankararaman, S. (2015). Significance, interpretation, and quantification of uncertainty in prognostics and remaining useful life prediction. *Mechanical Systems and Signal Processing, 52-53*, 228–247. doi:10.1016/j.ymssp.2014.05.029

Scheifele, S., Friedrich, J., Lechler, A., & Verl, A. (2014). Flexible, self-configuring control system for a modular production system. Procedia Technology, 15, 398–405.

Schweichhart, K. (2016). *Reference architectural model industrie 4.0 (rami 4.0). An Introduction.* Available online: https://www. plattform-i40. deI

Sedjelmaci, H., Guenab, F., Senouci, S. M., Moustafa, H., Liu, J., & Han, S. (2020). Cyber security based on artificial intelligence for cyber-physical systems. *IEEE Network, 34*(3), 6–7. doi:10.1109/MNET.2020.9105926

Sénéchal, O., & Trentesaux, D. (2019). A framework to help decision makers to be environmentally aware during the maintenance of cyber physical systems. *Environmental Impact Assessment Review, 77*, 11–22. doi:10.1016/j.eiar.2019.02.007

Serpanos, D. (2018). The cyber-physical systems revolution. *Computer, 51*(3), 70–73. doi:10.1109/ MC.2018.1731058

Setha, D., & Minhaj, A. A. (2018). Green manufacturing drivers and their relationships for small and medium(SME) and large industries. *Journal of Cleaner Production, 198*(10), 1381–1405. doi:10.1016/j.jclepro.2018.07.106

Sezer, O. B., Dogdu, E., & Ozbayoglu, A. M. (2017). Context-aware computing, learning, and big data in internet of things: A survey. *IEEE Internet of Things Journal, 5*(1), 1–27.

Shafique, M., Khalid, F., & Rehman, S. (2018). Intelligent Security Measures for Smart Cyber-Physical Systems. In *21st Euromicro Conference on Digital System Design*. Conference Publishing Services. 10.1109/DSD.2018.00058

Shahraki, A., Abbasi, M., Taherkordi, A., & Jurcut, A. D. (2021). *Active Learning for Network Traffic Classification: A Technical Survey*. arXiv preprint arXiv:2106.06933.

Shalendra Singh Rao, M. D. (n.d.). Impact of Foreign Direct Investment in Indian Capital Market. *International Journal of Research in Economics and Social Sciences, 7*(6), 172–178.

Shang, R., Ara, B., Zada, I., Nazir, S., Ullah, Z., & Khan, S. U. (2021). Analysis of Simple K-Mean and Parallel K-Mean Clustering for Software Products and Organizational Performance Using Education Sector Dataset. *Scientific Programming, 2021*, 1–20. doi:10.1155/2021/9988318

Shao, H., Jiang, H., Li, X., & Wu, S. (2018). Intelligent fault diagnosis of rolling bearing using deep wavelet auto-encoder with extreme learning machine. *Knowledge-Based Systems, 140*, 1–14. doi:10.1016/j.knosys.2017.10.024

Sharafaldin, I., Lashkari, A. H., & Ghorbani, A. A. (2018). Toward generating a new intrusion detection dataset and intrusion traffic characterization. *ICISSp, 1*, 108–116. doi:10.5220/0006639801080116

Compilation of References

Sharma, V. & Yasmin, N. (2018). An overview-comparative study of Hash Functions. *International Journal of Engineering Research, 5*(6).

Sharma, N., & Dadhich, M. (2014). Predictive Business Analytics: The Way Ahead. *Journal of Commerce and Management Thought, 5*(4), 652. doi:10.5958/0976-478X.2014.00012.3

Sharma, R., Kamble, S. S., Gunasekaran, A., Kumar, V., & Kumar, A. (2020). A systematic literature review on machine learning applications for sustainable agriculture supply chain performance. *Computers & Operations Research, 119*, 1–12. doi:10.1016/j.cor.2020.104926

Shatoori, M., Davidson, L., Kaur, G., & Lashkari, A. H. (2020, August). Detection of doh tunnels using time-series classification of encrypted traffic. In 2020 IEEE Intl Conf on Dependable, Autonomic and Secure Computing, Intl Conf on Pervasive Intelligence and Computing, Intl Conf on Cloud and Big Data Computing, Intl Conf on Cyber Science and Technology Congress (DASC/PiCom/CBDCom/CyberSciTech) (pp. 63-70). IEEE.

Shcherbakov, M. V., Glotov, A. V., & Cheremisinov, S. V. (2020). *Proactive and Predictive Maintenance of Cyber-Physical Systems. In Cyber-Physical Systems: Advances in Design & Modelling, Studies in Systems, Decision and Control, 259.* Springer. doi:10.1007/978-3-030-32579-4_21

Sheikhalishahi, E., Ebrahimipour, V., & Farahani, M. H. (2014). An integrated GA-DEA algorithm for determining the most effective maintenance policy for a k-out-of-n problem. *Journal of Intelligent Manufacturing, 25*(6), 1455–1462. doi:10.100710845-013-0752-z

Shen, Z., Shehzad, A., Chen, S., Sun, H., & Liu, J. (2020). Machine Learning Based Approach on Food Recognition and Nutrition Estimation. *Procedia Computer Science, 174*, 448–453. doi:10.1016/j.procs.2020.06.113

Shih, Chen, Yang, & Chiueh. (2012). Hardware-efficient evd processor architecture in fastica for epileptic seizure detection. *APSIPA*, 1–4.

Shiravi, A., Shiravi, H., Tavallaee, M., & Ghorbani, A. A. (2012). Toward developing a systematic approach to generate benchmark datasets for intrusion detection. *Computers & Security, 31*(3), 357-374.

Song, J.-L., Hu, W., & Zhang, R. (2016). Automated detection of epileptic eegs using a novel fusion feature and extreme learning machine. *Neurocomputing, 175*, 383–391. doi:10.1016/j.neucom.2015.10.070

Srinivasan, V., Eswaran, C., & Sriraam, N. (2014). Epileptic detection using artificial neural networks. *Int. Conf. on Signal Processing & Communications (SPCOM)*.

Staal, Abramoff, & Niemeijer, Viergever, & van Ginnesen. (2004). Ridge-based vessel segmentation in color images of the retina. *IEEE Transactions on Medical Imaging*.

Stolfo, J., Fan, W., Lee, W., Prodromidis, A., & Chan, P. K. (2000). Cost-based modeling and evaluation for data mining with application to fraud and intrusion detection. *Results from the JAM Project by Salvatore*, 1-15.

Subba, B., Biswas, S., & Karmakar, S. (2015, December). Intrusion detection systems using linear discriminant analysis and logistic regression. In *2015 Annual IEEE India Conference (INDICON)* (pp. 1-6). IEEE. 10.1109/INDICON.2015.7443533

Subramanian, K., & Prakash, N. K. (2020). Machine Learning based Cardiac Arrhythmia detection from ECG signal. *2020 Third International Conference on Smart Systems and Inventive Technology (ICSSIT)*. .921407710.1109/ICSSIT48917.2020.9214077

Sujatha, R., Chatterjee, J. M., Jhanjhi, N. Z., & Brohi, S. N. (2021). Performance of deep learning vs machine learning in plant leaf disease detection. *Microprocessors and Microsystems, 80*(December). doi:10.1016/j.micpro.2020.103615

Sun, M. (2009). Addressing safety and security contradictions in cyber-physical systems. *1st Workshop Future Directions Cyber-Physical Syst. Secur.*

Tang, H., & McMillin, B. M. (2008). Security property violation in cps through timing. *IEEE 28th Int. Conf.*

Tao, F., Qi, Q., Wang, L., & Nee, A. Y. C. (2014). Digital Twins and Cyber–Physical Systems toward Smart Manufacturing and Industry 4.0: Correlation and Comparison. *Engineering, 5*(4), 653–661. doi:10.1016/j.eng.2019.01.014

Teixeira, Shames, Sandberg, & Johansson. (2012). Revealing stealthy attacks in control systems. *Proc. 50th Annu. Allerton Conf. Communication, Control, Computing.*

Temko, A., Lightbody, G., Thomas, E. M., Boylan, G. B., & Marnane, W. (2012). Instantaneous measure of eeg channel importance for improved patientadaptive neonatal seizure detection. *IEEE Transactions on Biomedical Engineering, 59*(3), 717–727. doi:10.1109/TBME.2011.2178411 PMID:22156948

Thyago, Carvalho, Soaresa, Vita, & Francisco, Basto, & Alcal. (2019). A systematic literature review of machine learning methods applied to predictive maintenance. *Computers & Industrial Engineering, 137*. doi:10.1016/j.cie.2019.106024

Tian, Y., Ma, J., Lu, C., & Wang, Z. (2015). Rolling bearing fault diagnosis under variable conditions using LMD-SVD and extreme learning machine. *Journal of Mechanics and Machine Theory, 90*, 175–186. doi:10.1016/j.mechmachtheory.2015.03.014

Tobon-Mejia, D. A., Medjaher, K., & Zerhouni, N. (2012). CNC machine tool's wear diagnostic and prognostic by using dynamic Bayesian networks. *Mechanical Systems and Signal Processing, 28*, 167–182. doi:10.1016/j.ymssp.2011.10.018

Törngren, M., Grimheden, M. E., Gustafsson, J., & Birk, W. (2017). Strategies and considerations in shaping cyber-physical systems education. *ACM SIGBED Review, 14*(1), 53–60. doi:10.1145/3036686.3036693

Tripathi, A. K., Sharma, K., Bala, M., Kumar, A., Menon, V. G., & Bashir, A. K. (2020). A Parallel Military-Dog-Based Algorithm for Clustering Big Data in Cognitive Industrial Internet of Things. *IEEE Transactions on Industrial Informatics, 17*(3), 2134–2142.

Tripathi, S., & Gupta, M. (2021). Identification of challenges and their solution for smart supply chains in Industry 4.0 scenario: A neutrosophic DEMATEL approach. *International Journal of Logistics Systems and Management, 40*(1), 70–94. doi:10.1504/IJLSM.2021.117691

Truong, N. D., Kuhlmann, L., Bonyadi, M. R., Yang, J., Faulks, A., & Kavehei, O. (2017). Supervised learning in automatic channel selection for epileptic seizure detection. *Expert Systems with Applications, 86,* 199–207. doi:10.1016/j.eswa.2017.05.055

Tsai, C. F., Hsu, Y. F., Lin, C. Y., & Lin, W. Y. (2009). Intrusion detection by machine learning: A review. *Expert Systems With Applications, 36*(10), 11994-12000.

Tyagi, S. K. S., Mukherjee, A., Pokhrel, S. R., & Hiran, K. K. (2020). An intelligent and optimal resource allocation approach in sensor networks for smart agri-IoT. *IEEE Sensors Journal.*

Udmale, S. (2019). Application of Spectral Kurtosis and Improved Extreme Learning Machine for Bearing Fault Classification. *IEEE Transactions on Instrumentation and Measurement, 68*(11), 4222–4233.

Ullah, A., Anwar, S. M., Bilal, M., & Mehmood, R. M. (2020). Classification of Arrhythmia by Using Deep Learning with 2-D ECG Spectral Image Representation. *Remote Sensing, 12*(10), 1685. doi:10.3390/rs12101685

Umadevi, S., & Marseline, K. J. (2017, July). A survey on data mining classification algorithms. In *2017 International Conference on Signal Processing and Communication (ICSPC)* (pp. 264-268). IEEE. 10.1109/CSPC.2017.8305851

Usha, M. V., & Vidyashree, M. R. (2015). *Locating the optic nerve and blood vessel in a retinal image using graph partition method.* Academic Press.

Uthayashangar, S., Dhanya, T., Dharshini, S., & Gayathri, R. (2021). Decentralized Blockchain Based System for Secure Data Storage in Cloud. *2021 International Conference on System, Computation, Automation and Networking (ICSCAN).* 10.1109/ICSCAN53069.2021.9526408

Vegh & Miclea. (2014). Enhancing Security in Cyber Physical Systems through Cryptographic and Steganographic techniques. *IEEE International Conference on Automation, Quality and Testing, Robotics.*

Vinayakumar, R., Soman, K. P., & Poornachandran, P. (2017, September). Applying convolutional neural network for network intrusion detection. In *2017 International Conference on Advances in Computing, Communications and Informatics (ICACCI)* (pp. 1222-1228). IEEE. 10.1109/ICACCI.2017.8126009

Walker-Roberts, S., Hammoudeh, M., Aldabbas, O., Aydin, M., & Dehghantanha, A. (2020). Threats on the horizon: Understanding security threats in the era of cyber-physical systems. *The Journal of Supercomputing, Springer, 76*(4), 2643–2664. doi:10.100711227-019-03028-9

Wang, Q., & Megalooikonomou, V. (2005, March). A clustering algorithm for intrusion detection. In Data Mining, Intrusion Detection, Information Assurance, and Data Networks Security 2005 (Vol. 5812, pp. 31-38). International Society for Optics and Photonics. doi:10.1117/12.603567

Wang, T., & Tsai, S.-W. (2014). Optimizing bi-objective imperfect preventive maintenance model for series-parallel system using established hybrid genetic algorithm. *Journal of Intelligent Manufacturing*, 25(3), 603–616. doi:10.100710845-012-0708-8

Wan, J., Yan, H., Suo, H., & Li, F. (2011). Advances in cyber-physical systems research. *Transactions on Internet and Information Systems (Seoul)*, 5(11), 1891–1908. doi:10.3837/tiis.2011.11.001

Wei, Y., Qi, X., Wang, H., Liu, Z., Wang, G., & Yan, X. (2019). A Multi-Class Automatic Sleep Staging Method Based on Long Short-Term Memory Network Using Single-Lead Electrocardiogram Signals. *IEEE Access: Practical Innovations, Open Solutions*, 7, 85959–85970. doi:10.1109/ACCESS.2019.2924980

Wu, P., Lu, Z., Zhou, Q., Lei, Z., Li, X., Qiu, M., & Hung, P. C. (2019). Bigdata logs analysis based on seq2seq networks for cognitive Internet of Things. *Future Generation Computer Systems*, 90, 477–488.

Wurm. (2017). Introduction to Cyber-Physical System Security: A Cross-Layer Perspective. *IEEE Transactions on Multi Scale Computing Systems.*

Wu, Y., Song, P., & Wang, F. (2020). Hybrid Consensus Algorithm Optimization: A Mathematical Method Based on POS and PBFT and Its Application in Blockchain. *Mathematical Problems in Engineering*, 2020, 1–13. doi:10.1155/2020/7270624

Wu, Z., Guo, Y., Lin, W., Yu, S., & Ji, Y. (2018). A Weighted Deep Representation Learning Model for Imbalanced Fault Diagnosis in Cyber-Physical Systems. *Sensors (Basel)*, 18(4), 1096. Advance online publication. doi:10.339018041096 PMID:29621131

Xia, Y., Zhang, H., Xu, L., Gao, Z., Zhang, H., Liu, H., & Li, S. (2018). An Automatic Cardiac Arrhythmia Classification System With Wearable Electrocardiogram. *IEEE Access: Practical Innovations, Open Solutions*, 6, 16529–16538. doi:10.1109/ACCESS.2018.2807700

Xu, L. D., & Duan, L. (2019). Big data for cyber physical systems in industry 4.0: A survey. *Enterprise Information Systems*, 13(2), 148–169. doi:10.1080/17517575.2018.1442934

Yaacoub, J.-P. A., Salman, O., Noura, H. N., Kaaniche, N., Chehab, A., & Malli, M. (2020). Cyber-physical systems security: Limitations, issues and future trends. *Microprocessors and Microsystems, ELSEVIER*, 77, 1–33. doi:10.1016/j.micpro.2020.103201 PMID:32834204

Yadav, C. (2021). Design Engineering AES-Light Weight CP-ABE Based Privacy Protection Framework with Effective Access Control Mechanism in Cloud Framework. *Design Engineering.*

Yang, F.-N., & Lin, H.-Y. (2019). Development of A Predictive Maintenance Platform for Cyber-Physical Systems. *2019 IEEE International Conference on Industrial Cyber Physical Systems (ICPS)*, 331-335, , 2019.10.1109/ICPHYS.2019.8780144

Yeboah, T., Odabi, I., & Hiran, K. K. (2015, April). An integration of round robin with shortest job first algorithm for cloud computing environment. In International Conference On Management. *Tongxin Jishu*, 3(1), 1–5.

Compilation of References

Ying, X. (2019). An Overview of Overfitting and its Solutions. *Journal of Physics: Conference Series*, *1168*, 022022. doi:10.1088/1742-6596/1168/2/022022

You, Z., & Feng, L. (2020). Integration of industry 4.0 related technologies in construction industry: A framework of cyber-physical system. *IEEE Access: Practical Innovations, Open Solutions*, *8*, 122908–122922. doi:10.1109/ACCESS.2020.3007206

Yuan, Y., Xun, G., Jia, K., & Zhang, A. (2017). A multi-view deep learning method for epileptic seizure detection using short-time fourier transform. In *Proceedings of the 8th ACM International Conference on Bioinformatics, Computational Biology, and Health Informatics*. ACM. 10.1145/3107411.3107419

Zanero, S. (2017). Cyber-physical systems. *Computer*, *50*(4), 14–16. doi:10.1109/MC.2017.105

Zhang, H., & Zhou, R. (2017). The Analysis and Optimization of Decision Tree Based on ID3 Algorithm. *9th International Conference on Modelling, Identification and Control*. 10.1109/ICMIC.2017.8321588

Zhang, Q., Chen, Z., Lv, A., Zhao, L., Liu, F., & Zou, J. 2013, August. A universal storage architecture for big data in cloud environment. In *2013 IEEE International Conference on Green Computing and Communications and IEEE Internet of Things and IEEE Cyber, Physical and Social Computing* (pp. 476-480). IEEE.

Zhang, Q., Wang, X., Cao, R., Wu, Y. N., Shi, F., & Zhu, S. C. (2020). Extracting an explanatory graph to interpret a CNN. *IEEE Transactions on Pattern Analysis and Machine Intelligence*.

Zhang, Q., Zhu, C., Yang, L. T., Chen, Z., Zhao, L., & Li, P. (2017). An incremental CFS algorithm for clustering large data in industrial internet of things. *IEEE Transactions on Industrial Informatics*, *13*(3), 1193–1201.

Zhou, M., Jin, K., Wang, S., Ye, J., & Qian, D. (2018). Color retinal image enhancement based on luminosity and contrast adjustment. *IEEE Transactions on Biomedical Engineering*, *99*(3), 1. doi:10.1109/TBME.2017.2700627 PMID:28475043

Zhu, X., Srivastara, G., & Parizi, R. M. (2019). *An Efficient Encryption Algorithm for the Security of Sensitive Private Information in Cyber Physical System*. MDPI Electronics.

About the Contributors

Kamal Hiran is an Innovative and Enthusiastic Academic Professional having more than 14 years of experience in Academic Administration, Teaching and Research experience in India, Europe, and Africa. I have worked on various academic positions such as Lecturer, Sr. Lecturer, Asst. Professor, Associate Professor, Head IT, Head Academics, Founder, IEEE Liberia, IEEE Ghana Technical & Professional Activity Chair, IEEE SB Coordinator. I have done the tie-up with Academic-Industry collaboration as part of my jobs such as Turnitin (Plagiarism Checker), Founder IEEE Student Branch, Ghana, and Oracle WDP. I have published and presented the research papers in the Peer-reviewed journals as well as International Conferences in India, Denmark, USA, Germany, Jordan, Ghana, and Ethiopia. Working as a Reviewer and Member in the International Program Committee in the International Journals: Journal of Medical and Biological Engineering (JMBE), Springer, Germany, IJCA USA, IGI-Global USA, and IJERT, India.

* * *

Manish Choubisa received the B.E. degree in Computer Science & Engineering from Mohan Lal Shukhadiya University, Udaipur, India, in 2009 and the M. Tech. degree in Information Communication from Suresh Gyan Vihar University, Jaipur, India, in 2011. He is currently pursuing the Ph.D. degree in Computer Science & Engineering at Azteca University, Chalco, Mexico. His research interest includes the Image Processing, Machine Learning, IOT and Cyber Security. He awarded as Microsoft Innovative Educator (MIE) and Gold Partner Faculty by Infosys Campus Connect.

Ruchi Doshi has more than 16 years of academic, research and software development experience in Asia and Africa. Currently she is working as research supervisor at the Azteca University, Mexico and Adjunct Professor at the Jyoti Vidyapeeth Women's University, Jaipur, Rajasthan, India. She worked in the BlueCrest University College, Liberia, West Africa as Registrar and Head, Examination; BlueCrest

University College, Ghana, Africa; Amity University, Rajasthan, India; Trimax IT Infrastructure & Services, Udaipur, India. She worked as a Founder Chair, Women in Engineering (WIE) and Secretary Position in the IEEE Liberia Subsection. She worked with Ministry of Higher Education (MoHE) in Liberia and Ghana for the Degree approvals and accreditations processes. She is interested in the field of Machine Learning and Cloud computing framework development. She has published numerous research papers in peer-reviewed international journals and conferences. She is a Reviewer, Advisor, Ambassador and Editorial board member of various reputed International Journals and Conferences.

A. Finny Belwin, MCA, PhD, is a teaching professional living in Tamilnadu, India. Currently he is working as an Assistant Professor at Angappa College of Arts and Science, Coimbatore, India. He has more than 2 years of teaching experience. He has published many papers in National / International Journals and Conferences. His interested areas are Data mining and Internet of Things.

Sujith Jayaprakash is currently the Head of NIIT in Accra, Ghana.

Chitra K. is a seasoned computer science academician. She has almost a decade of teaching, programming, and administrative experience. She is presently an Assistant Professor at Rathnavel Subramaniam College of Arts and Science (Autonomous), Sulur, Coimbatore, in the School of Computer Studies (PG). She is a prolific researcher with a passion for technology. Her areas of expertise include Big Data, Machine Learning, Data Science, and other related fields. She also holds a doctorate in computer science. Chitra also possesses a number of professional certifications, including Big Data Engineering, Python and Data Structures and Algorithms.

Suganthi K. received the B.E. degree in Computer Science and Engineering from Madras University in 2001, M.Tech degree in Systems Engineering and Operations Research and Ph.D in Wireless Sensor Network from the Anna University in 2006 and 2016 respectively. She is currently working as Assistant Professor(Senior) in the School of Electronics Engineering (SENSE) at VIT University Chennai campus, India since 2016. She is the author of more than 25 scientific publications on peer reviewed journals and conferences. Her research interests include Wireless Sensor Network, Internet of Things, Data Analytics and AI. She is an active reviewer for journals published by Elsevier, IEEE Springer, and Nature.

Apinaya Prethi K. N. received the ME degree in Computer Science and Engineering from Anna University, Chennai in 2013. She is currently pursuing Ph.D. degree from the Department of Information and Communication Engineering in

Anna University, Chennai. She is an Assistant Professor in the Department of Computer Science & Engineering at Coimbatore Institute of Technology, India. Her current interest includes edge computing, network security, the area of ad-hoc wireless communications and sensor networks.

A. Kanagaraj, MCA, MSc., M.Phil., PhD, DIR, is a teaching professional living in Tamilnadu, India. Currently he is working as an Assistant Professor in the Department of Computer Science in Nallamuthu Gounder Mahalingam College, Pollachi, India. He has around two years of Industrial Experience, 3 years of Research Experience as Project Fellow and more than 6 years of Teaching Experience. He has experience in handling UGC - Major Research Project. He has published many papers in National / International Journals and Conferences. He is an author of book called 'Research Paradigm in Pervasive Computing'. He is a life member of Indian Science Congress, life member of Internet Society, life member of Indian Society for Technical Education, life member of International Association of Engineers, life member of Computer Science Teachers Association and Senior Member of International Society for Research and Development. His Research areas are Data mining, IOT and Pervasive Computing.

A. Linda Sherin is a teaching professional living in Tamilnadu, India. She is working as an Assistant Professor at AMJAIN College, Chennai, India. She has more than 2 years of teaching experience. She has published many papers in National / International Journals and Conferences. Her interested areas are Data mining, Software Testing and Internet of Things.

Kathiresan M. has almost two decades of teaching, academic administration, and research experience. He is presently an Associate Professor and Vice Principal (Administration) at Coimbatore's Dr. SNS Rajalakshmi College of Arts and Science. Dr. Kathiresan has supervised and directed several computer science research projects. He has over 25 articles in national and international journals to his credit. He also serves as an external PhD thesis examiner and a reviewer for several international journals. In addition to curriculum creation, affiliation and accreditation of programs, and quality assurance, Dr. V. Kathiresan has extensive experience in research. In the field of computer science, he has two patents to his name and has coauthored a few books. He belongs to the Association for Computer Machinery (ACM) and the Computer Society of India (CSI). Data Mining, Algorithms, Machine Learning, and Robotics are among his specialties.

Sangeetha M. is currently working as an Associate Professor at Coimbatore Institute of Technology, Coimbatore. She has 17 years of experience in teaching.

She has completed her Ph.D. in Computer Science & Engineering, Anna University, Chennai. She did her M.Tech Information Technology, Anna University of Technology, Coimbatore, 2009, Master of Business Administration (M.B.A), Bharathiar University, Coimbatore and Bachelor's in Computer Science Engineering at Jayam College of Engineering and Technology,2003. She has good proficiency in teaching Cyber Security, Digital forensics, Artificial Intelligence, Soft computing, Theory of computation, Software Engineering, Software Testing and Quality Assurance etc. She is guiding 8 Ph.D research scholars in Big Data, Networking and Artificial Intelligence domain. She is one of the Anna University Affiliation Committee Member. She is also act as academic council and Board of Study member at CIT and Sri Krishna College of Engineering and Technology, Program advisory committee member in Sri Ramakrishna Engineering College and United Institute of Technology. She is also act as Technical committee member and Session chair for various international conferences. "Award as "Best Professor" Girl Power Summit Awards, Entrepreneurs Council of India 2018, "Master Trainer for FSIPD programme" by NASSCOM and Anna University, 2016. and "Young Women Achiever (Engineering), Women Awards – VIWA 2016", Certified as "Patent Drafter" by CIPR, Chennai.

Prantosh Kumar Paul holds PhD-Information Science & Technology, MSc (Double), MBA-InfoSys, is actively engaged in the research and academic activities in the field of IST and Engineering Sciences related with Information Processing and Management. He is an alumnus of IIEST, Shibpur, NBU, SMU, VMU, and CVRU, India. He has been associated with Raiganj University, Raiganj, West Bengal for the teaching and learning activities. He is also CEO and VP of IST Foundation. Virtually he is among the few Indian Information Science professional who holds Post Graduate Qualification in all the dimensions of Information Sciences; ranging from Computer Sciences, Management Science, Library Science and Information Technology. He is also responsible for design country's first MBA-Information Management programme for VMS University, Sikkim. He has credited so many writing/research first and few among the Indian Researcher which including; written first paper on Cloud Computing Applications in Information Science, Systems, Information Centre/ Green Computing or Green IT in Information Field/ I-Schools aspects/ Usability Engineering in Information Science and Services/ HCI in Information Uses/ Information Science Educational aspects/ [IST]/ Information Scientist/ Geo-Information Science, Quantum Information Science and so on. He is in Editorial Board Member and Reviewer of more than 40 National and International Journals like- IJASE (Associate Editor in Chief), IJIDT (Editorial Board Member), and so on.

Suguna R. is working as Assistant Professor, Department of Computer Science and Engineering, Bannari Amman Institute of Technology, Sathyamangalam,

Tamilnadu. Her area of research includes Web Recommendation, Cloud Security and prediction of diseases.

Manoj Kumar Rajagopal received his B.E degree in 2003 from the University of Madras and his Ph.D. degree in 2012 from Telecom Sud Paris, France. Currently, he is working as Associate Professor in VIT University, Chennai Campus, India. His research interest includes Computer Vision, Machine Learning and Image processing, Affective Computing. He has published nearly 10 papers in peer-reviewed international journals and conferences.

Nithya S. received the ME degree in Computer Science and Engineering from Anna University, Chennai in 2013. She is currently pursuing Ph.D. degree from the Department of Information and Communication Engineering in Anna University, Chennai. She is an Assistant Professor in the Department of Computer Science & Engineering at Coimbatore Institute of Technology, India. Her current interest includes cyber physical system, unstructured database and cyber foraging.

Sharanya S. is currently working as Assistant Professor in the School of Computing at SRM Institute of Science and Technology. She has obtained her Doctorate in the domain of machine health prognostics using machine learning algorithms. She has made many note worthy publications in SCI indexed and Scopus indexed journals. She also holds a patent for equipment condition monitoring. Her research interests include machine learning, deep learning and cyber physical systems.

N. Shanmugapriya has almost two decades of expertise in computer science teaching, administration, and research. She has a PhD in computer science and has authored over 25 journal articles in national and international publications. She works at Dr. SNS Rajalakshmi College of Arts & Science in Coimbatore as an Associate Professor and Head of the Department of Computer Applications(PG). She is skilled in preparing bids for funding agencies, the affiliation procedure, curriculum development, regulations, and syllabus for undergraduate and postgraduate degree programs. She is a member of the Association of Computer Machinery (ACM) as well as the Computer Society of India (CSI). Dr. N. Shanmugapriya is an external PhD thesis assessor and a reviewer for a number of international journals. Speech Enhancement, Machine Learning, and Robotics are among her research interests, and she just submitted a patent relating to mobile sensors.

Bhavna Sharma received M.Tech degree in Computer Science from Banasthali Vidyapith in 2002 and Ph.D. degree in Computer Science & Engineering from Mohanlal Sukhadia University, Udaipur in 2015. Having experience of 18 years in various reputed Institutes and Universities, Presently working as Associate Professor in Department of Computer Science & Engineering, JECRC University, Jaipur. The main area of research interest includes Image Processing, Machine learning and Soft Computing. Presented and published more than twenty research articles in reputed International Journals and Conferences.

S. Sharmila, MCA, M.Phil., is a teaching professional living in Tamilnadu, India. Currently she is pursuing PhD and working as an Assistant Professor at Nallamuthu Gounder Mahalingam College, Pollachi, Coimbatore, India. She has more than 7 years of teaching experience. She has published many papers in National / International Journals and Conferences. Her interested areas are Data mining, Software Testing, Internet of Things and Green Computing.

Apratim Shukla is currently pursuing a B.Tech Degree specializing in Electronics and Computer Engineering, from Vellore Institute Of Technology, Chennai. His research interest includes Blockchain, Machine-Learning, Cryptography, and Information security.

Antony Selvadoss Thanamani, MSc., M.Phil., PhD., is presently working as Professor and Head, Dept of Computer Science, Nallamuthu Gounder Mahalingam College, Pollachi, Coimbatore, India (affiliated to Bharathiar University, Coimbatore). He has published many papers in international/national journals and written many books. His areas of interest include E-Learning, Software Engineering, Data Mining, Networking, Parallel and Distributed Computing. He has to his credit 34 years of teaching and research experience. His current research interests include Grid Computing, Cloud Computing, Semantic Web. He is a life member of Computer Society of India, Life member of Indian Society for Technical Education, Life member of Indian Science Congress, Life member of Computer Science, Teachers Association, New York and Member of Computer Science, Teachers Association, India.

Abhishek Thazhethe Kalathil is currently pursuing a B.Tech Degree specializing in Electronics and Computer Engineering, from Vellore Institute Of Technology, Chennai. His research interest includes Blockchain, Machine-Learning, Cryptography, and Information security.

Mayank K. Tolani is currently pursuing a B.Tech Degree specializing in Electronics and Computer Engineering, from Vellore Institute Of Technology, Chennai. His research interest includes Blockchain, Machine-Learning, Cryptography.

Kirubanand V. B. is currently working as Associate professor in CHRIST (Deemed to be University), Bangalore. He completed his undergraduate in Electronics and Masters in Computer Application from Bharathiar University, Coimbatore. He received his Master's in philosophy from Periyar University, Salem and Doctoral degree from Anna University, Chennai. He possesses two decades of experience in teaching and expertise in Wireless Networks and Internet of Things. Dr. V.B. Kirubanand has more than 60 papers research publications in international and National conferences, Scopus and ugc journals. He also acted as resource person for many conferences and seminars in reputed institutions. He is also part of various consultancy projects and research projects. He has acted as Senate Member of Bharathiar University in the year 2001-2004. He has received various awards like Vocational Service Excellence Award from Rotary Club, Coimbatore, India. 2010, Best Teaching Faculty Award, Sri Krishna College of engineering and technology, Coimbatore, India.2014, Best Alumini Award at Erode Arts and science college, Erode, India 2018.

Mishra Swapnil Vinod is currently pursuing a B.Tech Degree specializing in Electronics and Computer Engineering, from Vellore Institute Of Technology, Chennai. His research interest includes Blockchain, Machine-Learning, and Data Analytics.

Vinay Yadav is skilled in DevOps, Automation, Cloud Computing, Web Developer with one year of experience creating automation models and retraining systems and transforming data science prototypes to production-grade solutions. Consistently optimizes and improves real-time recommendation systems by evaluating strategies and testing changes in Docker. Consistently employs statistical methods and designs to yield real gains from model changes.

Index

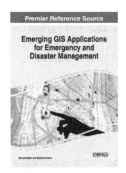 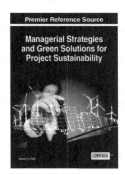  

IGI Global Author Services

Providing a high-quality, affordable, and expeditious service, IGI Global's Author Services enable authors to streamline their publishing process, increase chance of acceptance, and adhere to IGI Global's publication standards.

Benefits of Author Services:

- **Professional Service:** All our editors, designers, and translators are experts in their field with years of experience and professional certifications.
- **Quality Guarantee & Certificate:** Each order is returned with a quality guarantee and certificate of professional completion.
- **Timeliness:** All editorial orders have a guaranteed return timeframe of 3-5 business days and translation orders are guaranteed in 7-10 business days.
- **Affordable Pricing:** IGI Global Author Services are competitively priced compared to other industry service providers.
- **APC Reimbursement:** IGI Global authors publishing Open Access (OA) will be able to deduct the cost of editing and other IGI Global author services from their OA APC publishing fee.

Author Services Offered:

 English Language Copy Editing
Professional, native English language copy editors improve your manuscript's grammar, spelling, punctuation, terminology, semantics, consistency, flow, formatting, and more.

 Scientific & Scholarly Editing
A Ph.D. level review for qualities such as originality and significance, interest to researchers, level of methodology and analysis, coverage of literature, organization, quality of writing, and strengths and weaknesses.

 Figure, Table, Chart & Equation Conversions
Work with IGI Global's graphic designers before submission to enhance and design all figures and charts to IGI Global's specific standards for clarity.

 Translation
Providing 70 language options, including Simplified and Traditional Chinese, Spanish, Arabic, German, French, and more.

Hear What the Experts Are Saying About IGI Global's Author Services

 "Publishing with IGI Global has been *an amazing experience* for me for sharing my research. The *strong academic production* support ensures quality and timely completion." – **Prof. Margaret Niess, Oregon State University, USA**

"The service was *very fast, very thorough, and very helpful* in ensuring our chapter meets the criteria and requirements of the book's editors. I was *quite impressed and happy* with your service." – **Prof. Tom Brinthaupt, Middle Tennessee State University, USA**

Learn More or Get Started Here: For Questions, Contact IGI Global's Customer Service Team at cust@igi-global.com or 717-533-8845

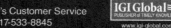 IGI Global
PUBLISHER of TIMELY KNOWLEDGE
www.igi-global.com

Publisher of Peer-Reviewed, Timely, and
Innovative Academic Research Since 1988

www.igi-global.com

IGI Global's Transformative Open Access (OA) Model:
How to Turn Your University Library's Database Acquisitions Into a Source of OA Funding

Well in advance of Plan S, IGI Global unveiled their OA Fee
Waiver (Read & Publish) Initiative. Under this initiative, librarians
who invest in IGI Global's InfoSci-Books and/or InfoSci-Journals
databases will be able to subsidize their patrons' OA article
processing charges (APCs) when their work is submitted and
accepted (after the peer review process) into an IGI Global journal.

How Does it Work?

Step 1: **Library Invests in the InfoSci-Databases:** A library perpetually purchases or subscribes to the InfoSci-Books, InfoSci-Journals, or discipline/subject databases.

Step 2: **IGI Global Matches the Library Investment with OA Subsidies Fund:** IGI Global provides a fund to go towards subsidizing the OA APCs for the library's patrons.

Step 3: **Patron of the Library is Accepted into IGI Global Journal (After Peer Review):** When a patron's paper is accepted into an IGI Global journal, they option to have their paper published under a traditional publishing model or as OA.

Step 4: **IGI Global Will Deduct APC Cost from OA Subsidies Fund:** If the author decides to publish under OA, the OA APC fee will be deducted from the OA subsidies fund.

Step 5: **Author's Work Becomes Freely Available:** The patron's work will be freely available under CC BY copyright license, enabling them to share it freely with the academic community.

Note: This fund will be offered on an annual basis and will renew as the subscription is renewed for each year thereafter. IGI Global will manage the fund and award the APC waivers unless the librarian has a preference as to how the funds should be managed.

Hear From the Experts on This Initiative:

"I'm very happy to have been able to make one of my recent research contributions *freely available* along with having access to the *valuable resources* found within IGI Global's InfoSci-Journals database."

– **Prof. Stuart Palmer**,
Deakin University, Australia

"Receiving the support from IGI Global's OA Fee Waiver Initiative *encourages me to continue my research work without any hesitation*."

– **Prof. Wenlong Liu**, College of Economics and Management at Nanjing University of Aeronautics & Astronautics, China

For More Information, Scan the QR Code or Contact:
IGI Global's Digital Resources Team at eresources@igi-global.com.